CONTENTS

List of Figures   vii
List of Tables   viii
List of Contributors   ix
Preface   xv
Table of Cases   xx
Table of Legislation   xxiv

PART I   Adult Guardianship   1

1   Adult Guardianship and Other Financial Planning
      Mechanisms for People with Cognitive Impairment in
      Australia   3
      TERRY CARNEY

2   The Role of Guardianship in Special Needs Plans in
      Saskatchewan, Canada   30
      JAMES H. GILLIS

3   Japanese Adult Guardianship Laws: Developments and
      Reform Initiatives   61
      MAKOTO ARAI

4   The Use of Trusts in Taiwan's Adult Guardianship
      System   87
      TAI YU-ZU

PART II   Lasting/Enduring Power of Attorney   115

5   Adult Guardianship and Powers of Attorney in England
      and Wales   117
      DENZIL LUSH

6   Supported Decision-Making and Enduring Powers:
     Innovations in Ireland   149
     ÁINE HYNES

7   Developments in Enduring Powers of Attorney Law in
     Australia   179
     TREVOR RYAN

8   Financial Planning Mechanisms Available to Persons with
     Special Needs in Singapore   212
     TANG HANG WU

     PART III   Special Needs Trust   237

9   What Will Happen When I'm Gone?   239
     DANA KATHERINE BIRKES

10   The Wispact Trusts: Making a Difference in a Means-Tested
     Support System   268
     ROY FROEMMING

11   SNTC's Operational Experience as Singapore's First
     Non-Profit Trust Company   303
     ESTHER TAN AND AMELIA LEO

12   A New Perspective on Adult Guardianship and Trusts
     in Korea   329
     CHEOLUNG JE

13   Reforming Enduring Powers and Launching a Special Needs
     Trust in Hong Kong   348
     LUSINA HO AND REBECCA LEE

     Index   365

SPECIAL NEEDS FINANCIAL PLANNING

Countries around the world are facing pressing needs to enhance financial planning mechanisms for individuals with cognitive impairment. The book provides the first comparative study of the three most common of such mechanisms, namely guardianship, enduring/lasting powers of attorney and special needs trusts. It involves not only scholarly overviews of the mechanisms in the jurisdictions studied, but also thorough, structured and critical reviews of their operational experiences.

This book aims at providing a useful source of reference for scholars, students, law and policymakers and practitioners in the fields of mental disability, healthcare and elder law. It is widely recognised in the field that books like this one are needed.

LUSINA HO is the Harold Hsiao-Wo Lee Professor in Trust and Equity at the Faculty of Law, The University of Hong Kong. She publishes widely in the fields of Equity and Trusts, and is the author of *Trust Law in China* (2003), the first comprehensive English-language monograph on the Chinese trust.

REBECCA LEE is Associate Professor at the Faculty of Law, The University of Hong Kong, where she teaches and researches in Equity and Trusts. Lusina Ho and Rebecca Lee co-edited *Trust Law in Asian Civil Law Jurisdictions: A Comparative Analysis* (2013), which critically examines the reception of trust in civil law jurisdictions in East Asia.

SPECIAL NEEDS FINANCIAL PLANNING

PLANNING

A Comparative Perspective

Edited by

LUSINA HO

The University of Hong Kong

REBECCA LEE

The University of Hong Kong

CAMBRIDGE
UNIVERSITY PRESS

CAMBRIDGE
UNIVERSITY PRESS

University Printing House, Cambridge CB2 8BS, United Kingdom

One Liberty Plaza, 20th Floor, New York, NY 10006, USA

477 Williamstown Road, Port Melbourne, VIC 3207, Australia

314–321, 3rd Floor, Plot 3, Splendor Forum, Jasola District Centre, New Delhi – 110025, India

79 Anson Road, #06–04/06, Singapore 079906

Cambridge University Press is part of the University of Cambridge.

It furthers the University's mission by disseminating knowledge in the pursuit of education, learning, and research at the highest international levels of excellence.

www.cambridge.org
Information on this title: www.cambridge.org/9781108481205
DOI: 10.1017/9781108646925

First published 2019

Printed and bound in Great Britain by Clays Ltd, Elcograf S.p.A.

A catalogue record for this publication is available from the British Library.

Library of Congress Cataloging-in-Publication Data
Names: Symposium on Special Needs Financial Planning (2017 : University of Hong Kong, Faculty of Law). | Ho, Lusina, editor. | Lee, Rebecca, 1979- editor. | University of Hong Kong. Faculty of Law, host institution.
Title: Special needs financial planning : a comparative perspective / edited by Lusina Ho, The University of Hong Kong; Rebecca Lee, The University of Hong Kong.
Description: Cambridge, United Kingdom ; New York, NY, USA : Cambridge University Press, 2019. | "Most of the chapters were presented as papers and discussed at a symposium held in October 2017 at the University of Hong Kong."–ECIP introduction. | Includes bibliographical references and index.
Identifiers: LCCN 2019001278 | ISBN 9781108481205 (hardback : alk. paper) | ISBN 9781108740449 (pbk. : alk. paper)
Subjects: LCSH: People with disabilities–Law and legislation–Congresses. | People with disabilities–Finance, Personal–Congresses. | Guardian and ward–Economic aspects–Congresses. | Trusts and trustees–Congresses. | People with disabilities–Services for–Law and legislation–Congresses.
Classification: LCC K637.A6 S96 2019 | DDC 346.01/8–dc23
LC record available at https://lccn.loc.gov/2019001278

ISBN 978-1-108-48120-5 Hardback

FIGURES

Figure 8.1 Special Needs Trust Company Scheme   222
Figure 8.2 Using the Special Needs Trust Company   222
Figure 11.1 Overview of SNTC Trust and the Parties Involved   304
Figure 11.2 Profile of SNTC's Beneficiaries   307
Figure 11.3 SNTC's Organisational Structure   308
Figure 11.4 Number of Trust Accounts Set Up over the Years   310
Annex A Summary Workflow of SNTC's Trust Service   327
Annex B Best Interests Framework   328
Figure 12.1 Delivery System for Developmental Disability Trusts   345

TABLES

Table 11.1 Year-on-Year Breakdown on the Number of Trust Accounts   306

Table 11.2 Funding Arrangements at Different Stages of the Trust Accounts   309

Table 11.3 Fees Payable to the Public Trustee (PT)   311

Table 11.4 Year-on-Year Projection on Trust Fund   312

Table 11.5 Description of SNTC's Trust Service at Different Stages   315

Table 12.1 Changes in Bed Numbers in Hospitals and Institutions for the Elderly and Disabled   331

Table 12.2 Number of Persons with Impaired Decision-Making Abilities, 2013   334

Table 12.3 Applications for and Acceptance of Full and Limited Incapacity Declarations from 2001 to 2012   334

Table 12.4 Number of Applications for Adult Guardian Appointments under New Adult Guardianship System   335

Table 12.5 Current Situation of Trust Contract Performance by the Korean Autism Association   346

CONTRIBUTORS

MAKOTO ARAI Professor, Chuo University, Japan. Professor Arai was formerly Dean of the Law School at the University of Tsukaba. He is currently Dean of the Graduate School of Law at Chuo University. His research interests include the use of the trust system in an aging society and the encouragement of better utilisation of adult guardianship. His major works include *Trust Law* (4th edition, 2014), *Visions of the Trust Law System* (co-author, 2011) and *Visions of the Adult Guardianship Law System* (co-author, 2011). Professor Arai has also authored numerous articles and is particularly noted for his work in comparative law. He received the Humboldt Research Award in 2006 and was awarded the Officer's Cross of the Order of Merit of the Federal Republic of Germany in 2010. He is also the president of the Japan Adult Guardianship Association and a standing director of the Japan Association for the Law of Trust. Professor Arai also serves as the Chair of the Agency for Cultural Affairs' Religious Juridical Persons Council.

DANA KATHERINE BIRKES Executive Director, Midwest Special Needs Trust, USA. Dana Katherine (Kathy) Birkes has experience in a broad range of public service spanning over 30 years, serving at Washington University in St. Louis for more than 10 years and 16 years in Missouri state government, culminating as director of the Missouri Department of Social Services. Ms Birkes's other positions in social services included federal controller, director of the Division of Budget and Finance and chief operating officer for Caring Communities. She served as auditor, strategic planner and telecommunications assistant manager with the Missouri Public Service Commission. Ms Birkes has also provided consultant services to the Center for the Study on Social Policy, the Danforth and Kauffman Foundations and the Missouri Alliance for Children and Families.

TERRY CARNEY Emeritus Professor, University of Sydney, Australia. Professor Carney was a long-serving director of research and past head of department at the University of Sydney Law School. He was the president (2005–2007) of the *International Academy of Law and Mental Health*, and chaired Commonwealth bodies such as the *National Advisory Council on Social Welfare* and of the Board of the *Institute of Family Studies*, along with various state enquiries on child welfare, adult guardianship and health law. His recent books include *Australian Mental Health Tribunals: Space for Fairness, Freedom, Protection & Treatment* (with David Tait, Julia Perry, Alikki Vernon and Fleur Beaupert, 2011), *Managing Anorexia Nervosa: Clinical, Legal and Social Perspectives on Involuntary Treatment* (with David Tait, Stephen Touyz, Miriam Ingvarson, Dominique Saunders and Alison Wakefield, 2006), *Social Security Law and Policy* (2006) and co-editor of *The Brave New World of Health* (with B. Bennett and I. Karpin, 2008).

ROY FROEMMING Consulting Attorney to Wispact, Inc., USA. Roy Froemming is an attorney in private practice, focused on assisting people with disabilities and their families on issues including estate planning, supplemental needs trusts and guardianship. Since beginning his private practice in 2003, Roy has assisted over 200 clients in creating accounts in Wispact trusts, as well as drafting over 250 free-standing supplemental needs trusts. He has represented over 160 families in petitioning for guardianship. As part of his practice, he regularly consults with the board and staff of Wispact, Inc., and has an office at Wispact. He was on the committee that originally drafted Wispact Trust I and is the drafter of the original Trust II and the original creation documents for both trusts. Roy has drafted amendments to both trusts over the years, including the most recent changes to the two trusts to clarify the management roles of Wispact, Inc., and the trustee. His background includes three years as co-director of the first elder benefit specialist program in Wisconsin, 20 years as staff and managing attorney at Disability Rights Wisconsin, three years as state coordinator of Wisconsin's Self-Determination Learning Project, and two years as trust attorney for Movin' Out, Inc., a housing organisation that promotes home ownership for people with disabilities and their families. He is currently a member of the Wisconsin Trust Code Study Group, a member of the Wisconsin Working Interdisciplinary Network of Guardianship Stakeholders Steering Committee, a member of the Board of the Wisconsin Chapter of the National Academy of Elder Law Attorneys, and an advisor to the Board of the Elder Law Section of the State Bar, of which he is a past chairperson.

JAMES H. GILLIS Lawyer, Saskatchewan, Canada. Mr Gillis has developed experience in corporate and commercial law, civil litigation and arbitration, as well in wills and estate planning. Mr Gillis's interest in advocacy for persons with disabilities has also allowed him to develop expertise in adult guardianship and estate planning for families with members who have special needs. He was a founder and incorporator of the Lions' Eye Bank of Saskatchewan – the first of its kind in Canada. As part of that process, he lobbied for and helped achieve amendments to the Human Tissue Gift Act and the Coroners Act. He is a director and past president of Cosmopolitan Industries, a sheltered workshop and activity centre for individuals with intellectual disabilities. He was also a founder and incorporator of Family and Friends of Cosmo & Elmwood Ltd., an organisation which advocates for persons with intellectual disabilities and their families. He served on a committee, which advised the provincial government in the drafting of legislation on adult guardianship.

LUSINA HO Professor, Faculty of Law, The University of Hong Kong. Professor Ho is the Harold Hsiao-Wo Lee Professor in Trust and Equity at the Faculty of Law, University of Hong Kong. She applies her expertise in both common law and civil law trusts to analyse laws and regulations pertaining to the use of trusts in China. Her book, *Trust Law in China*, published in 2003, is so far the only comprehensive critique of the Chinese Trust Law in the English legal literature and has enabled international experts to gain a thorough understanding of the subject. She is co-editor of Trust Law in Asian Civil Law Jurisdictions: A Comparative Analysis (with Rebecca Lee, Cambridge University Press, 2013). She has provided advice to both the Chinese Government on the enactment of the Chinese Trust Law and the Hong Kong Government on the reform of the Trustee Ordinance. She was a member of the Working Group on the Feasibility Study of Special Needs Trust established by the Hong Kong Government in 2016.

ÁINE HYNES Partner, St John Solicitors, Ireland. Áine Hynes is a partner specialising in Healthcare and Capacity Law. She advises Ireland's Health Service Executive in all aspects of capacity and disability law, including appearing before the High Court in Wardship matters. She was appointed by the former Minister for State for Mental Health and Disabilities, Kathleen Lynch, to the Expert Steering Group on the Review of Ireland's Mental Health Act 2001 (2012 to 2015). She is Vice-Chair of the Law Society of Ireland's Task Force on Mental Health and Capacity Law and has been involved in the formulation of Law Society submissions to government on legislative reform to mental health and capacity law. She held the position of Chair of the Irish Mental Health Lawyers Association from 2010 to 2015.

CHEOLUNG JE Professor, Hanyang University, Republic of Korea. Professor Je has served as the president of the Korean Institute for Guardianship Law and Policy until January 2016, for the proper implementation of the new Adult Guardianship Act 2011, which came into force in 2013. He has been a member of Disability Policy Consultation Committee at the National Human Rights Commission of Korea. In the arena of business and human rights, he has conducted lots of research since 2011 and consulted companies on how to implement the recommendations by the National Human Rights Commission of Korea on 'Business and Human Rights' into individual corporations. In the arena of human rights of persons with disabilities, he has published many articles in academic journals especially focused on adult guardianship and the reformation of private and public law for the protection of adults with impairments to decision-making ability since 2007.

REBECCA LEE Associate Professor, Faculty of Law, The University of Hong Kong. Ms Lee teaches and researches in Equity and Trusts (including comparative trusts and special needs trusts), contract and non-profit law. She has published articles in leading English and American law journals. She is co-editor of *Trust Law in Asian Civil Law Jurisdictions: A Comparative Analysis* (with Lusina Ho, Cambridge University Press, 2013) and contributing author to Kim Dayton (ed.), *Comparative Perspectives on Adult Guardianship* (2014). Since 2015, she has worked with NGO bodies to advocate for the setting up of the first special needs trust in Hong Kong.

AMELIA LEO Manager (Special Projects), Special Needs Trust Company Ltd, Singapore. Ms Leo graduated from the Singapore Management University's School of Law in 2012 and spent the next four years working in the Ministry of Social and Family Development (MSF). Her work at the MSF revolved around policymaking for vulnerable adults (i.e. persons with disabilities and elderly with poor social support) and the development of the recent amendments to the Mental Capacity Act and the new

Vulnerable Adults Act. She was seconded to her current post in mid-2016 to assist the Special Needs Trust Company in service development.

DENZIL LUSH Former Senior Judge of the Court of Protection, UK. Judge Lush was formerly a partner in Anstey & Thompson (now known as Foot Anstey), Solicitors, Exeter, and was a part-time chairman of the Social Security Appeals Tribunal from 1994 to 1996, before being appointed master of the Court of Protection in 1996. He became the senior judge of the Court of Protection when the Mental Capacity Act 2005 came into force in 2007. He is the author of *Elderly Clients: A Precedent Manual* (1996; 3rd edition, 2010), *Cohabitation: Law Practice and Precedents* (1993; 5th edition, 2012) and *Cretney & Lush on Lasting and Enduring Powers of Attorney* (6th edition, 2009). He is a judicial member of STEP (the Society of Trust and Estate Practitioners) and was presented with the Geoffrey Shindler Award for Outstanding Contribution to the Profession at the STEP Private Client Awards 2009/10. He is a patron of SFE (Solicitors for the Elderly), was formerly a trustee of the PEOPIL Foundation (Pan-European Organisation of Personal Injuries Lawyers) and was a member of the international team of lawyers who drafted the Yokohama Declaration on Adult Guardianship Law in 2010.

TREVOR RYAN Associate Professor, University of Canberra, Australia. Dr Ryan's research narrative evaluates law's response to an ageing society, drawing primarily from Japan's experience as the most rapidly ageing society in the world. His publications include adult guardianship, family trusts, retirement income disputes within families and the workplace, welfare entitlements of non-citizens and the contractualisation of welfare. He is currently working on tortious liability for accidents caused by dementia-related behaviours such a wandering, the political rights of persons with mental impairment and legal issues surrounding the housing supply for seniors. Dr Ryan's recent research publications include Trevor Ryan, Andrew Henderson and Wendy Bonython, 'Voting with an "Unsound Mind"? A Comparative Study of the Voting Rights of Persons with Mental Disabilities' (2016) 39 *University of New South Wales Law Journal*; Trevor Ryan, Bruce Baer Arnold and Wendy Bonython, 'Protecting the Rights of Those with Dementia through Mandatory Registration of Enduring Powers? A Comparative Analysis' (2015) 36(2) *Adelaide Law Review*; and Trevor Ryan, 'Administering Welfare in an Ageing Society' in Leon Wolff (ed.), *Who Judges Japan?* (2015), 108.

ESTHER TAN General Manager, Special Needs Trust Company Ltd, Singapore. Ms Tan works at Special Needs Trust Company Ltd (SNTC), a registered charity, and she been with the organisation since its inception in 2009. She brought with her years of experience with multinational companies in the area of legal and compliance. Under SNTC, Ms Tan journeys alongside caregivers with special needs dependents, empowering them with information that helps to safeguard their loved ones' financial security and welfare. As of 31 March 2017, 460 SNTC trust accounts have been set up. SNTC also administer the Special Needs Savings Scheme which allows parents to nominate their children with disabilities to receive monthly disbursements from the nominating parents' Central Provident Fund Savings Accounts after their death. As of 31 March 2017, 381 parents have applied for Special Needs Savings Scheme.

TANG HANG WU Professor, School of Law, Singapore Management University, Singapore. Professor Tang's research interests include research interests include property law, restitution, equity, trusts, charity and non-profit law. He has published widely, and his work has been relied on by all levels of the Singapore courts, the Federal Court of Malaysia, the Royal Court of Jersey, the Caribbean Court of Appeal, law reform committees in the Commonwealth, major textbooks and law journals. He is also frequently instructed to act as counsel and expert in contentious and non-contentious matters. He was described in a judgment by the Singapore Court of Appeal as 'a leading expert' who is 'well-known locally and internationally' in unjust enrichment and equity. Outside his work in academia and practice, Hang Wu is a member of the Strata Titles Board, a director of the non-profit Special Needs Trust Company and a volunteer assistant director at the Legal Aid Bureau.

TAI YU-ZU Associate Professor, Department of Law, National Taipei University. Dr Tai graduated from the University of Mainz in Germany. She specialises in assisted reproduction technology, adult guardianship and succession laws and has published extensively in these areas.

PREFACE

As a result of growing longevity and rapidly ageing populations, countries worldwide are facing a pressing need to enhance their planning instruments for individuals with cognitive impairment. Whether that impairment is inborn or the result of illness or accident, such individuals share the common need for assistance in managing financial assets available for their benefit. However, the growing prevalence of nuclear and single-parent families has rendered it increasingly difficult to rely solely on the families of the individuals concerned to provide the necessary support. Also, improvements in life expectancy for individuals born with intellectual disability such as Down Syndrome mean that they are more likely to survive their parents for longer periods of time than in the past and, thus, to face disruption to the care they previously enjoyed. Further, individuals with dementia are increasingly vulnerable to inheritance impatience, if not financial abuse, from their children. On top of these developments, signatory countries are grappling with implementation of Article 12 of the UN Convention on the Rights of People with Disabilities (CRPD), which moves away from substitute to supported decision-making for these individuals. All of these developments have generated healthy debate and, in some jurisdictions, innovative reforms that have attracted the attention of scholars, practitioners and policymakers alike.

This book seeks to provide a timely response to these developments. It examines the three most prominent legal tools that are affordable for individuals with modest wealth, namely statutory guardianship, lasting (or enduring) power of attorney and special needs trusts. The book provides a comparative perspective by reporting on jurisdictions in which the law concerning each of these tools is most advanced or in which new innovations have been or are being introduced. The chapters in each of the book's three parts focus predominantly on the legal tool addressed in that part, although comparison with other legal tools is also made where appropriate.

The book begins in Parts I and II with an examination of the traditional and internationally established financial planning tools of guardianship and lasting/enduring power of attorney. Part I focuses on statutory adult guardianship. A statutory guardianship order gives a guardian decision-making powers over the personal, healthcare and financial affairs of the individual with cognitive impairment. The respective chapters in Part I provide a general analytical understanding of the adult guardianship regimes in Australia, Canada, Japan and Taiwan. In addition to the major features of the respective adult guardianship regimes, two recurrent themes can be discerned. First, the authors locate their examination of this legal mechanism within the context of the legal, political and socioeconomic conditions of the jurisdiction in question. For example, in the chapter on Australia, Terry Carney compares adult guardianship to other available financial planning mechanisms for people with cognitive impairment in that country and demonstrates superbly how the configuration of these various mechanisms is a product of the values, strengths and limitations of the welfare state on the one hand and the acceptance of state responsibility for the funding of services for disabled people on the other. In a similar vein, in examining the use of the trust in the adult guardianship system in Taiwan, Tai Yu-Zu scrutinises the legal basis for the application of the trust, as well as the practical difficulties involved.

The second recurrent theme in the chapters in Part I is international developments in this field. As noted, the CRPD has served as a catalyst for guardianship reform around the world, prompting many jurisdictions to explore the potential of supported decision-making as a means of increasing the self-determination of individuals with cognitive impairment. Against this backdrop, James Gillis examines the law and practice of guardianship in the Canadian province of Saskatchewan, including its interplay with Henson Trusts (absolute discretionary trusts created for beneficiaries with a disability) and its attempts to balance the 'best interests' with the 'will, preferences and rights' of the subjects of guardianship orders. In a similar vein, Makoto Arai offers a critical examination of the Japanese adult guardianship system. In light of international developments in this field, he encourages the adoption in Japan of a human rights perspective on guardianship that emphasises self-determination rather than the traditional healthcare policy perspective, and further proposes a combination of the trust and adult guardianship systems to provide care for the country's greying population.

Part II focuses primarily on lasting/enduring powers of attorney. The donees of a lasting/enduring power of attorney can be given the power to manage the financial affairs of the donor when the latter no longer has the mental capacity to do so. Lasting/enduring power typically involves less formality and supervision than guardianship and, hence, is even more easily accessible. However, its convenience and utility also facilitate the exploitation of lasting/enduring powers as a vehicle for financial abuse, as Denzil Lush demonstrates in his critical assessment of lasting powers of attorney (LPAs) in the United Kingdom, which were introduced with the enactment of the Mental Capacity Act 2005. Since the enactment of that legislation, the number of LPAs has increased significantly. Lush reviews the policy considerations underpinning the legislation, critiques the developments in this area and explains his preference for deputyship to LPAs.

The UK Mental Capacity Act has served as a model law for jurisdictions in Asia to emulate. For example, Tang Hang Wu reviews, in addition to various financial planning mechanisms, Singapore's Mental Capacity Act 2010, which follows the English model closely and explains how the Singaporean Act has been refined to adapt to local culture. Although visionary at the time of its enactment, the UK Act adopts the 'best interest' model, which raises questions as to whether it complies with Article 12 of the CPRD. Such questions make comparison with state-of-the-art legislation in Ireland and the Australian state of Victoria particularly interesting. Áine Hynes examines how the Assisted Decision-Making (Capacity) Act 2015 of the Republic of Ireland complies with the CPRD and has introduced sweeping changes that align the duties and supervision of enduring powers with guardianship. Trevor Ryan then demonstrates how the innovative concept of 'supportive attorney' recently introduced to enduring powers in Victoria implements the principle of supported decision-making and examines its interplay with competing policy considerations concerning autonomy and protection.

After exploring the inherent limits of the more traditional legal tools of adult guardianship and enduring/lasting power of attorney, the book turns in Part III to examination of a recent and innovative alternative, namely the special needs trust. In the past few decades, particularly in the United States, special needs trusts have been created to provide affordable trust service by pooling assets together for investment to reduce administrative and investment costs. Only individuals with special needs are eligible to become beneficiaries under such trusts, which operate as pooled trusts with individualised accounts for clients. The pooled assets of the individual trust accounts are transferred to a trustee, who either manages the assets itself or does so with the help of a fund manager.

The trustee devises a care plan and budget for the special needs dependent in consultation with his or her caregiver. The budget provides the basis for the caregiver to apply for distributions for the dependent's maintenance. Dana Katherine Birkes's and Roy Froemming's chapters closely examine exemplary special needs trust models in the United States, namely the Midwest Special Needs Trust in Missouri and WisPact Trust in Wisconsin, respectively. Birkes's chapter offers practical insights of the background and operation of the Midwest Special Needs Trust, whereas Froemming also identifies best practices for jurisdictions considering setting up such a trust.

While the special needs trust originated in the United States, it has been adopted by other jurisdictions, most recently in Singapore and Hong Kong. Esther Tan and Amelia Leo's chapter reviews the issues and challenges involved in the creation, administration and monitoring of a special needs trust in Singapore. Drawing on the US and Singaporean experiences, Lusina Ho and Rebecca Lee's chapter investigates the latest developments and challenges in Hong Kong in launching a special needs trust. Given the developments in these two Asian jurisdictions, it is not surprising that there has been a burgeoning interest in special needs trusts in other jurisdictions in the region, including the Republic of Korea.[1] Cheolung Je considers an alternative approach adopted in that country, namely developmental disability trusts, and compares their relative advantages with those of special needs trusts in the United States.

The editors hope that this edited collection provides not only a detailed comparative study of the recent trends and developments in special needs financial planning mechanisms in Asia and the West, but also an understanding of the legal and operational difficulties involved in designing the ideal mechanism for the fiduciary management of the property of individuals with special needs. The book represents a modest attempt to highlight the significance of financial planning for such individuals and the insights of comparative analysis to encourage law and policymakers and practitioners in the fields of mental disability, healthcare and elder law to take the experience of other jurisdictions into account when reviewing and reforming their own laws.

This book could not have been produced without the goodwill and commitment of expert contributors from Australia, Canada, Ireland, Japan, Singapore, Korea, Taiwan, the United Kingdom and the United

---

[1] The Republic of Korea is also known as South Korea. For ease of reference, 'Korea' is used in this book.

States. We are extremely grateful to them for their thorough research and dedicated efforts. Most of the chapters were presented as papers and discussed at a symposium held in October 2017 at the University of Hong Kong. We have benefited tremendously from these engaging discussions and the contributors' generous sharing of their knowledge and expertise with us. We are also grateful to our student, Oscar Chan, who assisted with subediting work in a most meticulous and professional manner. Finally, we thank Joe Ng and Gemma Smith from Cambridge University Press, and gratefully acknowledge the financial support we received from the Research Grants Council of Hong Kong (GRF project number 17612916).

TABLE OF CASES

Australia

Alcazar-Stevens v. *Stevens* [2017] ACTCA 12,   208

Banks v. *Goodfellow* (1870) LR 5 QB 549, 565,   183

Burns v. *Corbett* [2017] NSWCA 3,   194

Cohen v. *Cohen* [2016] NSWSC 336,   200, 201

Daunt v. *Daunt* [2013] VSC 706,   192

Director of Income Maintenance Branch of Ministry of Community and Social Services
    v. *Henson* 28 ETR 121, 26 OAC 332, [1987] OJ No. 1121 (QL) (Div Ct),   25

Drake v. *Minister for Immigration and Ethnic Affairs (No. 2)* [1979] AATA 179; (1979)
    2 ALD 634),   14

Fear by His Mother Vanda Fear v. *National Disability Insurance Agency* [2015] AATA
    706,   14

Ghosn v. *Principle Focus Pty Ltd* [2008] VSC 574,   183

Gibbons v. *Wright* (1954) 91 CLR 423,   182

Greenland v. *Intellectually Disabled Citizens of Queensland* [2000] QSC 84,   200

Holt & Anor v. *Protective Commissioner* (1993) 31 NSWLR 227,   205

Hospital Products Ltd v. *United States Surgical Corp* (1984) 156 CLR 41,   202

JQJT v. *National Disability Insurance Agency* [2016] AATA 478,   14

Kang v. *Secretary, Department of Social Services* [2017] FCA 895,   18

Kelly v. *CA & L Bell Commodities Corporation Pty Limited* (1989) 18 NSWLR
    248,   202

Klotz & Klotz v. *Neubauer & Klotz* [2001] SASC 454,   200

McGarrigle v. *National Disability Insurance Agency* [2016] AATA 498,   14

Moylan v. *Rickard* [2010] QSC 327,   205

Ranclaud v. *Cabban* (1988) NSW Conv R 55–385,   183

R v. *Naidu* [2008] QCA 130,   208

Re BWA (Guardianship) [2016] VCAT 1002,   12

Re CDJ [2016] QCAT 509,   12

Re DTB [2016] NSWCATGD 35,   12

Re FGU (Guardianship) [2016] VCAT 1009,   12

Re GEM [2016] QCAT 123,   12

Re Giacomin v. *Secretary, Department of Social Services (Social services second review)*
 [2016] AATA 227, 20
Re HKO [2016] NSWCATGD 14, 13
Re JGM [2006] QGAAT 8, 12
Re Kang v. *Secretary, Department of Social Services (Social services second review)* [2016]
 AATA 829, 20
Re KCG [2014] NSWCATGD 7, 13
Re KJS [2003] QGAAT 27, 200
Re KTT [2014] NSWCATGD 6, 13
Re LBL [2016] NSWCATGD 22, 13
Re MCQ [2014] NSWCATGD 29, 206
Re NC (Guardianship) [2009] VCAT 2430, 12
Re NXO [2015] NSWCATGD 53, 208
Re R [2000] NSWSC 886, 206
 Re STS [2016] NSWCATGD 18, 12
 RJL [2011] NSWSC 200, 199
 RL [2012] NSWCA 39, 199
 Siahos & Anor v. *J P Morgan Trust Australia Limited* [2009] NSWCA 20, 206
 Scott v. *Scott* [2012] NSWSC 1541, 182
 Smith v. *Glegg* 2004 QSC 443, 203
 Smith v. *Smith* [2017] NSWSC 408, 207
 Spina v. *Permanent Custodians Ltd* [2008] NSWSC 561, 201
 Susan Elizabeth Parker v. *Margaret Catherine Higgins & Ors* [2012] NSWSC 1516, 209
 Taheri v. *Vitek* [2014] NSWCA 209, 201
 THBC v. *Secretary, Department of Families, Housing, Community Services and
 Indigenous Affairs* [2009] AATA 399, 23
 Thorn v. *Boyd* [2014] NSWSC 1159, 203
 Tobin v. *Broadbent* [1947] 75 CLR 378, 200
 Trevenar v. *Ussfeller* [2005] NSWSC 582, 203
 Watson v. *Watson* [2002] NSWSC 919, 185, 198, 200
 YPRM v. *National Disability Insurance Agency* [2016] AATA 1023, 14

Canada

Ontario (Ministry of Community and Social Services, Income Maintenance Branch)
 v. *Henson* [1987] OJ No. 1121, 25, 43
S.A. v. *Metro Vancouver Housing Corporation* 2017 BCCA 2 (37551), 43

England and Wales

A and B (Court of Protection: Delay and Costs) [2014] EWCOP 48; [2015]
 COPLR 1, 123
Breakspear v. *Ackland* [2008] EWHC 220 (Ch), [2009] Ch. 32, 221

Calvin's Case (1608) 7 Co Rep, 1a,   119
Drew v. Nunn (1878) 4QBD 661; [1874–80] All ER Rep 1144,   133
G v. E [2010] COPLR Con Vol. 470,   146
Re Gladys Meek; Jones v. Parkin and Others [2014] COPLR 535,   144
Re GM [2013] COPLR 290,   144
Re K, Re F [1988] Ch. 310, [1988] 1 All ER 358, [1988] 2 WLR 781,   137, 138
Re P [2010] EHWC 1592 (Fam); [2010] COPLR Con Vol. 922,   120
Re Windham (1862) 31 LJNS, Ch. 720,   123
Transparency in the Court of Protection: Publication of Judgments [2014] EWHC B2
    (COP); [2014] COPLR 78,   127

European Court of Human Rights

Shtukaturov v. Russia Application No 44009/05 (ECtHR, 27 March 2008),   165

New Zealand

Powell v. Thompson [1991] 1 NZLR 597,   185

Republic of Ireland

A.C v. Clare & Ors [2018] IECA 217,   177
Fitzpatrick v. F.K. [2008] IEHC 104,   151
Health Service Executive v. J.M. A Ward of Court & ors [2017] IEHC 399,   151
In re Ward of Court (withholding medical treatment) No. 2 [1996] 2 I.R. 79,   151
SCR – Power of Attorney [2015] IEHC 308:20/05/2015,   157, 158, 160, 165

Republic of Korea

Korean Supreme Court, 2004DA60072, 6008 (19 April 2007),   333
Korean Supreme Court decision 98DU16996 (28 January 2001),   332

Singapore

Chung Kin Chun K v. Yang Yin [2015] 5 SLR 467,   219
*Hsu Ann Mei Amy (personal representative of the estate of Hwang Cheng Tsu Hsu,
    deceased) v. Oversea-Chinese Banking Corp Ltd* [2011] 2 SLR 178,   232
Law Society of Singapore v. Wan Hui Hong James [2013] 3 SLR 221,   226
Public Prosecutor v. Yang Yin [2015] 2 SLR 78,   219
Re BKR [2013] 4 SLR 1257,   217
TDA v. TCZ [2016] 3 SLR 329,   219

Taiwan

Hualien District Court Case No. 9 of 2009,   100

Hualien District Court Case No. 79 of 2008 (Hualien District Court Case No. 9 of
    2009),   98

Hualien District Court Civil Case No. 79 of 2008,   100

Kaohsiung Juvenile and Family Court Case No. 000021 of 2015,   98, 99

Shiling District Court Case No. 64 of 2007,   98

Supreme Court of Taiwan Case No. 117 of 2015,   98, 101

Taichung District Court Case No. 105 of 2014,   98, 101

Taichung District Court Case No. 773 of 2013,   98, 101

Taipei District Court Case No. 72 of 2015,   98

Yilan District Court Case No. 141 of 2015,   98, 99

USA

Hutson v. *Mosier*, 401 P.3d 673 (Kan App 2017),   247

Lewis v. *Alexander*, 685 F 3d 325, 348 (3rd Cir. 2012),   261

TABLE OF LEGISLATION

Australia

Advance Care Directives Act 2013 (SA),   4
Advance Personal Planning Act (NT),   181, 186
Advance Personal Planning Regulation (NT),   13
Conveyancing Act 1919 (NSW),   200, 201
Disability Services Act 1993 (SA),   4
Guardianship Act 1987 (NSW),   7
Guardianship and Administration Act 1990 (WA),   181, 182, 186
Guardianship and Administration Act 2000 (Qld),   9, 11
Medical Treatment and Planning Act 2016 (Vic),   4
National Disability Insurance Scheme (Supports for Participants) Rules 2013,   14
National Disability Insurance Scheme Act 2013 (Cth),   15
Powers of Attorney Act 1998 (Qld),   181, 185–187, 198, 203, 205
Powers of Attorney Act 2000 (ACT),   181, 186
Powers of Attorney Act 2000 (Tas),   181, 182
Powers of Attorney Act 2003 (NSW),   181, 182, 187, 200, 205, 206
Powers of Attorney Act 2006 (ACT),   181, 185, 187, 198, 203, 205
Powers of Attorney Act 2014 (Vic),   4, 181–183, 185, 186, 198, 203, 204, 210
Powers of Attorney and Agency Act 1984 (SA),   181, 186
Social Security (Active Participation for Disability Support Pension) Determination 2014,   21
Social Security (Special Disability Trust – Trust Deed, Reporting and Audit Requirements) (FaHCSIA) Determination 2013,   19–20
Social Security (Special Disability Trust) (FaHCSIA) Guidelines 2011,   20
Social Security (Tables for the Assessment of Work-related Impairment for Disability Support Pension) Determination 2011,   21
Social Security Act 1991 (Cth),   18–21, 23

Canada

The Adult Guardianship and Co-Decision-Making Act, R.S.S. 1978, c A-5.3,   30–42, 54
The Dependant Adult's Act, Statutes of Saskatchewan, 1989–1990 c D-25.1,   33

The Dependants' Relief Act, 1996, R.S.S. 1976 c D-25.01,   47, 48, 53, 54
The Dependant's Relief Act, R.S.S. 1940 c 111,   43
The Saskatchewan Assistance Act, R.S.S. 1978 c s-8,   46
The Saskatchewan Assured Income for Disability Regulations, 2012 c s-8,   45, 46
The Trustee Act, 2009, R.S.S. 1978, c T23.01,   54

England and Wales

Court of Protection Practice Direction PD13,   123
Enduring Powers of Attorney Act 1985,   134–139, 142, 148, 350
Infants' Property Act 1830,   121
Lasting Powers of Attorney, Enduring Powers of Attorney and Public Guardian (Amendment) Regulations 2015 (Statutory Instrument 2015 No. 899),   139
Lunacy Act 1842,   124
Lunacy Act 1890,   121
Lunacy Act 1922,   124
Lunacy Regulation Act 1862,   123
Lunatics' Visitors Act 1833,   128
Mental Capacity Act 2005,   117, 124, 127–136, 139, 142, 203, 215, 349
Mental Health Act 1959,   123
Mental Health Act 1983,   117
Patients' Estates (Naming of Master's Office) Order 1947 (SR&O 1947 No. 1235/ L16),   21
Statute de Praerogativa Regis 1324,   119
Public Trustee Act 1906,   124
Public Trustee and Administration of Funds Act 1986,   124
Supreme Court Act 1981,   128
Tenures Abolition Act 1660,   124

Hong Kong

Continuing Power of Attorney Bill,   351–353
Director of Social Welfare Incorporation Ordinance (Cap 1096),   357
Enduring Power of Attorney Ordinance (Cap 501),   349–352
Mental Health Ordinance (Cap 136),   360

Japan

Act Concerning Establishment of Legal Frameworks in conjunction with the enforcement of the Partial Amendment of the Civil Code, Act No. 151 of 1999,   62
Act for Partial Amendment of the Civil Code, Act No. 149 of 1999,   62
Act on Guardianship Registration, Etc., Act No. 152 of 1999,   62
Act on Voluntary Guardianship Contracts, Act No. 150 of 1999,   62, 65

Act for Promoting the Use of the Adult Guardianship System, Act No. 29 of
    2018,   75, 76, 80
Act on Mental Health and Welfare for the Mentally Disabled, Act No. 123 of
    1950,   74

Republic of Korea

Amendment of Some Provisions in Korean Civil Code Act (Act No. 10429)
    2011,   335
Business of Trusts Act (Act No. 945) 1961,   332
Civil Code (Act No. 14409) 2016,   333, 336
Civil Code (Act No. 471) 1958,   329
Civil Code (Act No. 7428) 2005,   329
Constitution of the Republic of Korea,   340
Family Litigation Procedure Act (Act No. 14278) 2017,   339, 340
Family Litigation Regulation,   339
Financial Investment Services and Capital Markets Act (Act No. 8635) 2008,   332,
    342
Inheritance Tax and Gift Tax Act (Act No. 14388) 2016,   337
National Assistance Act (Act No. 14880) 2017,   347
Regulation of the Family Law Procedure Act,   336
Social Benefit Application, Its Provision and Discovery of the Entitled Recipients Act
    (Act No. 13994) 2016,   344
Trusts Act (Act No. 10924) 2011,   332
Trusts Act (Act No. 12592) 2014,   333, 347

Republic of Ireland

Assisted Decision-Making (Capacity) Act 2015,   147, 150, 161–176
Enduring Powers of Attorney Regulations (Personal Care Decision) Regulations 1996
    (S.I. No. 287/1996),   152, 153
Enduring Powers of Attorney Regulations 1996 (SI No. 196/1996),   152
Lunacy Regulations (Ireland) Act 1871,   149, 152, 155, 161, 164, 178
Powers of Attorney Act 1996,   149, 152–173
Rules of the Superior Courts (No. 1) (Powers of Attorney Act 1996) 2000 (S.I. No. 66 of
    2000),   152, 153
Succession Act 1965,   167

Singapore

Mental Capacity Act (Cap 177A, 2010 Revised Edn),   215–219
Mental Capacity Regulations 2010,   350
Mental Disorders and Treatment Act (Cap 178, 1985 Revised Edn),   215
Public Trustee Act (Cap 260, 1985 Revised Edn),   221, 312

Taiwan

(Physically and Mentally) Disabled Citizens Protection Act,   95
Civil Code,   88–90, 93–95, 98, 103, 106, 107, 109–111
People with Disabilities Rights Protection Act,   95–103
Senior Citizens Welfare Act,   95–103
Trust Law of the Republic of China,   90–92, 106–108

USA

21st Century Cures Act of 2016,   246
Achieving a Better Life Experience Act of 2014,   25, 263
Internal Revenue Code,   264
Omnibus Budget Reconciliation Act of 1993,   240, 261
Uniform Probate Code 1969,   133
Wisconsin Trust Code,   281

International Legislation

Optional Protocol to the United Nations Convention on the Rights of Persons with
    Disabilities,   177
The Hague Convention on the International Protection of Adults,   72, 83, 85
The United Nations Convention on the Rights of Persons with Disabilities,   3, 8,
    10–12, 16, 22–24, 61, 68–72, 74, 75, 122, 147, 149, 150, 151, 161, 174, 175, 177, 180,
    190, 197, 198, 211, 216, 300, 338, 339, 341, 353, 354
The Yokohama Declaration,   61, 72, 73, 75, 76, 81, 82, 85

PART I

Adult Guardianship

Adult Guardianship and Other Financial Planning Mechanisms for People with Cognitive Impairment in Australia

TERRY CARNEY[*]

I Introduction

Planning instruments for people with cognitive impairments in Australia reflect both its comparatively early adoption of principles of the least restrictive alternative and the need for personal advance planning devices – such as adult guardianship reforms and recognition of durable powers of attorney in the 1980s[1] – and the more recent embrace of principles of supported decision-making enshrined in the Convention on the Rights of Persons with Disabilities (CRPD).[2]

---

[*] Emeritus Professor of Law, The University of Sydney; Visiting Research Professor, University of Technology Sydney. A revised version of a paper presented at the 'International Symposium on Special Needs Financial Planning', Faculty of Law, The University of Hong Kong, 13–14 October 2017.

[1] T. Carney, 'The Limits and the Social Legacy of Guardianship' (1989) 18 *Federal Law Review* 231; T. Carney and D. Tait, *The Adult Guardianship Experiment: Tribunals and Popular Justice* (Sydney: Federation Press, 1997); T. Carney, 'Abuse of Enduring Powers of Attorney: Lessons from the Australian Tribunal Experiment?' (1999) 18 *New Zealand Universities Law Review* 481. One dilemma with enduring powers is that 'formality' preconditions or registration requirements have been found to discourage their use, boosting reliance on riskier informal arrangements, putting both parties at risk: C. Tilse et al., 'Older Peoples Assets: A Contested Site' (2005) 24 *Australasian Journal on Ageing* S51, S52. For gold standard legislation and analysis of how to balance take-up and protection: Law Commission of Ontario, *Legal Capacity, Decision-making and Guardianship: Final Report* (Toronto: Law Commission of Ontario, 2017), available from www .lco-cdo.org, pp. 169, 179–183.

[2] Convention on the Rights of Persons with Disabilities, New York, 30 March 2007, in force 3 May 2008, 2015 UNTS 3 (CRPD); T. Carney and F. Beaupert, 'Public and Private Bricolage-Challenges Balancing Law, Services & Civil Society in Advancing CRPD Supported Decision Making' (2013) 36 *University of New South Wales Law Journal* 175. To date, apart from some limited dabbling in South Australia, Victoria has been the only jurisdiction to seriously introduce new 'support' avenues (not conferring proxy decision-making power),

Financial planning for people with cognitive impairment unable to provide for themselves and reliant for their economic and social support on succession planning by their family members was hindered in Australia due to major roadblocks posed by Australia's needs-based income support arrangements, which tightly means-test all payments.[3] As a consequence, it was delayed for almost a quarter of a century after the guardianship and durable power reforms, until special legislation was passed in late 2006 providing limited avenues for skirting those roadblocks.[4] Why the delay? Part of the answer may be that not many families had the wealth to sufficiently fund the establishment of a trust to provide support after their death, that state residential care was adequate enough and that it was not easy to construct a scheme to relieve the income security traps. The traps being those of contributions being deemed to remain the property of the donor as being 'gifts' and for distributions to be counted as income of the disabled beneficiary for the purpose of reducing their rate of disability pension or other social security.

This chapter suggests that most of the explanation for the pace and design of Australian planning instruments can be attributed to the architecture of its welfare state.[5] This is because Australia's welfare state is a rather unique combination of a right to an austere level of social assistance based on needs assessment through tight means-testing but absent any expectation of family support[6]; and acceptance of state responsibility for funding of services for disabled people least able to care for themselves: initially through accessing state/territory-run or

---

confined so far to appointments made by the person, or health and mental health: Powers of Attorney Act 2014 (Vic), ss. 87–89; Mental Health Act 2014 (Vic), ss. 12–27; Medical Treatment and Planning Act 2016 (Vic), ss. 31–32, although Tribunal appointments are authorised under Part IV of its *Guardianship and Administration Bill 2018* (Vic), awaiting passage at the time of writing; also see Advance Care Directives Act 2013 (SA), s. 10(d); Disability Services Act 1993 (SA) as amended, s. 3A; T. Carney, 'Supported Decision-Making for People with Cognitive Impairments: An Australian Perspective?' (2015) 4 *Laws* 37.

[3] For details of means testing: T. Carney, *Social Security Law and Policy* (Sydney: Federation Press, 2006), Ch. 6. For the architecture of Australia's welfare state: T. Carney, 'Where Now Australia's Welfare State' (2013) *Diritto Pubblico Comparato ed Europeo (Journal of Comparative and European Public Law)* 1353.

[4] T. Carney and P. Keyzer, 'Private Trusts and Succession Planning for the Severely Disabled or Cognitively Impaired in Australia' (2007) 19 *Bond Law Review* 1.

[5] Carney, 'Where Now Australia's Welfare State', n 3.

[6] T. Carney, 'The Future of Welfare Law in a Changing World: Lessons from Australia and Singapore?' (2010) 32 *Sydney Law Review* 199; [2010] *Singapore Journal of Legal Studies* 22.

funded disability services, now the more generous personal packages under the National Disability Insurance Scheme (NDIS).[7]

II Background

Impairment of cognitive capacity arises in several ways: it may be due to congenital causes (such as intellectual disability); an acquired brain injury from a stroke, accident or other injury; degenerative conditions such as a dementia; or severe mental illness. The planning needs of such groups differ, as indeed do the circumstances and needs of individuals within each category. The standard legal planning toolkit of wills, trusts or powers of attorney offered little by way of effective options,[8] so Parliament stepped in. This had varying success,[9] not least because the needs and capacities of people differ significantly, as now explained.

People with an intellectual disability are likely to accumulate few financial or other resources of their own, being reliant on transfers from family or government, whereas people with dementia frequently will have accumulated assets and savings. People with dementia or even an acquired brain injury may have taken advantage of opportunities to use private planning instruments such as durable powers of attorney to direct their future personal and financial affairs; and even if not, they will have left a 'memory trail' of impressions of informed opinions and value preferences in the minds of family and friends which might be drawn

---

[7] For an accessible summary of the history and structure of the NDIS scheme, see D. Reddihough et al., 'The National Disability Insurance Scheme: A Time for Real Change in Australia' (2016) 58 *Developmental Medicine & Child Neurology* 66.

[8] Wills and testamentary trusts can give rise to problems such as family provision contests with other siblings, lack of expertise of the trustee, failure of surviving beneficiaries to care for their disabled sibling as expected or conflicts over testamentary wishes. Ordinary powers of attorney, for their part, subsist only while the donor retains capacity and cannot delegate day-to-day health or other 'care' responsibilities over adults: further, T. Carney and P. Keyzer, 'Planning for the Future: Arrangements for the Assistance of People Planning for the Future of People with Impaired Capacity' (2007) 7 *Queensland University of Technology Law and Justice Journal* 255; S. Booth, 'Providing for a Child with an Intellectual Disability' (1996) 34 *Law Society Journal* 63, 63.

[9] Enduring/durable powers of attorney survive loss of donor capacity but are of no assistance where the donor never acquires capacity; adult guardianship laws deal with immediate needs unable to be met in other ways and are not instruments for advance planning against anticipated contingencies; relatives entrusted with 'automatic' statutory powers for health may lack the qualities needed to make wise decisions or the decision may fall outside the more 'routine' care authorised: Carney and Keyzer, 'Planning for the Future', n 8.

on to guide future actions. People with intellectual disabilities, for their part, rarely will have displayed the capacity currently required to execute private advance planning instruments. Consequently, they are more likely to be reliant on public bodies like adult guardianship tribunals and associated legislation to make financial or personal management arrangements.

To further complicate the story, however, lived lives may contradict the best-laid plans. For instance, adult guardianship was revived and modernised in Australia in the 1980s in the expectation that its main caseload would be intellectually impaired former residents of congregate care institutions returning to community care under deinstitutionalisation measures,[10] but the overwhelming majority of the caseload turned out to be the frail aged,[11] with tribunals catering to just an estimated 2 per cent of the population of people with severe or profound cognitive impairments on the basis of Victorian modelling.[12] The same is true even for workhorse provisions such as durable powers of attorney (notable for low take-up[13]), representative payee (or other 'nominee') provisions, and

[10] For a good review of the parallel deinstitutionalisation of residential mental health institutions, see P. Gooding, 'From Deinstitutionalisation to Consumer Empowerment: Mental Health Policy, Neoliberal Restructuring and the Closure of the 'Big Bins' in Victoria' (2016) 25 *Health Sociology Review* 33.

[11] Victorian Law Reform Commission, *Guardianship: Final Report* (Report No. 24, 2012), pp. 34–38.

[12] Ibid., p. 37. Likewise Hong Kong's adoption of the law and administrative culture of adult guardianship laws from the Australian State of New South Wales attracted approximately one-tenth of the anticipated demand (based on per-capita projections from NSW), an outcome thought to be a product of greater cultural expectations of family rather than external care: M. Schyvens, 'Presentation' (Paper presented at the Second International International Conference on Capacity; International Congress of Psychogeriatricians, Berlin, 13 October 2015), available from www.ncat.nsw.gov.au, p. 5; L. Ho and R. Lee, 'Introducing the Special Needs Trust to Hong Kong' (2017) 23 *Trusts & Trustees* 1111 (just 280 applications filed in 2014–2015). Japan also has a low take-up: see Chapter 3 (203,551 in 2017, or approximately one-sixth of the expected 1 per cent of the population).

[13] Hong Kong's experience with enduring powers is emblematic, with only 55 registered in the first 15 years due to the barrier of almost 'wills level' formalities, and only 383 in a population of 7.5 million (0.005 per cent) in the first three years after formalities were eased somewhat: see Chapter 13; likewise in Singapore, even though registration is at the point of activation: see Chapter 8 (8,478 in a population of 5.7 million, or 0.15 per cent). By comparison, in England and Wales in 2016-2017, 635,540 durable powers were registered, bringing the total since 2009–2010 to 2,577,848 for a population of 58.3 million (or 4.42 per cent): see Chapter 5.

even statutory 'lists' of authorised proxy decision-makers for health: they too fail fully to cater to the needs of their intended target audiences.[14]

As a result, Australia planning for people with an intellectual impairment relies most heavily not on durable powers or adult guardianship, but on representative payee (payment nominee) provisions to redirect management of their social security payments[15] and any statutory 'lists' of authorised proxy decision-makers for health[16] or, for a minority, on a special needs disability trust (in the event their family has sufficient assets able to be set aside).

A   Australia's Governance and Welfare Context

As a federal system of government, law-making and administrative authority is divided between a national government with the strongest revenue base but constitutional responsibility only over defined matters such as income support (but not welfare, health or disability services as such), and state or territory governments with plenary law-making powers over all matters not allocated to the national government.

---

[14] For a recent review of differences between Australia, China, Thailand and Japan with regard to legal systems, sociocultural influences and take-up of various measures, see J. Tsoh et al., 'Comparisons of Guardianship Laws and Surrogate Decision-Making Practices in China, Japan, Thailand and Australia: A Review by the Asia Consortium, International Psychogeriatric Association (IPA) Capacity Taskforce' (2015) 27 *International Psychogeriatrics* 1029 (citing that only 21 durable powers of appointment cases were reported for Hong Kong in the first decade from introduction of the laws in 1997, compared to nearly 19,500 in a single year (2006) in England and Wales: ibid., pp. 1035–1036); also L. Willmott et al., 'Guardianship and Health Decisions in China and Australia: A Comparative Analysis' (2017) 12 *Asian Journal of Comparative Law* 371.

[15] Further: Carney, 'Supported Decision-Making for People with Cognitive Impairments', n 2; T. Carney, 'Supporting People with Cognitive Disability with Decision-Making: Any Australian Law Reform Contributions?' (2015) 2 *Research and Practice in Intellectual and Developmental Disabilities* 6.

[16] Such provisions 'list' and establish a 'hierarchy' of close relatives, spouses, etc. who are automatically authorised in advance to consent to basic medical or dental care of a person otherwise unable to give their own consent outside an emergency, under provisions such as Part 5E of the Guardianship Act 1987 (NSW), or s 55(3) of the Victorian Medical Treatment Planning and Decisions Act 2016 and the former Part 9 of the Victorian Guardianship and Administration Act 1986: further, B. White, L. Willmott and S. Then, 'Adults Who Lack Capacity: Substitute Decision-Making' in B. White, F. McDonald and L. Willmott (eds.), *Health Law in Australia*, 3rd edn (Sydney: Thompson Reuters Law-book Co, 2018) 207, 261–265; Victorian Law Reform Commission, *Guardianship: Final Report*, n 11, pp. 276–301.

As a consequence of the federal distribution of governance authority, the lion's share of responsibility lies with States and Territories: they make the laws about adult guardianship, durable powers of attorney and statutory 'lists' of authorised proxy decision-makers for health, as well as carrying a major responsibility for funding and delivery of disability services (now shared for NDIS clients); all of which differ between jurisdictions. Representative payee (nominee) appointments are available under national social security legislation (either to simply deal with correspondence or to administer payments), as also under the NDIS (recently enacted under the insurance and other powers of the national government). Special disability trusts to alleviate some of the social security pitfalls of their use are also national.

So our narrative necessarily begins with adult guardianship.

B   Modernising Adult Guardianship and Safeguards from the 1980s

Australia's adult guardianship model offers accessible, cost-free tribunal hearings about whether there are workable alternatives to avoid the need to appoint a substitute decision-maker as financial manager or a guardian of personal affairs (such as where to live or healthcare)[17]; though, as explained later, it is not fully CRPD compliant and retains an outdated best-interest test in place of modern preferences for being guided by the 'will and preferences' of the person. Prior to the enactment of the new model, guardianship relied on rarely used and costly superior court applications (the equitable jurisdiction to appoint a 'committee' of the estate or person traceable back to the thirteenth century), automatic financial appointments consequent on acquisition of the status of involuntary patient, or in some jurisdictions, medical certification processes.[18] Ontario, with a similar inheritance, took a different (and less adequate) reform path, but has recently favoured the Australian tribunal model.[19]

Hearings under the new guardianship model are informal. Procedures are flexible and inquisitorial (proactive) in style, and legal representation, while permitted, is not essential. Decision-makers are drawn from

---

[17] Carney, 'Supported Decision-Making for People with Cognitive Impairments', n 2.

[18] For details, T. Carney, 'Civil and Social Guardianship for Intellectually Handicapped People' (1982) 8 *Monash University Law Review* 199. The Canadian province of Ontario still relies heavily on such status and statutory guardianship avenues: Law Commission of Ontario, *Legal Capacity, Decision-Making and Guardianship: Final Report*, n 1, pp. 253–254, 259–260, 268–274.

[19] Ibid., pp. 215–229.

various professional backgrounds, and case-management and conciliation turns away some of the unnecessary applications,[20] while tribunal
staff or pre-hearing procedures gather information on cases going on to a
hearing. Applications are decided in accordance with principles such as
those of intervention as a last resort and in the least restrictive manner,[21]
the wishes of the person subject to the application must be ascertained
and considered, and any orders must be periodically reviewed.[22]

Critically significant is the strong presumption towards appointing a
human being as a financial administrator (managing assets and finances)
and/or guardian of the person (dealing with issues such as where a
person lives, services received or their social interaction), and the pre-
ferencing of members of the family or others who know the person. The
two orders are quite separate, are only made where informal arrangements currently are not working (not in anticipation of future problems)
and, if both are made, may be held by the same or by different people
(e.g. where one family member is more competent with finances while
another is better able to read the person's personal guardianship needs,
such as for personal care). Only when no such person is suitable will a
bureaucratic agency be appointed in the form of the Public Trustee or
Public Guardian. Financial administrators are not limited in the size or
complexity of affairs administered, but highly taxing or complex portfolios are often placed in the hands of the Public Trustee or equivalent.
Personal guardians cannot be authorised to make some very sensitive
decisions, such as writing a will or voting, but otherwise can deal
with most matters as assigned (commonly to deal with needs such as
admission to residential aged care, or a medical issue). Orders are often
time-limited and confined to stipulated matters (partial orders), though
financial orders are usually plenary. The tribunal is complemented by a
'watchdog' and advocacy agency, the Office of the Public Advocate

---

[20] C. Thurstans, 'ADR in VCAT's Guardianship and Residential Tenancies Lists: Room for
improvement?' (2016) 27 *Australasian Dispute Resolution Journal* 125.

[21] See, for example, Guardianship and Administration Act 2000 (Qld), ss. 11 (application of
'general principles' in Schedule 1), 12. Among the principles laid out in schedule 1 are the
presumption of capacity (cl. 1), participation in community life and encouragement of
self-reliance (cl. 5–6) and that of 'maximum participation and minimal limitations' (cl. 7).

[22] T. Carney and D. Tait, *Balanced Accountability: An Evaluation of the Victorian Guardianship and Administrative Board* (Melbourne: Office of Public Advocate, 1991); Carney
and Tait, *The Adult Guardianship Experiment*, n 1; T. Carney and D. Tait, 'Adult
Guardianship: Narrative Readings in the "Shadow" of the Law?' (1998) 21 *International
Journal of Law and Psychiatry* 147.

(OPA), which in Victoria has jurisdiction over any vulnerable citizen, whether or not subject to an order.[23]

The guardianship tribunals reform model was rapidly copied from Victoria by other Australian jurisdictions,[24] while the complementary watchdog and advocacy bodies took various forms (in NSW and some other jurisdictions responsible only for those under an order). Adapted from an Alberta equivalent[25] and clothed with ombudsman-like powers,[26] Victoria's OPA, for instance, is a highly regarded proactive body for tackling individual or systemic concerns of people with cognitive impairments.[27] However, pressures of rising demand, limited budgets and risk adverse service cultures, together with lack of conformity to CRPD supported decision-making, have contributed to some rethinking of the 1980s guardianship model and its associated institutions,[28] along with calls for greater harmonisation across the federation.[29]

Writing in 2012 about caseload trends revealed by its commissioned modelling into future demands on the Victorian guardianship system, the Victorian Law Reform Commission observed that '[p]eople with dementia, people with mental illness and people with acquired brain injury are now the major users of legislation designed initially with the needs of people with intellectual disabilities primarily in mind. People with dementia are likely to be the major users of guardianship laws over the next 20 years'.[30] The 'equality' principle of Article 12 of the CRPD,

---

[23] For its origins, see Victoria Minister's Committee on Rights & Protective Legislation for Intellectually Handicapped Persons, *Report of the Minister's Committee on Rights and Protective Legislation for Intellectually Handicapped Persons* (Melbourne: Government Press, 1982), available from http://u.b5z.net/i/u/10196230/f/LISA_Cocks_Report_on_Guardianship_1982.pdf.

[24] Victorian Law Reform Commission, *Guardianship: Final Report*, n 11.

[25] Victoria Minister's Committee on Rights & Protective Legislation for Intellectually Handicapped Persons, *Report of the Minister's Committee on Rights and Protective Legislation for Intellectually Handicapped Persons*, n 23.

[26] A. Abraham, 'Making Sense of the Muddle: The Ombudsman and Administrative Justice, 2002–2011' (2012) 34 *Journal of Social Welfare and Family Law* 91.

[27] M. Feigan, 'The Victorian Office of the Public Advocate: A First History 1986–2007', PhD thesis, La Trobe University (2011).

[28] J. Chesterman, 'The Review of Victoria's Guardianship Legislation: State Policy Development in an Age of Human Rights' (2010) 69 *Australian Journal of Public Administration* 61.

[29] J. Chesterman, 'The Future of Adult Guardianship in Federal Australia' (2013) 66 *Australian Social Work* 26.

[30] Victorian Law Reform Commission, *Guardianship: Final Report*, n 11, p. 34, para. [4.16]. The Commission cited 2010–2011 figures showing one-third of people with an order had dementia (33 per cent) followed by acquired brain injury (18 per cent), mental illness (17

for its part, is interpreted by its UN monitoring committee as requiring immediate repeal of traditional guardianship in favour of reliance on support for decision-making: replacing orders authorising proxy decision-making on behalf of people with new ways of enabling individual will and preferences (or a person's rights) to find expression.[31] Australia, however, entered an interpretive declaration that Article 12 'allows for fully supported or substituted decision-making arrangements ... only where such arrangements are necessary, as a last resort and subject to safeguards'.[32] There is a large literature debating the correctness or otherwise of such interpretations of CRPD requirements, but it is a matter of record that for whatever reasons international progress on supported decision-making and guardianship reform has been glacial.[33]

One small innovation, aimed mainly at reducing pressure on guardianship tribunals while reinforcing informal arrangements, is the so-called intermediate option of obtaining tribunal ratification of larger decisions made by informal decision-makers. Queensland, for instance, enacted its Law Reform Commission recommendation,[34] enabling ratification of informal decisions made (or to be made) by an incapacitated person's friends or 'support network'.[35] Various law reform proposals to make adult guardianship more compliant with CRPD thinking have been made at the state and federal levels,[36] but legislative action has been sparse. The most promising are the 2018 recommendations of the NSW Law Reform Commission. While not meeting the complete abolition

---

per cent) and intellectual disability (1 per cent). By the same year, 36 per cent of people on an order were older than 80 years (a rise from 26 per cent in 1988): ibid., p. 35, paras. [4.18], [4.19].

[31] UN Committee on the Rights of Persons with Disabilities, *General Comment No. 1 (2014)*, CRPD/C/GC/1, available from www.ohchr.org, para. 28.

[32] Quoted and discussed in Australian Law Reform Commission, *Equality, Capacity and Disability in Commonwealth Laws: Final Report* (ALRC Report 124, 2014), pp. 48–49, paras. [2.57]–[2.59].

[33] T. Carney, 'Prioritising Supported Decision-Making: Running on Empty or a Basis for Glacial-to-Steady Progress?' (2017) 6(4) *Laws* 18.

[34] Queensland Law Reform Commission, *Assisted and Substituted Decisions: Decision-Making by and for People with a Decision-Making Disability* (Report No. 49, 1996); B. White and L. Willmott, 'Will You Do as I Ask? Compliance with Instructions about Health Care in Queensland' (2004) 4(1) *Queensland University of Technology Law and Justice Journal* 77.

[35] Guardianship and Administration Act 2000 (Qld), ss. 9(1), 154.

[36] Victorian Law Reform Commission, *Guardianship: Final Report*, n 11; *Australian Law Reform Commission, Equality, Capacity and Disability in Commonwealth Laws: Final Report*, n 32.

interpretation of the CRPD monitoring committee, if enacted, there would be a new Assisted Decision-Making Act providing both for supported decision-making and (as a last resort) substitute decision-making.[37] Respect for autonomy and the will and preferences of the person would be implemented wherever possible, the concept of 'decision-making ability' would replace 'capacity' (with ability presumed), a finding of disability would no longer be a precondition to orders, and preference would be accorded to a 'support' agreement made by the person or by the tribunal (neither of which confer proxy decision-making powers, but merely facilitate decision-making), with tribunal 'representation orders' a last resort. Although representation orders would continue to authorise substitute decision-making as with current guardianships, they would always stipulate the specific areas covered (never conferring plenary authority), and safeguards would be strengthened over both these or any personal planning instrument granting such powers (the newly named 'representation agreements' replacing enduring powers).[38]

With its orders covering a fraction of people living with significant cognitive impairments, it is clear that even traditional adult guardianship is a small (if important) contributor to planning needs. Certainly its financial management orders cater to the needs of some, either through appointment of a family member or the Public Trustee or Public Guardian by default. However, it also serves a 'normative' function of policing the boundaries, such as deciding when informal or other arrangements are unworkable as alternatives to making an order,[39] or are unnecessary because informal arrangements remain perfectly

---

[37] New South Wales Law Reform Commission, *Review of the Guardianship Act 1987* (2018), available from www.lawreform.justice.nsw.gov.au/Documents/Current-projects/Guardianship/Report/Report 145.pdf, pp. xxii–xxxi.

[38] Ibid., pp. 1–2, 25–34, 41–46, 48–49, 56–59, 71–91, 93–97, 105–107, 121–152.

[39] In cases all of which involved intellectually impaired people (before guardianship tribunals in the three most populous states of Victoria, Queensland and NSW, respectively), see: *Re FGU (Guardianship)* [2016] VCAT 1009 (no further decisions required so guardian revoked); *Re BWA (Guardianship)* [2016] VCAT 1002 (administrator, excluding pension, but no need for guardian); *Re NC (Guardianship)* [2009] VCAT 2430 (informal management least restrictive]; *Re CDJ* [2016] QCAT 509 (interim order not warranted]; *Re GEM* [2016] QCAT 123 (no need for order to facilitate transition to supported accommodation); *Re JGM*, [2006] QGAAT 8 (informal arrangements for intellectually disadvantaged person not least restrictive); *Re DTB* [2016] NSWCATGD 35 (informal arrangements and person responsible powers for health sufficient); *Re STS* [2016] NSWCATGD 18 (financial manager appointed for pending lump-sum compensation, but social security excluded to allow self-management). All decisions are accessible at www.austlii.edu.au.

satisfactory and orders are being sought for the wrong reasons, such as to give a parent greater leverage by becoming a nominee to negotiate NDIS plans.[40] And as discussed later,[41] agencies such as OPA Victoria have posted discussion papers and guidelines to assist educating people about the interaction between state guardianship and the federal NDIS.

These new schemes and legislative options pose some interesting issues, as discussed in the next section.

III   New Parts of the Australian Architecture

In the last few decades, some significant new additions have been made to Australia's provisions for people with cognitive impairments.

A   The NDIS and Cognitive Impairment

The NDIS was enacted in 2013.[42] Implementation began in pilot sites before full roll-out commenced in 2016, optimistically slated for completion by 2019. Of an estimated 475,000 participants, 60 to 70 per cent are anticipated to have an intellectual impairment.[43] The scheme was funded federally by raising the taxation levy that helps fund universal healthcare (Medicare) from 1.5 per cent to 2 per cent, with half the cost contributed by the states and territories.[44] It is, of course, not strictly an 'insurance'

---

[40] Most recently the thorough review in *Re LBL* [2016] NSWCATGD 22; *Re KTT* [2014] NSWCATGD 6, paras. 29–33. In *Re KCG* [2014] NSWCATGD 7 the issues at stake in an NDIS plan were, however, concluded to be weighty enough to warrant appointing a guardian: para. 67; also *Re HKO* [2016] NSWCATGD 14, paras. 17–26.

[41] See n 55 and accompanying text.

[42] The government broadly accepted the design proposals of the Productivity Commission for a *National Disability Insurance Scheme* and associated National Injury Insurance Scheme but rejected its recommendation that it be fully funded by the national government: Productivity Commission, *Disability Care and Support*, 2 vols. (Canberra, Productivity Commission, 2011) available from www.pc.gov.au/inquiries/completed/disability-support/report; T. Kirby, 'Hope for Young Disabled Australians in Elderly Care Homes' (2011) 378 *The Lancet* 387. The National Disability Insurance Scheme (NDIS), providing long-term care and support for the disabled was estimated to cost AUD6.3 billion dollars annually. The National Injury Insurance Scheme (NIIS) will provide no-fault support for catastrophic accident or medical injury cases.

[43] S. Collings, A. Dew and L. Dowse, 'Support Planning with People with Intellectual Disability and Complex Support Needs in the Australian National Disability Insurance Scheme' (2016) 41 *Journal of Intellectual and Developmental Disability* 272, 272.

[44] This has been criticised as inferior to funding through a fully hypothecated tax: H. Ergas, 'National Disability Insurance Scheme Funding: The Case for Hypothecation' (2013) 46 *Australian Economic Review* 338.

scheme in the European sense, with taxpayers bearing the actuarial risks and uncertainties of its planning assumptions.[45]

The scheme is designed to enhance personal choice and control over the resources a person needs as a result of their impairment. It can cover supports in the form of coordination, strategic and referral services, and funding of persons or organisations[46] to facilitate participation in economic and social life, including funding for 'reasonable and necessary supports' for eligible participants.[47] Decisions about eligibility to be a participant and the content of plan packages are reviewable on their merits by the federal Administrative Appeals Tribunal (AAT) once internal review processes are completed.[48] The personal budget model necessarily presumes capacity of the person to negotiate a plan to reflect their needs and the ability to then devote those resources responsibly to realise their values and preferences. So provision is made for assistance, including through appointment of a 'nominee', should circumstances warrant it.

Plan or correspondence 'nominees', appointed under Part 5 of the NDIS legislation, deal with some very 'weighty' issues by comparison with those handled by nominees in other contexts (such as social security,[49] important as that is). Here they deal with issues going to the very

---

[45] See, for example, J. Walsh and S. Johnson, 'Development and Principles of the National Disability Insurance Scheme' (2013) 46 *Australian Economic Review* 327.

[46] The package may either stipulate service entitlements or be 'cashed out' (self-directed funding) to allow the person to select their own providers or ways of obtaining support: Reddihough et al., 'The National Disability Insurance Scheme: A time for real change in Australia', n 7, p. 68.

[47] Eligible participants are defined in ss. 9, 21 of the National Disability Insurance Scheme Act 2013 (Cth)('NDIS Act'). Reasonable and necessary supports are defined in s. 34(1) of the NDIS Act (including that it is not more appropriately funded elsewhere: s. 34(1)(f)), as supplemented by the National Disability Insurance Scheme (Supports for Participants) Rules 2013 ('Supports for Participants Rules') which form part of the law. There are also operational guidelines promulgated by the administering agency, which, while not part of the law as such, will be applied by review tribunals unless there is a cogent reason for departing from that policy (the 'Drake principle' from *Drake* v. *Minister for Immigration and Ethnic Affairs (No. 2)* [1979] AATA 179; (1979) 2 ALD 634).

[48] For recent reviews see: *McGarrigle* v. *National Disability Insurance Agency* [2016] AATA 498; *JQJT* v. *National Disability Insurance Agency* [2016] AATA 478 (transport costs for persons with autism and intellectual disability); *Fear by His Mother Vanda Fear* v. *National Disability Insurance Agency* [2015] AATA 706 (oximeter and suction machines for a person with ABI); *YPRM* v. *National Disability Insurance Agency* [2016] AATA 1023 (early intervention for diabetes best funded by the general health system).

[49] See Section IV.

core of the welfare of the person: major life-course-shaping issues about the resources to realise aspirations of engaging in community, training, work, leisure and lifestyle domains; these are core issues akin to those dealt with by adult guardianship orders or as significant to welfare and lifestyle as is the case in navigating the complexity of Canada's Registered Disability Savings Plans.[50] Although not perfect,[51] the existing guidelines for the operation of NDIS nominees when handlings these big-ticket areas of life generally mirror or surpass the principles set down for adult guardianship.[52] The option of appointing 'plan nominees' for the negotiation and administration of individualised personal plans[53] has however been little utilised.[54] In practice, application instead is made for financial

---

[50] Law Commission of Ontario, *Capacity of Adults with Mental Disabilities and the Federal RDSP* (Toronto: Law Commission of Ontario, 2013), available from www.lco-cdo.org/rdsp-discussion-paper.pdf. Section 78 of the NDIA Act provides that unless the instrument of appointment of a plan nominee otherwise provides, a plan nominee can make any decision open to a participant regarding the 'preparation, review or replacement' of a plan or 'the management of the funding for supports' under that plan.

[51] The ALRC found the principles to be lacking in some respects (such as their regard for 'wishes' rather than on will, preferences and rights) and in failing to provide for a genuine 'supporter': Australian Law Reform Commission, *Equality, Capacity and Disability in Commonwealth Laws*, n 32, paras. [6.18], [6.23]–[6.27].

[52] Thus, s. 80(1) of the National Disability Insurance Scheme Act 2013 (Cth) provides that it is the 'duty of a nominee of a participant to ascertain the wishes of the participant and to act in a manner that promotes the personal and social wellbeing of the participant'. Subsection (4) authorises promulgation of rules prescribing 'other duties', including a duty 'to support decision-making by the participant personally' or 'to have regard to, and give appropriate weight to, the views of the participant: ss. 80(4)(a), (b). The appointment of a nominee may not be made without the written consent of the participant after taking account of the participant's wishes: ss. 88(2)(a), (b). The appointment must also 'have regard to' the existence of any person already empowered under guardianship order or other appointment conferring power to make decisions for the person: ss. 88(4)(a), (b) (this would include an existing Centrelink nominee). The rules may prescribe persons 'who must not be appointed' and lay down 'criteria to which the CEO is to have regard' in making appointments: ss. 88(6)(a), (b).

[53] National Disability Insurance Scheme Act 2013 (Cth), ss. 78, 84. Further C. Purcal, K. Fisher and C. Laragy, 'Analysing Choice in Australian Individual Funding Disability Policies' (2014) 73 *Australian Journal of Public Administration* 88.

[54] The ALRC found few nominee appointments at NDIS trial sites, instead relying mainly on family carers or other informal supporters: *Australian Law Reform Commission, Equality, Capacity and Disability in Commonwealth Laws*, n 32, paras. [5.17], [5.30]. One concern was that family members of people found to have low needs would subsequently apply for appointment to resolve disagreements about levels of funding: M. O'Connor, 'The National Disability Insurance Scheme and People with Mild Intellectual Disability: Potential Pitfalls for Consideration' (2014) 1 *Research and Practice in Intellectual and Developmental Disabilities* 17.

or personal guardianship orders – highly controversial because it may breach the principle of the least restrictive alternative.[55] Of course, since equivalent major life issues at the state or territory level are dealt with by a sophisticated (if outdated to CRPD eyes) set of guardianship tribunals and offices of the public advocate (or equivalent), with access to state and territory public trustees should a suitable individual not be available for appointment as a financial manager, serious problems and doubts arise about how the two systems interact or how the 'orphan' protections at federal level could replicate necessary checks and balances found at the state and territory level.[56] Another concern has been that the NDIS may lead to 'net-widening' guardianship-order appointments for people who do not require them,[57] as subsequently discussed.

Before addressing these issues, there is another poorly received and underused recent addition to the planning toolbox in Australia's version of the special needs trust.

B   Special Needs Trusts

Australian law always permitted establishment of a discretionary trust in favour of a beneficiary with cognitive impairment or other disability, and unlike some countries, its rules about legal personality were no bar to creation of 'pooled' trusts designed to achieve economies of scale and expert administration of the trust by people knowledgeable about intellectual disability.[58] Nor has Australia historically lacked access to

---

[55] Office of the Public Advocate, *Guardianship and the National Disability Insurance Scheme* (September 2014) Office of the Public Advocate, available from www.publicadvocate.vic.gov.au/advocacy-research/ndis.

[56] As the ALRC wrote, 'one of the key difficulties in applying the Commonwealth decision-making model to the NDIS is determining how NDIS supporters and representatives interact with state and territory appointed decision makers': Australian Law Reform Commission, *Equality, Capacity and Disability in Commonwealth Laws*, n 32, para. [5.88]; a concern shared by the Victorian Office of the Public Advocate: Office of the Public Advocate, n 55, p. 26.

[57] By late 2014, 85 such applications had been made in the small NSW Hunter region trial site: Australian Law Reform Commission, *Equality, Capacity and Disability in Commonwealth Laws*, n 32, para. [5.94].

[58] There was no equivalent of the barrier posed in Chinese trust law (though not in Hong Kong, under the one country two laws arrangement preserving common law to 2047) by failure to recognise voluntary organisations as being a legal person capable of being appointed as a trustee: T. Simmons, 'The Wrongheadedness of the POMS Pooled Trust Rules and an Unfortunate but Recently Noted Chinese Parallel' (2015) 43 *Rutgers Law Record* 117, 118–119. Nor did Australia face the state banking restrictions on voluntary

competent agencies of the Public Trustee as a backstop for those unable to set up a private arrangement. Due to lack of competent private trustees or concerns about accountability of corporate trustees (where permitted), Commonwealth countries such as India, New Zealand, some Australian States and England long ago established a low-fees government guaranteed 'Office of Public Trustee', as an alternative (in the closing decades of the nineteenth century in India, New Zealand and South Australia; in the early 1900s in New South Wales and England).[59]

However, while in many countries (but not all, as witness Singapore[60]) individual or pooled special needs trusts need an exemption from the counting of distributions for social assistance means-testing, construction of Australia's scheme faced additional hurdles. Those additional hurdles were the decades-old anti-avoidance provisions bringing back into account as 'gifts', over the five years from disposition, any capital amounts transferred to settle or contribute to a trust or entity (affecting settlors' pension rights); the rule that half of any compensation settlement of damages[61] is deemed to be for loss of earnings and thus for

organisations acting as trustees in the way described after the US social security administration issued new administrative guidelines in 2012: ibid., pp. 123–126. For a short review of mainland China's 'shapeless' trust reform: A. Hofri-Winogradow, 'Shapeless Trusts and Settlor Title Retention: An Asian Morality Play' (2012) 58 *Loyola Law Review* 135.

[59] E. Trevelyan et al., 'The Public Trustee in India, New Zealand, Australia, and England' (1916) 16 *Journal of the Society of Comparative Legislation* 110; M. Jacobs and E. Cahn, 'The Fiduciary of the Future' (1930) 5 *St. Johns Law Review* 32, 40–41.

[60] See, for instance, the Singapore Special Needs Trust Corporation ('SNTC'), a not-for-profit charitable trust established in 2009 to meet family concerns about the risk of monies being 'frittered away' after parents die: H. W. Tang, 'Setting Up a Non-Profit Trust Company: The Special Needs Trust Company in Singapore' (2014) *Elder Law Journal [UK]* 14; the main benefit conferred is that management fees are very low, due to government subsidising 90–100 per cent of administrative overheads, but payments are made only until cash holdings are exhausted (it only manages cash, and the funds themselves are invested by the Public Trustee). Also see: www.sntc.org.sg. In 2012, those not able to afford the minimum capital amount to settle a pooled trust were enabled to set up a 'special needs savings scheme' (SNSS) under the Central Provident Fund – a scheme akin to Australia's compulsory superannuation scheme – so that an earmarked monthly amount would be payable to a disabled nominee, rather than the person receiving the usual lump sum CPD payout on death of parents: Tang, ibid.; J. Tai, 'Children get monthly payout from CPF after parents' death', The Straits Times, 4 May 2012, available from http://ifonlysingaporeans.blogspot .com.au/2012/05/special-needs-savings-scheme-snss-98.html.

[61] In the case of court awards after a full hearing (as distinct from settlements of actions) the actual loss of earnings figure becomes the amount to be used to meet living expenses: T. Carney, 'Social Security (title 22.3)' in M. Kirby (ed.), *Laws of Australia* (Sydney: Thompson Reuters, 2013), para. [22.3.4020].

meeting living expenses of the disabled or injured person (precluding social security payments for its duration); and, finally, the 2002 'veil-piercing' measures enabling the underlying economic substance of private trust or company entities (and any indirect control of them) to also be attributed to the real owners or beneficiaries.[62]

The 2006 special disability trusts reforms[63] removed, for qualifying individual trusts below a stipulated ceiling amount of AUD500,000 (indexed, currently AUD647,500),[64] the liability of settlors or beneficiaries to be means-tested on the amount contributed to the trust, or for beneficiaries to be means-tested on their beneficial entitlement under a trust (including widened 'veil piercing' which caught discretionary trusts[65]). However, the reforms leave untouched the preclusion rules for compensation awards.[66] As a result, not only must half of any compensation award be used for living expenses (the preclusion period

---

[62] Carney, *Social Security Law and Policy* n 3, pp. 107–109 (attribution of income and assets of controlled private trusts and companies), pp. 117–118 (gifts), pp. 164–168 (compensation preclusion). Also Carney, 'Social Security (title 22.3)', ibid., paras. [22.3.3080]-[22.3.3110] (controlled trusts and companies), paras. [22.3.3420]-[22.3.3480] (gifts), paras. [22.3.3970]-[22.3.4050] (compensation preclusion), para. [22.3.3560] (special disability trust dispensations).

[63] Further: Carney and Keyzer, 'Private Trusts and Succession Planning for the Severely Disabled or Cognitively Impaired in Australia', n 4; R. Ward, 'Setting up Special Disability Trusts' (2006) 44 *Law Society Journal* 48; Social Security Act 1991 (Cth), Part 3.18A, ss. 1209L-1209ZE.

[64] The 'principal home' of the beneficiary is excluded from being counted in the value of trust assets (s. 1209Y(4)) but any surplus is caught by the standard rules: surplus donations by qualified family members, made in excess of the AUD500,000 cap, are treated in the usual way – that is, the excess becomes caught by gifting or disposition rules: Social Security Act 1991 (Cth), ss. 1209ZA(1), (2).

[65] This latter is done by stipulating that the *only* attributable stakeholder in such trusts is the beneficiary, along with specific provisions dealing with the (non)attribution of trust income or assets: Social Security Act 1991 (Cth), ss. 1207X(2A) 1209V, 1209Y. The necessity of such exemptions, even in the case of a trust for administration of a residence for a severely cognitively impaired person lacking ability to control the trust, is illustrated by *Kang v. Secretary, Department of Social Services* [2017] FCA 895 (McKerracher J), where the potential to receive other benefits later on was relevant (and a relevant aspect not addressed by the AAT).

[66] Original failures to adjust capital gains tax rates on establishment or personal tax rates on closure of funds were partially rectified in subsequent years. For a summary of the changes and dates of effect: www.dss.gov.au/our-responsibilities/disability-and-carers/program-services/special-disability-trusts.

calculated by dividing the amount by a pension rate), but also no portion of such an award may be contributed to the trust.[67]

Settlors must have reached retirement age and be of retirement age and in receipt of a pension,[68] or have its operation deferred until both conditions are met, thus prejudicing any access by settlors to working age payments due to the assets being brought back into account.[69] A qualifying special disability trust may only be established for a person who is either a child who is 'severely disabled' and whose parent is qualified as providing 'intense' care as defined, or for an adult who has an impairment level sufficient to qualify the person for Disability Support Pension (DSP), is living in residential care or a hostel or has a care need that would qualify someone for Carer Payment (CP) or Carer Allowance (CA), and has an inability to work for more than seven hours a week.[70] These trusts therefore do not assist people with less severe impairments or people with episodically severe conditions. Transfers must be made by 'immediate' family members as defined,[71] other than very *limited* circumstances of recent bequests,[72] though transfers may be made by the beneficiary or their partner (expressly excluding compensation monies).[73]

To further immunise special disability trusts from misuse for tax minimisation or social security planning and rule avoidance, trusts must meet several conditions, including that they contain the 'model' clauses,[74]

---

[67] Social Security Act 1991 (Cth), s. 1209R(2) 'The assets of the trust must not include any compensation received *by or on behalf of* the principal beneficiary' [emphasis added]. However other assets of the beneficiary (or their partner) can be transferred free of the 'disposition' rules provided the transfer is unconditional: s. 1209ZC.

[68] Ibid., s. 1209Z(1)(b).

[69] Ibid., s. 1209ZB(1).

[70] Ibid., s. 1209M. For summary outline of the tight conditions for qualification for DSP, see n 85; conditions for payment of CP (ss. 197, 197A (overview)) and CA (ss. 952, 953, 954) are also governed by 'disability load' rating instruments: Carney, 'Social Security (title 22.3)', n 61, paras. [22.3.1460]-[22.3.1470] (CP), [22.3.1570] (CA).

[71] Section 23(1) of the Social Security Act 1991 (Cth) defines an 'immediate family member' of a person as their natural parents, adoptive or step-parents (subs. (a)), persons who are legal guardians of the person (or were when the person was under 18 years of age) (subs. (b)), grandparents (subs. (c)) or siblings of the person (subs. (d)). In its turn, s. 23(1) defines a 'sibling' to include 'half-brother, half-sister, adoptive brother, adoptive sister, stepbrother or stepsister of the person, but [not] a foster-brother or foster-sister of the person'.

[72] Ibid., s. 1209R(1).

[73] Ibid., s. 1209ZC(1).

[74] Ibid., s. 1209P(2). The required content is prescribed by the Social Security (Special Disability Trust – Trust Deed, Reporting and Audit Requirements) (FaHCSIA)

and satisfy objects and accountability requirements. The nine requirements are that the trust be 'protective' in character; have only one
principal beneficiary[75] who meets the previously outlined severity of
disability test;[76] provide only for reasonable accommodation and care
needs of that person;[77] include the model clauses;[78] have an independent
trustee or more than one trustee;[79] comply with investment restrictions;[80] provide annual financial statements from an independent qualified accountant;[81] and undergo independent audits by a separate
qualified auditor.[82] Since 2011, trusts have been authorised to spend an
indexed AUD10,000 (currently AUD11,500) on 'discretionary items
unrelated to care and accommodation', such as for 'health, wellbeing,
recreation, independence and social inclusion'.[83] All of these conditions
are strictly applied.[84]

Determination 2013 (F2013L01026), Part 2. Guidelines are set in the Social Security
(Special Disability Trust) (FaHCSIA) Guidelines 2011 (F2016C00702). The model trust
deed and the provisions which must be included in the model trust deed (s. 2.2(1)) are
available at www.dss.gov.au/our-responsibilities/disability-and-carers/publications-art
icles/model-trust-deed-for-special-disability-trusts.

[75] Social Security Act 1991 (Cth), ss. 1209L(a), 1209M(1).

[76] Ibid., ss. 1209L(a), 1209M(2).

[77] Ibid., ss. 1209L(b), 1209N.

[78] Ibid., ss. 1209L(c), 1209P.

[79] The requirement is that the trustee (or directors of a corporate trustee) be Australian
residents and not be disqualified as directors: Social Security Act 1991 (Cth), ss. 1209L(d),
1209Q(1), (2).

[80] Ibid., ss. 1209L(e), 1209R. These policies essentially restrict investments to those permitted for superannuation purposes, but also prevent investments in 'in-house' assets (other
than those in the beneficiary's home), or owning business property of a 'related party'
(other than the beneficiary).

[81] Ibid., ss. 1209L(f), 1209S. Social Security (Special Disability Trust – Trust Deed,
Reporting and Audit Requirements) (FaHCSIA) Determination 2013 (F2013L01026),
para. 3.1(a)(i), (ii).

[82] Ibid., s. 1209T. Social Security (Special Disability Trust – Trust Deed, Reporting and
Audit Requirements) (FaHCSIA) Determination 2013 (F2013L01026), paras. 4.2(b), (c)
(independence), 4.3 (information to be contained in audit).

[83] Social Security (Special Disability Trust) (FaHCSIA) Guidelines 2011 (F2016C00702),
para. 2.7(b).

[84] See for instance the Administrative Appeals Tribunal reviews of social security issues in
Re Kang v. Secretary, Department of Social Services (Social services second review) [2016]
AATA 829 (a debt found to be fully recoverable although the trust was expressly intended
to operate as a special disability trust, because requirements not satisfied); Re Giacomin
v. Secretary, Department of Social Services (Social services second review) [2016] AATA
227 (family trust unable to be characterised as a special disability trust for a settlor father
who became disabled).

The next question is what alternatives exist when this newer planning machinery proves to be beyond ordinary families of average to limited means.

IV   Catering for the 'Ordinary' Case

Special disability trusts are of no assistance at all to ageing parents of people with a disability who lack the means to take advantage of the concessions. For many cognitively impaired Australians, their most likely 'planning' encounter with a legal instrument will instead be a correspondence nominee or payment nominee appointed in relation to their disability pension.[85]

A   Representative Payee/Payment Nominees

Provisions enabling nomination of a substitute decision-maker to receive and manage social security payments of a person unable to manage for themselves have long been part of Australian and US social security law.[86] Australia added a less drastic option of a 'correspondence' nominee to overcome privacy restrictions on communication by third parties with the administrative agency (Centrelink). Correspondence nominees can receive and provide information, including taking responsibility for reporting changed circumstances or income.[87] As already discussed, both powers are replicated in the NDIS, including appointment of 'plan

---

[85] The most common payment is the DSP, which requires obtaining 20 impairment points under rating Tables (for cognitive impairment either Table 9 for 'Intellectual function' or Table 7 for 'Brain function', found in the Social Security (Tables for the Assessment of Work-related Impairment for Disability Support Pension) Determination 2011), along with an inability to undertake 15 hours a week of any work of any kind, irrespective of factors such as education or location (an abstract, not a real labour-market testing): Social Security Act 1991 (Cth), ss. 94(1)(a) and 94(1)(b)(i) respectively. Unless a person has a 'severe' impairment (defined as obtaining at least 20 points under a *single* Table) it is also necessary to complete 18 months of participation with a job provider (training and placement agency) *specialising in disability* in the three years immediately prior to the application: ss. 94(2)(aa), (3C), Social Security (Active Participation for Disability Support Pension) Determination 2014 (F2015L00001).

[86] Called 'representative payee' schemes in the US: R. Creyke, 'Whose Pension Is It: Substitute Payees for Mentally Incompetent Pensioners' (1990) 10 *University of Tasmania Law Review* 102.

[87] Carney, 'Supported Decision-making for People with Cognitive Impairments', n 2, paras. [12]–[15].

nominees' for negotiation and administration of resources allocated under individualised personal plan entitlements.[88]

The Australian Law Reform Commission (ALRC) found that correspondence nominees were most in tune with the strong preference of the CRPD for supported rather than substitute decision-making (interpreted by many as the *only* compatible model[89]), adapting it to become a newly named 'supporter'. While accepting that some substitute decision-making options were needed as a last resort (appointment of a representative), the ALRC rewrote both its supporter and its representative powers[90] in an attempt to better address the criticism of lack of attention to fiduciary obligations or safeguards against abuse.[91]

B   Safeguards

The need for safeguards against miscarrying of low-cost tools pitched at the routine needs of the many is a significant challenge.[92]

---

[88] See n 53 and accompanying text.

[89] For extended discussion of the requirements, Carney, 'Supported Decision-making for People with Cognitive Impairments?', n 2; P. Gooding, 'Navigating the 'Flashing Amber Lights' of the Right to Legal Capacity in the United Nations Convention on the Rights of Persons with Disabilities: Responding to Major Concerns' (2015) 15 *Human Rights Law Review* 45; EAP, 'Three Jurisdictions Report: Towards Compliance with CRPD Art. 12 in Capacity/Incapacity Legislation across the UK' (Essex, UK: The Essex Autonomy Project, University of Essex, 2016), available from http://autonomy.essex.ac.uk/eap-three-jurisdic tions-report.

[90] Australian Law Reform Commission, *Equality, Capacity and Disability in Commonwealth Laws*, n 32, pp. 99–119. The model includes detailed specification of statutory objects and fundamental principles, reinforced by finely crafted formulations of guidelines (ibid., para. [3.4] and ch. 3 generally).

[91] For the deficiencies of existing arrangements: S. Ellison et al., *The Legal Needs of Older People in NSW* (NSW Law and Justice Foundation, 2004), ch. 9; Legal and Constitutional Affairs Committee, *Inquiry into Older People and the Law* (Canberra: Legal and Constitutional Affairs Standing Committee of the House of Representatives, 2007), available from www.aph.gov.au, para. [3.120]; Commonwealth Ombudsman, *Commonwealth Ombudsman Annual Report 2007–2008* (Canberra, Commonwealth Ombudsman, 2008), available from www.ombudsman.gov.au/publications/annual/all-commonwealth-ombudsman-reports/annual_report_07-08, ch. 7; Australian Law Reform Commission, *Family Violence and Commonwealth Laws – Improving Legal Frameworks* (ALRC Report 117, 2011), paras. [9.40]ff. Existing protocols and protections are found in the Centrelink policy guide: http://guides.dss.gov.au/guide-social-security-law/8/5.

[92] Further T. Carney, 'Australian Guardianship Tribunals: An adequate response to CRPD disability rights recognition and protection of the vulnerable over the lifecourse?' (2017) 10 *Journal of Ethics in Mental Health*, available from www.jemh.ca/issues/v9/ theme3.html.

That challenge is best highlighted by an all-too-common social security example. Namely, appointment as correspondence or payment nominee of a well-meaning but ill-informed parent or sibling, who then fails to report or detect errors in the payment being made – such as that Centrelink (the payment agency) had ceased to record part-time earnings at all or had understated them. Such oversights can generate overpayment debts running to several thousand dollars within a short period of a year or so, and that debt is usually fully recoverable.[93] The ability legally to waive such debts is extraordinarily rare, though in one case where a parent was appointed as payment nominee for her intellectually disabled adult son who would 'withdraw' that appointment on a rather erratic basis and instead provided his own information to Centrelink, a portion of a resultant overpayment debt was waived under the 'special circumstances' discretion.[94]

Such challenges of providing adequate safeguards are heightened when 'supporters' (without any decision-making powers) replace substitute decision-making responsibilities of 'representatives' such as payment nominees.[95] This is because, consistent with the equality principle of article 12 of the CRPD, the object is to replicate for people with impairments the same 'informal' supports other citizens routinely tap into in their everyday lives, as they seek or receive advice from friends and families.[96] However, by locating the process further into civil society (subject only to any monitoring or reporting obligations imposed on supporters) any misuse is rendered less 'visible'. For people with intellectual impairment, this risk is compounded by – often unconscious – continuation by carers of their paternalist and risk-adverse overprotective care and management, and by ingrained 'dependency' and lack of

---

[93] This is because the debt is not solely (i.e., exclusively) due to agency error (which precludes recovery when other conditions such as good faith receipt are met) and the circumstances of the person rarely satisfy 'special circumstances' tests to permit discretionary waiver: see Social Security Act 1991 (Cth), ss. 1237A, 1237AAD respectively; further Carney, 'Social Security (title 22.3)', n 61, para. [22.3.4480]; Carney, 'An adequate response to CRPD disability rights recognition and protection of the vulnerable over the lifecourse', n 92.

[94] THBC v. Secretary, Department of Families, Housing, Community Services and Indigenous Affairs [2009] AATA 399 (Administrative Appeals Tribunal, Senior Member Hunt).

[95] For an outline of proposed Safeguards Guidelines, see Australian Law Reform Commission, Equality, Capacity and Disability in Commonwealth Laws, n 32, pp. 13, 64, 86–89.

[96] T. Carney, 'Supported Decision-Making in Australia: Meeting the Challenge of Moving from Capacity to Capacity-Building?' (2017) 35 Law in Context 44.

confidence of the person cared for.[97] The adult guardianship model from the 1980s continues to offer some accountability safeguards, but at the price of disrespecting CRPD values of honouring the 'will, preferences and rights' of people with disabilities by appointing a substitute decision-maker, along with several other unacceptable features such as retention of best interests and capacity tests. By contrast, the NSW Law Reform Commission proposals for supported decision-making and representation arrangements (by agreement or tribunal appointment) are complemented by a far stronger set of accountability safeguards, more capable of dealing with the heightened and less visible risks of supporter arrangements.

V   Conclusion

No planning instrument, however sophisticated or subsidised to encourage use, can provide low-income parents with assets they do not have to set up a trust, or the spare income to put away during their lifetime to pump-prime a savings plan for maintenance of their disabled daughter or son after their death.[98] Nor does it displace the case for payment of a state-funded disability pension or other carer payments of the type provided in Australia,[99] or provision of the more extensive portfolio of supports now able to be assembled under an NDIS plan.

One of the most important lessons in law reform and comparative policy studies, however, is exposing the naivety of the idea that transplanting an institution from another jurisdiction will yield equivalent change (witness Hong Kong adoption of NSW adult guardianship)[100] or

---

[97] B. Curryer, R. Stancliffe and A. Dew, 'Self-Determination: Adults with Intellectual Disability and Their Family' (2015) 40 *Journal of Intellectual and Developmental Disability* 394, 396; further, J. Craigie, 'A Fine Balance: Reconsidering Patient Autonomy in Light of the UN Convention on the Rights of Persons with Disabilities' (2015) 29 *Bioethics* 398, 404; A. Arstein-Kerslake, 'An Empowering Dependency: Exploring Support for the Exercise of Legal Capacity' (2016) 18 *Scandinavian Journal of Disability Research* 77, 77.

[98] T. Ho, *Financial Planning for the Future of Your Special Needs Loved Ones*, available from http://dollarsandsense.sg/financial-planning-for-the-future-of-your-special-needs-loved-ones/.

[99] Ibid.

[100] The phenomenon of lack of replication of impacts from transplanted institutions and general resistance to reform initiatives is a complicated story, described in the literature as 'path-dependence' of policy settings. For a welfare state example, C. Deeming, 'The Working Class and Welfare: Francis G. Castles on the Political Development of the Welfare State in Australia and New Zealand Thirty Years On' (2013) 47 *Social Policy &*

that adoption of a similarly named instrument (such as a special needs trust) involves real equivalence. They do not, as Australia's pathetic special needs trust demonstrates. By comparison with the advantages of planning through supplemental needs trusts,[101] the tax-free savings vehicle of the ABLE accounts in the USA[102] or Canada's Registered Disability Savings Plans (RDSP),[103] the concessions under Australia's special needs trusts are far less generous (and qualification conditions far tighter), and they are confined to 'individual' trusts (there is no provision for pooled trusts or transfers of entitlements of one beneficiary to surviving beneficiaries, as in the USA[104]).

In short, Australia's special needs trusts are a far cry from the 'service trusts' described by Robert Hodgson nearly 45 years ago, based around non-government advocacy organisations pooling parental funds and delivering or organising a suite of services such as housing, social and recreational activities, medical care and service plans;[105] or even from Canada's Henson trust, with its capacity to preserve social security benefits.[106] A service trust, with its civil society social policy base and mandate, also differs from measures mainly providing benefits of economies of scale in trust administration (e.g., Singapore's SNTC trust to

---

Administration 668. For a recent Australia/China review: Willmott et al., 'Guardianship and Health Decisions in China and Australia: A Comparative Analysis', n 14, pp. 4, 20–21.

[101] K. Birkes, 'What Will Happen When I'm Gone?': Chapter 9 of the present volume; R. Froemming, 'The Wispact Trusts: Background, Features and Operation': Chapter 10 of the present volume.

[102] Such trusts had been established in approximately 30 states at the time of writing, under the federal Achieving a Better Life Experience Act of 2014: further www.ablenrc.org; Froemming, ibid.; Birkes, ibid.

[103] See Law Commission of Ontario, *Legal Capacity, Decision-making and Guardianship: Discussion Paper* (Toronto: Law Commission of Ontario, 2014); *Law Commission of Ontario, Capacity of Adults with Mental Disabilities and the Federal RDSP*, n 50. The challenge addressed is to find alternatives to adult guardianship to supply advice about what was characterised as the 'demanding' and 'complex' (ibid., p. 18) decisions and investment choices involved in setting up and dealing with fund distributions from tax advantaged RDSPs, but do so at negligible cost to government (ibid., p. 40).

[104] Simmons, 'The Wrongheadedness of the POMS Pooled Trust Rules', n 58, p. 122.

[105] R. Hodgson, 'Guardianship of Mentally Retarded Persons: Three Approaches to a Long Neglected Problem' (1973) 37 *Albany Law Review* 407, 430.

[106] So-called after the ruling of the Ontario Supreme Court in *Ontario (Ministry of Community and Social Services, Income Maintenance Branch)* v. *Henson* (1989), 36 ETR 192 (Ont CA), affirming *Director of Income Maintenance Branch of Ministry of Community and Social Services* v. *Henson* 28 ETR 121, 26 OAC 332, [1987] OJ No. 1121 (QL) (Div Ct). Further, J. Gillis, 'The Role of Guardianship in the Special Needs Plans in Saskatchewan, Canada': Chapter 2 of the present volume.

prevent the frittering away of resources after parents pass on[107]), and from tax-advantaged long-term savings pooled trust measures (e.g., Canada's generous RDSP or Singapore's less generous SNSS, essentially a state-guaranteed savings 'vehicle'[108]). These models also offer more benefits than mainly just the relief from social security rules obtainable under Australia's sole-beneficiary special needs trust.

Of course, these special needs trust limitations are less acute for some Australian families since the introduction of the NDIS. For the NDIS offers *state-funded* plans that enable the lucky few (or their supporters) to organise packages akin to those of a service trust (without the pooling). But this leaves those not eligible for the NDIS to get by with assistance of correspondence or payment nominees in managing meagre income support – or resorting to financial guardianship appointments of a financial manager (or the Public Trustee if no individual is suitable) – while just a few individuals from wealthier families may derive benefit from special needs trusts.

By contrast, the 'unique' design of Canada's tax-advantaged RDSP pursues a suite of policy objectives, summarised by the Law Commission of Ontario as

> Long-term financial security for those who bear the high costs of disability ... [,] encouraging self-sufficiency through a contributory benefit structure, promoting active citizenship as consumers of mainstream financial services, and developing a partnership among families, the government and the private sector 'to share the responsibility for securing a good life for people with disabilities'.[109]

The savings scheme, for residents who meet the eligibility test for Disability Tax Credit,[110] commenced at the end of 2008 and by

---

[107] Introduced from 2009 as an outsourced or NGO service, as at the date of writing there were 454 trusts of which 25 had been activated: E. Tan and A. Leo, 'SNTC's Operational Experience as Singapore's First Non-Profit Trust Company': Chapter 11 of the present volume.

[108] H. W. Tang, 'Financial Planning Mechanisms Available to Persons with Special Needs in Singapore': Chapter 8 of the present volume.

[109] Law Commission of Ontario, *Capacity and Legal Representation for the Federal RDSP: Final Report* (Toronto: Law Commission of Ontario, 2014), p. 10, available from www.lco-cdo.org/en/rdsp-final-report.

[110] The non-refundable Disability Tax Credit is available to both family and carers, as well as the person with a disability, to offset income tax otherwise payable: Canada Revenue Agency, *Disability Tax Credit*, available from www.canada.ca/en/revenue-agency/ser vices/tax/individuals/segments/tax-credits-deductions-persons-disabilities/disability-tax-credit.html.

2014 had more than 80,000 participants,[111] compared to 687 operative special needs trusts in Australia in February 2018,[112] or (for different reasons) Korea's mere 20 over nearly two decades.[113] The Canadian success results from several features. Plans in Canada are regulated by the tax office but are offered by banks or credit unions along with their other investment products, and the plan contract is made with the provider. Periodic benefits generally are not available until a person turns 60, but contributions are leveraged by generous government subsidies (at up to 300 per cent of contributions of CAD3,500 p.a., capped at CAD70,000 over a lifetime) and tax concessions. Low-income families unable to contribute at all receive 'bond' payments into the RDSP of CAD1,000 p.a. (capped at CAD20,000 in a lifetime).[114] A single drawdown (Disability Assistance Payment) is permitted prior to turning 60 without attracting penalty (with reductions if within 10 years of commencement). Neither capital contributions nor the periodic payments at 60 (called Lifetime Disability Assistance Payments) are counted as assets or income for the purpose of income support (including provincial income support payments in addition to those the federal government is constitutionally responsible for).[115]

Countries lacking extended income support for people with disabilities, or which do not condition such support on tight means-testing,[116] do not, of course, share Australian and US or Canadian needs to design

---

[111] Law Commission of Ontario, *Capacity and Legal Representation for the Federal RDSP: Final Report*, n 109, p. 11; L. Pennisi, *Understanding Special Disability Trusts*, available from www.qls.com.au.

[112] SNTs reportedly held a total of AUD158,899,516 of assets, or an average of approximately AUD231,000 per trust. Of the 773 SDTs 'approved' (with 31 rejected) 86 had been wound up, 16 had become non-compliant over time, and 59 trusts had vested: Personal communication, 'Special Disability Trust Aggregated Totals', S. Owen, Department of Human Services, 25 June 2018. By contrast, registration (required to qualify for the tax concession) under the national register of Australian Business Names (ABN) disclosed 160 by 2014 and 187 by 2017: www.abr.business.gov.au.

[113] C. Je, 'A New Perspective on Adult Guardianship and Trusts in Korea': Chapter 12 of the present volume.

[114] The subsidies are called the Canada Disability Savings Grant and the Canada Disability Savings Bond respectively: Law Commission of Ontario, *Capacity and Legal Representation for the Federal RDSP: Final Report*, n 109, p. 9.

[115] Ibid, pp. 2, 9–12.

[116] Hong Kong's Social Security Allowance scheme is not means-tested, but qualification on the basis of disability is very strict, appearing to require close to 100 per cent incapacity; payments under the 'minimum safety net' scheme, the Comprehensive Social Security Assistance Scheme, are means-tested: www.swd.gov.hk/en/index/site_pubsvc/page_soc secu/sub_comprehens/.

special needs trusts to provide relief from such rules while avoiding creation of loopholes for astute tax avoidance planners. As social contexts change, so do the form and the function served by any new laws. For example, the most pressing need in Hong Kong may be for a specialist low-cost trustee service, given the restrictions on the levels of assets and other services currently able to be provided under guardianship orders.[117] With its unrestricted financial management orders under guardianship and its longer history of 'full-service' public trustee institutions, most Australian jurisdictions are already adequately served in that regard. However, to take another example, some US commentators have argued that pooled special needs trusts should be the intestacy default creation in the event that an intestacy favours a person with a cognitive disability in that country,[118] a suggestion that could be considered in Australia.

As shown in this review of Australia's planning options for people with cognitive impairments, the number and types of instruments, and the timing of their introduction, has been shaped by the architecture of its welfare state. Australia's somewhat unique combination of extensive access to tightly means-tested income support (and reforms to overcome tax minimisation or avoidance) made it difficult to craft a special disability trust offering benefits beyond amelioration of social security impacts or one catering to other than a narrow group of people with severe disability. A history of extensive welfare state services and an absence of expectations of significant family support has seen the provision of strong public sector agencies such as guardianship tribunals, offices of public trustees, public guardians and advocacy/ombudsman-like agencies such as the office of public advocate. Disability and carer payments – dating from 1908 for DSP, with 1983 (CP) and 1974 (CA)

---

[117] I. Cheng, *Public Trust Services for Persons with Intellectual Disabilities*, available from www.legco.gov.hk/research-publications/english/essentials-1617ise04-public-trust-services-for-persons-with-intellectual-disabilities.htm, para. [1] (restricted to managing 'cash assets up to a limit of HK$15,000 per month for the benefits and maintenance of the incapacitated person ... However, some parents [intending to bequeath assets] consider that the financial power of an appointed guardian is too limited. For example, a guardian is not empowered to handle non-cash assets such as real estate and stocks, or manage other financial affairs such as making investments for their children').

[118] J. Sullivan, 'Pooled Special-Needs Trusts: An Exemption that Should Be the Rule to Protect Adults with Developmental Disabilities' (2009) 27 *Law and Inequality* 441, pp. 444, 453–463.

origins of the since-expanded carer payments[119] – along with the more recent rolling out of the NDIS, reflect acceptance of state responsibility for funding of services for disabled people least able to care for themselves.

While anything but perfect, given the incomplete operationalisation of fiduciary obligations and accountability protections around payment and other 'nominee' appointments, the configuration of planning options for Australians with a cognitive impairment is nevertheless a product of the values, strengths and limitations of its welfare state.[120] The planning instruments, and the timing of their introduction, reflects adaption to that welfare architecture, including its somewhat unique combination of extensive access to tightly means-tested income support (and reforms to overcome tax minimisation or avoidance), the absence of any expectation of family support and acceptance of state responsibility for funding of services for disabled people least able to care for themselves.

---

[119] B. Edwards et al., *The Nature and Impact of Caring for Family Members with a Disability in Australia* (Melbourne: Australian Institute of Family Studies, 2008), pp. 5–7, available from https://aifs.gov.au/publications/nature-and-impact-caring-family-members-di.

[120] Carney, 'Where Now Australia's Welfare State', n 3; Carney, 'The Future of Welfare Law in a Changing World', n 6. See also the analysis of planning instruments in Asia and the way they reflect cultural, institutional and other forces: Tsoh et al., 'Comparisons of Guardianship Laws and Surrogate Decision-making Practices', n 14.

2

The Role of Guardianship in Special Needs Plans in Saskatchewan, Canada

JAMES H. GILLIS*

I Introduction

This chapter examines the law and practice of guardianship in the Canadian province of Saskatchewan.[1] Its main purpose is to show how, in the Saskatchewan context, guardianship can be made to work in conjunction with family estate-planning and government funding sources in securing the well-being of persons with cognitive impairments.[2] The chapter concludes with a brief discussion of the role that guardianship may play in jurisdictions that, unlike Saskatchewan, have established a broad-based special needs trust to assist families in planning for the financial needs of an affected family member.

Section II examines the scope, effect and practical application of The Adult Guardianship and Co-decision-making Act,[3] Saskatchewan's governing legislation in this area. The emphasis here is on the legal and

---

* Lawyer, Saskatchewan, Canada.

[1] Saskatchewan is one of the 10 provinces and three territories in the federation of Canada. Through the constitutional division of powers between the Canadian federal government and the provincial and territorial legislatures, jurisdiction over the issues of guardianship and management of the affairs of persons with intellectual disabilities rests with the provinces and territories. For this reason, there is considerable divergence across Canada in the laws governing those issues.

[2] This chapter deals primarily with one type of cognitive impairment, namely 'intellectual disability', which refers to a condition typically occurring at or near birth that limits the capacity of the affected individual to understand or make informed decisions about his or her life circumstances. For some, their intellectual disability affects them to the extent that they require ongoing or frequent intervention from others to manage their day-to-day life. Such individuals typically remain financially dependent on others over their lifetimes and, therefore, never acquire estates of significant value other than through inheritance. In addition, they typically do not marry or have children, and thus estate succession is not an issue for them. The primary focus of this chapter is on individuals fitting this particular profile.

[3] R.S.S. 1978, c A-5.3 (hereafter the 'Guardianship Act').

social aspects of guardianship rather than on its financial aspects. The past 25 years have seen guardianship's steady development in Saskatchewan from a highly intrusive, rigid instrument to one that seeks to enable flexible solutions that maximise independence and free choice.

Section III looks at how guardianship can be integrated with financial and other planning tools within the legal and social context of Saskatchewan. This examination focusses on trusts funded through various means – such as legacies, life insurance and tax-planned investment programmes – and on coordinating those trusts with both government financial assistance plans and programmes offered by residential and vocational service providers. Concurrent with the evolution of its guardianship laws, Saskatchewan has moved from an environment that assigns the primary financial responsibility for individuals with cognitive impairments to their families to one that recognises those individuals' right, as citizens of the province, to the benefit of government financial support and, where the family can provide it, enhanced quality of life.

Finally, Section IV concludes by looking beyond the context of Saskatchewan to consider whether guardianship plays a necessary or useful role in jurisdictions that have implemented special needs trusts.

A central consideration of this chapter is the role of government in the affairs of individuals with intellectual disabilities. In Saskatchewan, the primary governmental actors in this arena are the Public Guardian and Trustee ('PGT') and the Department of Social Services ('Social Services'). Operating within the Department of Justice, the PGT plays a central role in the guardianship process, as well as being tasked with general oversight of the legal affairs of those with diminished mental capacity. Within Social Services, a dedicated department called the Community Living Division is responsible for providing social and financial support to persons with cognitive impairments.

Except in hardship situations, Canadians generally prefer to avoid the involvement of government in family matters. It is thus interesting to examine how the line is drawn between government and the individual in addressing the affairs of those with intellectual disabilities in Saskatchewan.

II Scope, Effect and Application of the Guardianship Act

A Terminology

In this chapter, the familiar term 'guardianship' is used to refer generally to the legal authority acquired by one person to intervene in another's right to make decisions for him or herself. However, as we will see, in the Guardianship Act, 'guardianship' has a specific legal meaning, referring to the particular level of legal authority that enables *substituted decision-making*. The Guardianship Act also makes provision for 'co-decision-making', a less intrusive level of legal authority that enables *supported decision-making*. Guardians and co-decision-makers are referred to together in the Guardianship Act as 'decision-makers'.

Although the age threshold for guardianship in Saskatchewan (16 years) is two years younger than the province's age of majority, the Guardianship Act refers to the subject of a guardianship application or order as an 'adult'. That term will thus be used throughout the chapter for economy of language.

B   Towards Self-Determination

In a keynote address delivered to the Guardianship Conference of Hong Kong in February 2017,[4] Malcolm Schyvens, Chair of the Australian Guardianship and Administration Council, stated:

> A person's ability to determine their own future and to make choices about their own life and circumstances strikes at the very heart of what it means to be human. So what happens when a person's capacity to make decisions for themselves about important issues affecting their everyday life and the management of their assets is impaired? How are questions like these answered?: 'Where should the person live?', 'What medical treatment and services should they receive' and 'How is their money to be managed?' Who should provide the assistance that a person needs and in what circumstances should that assistance be provided? Whose values or standards or what decision making framework is to be applied in making such decisions? How is the desire to prevent the risk to or the exploitation of vulnerable people balanced against a person's freedom to make their own decisions? And even before that, what tests should be applied to determine the level of capacity required to make these everyday decisions? Should a person be free to make decisions that may not accord with a 'best interests' standard? These are not new questions but have their origins in the time of the Chancery where the common law started to try to find ways to answer these questions through formal legal structures and the formation of administrative law.

---

[4] M. Schyvens, 'Trends in Legal Development of Guardianship: A Transition or a Destination' (Keynote speech at the 2nd Guardianship Conference of Hong Kong, Hong Kong, 18 February 2017).

> In recent times, these questions have received a renewed attention and
> focus, propelled by the UN Convention on the Rights of Persons with
> Disabilities ('the Convention'), which came into being in 2008.
> . . .
> International law and thinking on the rights of persons with disabilities
> now favours a model that puts the 'will, preferences and rights' of the
> person concerned at the centre of the decision making process.
> A *supported* decision making model is preferred to the current *substitute*
> decision-making model, in keeping with the Convention. *(footnotes omit-*
> *ted and emphasis added)*

Since the enactment of the Guardianship Act's predecessor legislation,
The Dependant Adult's Act,[5] in 1990, the issues raised in Schyvens's
statement have been part of an ongoing discussion in Saskatchewan. The
Guardianship Act came into force on 15 July 2001 – in the midst of a
vigorous debate between, on the one side, community-based organisations providing residential and vocational services to individuals with
intellectual disabilities and, on the other side, advocates of inclusion and
free choice for those individuals. That debate centred primarily on the
prospect of 'deinstitutionalisation', which advocated the closure of facilities providing services in congregated settings, in the hope that such a
move would lead to the greater inclusion of persons with intellectual
disabilities in mainstream society. Some proponents of deinstitutionalisation regarded guardianship as an unwarranted intrusion on the legal
rights of those affected and, therefore, opposed it on principle. Its
opponents, in contrast, tended to prefer practicality over legal principle,
and favoured simplifying and streamlining the guardianship process to
make it more accessible to the general public.

The Guardianship Act constitutes a synthesis of these opposing views.
It enhanced the protections provided by its predecessor legislation in a
number of ways, including the addition of a 'supported decision-making'
component (co-decision-making) to complement the traditional 'substituted decision-making' component (guardianship). It established an
assessment protocol requiring specific examination of the nature and
extent of decision-making intervention required and introduced an
objection process. It provided for scrutiny by advocacy groups, giving
greater emphasis to the wishes of the subject, and included a statement of
legal principles governing whether and how guardianship orders should
be made. At the same time, however, the Guardianship Act retained,

---

[5] Statutes of Saskatchewan, 1989–1990 c D-25.1.

albeit with some refinement, the relatively simple procedure in the predecessor legislation enabling 'routine' consideration of guardianship applications by the courts in the substantial majority of cases involving persons with moderate to severe intellectual impairment, where the need was clear and the application had the support of all family members concerned.

Over the intervening years, Saskatchewan has emerged as a progressive jurisdiction in supporting the rights and interests of those with cognitive impairments. In 2009, Social Services implemented the Saskatchewan Assured Income for Disability (SAID) programme, which effected significant improvements in the previous income assistance plan covering persons with disabilities. The province's disability strategy, announced in June 2015 and entitled 'People before Systems',[6] is strong affirmation of full citizenship and inclusion for all persons with disabilities. Saskatchewan is also blessed with a wealth of high-quality residential and vocational services serving the population of intellectually disabled persons, provided in large measure by non-governmental organisations run by volunteer boards of directors.

The past 25 years have also seen significant developments in guardianship legislation in other parts of Canada. Although there is remarkable variety in the way that various Canadian provinces have addressed the issue, they are quite consistent in attempting to find a balance between the 'best interests' and 'will, preferences and rights' of the subjects of guardianship orders. All Canadian jurisdictions require guardians to act in the best interests of subjects, but they vary in the degree to which they also require them to take subjects' wishes into account. The way in which Saskatchewan's governing legislation seeks this balance is examined in greater detail in the following sections.

C   Key Features of the Guardianship Act

The Guardianship Act makes guardianship available to any person 16 years of age or older. As noted earlier, the Act creates two levels of decision-making authority, guardianship and co-decision-making, and uses the term 'decision-maker' to refer to the recipient of either level.

The most important features of the Guardianship Act can be summarised as follows.

---

[6] Government of Saskatchewan, *People before Systems: Transferring the Experience of Disability in Saskatchewan* (Regina: Government of Saskatchewan, 2015).

1   Focus on Function

In some jurisdictions, guardianship legislation distinguishes between intellectual disability ('mental handicap') and impaired decision-making arising from mental illness or brain injury ('mental disorder'). This is the case with Hong Kong's Mental Health Ordinance, for example. The Guardianship Act, however, focusses on impairment of capacity, irrespective of its cause or diagnosis, defining capacity as 'the ability to understand information relevant to making a decision, and to appreciate the reasonably foreseeable consequences of making or not making a decision'.[7] This focus allows the Act to apply to the full spectrum of cognitive impairments – including dementia, brain injury, addiction issues, mental illness and other causes of impairment – as well as to intellectual disability.

2   Comprehensiveness and Uniformity

Some jurisdictions differentiate between personal affairs and property-related matters in their approach to guardianship, sometimes covering them under different legislation, prescribing different assessment standards or methods for them, and placing them in different hands, be they those of the state or individuals, or assigning their adjudication to different decision-makers as between the courts, administrative tribunals and healthcare professionals.

The Guardianship Act covers both personal and property matters, uniformly places guardianship over both in the hands of family members or other interested individuals (with the PGT playing a role only in the absence of any suitable candidate for guardian), prescribes the same assessment method for both and places the adjudication of both in the hands of the court.

3   Balance of 'Best Interests' with 'Will, Preferences and Rights'

Section 3 of the Guardianship Act states the following principles.

(a) [A]dults are entitled to have their best interests given paramount consideration;

(b) adults are entitled to be presumed to have capacity, unless the contrary is demonstrated;

(c) adults are entitled to choose the manner in which they live and to accept or refuse support, assistance or protection, as long as they do

---

[7] Guardianship Act, s. 2(c).

not harm themselves or others and have the capacity to make decisions about those matters;

(d) adults are entitled to receive the most effective, but the least restrictive and intrusive, form of support, assistance or protection, when
they are unable to care for themselves or their estates;

(e) adults who have difficulty communicating because of physical or
mental disabilities are entitled to communicate by any means that
enables them to be understood; [and]

(f) adults are entitled to be informed about and, to the best of their
ability, participate in, decisions affecting them.

Sections 25 and 50 of the Guardianship Act address the duties of
personal decision-makers and property decision-makers, respectively,
in the following terms.

> A personal [or property] decision-maker shall exercise the duties and
> powers assigned by the court diligently, in good faith, in the best interests
> of the adult [or the adult's estate] and in a manner so as to:
>
> (a) ensure that the adult's civil and human rights are protected;
> (b) encourage the adult to:
> (i) participate to the maximum extent in all decisions affecting the
> adult's estate; and
> (ii) act independently in all matters in which the adult is able to; and
> (c) limit the personal [or property] decision-maker's interference in the
> life of the adult to the greatest extent possible.

These provisions illustrate the legislators' effort to strike a balance
between substituted and supported decision-making in the discharge of
a decision-maker's duties, a balance that can be difficult to strike.

For the most part, the Guardianship Act uses 'best interests' terminology
in defining the powers of the court in dealing with guardianship applications, which suggests that the *parens patriae* jurisdiction traditionally
exercised by the courts over minors and adults with impaired capacity
remains intact in Saskatchewan. However, sections 13 and 39, which
address the court's mandated inquiry when considering applications for
personal and property decision-making orders, specifically require the
court to take into account 'the wishes of the adult, having regard to his
or her capacity respecting matters relating to his or her person [*or estate*]'.

In addition, the Guardianship Act gives the PGT, as part of its
mandated role, the discretion to contact the adult to determine his or
her wishes to be represented in the proceedings.[8]

---

[8] Ibid., ss. 11(2) and 37.

Perhaps the Guardianship Act's most significant shift in emphasis towards an adult's will and preferences is its provision of a choice between substituted decision-making (guardianship) and supported decision-making (co-decision-making). The language used in the Act to distinguish between the two is remarkably simple:[9]

- a co-decision-making order will be made for any matter in respect of which the adult's capacity is impaired to the extent that he or she *requires assistance in decision-making in order to make* reasonable decisions' with respect to that matter; and
- a guardianship decision-making order will be made for any matter in respect of which the adult's capacity is impaired to the extent that he or she is *unable to make* reasonable decisions' with respect to that matter. (*emphasis added*)

While the enactment of the Guardianship Act preceded the coming into force of the UN Convention on the Rights of Persons with Disabilities (CRPD) by about seven years, it is clear from the foregoing, and from the other features of the Guardianship Act referred to in this section, that the issues embraced in article 12 of the CRPD were in the view of the framers of the Saskatchewan legislation. Exercise of will and preference, minimal intrusiveness, safeguards against conflict of interest, provision for review of court orders and the presumption of capacity are all provided for in the Guardianship Act, reflecting a major departure from its predecessor legislation. This shift occurred in the context of a strong and persistent campaign across Canada by the Canadian Association of Community Living and other advocacy organisations that began in the 1980s and gained considerable force in the 1990s. As mentioned in Section II, one of the key features of that campaign in Saskatchewan and elsewhere in Canada was a drive to close down congregate residential and vocational services because of their 'institutional' nature. Another important issue, however, was the whole question of adult guardianship. In the mid-to-late 1990s advocacy groups began to intervene on behalf of cognitively impaired individuals whose families were seeking court-ordered guardianship for them. Guardianship was seen by these groups as the wrong solution in every instance because it stripped away the affected individual's legal rights. The Saskatchewan government of the day was sensitive to the controversy around these issues, and initiated a

---

[9] Ibid., ss. 14(1) and 40(1).

public consultation process in or around 1998 that led to the passage of the Guardianship Act in 2000, coming into force in 2001.

While the Guardianship Act established a framework for observance of article 12 of the CRPD, it is not entirely clear that its practical implementation has fully lived up to its promise. There is no doubt that higher-functioning individuals with cognitive impairment have benefited from it. Over the years there seems to have been a growing willingness and interest among those who provide the required professional assessments to ensure through their recommendations to the court that the spirit and intent of the Act is embodied in the orders they make. For those with more significant impairment, however, the Act continues to serve as a reasonably expedient means to achieving orders that are not significantly different from those which would have arisen under the predecessor legislation. In many cases, this is likely the appropriate result. However, as always, the difficult balance between justice and expediency must be watched closely. Under Saskatchewan law, this function is ultimately entrusted to the professional assessors and the courts. There is no recent indication from the advocacy groups, or from any other interested members of the public, that these functionaries are failing in any way in their important roles.

The guardian's authority[10] is straightforward. He or she may do on behalf of the subject adult anything that that adult would ordinarily have the legal authority to do in relation to any matter covered by the guardianship order, with the adult ceasing to have any legal authority over any aspect of that matter. Section II.C.4 contains a general description of the things that can be covered in a guardianship order. The order as it relates to property and financial matters is all-inclusive, although it can be modified or restricted to allow an individual to retain legal control over certain aspects of his or her affairs, such as making routine purchases or engaging in transactions of less than a certain value. Authority over personal issues is treated differently. Specific aspects of personal life are delineated in the Act, and the court order must mention each aspect for which guardianship is needed.

The co-decision-maker's authority is more nuanced, with section 17 providing:

> 17(1) Subject to section 22, the personal co-decision-maker may advise the adult respecting the matters the court determines are within the

---

[10] Ibid., ss. 18 and 43.

personal co-decision-maker's authority and, subject to subsection (2), shall share with the adult the authority to make decisions respecting those matters and may do all things necessary to give effect to the authority vested in him or her.

(2) A personal co-decision-maker shall acquiesce in a decision made by the adult and shall not refuse to sign a document mentioned in section 16 if a reasonable person could have made the decision in question and no harm to the adult is likely to result from the decision.

Section 42 outlines a corresponding provision for property co-decision-making. Co-decision-making thus falls somewhat short of according full force and effect to the adult's will and preference, as the co-decision maker is empowered to override a decision by the adult if it does not fall within the range of decisions that a reasonable person would make in the circumstances and the outcome is likely to be harmful to the adult. While conceptually clear enough, this is an extremely difficult provision to apply, since, when differences arise between adult and co-decision-maker, there will normally be no practical means to adjudicate whether or not the adult's wishes should be overridden.

It is safe to say that co-decision-making is not well understood by the general public in Saskatchewan. The Guardianship Act leaves many unanswered questions as to the legal effect of contracts made by persons who are the subject of co-decision-making orders. It is difficult to distinguish between the Act's general admonition to respect the wishes of the subject of any order made under it and the specific requirement to involve the subject of a co-decision-making order in the decision-making process. There are no reported court decisions on these questions.

It may be that the most important role of co-decision-making is in giving specific recognition of the need to respect and conserve the legal personality of persons with cognitive impairment as much as is possible to do, and in providing principle and guidance to anyone who steps into the role of caring for a person with cognitive impairment in this special way.

4 Least Restrictive and Intrusive Support

As seen previously, the principles stated in section 3 of the Guardianship Act include a requirement that the subject of a guardianship application be entitled to 'the most effective, but the least restrictive and intrusive' decision-making support available. Sections 13, 14, 39 and 40 require the court, in considering an application for guardianship or co-decision-making, to also consider whether less intrusive support or assistance is available to meet the adult's needs, and preclude it from granting a decision-making order unless less intrusive means have been tried or carefully considered.

The order-making powers conferred upon the court in the Guardianship Act are designed to enable the court to construct an order that is 'tailor-made' to the particular needs and abilities of the adult in question. In simple terms, the Guardianship Act divides the adult's affairs into two major categories – personal matters and property matters – and further subdivides personal matters into numerous subcategories – including healthcare decisions; decisions about where to live; who to associate with; and which social, vocational and educational activities to engage in; and other decisions of a personal nature.[11] For each category or subcategory, the court must determine whether the adult needs any decision-making assistance in relation to it and, if so, whether that assistance should come in the form of co-decision-making or guardianship. Section 22 permits the court to add further conditions to or limitations upon a personal decision-making order, enabling further refinement.

Whilst there are no corresponding subcategories in decision-making about property matters, section 40 of the Guardianship Act permits the court to add further conditions or limitations to a property decision-making order and, in particular, to set a minimum value threshold to the property guardian's authority, thereby reserving an appropriate degree of autonomy for the adult under guardianship.

The combinations available to the court in granting a guardianship order demonstrate the Guardianship Act's flexibility in accommodating the particular abilities and needs of the adult in any application.

5   Parties and Procedures

The Guardianship Act allows any person who in the court's opinion has a sufficient interest in the personal or financial welfare of the adult to apply for a personal or property decision-making order, with preference afforded to persons with a long-standing caring relationship with him or her. It also empowers the PGT to apply for such an order. Finally, the Act enables the government to designate agencies with the authority to apply for a personal or property decision-making order, although no such designation has been made to date.[12]

Although the PGT has the statutory authority to apply for guardianship of an adult or to object to the guardianship application of any

[11]   Ibid., s. 15.
[12]   Ibid., ss. 6 and 30.

person, in practice it always favours guardianship by family members or others with a genuine interest in the adult in question. Accordingly, the PGT's main interest in a guardianship application is normally to ensure that adequate financial safeguards are in place in cases in which a fund has been established for the adult's financial benefit. The PGT will intervene to ensure that the guardian has posted a sufficient bond to secure the performance of his or her duties and that he or she submits a financial report in prescribed form to the PGT annually.[13]

The PGT must be notified of all guardianship applications.[14] One of its duties upon receipt of such notification is to advise any 'advocacy group' identified in the Adult and Co-decision-making Regulations ('the Regulations' hereafter) as having an interest in the subject of the application.[15] The involvement of advocacy groups is a feature of the Guardianship Act that arose from the debate between advocates and community-based organisations that was ongoing at the time the legislation was passed.[16] It was specifically included in the legislation at the request of representatives of advocacy groups who participated in the consultation process that preceded the passage of the Act. It is there to provide an additional safeguard against the granting of unnecessary or overly intrusive guardianship orders. To date, there are no reported decisions involving intervention by an advocacy group.

Anyone served with notice of a guardianship application, as well as anyone who claims a sufficient interest in the affairs of the subject of such an application, may file a statement of objection to the requested order.[17] In the case of objection, the court will set the matter down for a hearing if it considers it necessary to do so.[18] However, objections very seldom occur when applications are made in the context of a well-worked-out family plan. Barring any basis for challenging the suitability of an applicant/applicants, and with a suitable financial bond in place, the PGT will generally not oppose to the application. The adult in question will in most cases not object, and no advocacy group will object on his or her behalf. With no resistance on any front, the court is left to consider the application solely on the basis of the materials filed by the applicant(s),

---

[13] Ibid., ss. 44(6) and 54.
[14] Ibid., ss. 7 and 31.
[15] Ibid., ss. 11(1) and 36.
[16] See Section II.B.
[17] Guardianship Act, ss. 8 and 32.
[18] Ibid., ss. 9 and 33.

and the guardianship order will generally be granted without any formal hearing on all or substantially all of the terms requested.

6   Assessment and Adjudication

A guardianship application must also include two independent professional assessments of the adult in question. Those assessments must comprise detailed statements in a prescribed form made by healthcare or related specialists identified in the Regulations[19] – including medical doctors, registered psychologists, registered nurses and psychiatric nurses, registered occupational therapists, registered social workers, and registered speech pathologists [20] – and are of central importance to the application.

The prescribed form directs the assessor to make a recommendation to the court as to whether the assessed adult requires the intervention of either a guardian or a co-decision-maker in relation to each aspect of the adult's personal life listed for consideration in the Guardianship Act and in relation to his or her financial affairs.

As already noted, most guardianship applications involving persons with cognitive impairments proceed without objection and are considered by the court based only on the evidence presented by the applicant(s). The assessors' recommendations are thus typically the most significant determinants of the application outcome. Whilst the court may question certain practical aspects of an application, there are seldom any grounds for it not to follow recommendations made by duly qualified professionals prescribed under legislation created for that very purpose.

Accordingly, whilst the judicial process established under the Guardianship Act engages the Act's legal principles and assures due process, the substantive determination in the majority of applications is entrusted to the caring professions who often work most closely with the affected individuals.

III   Guardianship in the Overall Plan

A   The Financial Plan

1   The Henson Trust and the Social Contract

Prior to the late 1980s, it was well established in Canada that the parents of individuals with disabilities that prevented them from being financially self-sufficient had a legal responsibility to provide financial support for

---

[19] The Adult and Co-decision-making Regulations ('Regulations') A-5.3 Reg. 1.
[20] Guardianship Act, s. 5.

those individuals through their estates. From 1940 until its repeal in 1996, that responsibility was enforced in Saskatchewan through legislation entitled The Dependants' Relief Act,[21] which relieved the government of any financial responsibility for the individual concerned until his or her deceased parents' estates had been depleted. The legislation left parents in an unenviable position. Not only was their ability to benefit any of their other children restricted, but the sum they were required to direct to the support of their disabled child offered no tangible benefit to that child because its sole purpose was to fund the necessaries of life that would otherwise have been covered through government assistance. In effect, the government was often the primary beneficiary of the estates of parents in this position.

The conundrum led to some creative approaches being devised by lawyers and estate planners. The most successful approach, and the one most commonly used today, is known in Canada as the Henson trust. It is named for Ms Audrey Joan Henson, a woman with an intellectual disability who lived in the province of Ontario and was the beneficiary of a trust created under the terms of her father's will. The trust contained features intended to make adequate provision for Ms Henson – as her father was legally obliged to do – without impairing her continued receipt of social assistance after his death. Following his death, the Ontario Department of Social Services challenged the efficacy of the trust, leading to a 1987 Supreme Court of Ontario decision cited as *Ontario (Ministry of Community and Social Services, Income Maintenance Branch)* v. *Henson.*[22] The decision, which to some extent upheld the intended effect of the trust, established a legal basis for the use of a trust as a means of enabling parents to enhance the quality of life of their children with cognitive impairments through their estates while protecting those children's entitlement to government support for basic necessities. As discussed in the following paragraphs, it took years for what subsequently became known as the Henson trust to be recognised in Canada as a legitimate estate-planning tool for that purpose. Today, its use is firmly established in Saskatchewan and in most other provinces of Canada.

At the time of writing this chapter, a decision of the Court of Appeal of the Province of British Columbia named *S. A.* v. *Metro Vancouver Housing Corporation,*[23] awaits hearing by the Supreme Court of Canada,

---

[21] R.S.S. 1940 c 111.
[22] [1987] OJ No. 1121.
[23] 2017 BCCA 2 (37551).

with no date yet set for hearing. The dispute is over whether or not a fund held in a Henson trust for S. A. (an individual with a disability that prevents her from earning a livelihood) constitutes an 'asset' which must be taken into account in determining her eligibility for provincially subsidized housing. While this dispute may ultimately require examination of the legal efficacy of the Henson trust, the issue before the Court at this stage is limited to whether S. A. is required to disclose information about the trust in her housing application. If the Supreme Court limits its consideration to these disclosure requirements, its decision may cast no light on the efficacy of the Henson trust itself. It is noted as well that the trust in the S. A. case lacks one of the essential components of a Henson trust discussed in the next paragraphs, namely the requirement to limit its use to supporting things that enhance the beneficiary's quality of life as opposed to meeting his or her basic needs. (The stated purpose of S. A.'s trust is to provide for the 'care, maintenance, education or benefit' of the beneficiary. While this wording is commonly used, it must be avoided if the intention is to avoid impairing the beneficiary's access to income assistance, since 'maintenance' means meeting basic needs, thus obviating the need for income assistance.) As such, even an adverse finding on the efficacy of the trust in S. A.'s case would not necessary impact properly drafted Henson trusts. Despite all of this, the outcome of S. A.'s case will be of great interest to those who assist in planning for families with members who have need of Henson trusts.

The Henson trust accomplishes its objective to preserve the beneficiary's entitlement to social assistance through the following key features.

- It vests the bequest in the trustee, meaning the funds concerned are not legally the property of the beneficiary;
- it places the use of those funds at the unfettered discretion of the trustee, meaning the beneficiary never enjoys an enforceable right to all or any part of the funds;
- it specifies that the trustee should *not* apply the funds to meeting the beneficiary's *basic needs*, but *only* to things that enhance his or her *quality of life* beyond meeting those needs; and
- it provides for a 'gift over' of the residue of the trust funds to others upon the beneficiary's death.

The end result is that no part of the trust can ever be seen to vest in the beneficiary, and hence the government social assistance provider cannot take any part of it into account in means-testing to establish benefit entitlement. As the trustee is not permitted to direct any part of the trust funds to meeting the beneficiary's basic needs, the government is not relieved of its responsibility for meeting those needs under its basic social assistance obligation.

Sample wording for a Henson trust is attached in the Appendix to this chapter. For the sake of comprehensiveness, the sample wording contains a long list of the purposes to which a trust of this nature might be directed, although it is doubtful that any individual case would include all of those purposes.

As a Henson trust is normally funded only after the death of the beneficiary's parents, it is usually set up in the parents' wills. However, if the trust is funded through a 'joint and last to die' life insurance policy or through an investment vehicle that contains a beneficiary designation, it is also possible to establish it through a trust agreement made with the designated beneficiary. This method generally enables a Henson trust to be established more quickly and at less cost than establishment in a will, as the trust funds form no part of the deceased parent's estate. It may also enable the funds to avoid the claims of creditors.

Saskatchewan's acceptance of the Henson trust is expressed partly in policy and partly by regulation. Subsection 14.3 of The Saskatchewan Assured Income Disability Regulations, 2012, provides that discretionary trusts are not considered as assets of an applicant for the purpose of determining eligibility for SAID benefits, nor are payments from such trusts that are used for purposes other than ordinary living expenses. Section 20.1.6 of the Saskatchewan Assistance Program Policy provides:[24]

> Discretionary Trusts – A trust established as a result of a will where an individual named in the will as trustee has complete control over the disposition of the funds. These are usually set up by the family for a family member with a disability. Funds released for the client's basic needs are income. A copy of the will should be sent to Central Office for review.

As can be seen from this policy statement, even now the regulatory acceptance of the trust's intended operation is closely guarded. A will purporting to create a Henson trust is reviewed by Social Services' legal counsel to determine whether it meets the legal requirements for such a trust. Social Services requires annual reports from the recipients of benefits (or their guardians) and scrutinises the use of trust funds. Anything used to meet 'basic needs' is classed as 'income', and if the recipient's total income determined on that basis exceeds his or her

---

[24] Ministry of Social Services, Saskatchewan.

threshold under the programme, social assistance benefits are held back or required to be repaid.

The foregoing approach is part of a policy-based consensus between Social Services and the PGT as to how they discharge their respective legal mandates for those with cognitive impairments. This consensus is referred to herein as a 'social contract', as it is intended to reflect society's current view of the proper balance between fiscal responsibility and the rights of citizens with disabilities. It arises from the following legal considerations.

- Under The Saskatchewan Assistance Act[25] and The Saskatchewan Assured Income for Disability Regulations, 2012,[26] an adult with a cognitive impairment that prevents him or her from earning a livelihood is entitled to government-funded assistance benefits aimed at meeting his or her basic needs.
- Under The Dependants' Relief Act, an adult child of a deceased parent is entitled to the provision of 'reasonable maintenance' (which refers to the meeting of basic needs) from the parent's estate.

Social Services is mandated to provide financial assistance, whereas the PGT is mandated to enforce 'reasonable maintenance' claims against the estates of deceased parents who have not made adequate provision for their adult children with disabilities.

Until the late 1980s, the prevailing attitude of both Social Services and the PGT was that parents' financial duty under The Dependants' Relief Act took precedence over Social Services' duty to provide financial assistance in these circumstances. Thus, in cases in which deceased parents had not made adequate provision for a disabled child's basic needs, the PGT would require the administrators of their estates to set aside funds sufficient to meet those needs, over the child's lifetime if possible or at least until the estate funds had been exhausted, with Social Services restoring social assistance to the child only at that point. The end result was that parents were unable to leave their disabled children a legacy that provided them with any tangible benefit – that is, funds sufficient to enhance their quality of life beyond mere subsistence.

The implicit assertion of the Henson trust was that, by specifying that their legacy was to be used only to enhance the beneficiary's quality of life, parents had in fact provided 'reasonable maintenance' for the

[25] R.S.S. 1978 c s-8.
[26] c s-8 Reg. 11.

beneficiary, as required under The Dependants' Relief Act. If that were the case, then the PGT would have no basis for seeking further contributions from the parents' estate. Reaching that outcome required a new interpretation of 'reasonable maintenance' under The Dependants' Relief Act, as the traditional interpretation clearly pointed to meeting basic needs. Consensus between Social Services and the PGT to adopt the new interpretation was obviously required.

That consensus was achieved following the enactment of new legislation entitled The Dependants' Relief Act 1996,[27] section 9 of which empowers the court, in proceedings against estates wherein a deceased parent has not made adequate provision for an adult child with a disability, to establish a special trust for that child. This 'Section 9 trust' is in effect equivalent to a Henson trust. The amount that can be put into a Section 9 trust is capped by regulation. Originally set at CAD50,000, the cap currently stands at CAD100,000.[28]

Whilst The Dependants' Relief Act 1996 still enables the court to require an estate to provide 'reasonable maintenance', following its passage the PGT adopted the view that entitlement to government assistance in appropriate circumstances is a basic and ongoing right. As such, the only needs the PGT requires a parent's estate to meet are those that enhance the beneficiary's quality of life, with his or her basic needs continuing to be met through government assistance. Where the PGT sees a need to challenge the estate of a deceased parent on behalf of a beneficiary with cognitive impairments, it will typically seek a Section 9 trust, leaving the beneficiary's financial situation roughly the same as if the deceased parent had established a Henson trust in the appropriate amount. The main difference is that the Section 9 order will name the PGT as the trustee of the fund, whereas a Henson trust would have named a trustee chosen by the parent.

Consistent with this approach, the PGT now supports estate planning for adults using Henson trusts. When an adequate Henson trust has been created in a deceased parent's will, the PGT will not pursue any additional 'reasonable maintenance' or pursue any course of action aimed at eliminating or reducing the affected beneficiary's entitlement to social assistance. This remains the case regardless of the amount placed in the trust.

The PGT has developed guidelines on what constitutes 'reasonable maintenance'. These guidelines attempt to balance the needs of an adult

[27] R.S.S. 1976 c D-25.01.
[28] The Dependants' Relief Trust Fund Regulations, 1997, c D-25.01 Reg. 1, s. 2.

beneficiary with cognitive impairment with society's view of what his or her siblings ought to receive from their parents. Under Saskatchewan law, a child ordinarily has no legal right to share in the estate of a deceased parent. Parents are not obligated to treat their children equally in their wills or to include all or any of them in the distribution of their estates. The only exceptions are the parental obligation, under The Dependants' Relief Act 1996, to support minor children and adult children who are economically dependent upon them due to disability. Accordingly, when a parent dies, leaving both an adult child with cognitive impairments and other adult children of ordinary ability, only the former has a legal right to participate in the parent's estate, a situation that is not aligned with social expectations of how parents should treat their children in their wills. The PGT has thus adopted the following guidelines to take those expectations into account.

- For estates less than CAD100,000, the beneficiary, that is, the adult child with cognitive impairments, should receive a share equal to that of his or her siblings.
- For estates more than CAD100,000, the beneficiary should receive the greater of the 'equal share' and the amount required to meet his or her 'quality of life' needs. The PGT may request that a needs assessment of the beneficiary be performed at the estate's expense by an occupational therapist or other qualified health professional.
- If the beneficiary is the testator's only child or the testator has disinherited his or her other children, a needs assessment should be performed to determine the beneficiary's proper share of the estate.

When the PGT decides to intervene in an estate, it seeks a court order allowing it to manage the first CAD100,000 of the amount claimed against the estate under a Section 9 trust and requests that any additional amount in the claim be added to the special needs beneficiary's Henson trust if there is one, or otherwise managed insofar as possible to avoid adversely impacting the beneficiary's entitlement to social assistance.

The PGT has indicated that the 'equal division' principle is only one of several factors to be taken into account in achieving the main objective, which is to meet the beneficiary's needs. For example, all of the resources available to the beneficiary, whether or not they come from the estate, are taken into account in the needs assessment. The amount to be set aside in the parent's estate, in conjunction with the beneficiary's anticipated government assistance and any other assets, must be sufficient to cover the beneficiary's needs (including both basic needs and quality of life enhancements) for his or her lifetime. As it is difficult to predict with any accuracy the overall sum needed to meet the aforementioned objective, the equal share rule is applied (at least for larger estates) to ensure that money is always available to the beneficiary. If his or her parents established a fund through a Henson trust, then any excess at the beneficiary's death will in any event find its way back to the parents' other beneficiaries or their families, or to charities or other entities supported by the parents, through the terms governing the disposition of any remainder of the trust on the beneficiary's death. If the fund was established through any means other than a Henson trust, then the remainder will most likely remain in the beneficiary's estate, with its disposition governed by Saskatchewan's intestacy laws, as the beneficiary's lack of mental capacity will normally have precluded making a will.

2   The Planner's Toolbox

Since the creation of the Section 9 trust and the complementary policy approaches subsequently adopted by the PGT and Social Services, parents in Saskatchewan, or their professional advisors, have been able to plan with confidence for the financial security of their children with disabilities while also benefiting other family members in line with social expectations. The policies and practices established by the PGT have afforded guidance in such planning to avoid the cost and difficulties of a posthumous legal challenge by the PGT. In the years following that creation, two new developments have expanded parents' options beyond the will-based Henson trust: the Government of Canada's launch of the Registered Disability Savings Programme (RDSP) in 2008 and, in Saskatchewan, Social Services' implementation of the SAID programme in 2009.[29]

The RDSP enables the establishment of pension plans for individuals who are prevented by disability from earning an income, and allows joint contributions by government and family members. The pension can accumulate on a tax-sheltered basis over the beneficiary's lifetime and, like a conventional pension, has the potential to grow into an asset sufficient to sustain the beneficiary in his or her senior years and leave a significant estate upon his or her death.

The SAID programme contains many improvements over the previous income plan available to persons with cognitive impairments. Of greatest relevance to estate planning is that it permits a beneficiary to receive a

---

[29] See n 26.

lump sum by way of a legacy, legal settlement or other one-time event, of up to CAD100,000 without any impact on his or her monthly support benefits. This means that a parent may leave a legacy of up to that amount to a child with cognitive impairment without having to place it in a Henson trust. However, doing so will be of limited practical value unless the child has some capacity to manage the legacy's use without the intervention of a trustee.

Rather than setting aside funds, another way for parents to financially benefit children with cognitive impairments without affecting their social assistance provision is to purchase real or personal property for them. In conducting means-testing for social assistance eligibility, Social Services takes into account only the amount of cash or near-cash held by the recipient. The ownership of such assets as a home, wheelchair van or other property of potential significance to the recipient's well-being will not jeopardise his or her entitlement to such assistance. Therefore, one part of a parent's estate plan to benefit an adult child with cognitive impairments may be to direct the purchase of such an asset from the parent's estate.

In sum, the following are the estate-planning tools and approaches available to parents in Saskatchewan who wish to make adequate provision for children with cognitive impairments without affecting the children's entitlement to social assistance.

(a) A straight bequest of up to CAD100,000 (the exempt amount specified by Social Services under the SAID programme).
(b) Henson trust created by a will or through a life insurance or beneficiary designation.
(c) An RDSP plan.
(d) The purchase of assets to meet basic needs and enhance quality of life.

An estate plan should normally follow the PGT's equal division principle, keeping in mind that the value of the benefit to be provided to the adult with cognitive impairments will include not only the value of the estate share that he or she will receive, but also the value of all assets outside the estate made available for the adult's benefit through the parents' efforts, including trusts funded by life insurance proceeds or beneficiary-designated investments, RDSP plans and major capital assets purchased by the parents through their estates or during their lifetimes. These additional benefits to the adult allow parents to provide a greater-than-equal share of their estates to their other children.

Whilst the equal division principle proposed by the PGT is a sound basis for planning, there are times when it may be inappropriate. For example, a special needs beneficiary with very limited capacity may be unable to benefit significantly from the expenditure of money. In a large estate, an equal distribution to that beneficiary would thus simply tie up resources unnecessarily or require the estate to liquidate land or other assets earmarked for other beneficiaries. Of course, planning a less-than-equal distribution for a special needs beneficiary may invite PGT intervention, although the application of a proper needs test might persuade the PGT to endorse a distribution other than that normally prescribed.

It may be that in many cases, equality rules end up being followed simply because of the difficulty of establishing a more precise 'needs-directed' plan. It is beyond the scope of this chapter to examine how such a plan might be undertaken. However, it is safe to say that past and present practice within the family can serve as a guide to future needs. Parents typically spend money on 'quality of life' purchases for their special needs children, and their rate of spending will thus go a long way towards identifying those children's 'extra amenities' needs. A plan meant to continue after the parents' death might include a provision for periodic visits by out-of-town family members. The list of purposes in the sample Henson trust in the Appendix suggests other potential elements of a well-constructed plan.

B The Role of Guardianship

1 Is Guardianship Really Necessary?

It is quite possible in Saskatchewan for parents or other family members, through the use of trusts, to establish an effective long-term financial plan for an adult with cognitive impairment without establishing legal guardianship. Although a property guardianship order is generally not difficult to obtain in the case of an individual with moderate to severe impairment, the process is time-consuming and usually requires the assistance of a lawyer. Not surprisingly, families are sometimes reluctant to incur the expense and effort of pursuing legal guardianship. Elderly parents who have successfully managed the affairs of their disabled child for many years without the benefit of guardianship tend to be particularly sceptical of the need for it.

'Do we really need to apply for guardianship?' is a question the author of this chapter is regularly asked in his practice. In the past, the question was difficult to answer objectively because families with cognitively impaired members generally seemed able to function well without it.

However, the question no longer poses much difficulty. Increased concern over privacy, identity theft and a host of other twenty-first century issues has raised the level of bureaucratisation in everyday life to the point where the informal recognition of parents' moral authority to speak for their adult children with cognitive impairments is no longer routinely expected, and formal decision-making authority is becoming increasingly important. Such authority becomes even more important after the parents have passed away, and the task of managing those adult children's affairs falls to their siblings or other family members.

The three pillars of any parent's plan to secure the future of his or her adult child with cognitive impairments are

- The provision of advocacy and support to ensure that adult's vocational, medical and social needs are met.
- The establishment of a secure source of funding sufficient to meet both the adult's 'basic' and 'quality of life' needs.
- The establishment of responsible management of the adult's funds.

It is difficult to imagine an effective plan that does not include some measure of decision-making authority in relation to the affairs of an adult with cognitive impairment, particularly when we consider that the plan will normally be expected to operate beyond the parents' lifetimes, when the centre of moral authority to speak for that adult will no longer be so clearly identifiable. Even where funds are managed for the adult in a Henson or Section 9 trust (for which property guardianship is not required), there is a very obvious need for advocacy in relation to such personal matters as dealing with healthcare professionals and social workers and providing for residential and vocational services.

2   Power of Attorney: Alternative or Adjunct?

Power of attorney is a simpler, less expensive planning approach than guardianship. Traditionally, the two approaches have been seen as mutually exclusive, as establishing power of attorney generally requires a level of capacity that must be absent to justify a guardianship order. There may be times, however, when a subject has sufficient capacity to grant power of attorney while at the same time requiring supported or substituted decision-making intervention in some aspects of his or her life. The level of capacity required to grant power of attorney is lower than that required to make a will because the issues to be decided are narrower and simpler. With the emergence of guardianship legislation that enables a restricted scope of authority and supported rather than substituted decision-making, one can imagine a person with cognitive impairment having the capacity to grant property power of attorney (because the need is clear and obvious) while requiring a substituted or supported decision-maker in relation to other, more nuanced decisions such as those about financial and healthcare matters or residential arrangements.

A full examination of legal capacity in the will and power of attorney arenas is beyond the scope of this chapter. However, family planning for members with cognitive impairments should include consideration of whether there is proper scope for the use of power of attorney as an alternative or adjunct to guardianship, either permanently or provisionally.

3   Property Guardian as Advocate and Gatekeeper

As already noted, a properly constituted Henson trust does not require a court-appointed property guardian to administer it because all necessary powers and appointments needed for that purpose have been created and effected in the instrument establishing the trust. However, those powers and appointments apply only to funds settled in that instrument. Funds that accrue to the adult in question from other sources remain vested in and under the legal control of the adult in the absence of a property guardianship order.

Those other sources include all income earned by the adult, as well as all social assistance, RDSP payments and any other financial benefits to which he or she may become entitled. Also included are bequests from well-meaning members of the adult's family who have included him or her in their estates but not settled them in a Henson trust. Funds from some of these sources could be included in the adult's income for means-testing purposes, with the potential to impair his or her social assistance entitlement. Another source of funds that could potentially affect such entitlement in the absence of an established Henson trust would be any amount payable to the adult under his or her Dependants' Relief Act claim in excess of the CAD100,000 allocated to a Section 9 trust. The risk of these adverse outcomes can be eliminated by a property guardianship order that affords the guardian the discretion to restrict expenditures on the adult's behalf to things that enhance his or her quality of life in the same manner as a Section 9 trust.

In addition, the RDSP rules are unclear about the nature and extent of authority needed by a third party to activate an adult's claim to pension benefits if the adult is unable to activate it him or herself. Many financial advisors to the families setting up RDSP plans are now suggesting to them that someone in the family who is likely to be alive when those benefits commence should obtain a property guardianship order to ensure the adult's prompt and effective access to the funds when they are needed.

Property guardianship is needed to ensure that the funds an adult receives from Social Services and RDSP plans are directed towards his or her basic needs, whilst funds received from a Henson trust and other sources are never directed towards that purpose. As long as this gate-keeping function is exercised, Social Services will have no reason to reduce future assistance payments or require the repayment of funds already advanced. Further, if the guardian is not also the Henson trustee, he or she can serve as an advocate for the adult in ensuring that the purposes of the Henson trust are fulfilled.

4   Managing Conflicts of Interest in Estate Claims

As stated earlier, one of the PGT's roles is monitoring the estates of persons who have left behind adult beneficiaries with cognitive impairments, as well as asserting claims against those estates when adequate provision for those beneficiaries has not been made. A potential claim is inherent in every estate involving a special needs beneficiary. When the beneficiary lacks the capacity to participate, and no property guardian has been appointed, the question of how a potential claim will be handled arises.

The Guardianship Act prohibits the appointment as guardian of any person whose interests are in conflict with those of the special needs beneficiary.[30] Generally speaking, adult children are chosen as executors of their parents' estates and as Henson trustees, and as property guardians for their special needs siblings, because they are considered the best suited for those tasks. They are selected as the beneficiaries of their parents' estates for obvious reasons. Conflicts of interest with regard to a special needs beneficiary's claim under The Dependants' Relief Act 1996 are thus both natural and inevitable.

The problem can be managed with an effective estate plan. In addition to implementing one or more of the planning tools described earlier, it would be of great assistance to the 'conflicted' family member(s) who will be assuming authority over the estate and stewardship of the special needs beneficiary's legacy to obtain a property guardianship order with a provision permitting them to represent the interests of that beneficiary in the parents' estate notwithstanding their own estate-related interests and duties, subject to the supervision of the court in the administration of the estate. Despite the proscription against conflicts of interest in the Guardianship Act, the Trustee Act 2009 of Saskatchewan enables a

---

[30] Guardianship Act, ss. 21, 46.

trustee with a conflict of interest to continue to act in the capacity of trustee on conditions prescribed by the court.[31]

IV   Concluding Remarks – Guardianship and the Special Needs Trust

It was concluded in Section III.B.1 of this chapter that, at least for residents of Saskatchewan, there remains a proper and necessary role for legal guardianship in succession planning for individuals with cognitive impairments, even when the succession plan also includes trust funds and other sources of income for those individuals. However, there is no formalised use of special needs trusts in Saskatchewan. Would that conclusion differ in jurisdictions in which a state-sponsored or other broad-based special needs trust is available?

A comprehensive answer to that question would require a broad evaluation of the ways in which special needs trusts operate, which vary considerably across the jurisdictions in which they are available. Therefore, only a few general comments are offered here. As we have seen, the legal regime in Saskatchewan affecting financial planning for persons with cognitive impairments has evolved over the years as a patchwork of court decisions coupled with various federal and provincial laws, policies and initiatives, all aimed at specific issues. Lacking any central plan, the legal path guiding the financial affairs of Saskatchewan residents with cognitive impairments is replete with pitfalls and inconsistencies requiring legally mandated management. The issues needing such management include the following.

- Ensuring that financial support and expenditures are structured and managed to avoid impairing entitlement to social assistance.
- Establishing the appropriate level of support required to be provided to an individual with cognitive impairments in a deceased parent's estate.
- Managing conflicts of interest in determining entitlement to participate in a parent's estate.
- Dealing with confidentiality in relation to the personal and financial information of the individual in question.
- Ensuring the individual's compliance with legal obligations such as making income tax or social assistance-related filings.

Obviously, the more settled and straightforward the legal environment those individuals face, the less need there is for such management.

---

[31] R.S.S. 1978, c T23.01, s. 10.

A regime in which a special needs trust operates in the context of a clear plan for dealing with the aforementioned issues would go some way towards eliminating the need for property guardianship.

However, absent a clear legislated programme covering those issues, no one will be in a position to make decisions if the affected individual lacks the capacity to do so and no guardian is appointed on his or her behalf. The settling of a trust, even with a comprehensive personal plan for the individual, does not of itself legally empower the trustee to make these sorts of decisions. In addition, there will always be issues falling outside the scope of financial control, such as the subcategories of personal matters listed in Section II(C)(4).

Even if special needs trustees, or the family members working with them, were given legal decision-making power for their beneficiaries, questions remain over whether the result would be in keeping with current thinking regarding the rights of persons with disabilities. Empowering trustees and family members to manage the personal and property affairs of such persons necessarily entails removing those persons' power to do so for themselves. However constituted, the legal act of removing or impairing the right of persons with disabilities to make decisions for themselves cannot take place in the absence of a due legal process aimed at minimal intrusion and establishing the appropriate mix of substituted and supported decision-making. Alternate decision-making authority should never arise as an adjunct to a parent's decision to establish a trust fund for an affected individual, no matter how well meaning or properly directed the parent may be.

In conclusion, any legal regime that promotes the well-being of individuals with cognitive impairments must include a provision for an adjudicative process that establishes and appropriately limits the power of others to make or assist in making decisions for those individuals. It is unlikely that organisations serving as special needs trustees would be anxious to assume that legal responsibility in addition to their responsibility to administer the trusts in accordance with their terms. There will always be a need for advocates to hold trustees accountable to trust beneficiaries, and those advocates require the legal authority to enforce their obligations and to make or assist in making decisions about enforcement. Advocates also need the authority to make or assist in making the myriad decisions concerning the personal affairs of special needs trust beneficiaries.

Put simply, individuals with cognitive impairments will always need legal guardians in one form or another to address both their personal affairs and property-related matters, whether or not they are beneficiaries of a special needs trust.

Appendix

Sample Henson Trust

I DIRECT ——————————, to be referred to in this paragraph as my Discretionary Trustee, to hold and administer upon the trusts herein-after specified the share of my Estate set aside for my son, **AB**, given under the provisions of paragraph — of this my Will. My Discretionary Trustee shall keep the same invested and in trust during the lifetime of the said AB. My Discretionary Trustee may pay to the said AB, or spend on his behalf, so much of the income or capital thereof, in varying amounts and from time to time, as my Discretionary Trustee in her absolute and unfettered discretion considers appropriate for the welfare, support, and benefit of the said AB other than for basic necessaries of life, the purposes of my Discretionary Trustee's uses of such funds to include education, provision for medical needs, travel, social and recreational activities, maintaining contact with family members and friends, occasional gifts to AB and to those to whom it would be appropriate to give gifts on her behalf, provision for extra comforts, benefits and amenities of life, and helping her to achieve independence.

Without restricting the generality of the foregoing, it is my wish that my Discretionary Trustee shall from time to time, exercise in her absolute discretion, all or any one or more of the following powers for the benefit of AB:

(a) My Discretionary Trustee shall be empowered to use the said funds and interest income to cover the cost of travel, food, accommodation and such other expenses as are rea-sonably required to enable AB's siblings, ———— and —————, and their respective spouses and children, to maintain regular contact with AB; and

(b) My Discretionary Trustee shall be empowered to use the said funds and interest income to cover the cost of appli-ances, furnishings, or other amenities for the enjoyment of those living at the residence in which AB primarily resides.

(c) My Discretionary Trustee shall be empowered to use the said funds and interest income for AB's benefit, including but not limited to the cost of memberships, participation fees, program fees, subscriptions, expenses for travel, meals, accommodations, fees to tutors, personal attendants, advocates, companions, rentals, whether the purposes thereof are educational, therapeutic, athletic, recreational, religious, social, or for vocational training, so long as the same are for the benefit of AB;

(d) My Discretionary Trustee may maintain a timely inspection program regarding the requirements of AB in respect of general health, including dental needs, eyeglasses, skin and scalp care, and any personal appliances he may require so that the same are purchased and adequately maintained at all times;

(e) My Discretionary Trustee may select appropriate advocates and professionals experienced in community living, integration, and personal development for persons with intellectual disabilities, from time to time, and for the purpose of maintaining such general service plan and individual program plan for the enhancement of the quality of life of AB as may be recommended from time to time by the advocate or any caregiver in consultation with professionals, with reviews from time to time. In so doing, my Discretionary Trustee may seek out advocates and professionals experientially involved with AB in current methodologies from time to time hereafter, based on quality of life and the least restrictive alternatives that would be personally appropriate to AB. AB should be viewed not only as a person with an intellectual disability, but also as a whole human being in need of some support to be an active participant in recreation, leisure, higher education, work and other aspects of community living. AB should be given the opportunity to make friends, to benefit from a variety of community supports and activities and be expected to contribute to the community by his presence;

(f) My Discretionary Trustee may encourage and assist any advocate or caregiver in seeking out available funding to have the advocate or caregiver, and my Discretionary Trustee may from time to time attend such conferences or workshops or seminars pertaining to current methodologies concerning AB that are likely to lead to the benefit of my said son, with authority to supplement such funding;

(g) My Discretionary Trustee may make available the opportunity in consultation with AB for up to TWO (2) major trips per year to visit with my other children and their families;

(h) My Discretionary Trustee shall be authorised to pay the expenses of AB for admission to any sporting or athletic and entertainment events including any meals or travel expenses;

(i) My Discretionary Trustee shall be authorised to pay the expenses for herself and up to one additional person for travel to the location where AB is residing from time to time provided the main purpose of that trip is in order to visit with AB, insofar as the expense relating to the same being reasonable based on the income from this trust;

(j) My Discretionary Trustee may, depending on the net income of this Trust, arrange for AB to purchase reasonably priced gifts for special occasions such as birthdays, Christmas, graduations, weddings and other similar events or occasions for members of his family, and his friends;

(k) My Discretionary Trustee may arrange for money allowance for AB to go on shopping trips at least twice per year for the purposes of purchasing new clothing in current styles for himself, but in doing so the same should be for purchasing items over and above what would be allowed in the event that AB is then currently receiving public assistance from the jurisdiction where he is residing;

(l) My Discretionary Trustee shall also be entitled, in their sole discretion from the trust income, to adequately insure against all risks any assets owned by AB;

(m) My Discretionary Trustee shall be empowered, from time to time, in her discretion, to provide AB with amounts of money from the said funds and interest being income that he will manage himself, and if, in the sole discretion of my Discretionary Trustee, he shows an ability to properly manage his funds within reason, then such amounts may be increased from time to time, but not in amounts so as to interfere with appropriate levels for maintaining governmental assistance for AB;

(n) My Discretionary Trustee may, from time to time, pay all or any portions of premiums payable on behalf of AB to maintain sickness and health insurance coverage; and

(o) My Discretionary Trustee may, from time to time, pay all or any portions of drugs, prescriptions, medications and professional fees of dental and healthcare providers on behalf of AB, but only to the extent that this will not interfere with the appropriate levels for maintaining government assistance for AB.

In determining the manner in which this discretion is to be exercised, my Discretionary Trustee may take into account any other source of income and government assistance to which the said AB may be or become entitled, and insofar as possible, my Discretionary Trustee shall exercise such discretion so as not to impair such income or entitlement to government assistance. Any income upon the trust fund not paid out in any year shall be accumulated and added to the capital thereof. No interest in the trust fund, nor in any of the income thereon, shall vest in the said AB unless actually paid to or for her by my Discretionary Trustee.

Upon the death of the said AB, my Discretionary Trustee may pay from the trust fund his funeral expenses and related costs, and thereafter this trust shall terminate, and so much of the trust fund as may then remain undistributed by my Discretionary Trustee shall be distributed *[in equal shares between my children, — and ——] or [to the charitable organisation designated in paragraph - of this my Will, or otherwise as the case may be].*

I declare that the primary purpose of the trusts herein contained is to enhance AB's quality of life through the expenditures herein authorised, and I relieve my Discretionary Trustee of the duty to maintain an even hand between AB as life beneficiary of this Trust and those entitled to share in the remainder thereof on the death of AB.

In constituting this trust fund for the said AB, I have taken into account that he suffers from disabilities rendering him unable to earn income to support himself, and that he will throughout her lifetime be dependent upon the financial support of others. I have further taken into account that the well-being of the said AB will be best served if the trust fund is applied so as to purchase goods and services for the said AB in addition to and not in substitution for those which are or may be purchased for him through any government assistance to which he is or may become entitled.

3

Japanese Adult Guardianship Laws: Developments and Reform Initiatives

MAKOTO ARAI*

I Introduction

Adult guardianship is a legal system developed to protect adults who lack sufficient capacity to make sound judgements such as those suffering from age-related dementia, impaired intelligence or a mental disorder. Until 2000, the Japanese Civil Code provided protection for such people through guardianships or curatorships based on the concepts of incompetence and quasi-incompetence. However, the emphasis these protective arrangements placed on the protection of principals and their lack of flexibility rendered them difficult to use in practice. In addition, the rapid greying of Japanese society and heightened concern over the welfare of people with impaired intelligence or mental disorders furthered social demand for an overhaul of the traditional system to produce a more flexible, user-friendly system.

A new system of adult guardianship came into effect in Japan on 1 April 2000. This chapter critically examines the development of the Japanese adult guardianship system and suggests further reform initiatives in light of recent international developments in this field, most notably the United Nations Convention on the Rights of Persons with Disabilities[1] and the Yokohama Declaration.

II Enactment and Operation of Japanese Adult Guardianship Laws

A The New Adult Guardianship System and Its Guiding Principles

The new adult guardianship system that took effect in April 2000 followed the enactment of four laws in December 1999: the Act

---

* Professor, Chuo University, Japan.
[1] Hereafter CRPD. The CRPD was adopted on 13 December 2006 and entered into force on 3 May 2008. Japan ratified the CRPD on 20 January 2014.

for Partial Amendment of the Civil Code,[2] the Act on Voluntary Guardianship Contracts,[3] the Act Concerning Establishment of Legal Frameworks in conjunction with the enforcement of the Partial Amendment of the Civil Code[4] and the Act on Guardianship Registration, etc.[5] The new system substantially revised the 'system for adjudication of [incompetent] and quasi-incompetent persons'[6] that had prevailed under Japanese civil law until that point. The previous system for determining incompetence and quasi-incompetence was limited in application to those with serious cognitive impairments, and the substance of the protection afforded was uniform and rigid. Further, because a person judged to be incompetent or quasi-incompetent was also identified as such on the official family register, many were fiercely resistant to the system. Finally, the cost in time and money involved imposed a heavy burden on the parties concerned and rendered the system difficult to use.[7]

The new adult guardianship system broadly consists of statutory guardianship and continuing power of attorney. Statutory guardianship is imposed through legal action and takes the form of either advisorship – a new device – or guardianship and curatorship – existing devices that have been extensively reformed. Under statutory guardianship, if the court deems that a principal has become insufficiently capable of making sound judgements, it appoints an advisor, curator or guardian as protective agent, based on the relevant provisions of law, and grants him or her necessary powers. Continuing power of attorney, in contrast, is a contract-based protective arrangement, and as such its use is optional. Any person with sufficient capacity to make judgements may appoint a voluntary guardian by contract in preparation for the eventual loss of full capacity and grant him or her the powers desired. Continuing power of attorney respects the autonomy of the principal to the greatest extent

---

[2] Act no. 149 of 1999.

[3] Act no. 150 of 1999.

[4] Act no. 151 of 1999.

[5] Act no. 152 of 1999.

[6] M. Arai (ed.), *Seinenkoken (Adult Guardianship)* (Tokyo: Yuhikaku, 2000), pp. 1–2.

[7] The author's English-language works on the subject of Japan's adult guardianship law include M. Arai, 'Japan's New Safety Network: Reform of Statutory Guardianship and the Creation of Voluntary Guardianships' (Fall 2000) *NAELA Quarterly* 5, and M. Arai, 'Ten Years' Experience of Japan's Adult Guardianship Law of 2000', in M. Arai, U. Becker and V. Lipp (eds.), *Adult Guardianship Law for the 21st Century: Proceedings of the First World Congress on Adult Guardianship Law 2010* (Baden-Baden: Nomos, 2013), pp. 15–23.

possible and is compatible with the principle of private autonomy. In principle, it is therefore applied in preference to statutory guardianship, which is reserved for situations in which the principal does not opt for continuing power of attorney or in which that option would not fully protect the principle's rights and interests.

As noted, Japan's current adult guardianship system is a new system designed to support those who require protection. It is underpinned by several guiding principles: normalisation, respect for the right to self-determination and emphasis on livelihood protection. 'Normalisation' refers to guaranteeing a prejudice-free, normal-as-possible way of life for people with disabilities. The idea is to move away from protecting these people while depriving them of their abilities towards offering them a helping hand and allowing them to keep their dignity intact. The concept of respect for the right to self-determination contains two meanings. First, even in cases in which the principal's competence is impaired, maximisation of his or her residual competence is sought. Second, self-determination concerning matters that arise after the principal loses competence is sought while he or she still retains his or her mental faculties. Finally, emphasis on livelihood protection stresses not only the protection of financial assets but also support for daily life and the ability to help oneself. It can also be described as an approach to adult guardianship that seeks to improve the quality of life of the individual concerned.

What follows is an outline of the distinctive features of Japan's new adult guardianship system.

B   Addition of Advisorship to Legal Guardianship System

The new adult guardianship system provides for three types of protection – namely guardianship, curatorship and advisorship – to enable flexible, resilient responses to the circumstances of the person concerned, including his or her mental capacity, the necessity for protection and so on. These three types of protection are defined under civil law and collectively referred to as the 'legal guardianship system'.

A new system of advisorship was introduced to fill a gap in the existing arrangements, which covered only those with significant mental deterioration. The new provisions replace the grounds of incompetence or quasi-incompetence with a family court hearing that determines whether the person concerned is insufficiently capable of making sound judgements owing to impaired mental faculties. If so, advisorship may commence.

The persons authorised to apply to initiate such a proceeding include the principal, the principal's spouse and his or her relative within the fourth degree of kinship. If a petition is filed by a person other than the principal, the proceeding is conditional upon the principal's consent, as any action against a principal's will is considered to be incompatible with the ideal of respect for autonomy. The advisor is granted the power of consent or representation only with respect to certain juristic acts. Once that power has been exercised, and the need for it ceases to exist, the advisorship is effectively rescinded and has no practical utility or merit.

The provisions for incompetence and quasi-incompetence have been renamed guardianship and curatorship, respectively – classifications that are easier to work with. Persons considered 'prodigals', who had previously been classified as quasi-incompetent, are now excluded. In other words, prodigals with sufficient mental capacity to manage their affairs are not subject to the curatorship system because, for instance, it is considered undesirable for the court to interfere in such persons' use of their own property. The curatorship arrangements are intended to help persons with significantly insufficient capacity to make sound judgements owing to impaired mental faculties, thus replacing the traditional arrangement based on quasi-incompetence, which also covered spendthrifts. In light of guardianship's focus on supplementing the judgement capacity of persons who have difficulty making decisions, spendthrifts capable of making sound judgements are excluded from its coverage. A curator holds the power of consent with respect to important juristic acts, as specified in the Civil Code, but not to those pertaining to daily life.

C   Introduction of Continuing Power of Attorney System

The creation of a continuing power of attorney system constitutes a major reform, as there are no court precedents in Japan concerning the possibility of using a mandate contract to commission a mandatary to act as a guardian with power of representation in the event that the mandator's judgement capacity has become insufficient.[8] The continuing power of attorney system can be described as follows.

The person concerned takes steps in advance, that is, while still in possession of sufficient mental capacity, to conclude a continuing power

---

[8] For details, see M. Arai and A. Homma, 'Guardianship for Adults in Japan: Legal Reforms and Advances in Practice' (2005) 24 *Australasian Journal on Ageing* 19.

of attorney contract as a notarised document that grants to a voluntary guardian (the mandatary of the continuing power of attorney system), who acts as that person's agent, the authority of representation to handle property management, personal supervision and other such matters. Thereafter, if the mental capacity of the person concerned becomes insufficient owing to dementia or a similar reason, the contract becomes effective when the family court appoints a supervisor of the voluntary guardian, enabling that person to receive support from the guardian under the supervisor's supervision. The notarised document in question must be prepared by a notary public in the notary public's office. Law No. 150 of 1999 defines such a contract as a mandate contract under which the mandator entrusts the mandatary with the handling, in whole or in part, of his or her affairs pertaining to livelihood, medical treatment, and care and asset management when he or she becomes incapable of making sound judgements owing to impairment of his or her mental faculties. Under the terms of that contract, the mandator gives the power of representation (power of attorney) to the mandatary regarding the entrusted affairs and prescribes that the contract take effect if a guardian supervisor is appointed by a family court.

Because a continuing power of attorney contract is a mandate contract, the scope of power that can be granted and the types of juristic acts that can be performed pursuant to power of attorney are questions that can be raised about any mandate contract. Power of attorney can thus be considered a voluntary power of representation, whilst the power granted to an advisor, curator or guardian constitutes a statutory power of representation. Continuing power of attorney in principle takes precedence over statutory guardianship. If a voluntary guardianship contract has been registered, a family court may commence statutory guardianship only if it deems doing so to be necessary to protect the principal's interests, for example, in a case where the scope of the power of attorney afforded under the voluntary guardianship contract is too narrow to protect the principal's rights and interests.

D   Other Steps Taken to Improve the Guardianship System (Adult Guardianship, Curatorship, Advisorship)

A number of other steps were taken to improve the adult guardianship system. For example, to improve the arrangements for supporting persons with cognitive impairments, the adult guardianship system now allows the family court to select an appropriate adult guardian, curator or advisor, depending on the situation at hand. It also allows for the appointment of multiple guardians or the selection of a corporate entity. In the event that a person of insufficient mental capacity has no spouse and no relatives within the fourth degree of kinship, or has such relatives but is not in communication with them, the mayor of the given municipality can petition for a determination to initiate legal guardianship if he or she recognises the necessity of taking such a step to enhance the person's welfare.

Furthermore, a new registration system for both statutory guardianship and continuing power of attorney was established. The traditional method of the proclamation of guardianship, by which a guardian's name was entered in the family register pursuant to the provisions of the Family Registration Law, was abolished. Adjudications of incompetence and quasi-incompetence are no longer recorded in the official family register. In accordance with the Act on Guardianship Registration, Etc., the authority of the guardian, content of the continuing power of attorney contract and related matters must be registered under the new adult guardianship system. The procedure is as follows. Following a commission (request) from the family court or a notary public to initiate guardianship or the preparation of a continuing power of attorney contract as a notarised document, the guardian's authority, content of the continuing power of attorney contract and other matters are registered, with the registered information disclosed when the registrar issues a certificate. He or she can also certify that no such registration has occurred.

E   Operation of the Adult Guardianship System

According to the Supreme Court of Japan's *Summary of Guardianship Cases* in 2017,[9] a few observations on Japan's new adult guardianship system can be made.

First, only 203,551 people used the adult guardianship system in 2017, which is an astonishingly small number. To the best of the author's knowledge, internationally, at least 1 per cent of the population can be expected to be latent users of such systems. In Japan, the number of guardianship users in 2017 was 161,307, the number of curatorship users 30,549, the number of assistance users 9,234 and the number of continuing power of attorney users 2,461, for a total figure that is no more than

---

[9] The General Secretariat, 'Overview of Cases Related to Adult Guardianship', Family Bureau, Supreme Court of Japan.

one-sixth the 1.27 million users that would be expected if the country followed the international pattern. Promoting greater utilisation of the adult guardianship system is thus an important issue for Japanese society as a whole.

Second, there has been minimal recourse to the advisorship type of protection, which was the main feature of the adult guardianship system reform and continuing power of attorney system. Continuing power of attorney is overwhelmingly the most common type of protection sought under the legal guardianship system in Japan, with the utilisation of advisorship, in contrast, accounting for as little as 5 per cent of guardianship cases. The current situation has thus diverged widely from the basic intention of the system's framers – who declared that the newly established advisorship would function primarily as a system, making it possible to select a flexible partial authority of representation that does not involve a system of legal capacity.

The trend internationally is for adult guardianship laws to move towards further utilisation of continuing power of attorney systems. In Japan, however, the number of continuing power of attorney contracts concluded and registered is by no means large. The number, 2,461, could in fact be described as extremely small. The continuing power of attorney system was supposed to be the core of the new adult guardianship system, and it is thus very much cause for concern that its utilisation is at such a low ebb.

Third, the selection of persons other than relatives as third-party guardians is on the rise, with third-party guardians accounting for 71.9 per cent of all guardians selected in 2017. This tendency is very much marked in comparison with other countries, where relatives are most commonly chosen. It cannot be denied that relatives are, in most cases, the parties best suited to serve as adult guardians. The large percentage of third-party guardians in Japan is likely not the result of the population rejecting the notion that adult guardianship is a matter to be handled by families or broadly accepting the notion that it is the responsibility of the wider society, but rather the result of the courts avoiding the appointment of relatives as guardians because of concerns over potential abuses of authority by such guardians.

Last but not least, there has been an increase in petitions by municipal mayors, which accounted for 6,466 of adult guardianship cases in 2017, representing 18.8 per cent of the total. Petitions by municipalities are a direct expression of the notion that adult guardianship is a function of society, and their increase is thus a desirable trend. It is hoped that the active filing of petitions by municipal mayors will continue in future.

The preceding observations suggest that Japan's adult guardianship system requires fundamental reform. The route by which such reform should be approached is discussed in the following section.

III Impetus for Further Reform Initiatives

A Convention on the Rights of Persons with Disabilities

1 Paradigm Shift and Adoption of a Social Model

The CRPD has prompted a major re-examination of the conceptual approach underpinning adult guardianship law worldwide. This section first clarifies the content of the CRPD and discusses its relationship to adult guardianship law. It then outlines a possible future direction for adult guardianship law in Japan while keeping the CRPD's perspective firmly in view.

The CRPD was adopted unanimously by the General Assembly of the United Nations in its 61st session on 13 December 2006 and took effect on 3 May 2008.[10] Historically, persons with disabilities have been considered subject to protection and care, as international documents attest. The basic purpose of measures aimed at such persons is the provision of welfare and healthcare. In international terms, these measures have been under the jurisdiction of the World Health Organisation and United Nations Economic and Social Council.

The CRPD was the first international document to consider persons with disabilities from the human rights perspective rather than from the traditional social policy or healthcare policy perspective. Whilst recognising that persons with disabilities face special problems with the activities of daily living, the CRPD treats disability as the interaction between an individual's personal condition and environmental factors, which together affect how he or she engages with society. This human rights perspective signifies a major shift in the conventional approach to

[10] For a comprehensive understanding of the CRPD, see V. Della Fina, R. Cera and G. Palmisano (eds.), *The United Nations Convention on the Rights of Persons with Disabilities: A Commentary* (Cham: Springer, 2017). For a document in legal language, see the informative R. Matsui and S. Kawashima (eds.), *Summary of the Convention on Rights of Persons with Disabilities* (Kyoto: Horitsu bunka sha, 2010). Another very valuable source is T. Sai, 'The Convention on the Rights of Persons with Disabilities and the Act for Support of the Independence of Persons with Disabilities: An Examination in Terms of Contract Provisions for Independent Living' in N. Ibaraki, et al. (eds.), *Prospects of the Act for Comprehensive Welfare Services for Person with Disabilities* (Kyoto: Minerva shobo, 2009), pp. 198–219.

persons with disabilities, as well as a shift in two major paradigms: (1) a shift from the traditional notion of integration to the notions of inclusion and empowerment, and (2) a shift from a person with disability being the object of care to being an agent who enjoys equal rights, including the rights of independence and self-determination.

In theory, conventions on human rights prior to the CRPD already afford protection to the rights of persons with disabilities. In reality, however, such persons have long been discriminated against. What the CRPD sought to clarify was the concrete substance of the rights granted to persons with disabilities together with the methods for realising that substance. In fact, the CRPD defines that objective in article 1. It treats the concept of disability broadly, viewing disability not simply as a medical fact but, rather, as a social circumstance arising from a bodily state, which confers a broad scope of applicability that surpasses the traditional medical understanding. The CRPD can thus be said to advocate the adoption of a social rather than medical model of disability,[11] which is closely related to the question of how far the scope of the existing conventions on human rights other than CRPD should be extended. In the conventional view of disability as leading to diminished capacity or social disadvantage, the means of eliminating that unfavourable state is to overcome the disability. Therefore, persons with cognitive impairments can only be objects of medical treatment, protection and/or rehabilitation. The social model, in contrast, posits that the way to eliminate diminished capacity/social disadvantage is to eliminate the societal barriers to those persons' full participation in society.[12]

2 Special Provisions Relating to Adult Guardianship

Article 12 of the CRPD establishes the following special provisions relating to adult guardianship.

Article 12: Equal recognition before the law

1. States Parties reaffirm that persons with disabilities have the right to recognition everywhere as persons before the law.

---

[11] S. Kawashima and T. Higashi, 'The Formation of the Convention on the Rights of Persons with Disabilities' in O. Nagase, T. Higashi and S. Kawashima (eds.), *The Convention on the Rights of Persons with Disabilities and Japan: Overview and Prospects* (Tokyo: Seikatsu shoin, 2008), p. 20.

[12] Sai, 'The Convention on the Rights of Persons with Disabilities and the Act for Support of the Independence of Persons with Disabilities', n 10, 201.

2. States Parties shall recognise that persons with disabilities enjoy legal capacity on an equal basis with others in all aspects of life.
3. States Parties shall take appropriate measures to provide access by persons with disabilities to the support they may require in exercising their legal capacity.
4. States Parties shall ensure that all measures that relate to the exercise of legal capacity provide for appropriate and effective safeguards to prevent abuse in accordance with international human rights law. Such safeguards shall ensure that measures relating to the exercise of legal capacity respect the rights, will and preferences of the person, are free of conflict of interest and undue influence, are proportional and tailored to the person's circumstances, apply for the shortest time possible and are subject to regular review by a competent, independent and impartial authority or judicial body. The safeguards shall be proportional to the degree to which such measures affect the person's rights and interests.
5. Subject to the provisions of this article, States Parties shall take all appropriate and effective measures to ensure the equal right of persons with disabilities to own or inherit property, to control their own financial affairs and to have equal access to bank loans, mortgages and other forms of financial credit, and shall ensure that persons with disabilities are not arbitrarily deprived of their property.

The CRPD is significant in a number of respects. First, in addition to article 12, article 5 of the CRPD prohibits 'all discrimination on the basis of disability'. In conjunction with article 12 – which stipulates that 'persons with disabilities have the right to recognition everywhere as persons' and, accordingly, that they should be free to decide when to exercise their right to self-determination – the prohibition means that disability does not constitute the basis for appointing guardians, nor does it constitute a reason for limiting the legal capacity of the persons concerned. Only when a person is deemed incapable of independent decision-making can guardians be appointed and legal capacity limited.

Second, the CRPD recognises that the right to self-determination is meaningful only if the person concerned actually makes decisions for him or herself. If a person lacks the capacity for self-determination, then the state should provide the support required to allow him or her to exercise that right. In the author's view, there is self-contradiction in article 12 of the CRPD. On the one hand, it recognises a person's right to resist interference by the state or other parties if he or she can make decisions independently. On the other hand, it recognises that if he or she cannot make decisions independently, then he or she has the right to obtain decision-making support.

Third, the CRPD outlines specific guidelines relating to the methods of support in article 12(4). It states that the rights, will and preferences of the person concerned are to be respected, that conflicts of interest are to be avoided, that undue influence is to be eliminated, that the person's circumstances are to be taken into consideration, that safeguards are to be applied for the shortest time possible, and that those safeguards are to be subject to regular review by an independent and impartial authority or judicial body.

The foregoing requirements specified in article 12 of the CRPD raise questions over the potential discriminatory nature of Japan's adult guardianship system, which might violate a ward's independent right to self-determination. The conceptual approach in traditional adult guardianship, which can be described as 'substituted decision-making', has been criticised for possibly infringing independence and self-determination. In article 12(3), the Convention provides for the alternative conceptual approach of 'supported decision-making', and the dominant position today is that only this kind of decision-making is permitted.[13] Hence, we are now in the middle of a conflict between supported and substituted decision-making, with Japan's adult guardianship law – based as it is on traditional, extremely conservative thinking – being subjected to rigorous scrutiny to determine whether it does in fact accord with the spirit of the CRPD. The author's personal opinion is that the Japanese system does not comply with the demands of the CRPD. This is because the appointment of guardians accounts for an overwhelming share of cases and the use of continuing power of attorney is virtually stagnant; furthermore, the system centres on asset management while support for daily life and the ability to help oneself is not adequately functioning.

Whilst the direction the CRPD seeks to take is innovative in the extreme, and it is likely that full acceptance of its principles and spirit will involve considerable difficulty, the author nonetheless declares his full support for its intentions. It must be emphasised that the CRPD does not instruct us to repeal the adult guardianship law per se. An adult guardianship system is essential for those incapable of making their own decisions, and the demand for such a system is particularly great in Japan, where an overwhelmingly large proportion of cases involve the appointment of guardians and the concept of supported decision-making has yet to become widely popular. However, the Japanese adult

---

[13] See Principle 3 of Committee of Minister of the Council of Europe, *Principles Concerning the Legal Protection of Incapable Adults* (Recommendation No. R (99)4, 1999).

guardianship system as it stands today requires reform before it can fit into the new container demanded by the CRPD. Determining how that reform can be realised is the issue we now face.

B   The Yokohama Declaration

The Yokohama Declaration provides a useful starting point for further reform initiatives.[14] Ten years after implementation of Japan's current adult guardianship system, and despite widespread calls for the system's fundamental reform in terms of both theory and practice, no signs of movement towards implementing specific reforms can be seen. Against this backdrop, the author, who serves as President of the Japan Adult Guardianship Law Corporate Association, organised the world's first World Congress on Adult Guardianship in Yokohama from 2 to 3 October 2010 with the intention of issuing a declaration calling for reform of the global adult guardianship system. Approximately 500 people from 16 countries took part in the World Congress, holding frank and meaningful discussions about current issues concerning the adult guardianship system internationally, including the domestic cir- cumstances of the attendees. Publication of the Yokohama Declaration was approved as a summation of the discussion at the Congress.

The Yokohama Declaration constitutes the world's first declaration in the adult guardianship law arena. It consists of three parts: a 'Preamble', 'International Part' and 'Japanese Part'. This chapter addresses only the International Part and the Japanese Part, which was retained in the revised version of the Yokohama Declaration agreed at the 4th World Congress on Adult Guardianship held in Berlin in September 2016.

Two main points should be emphasised. First, the Declaration con- firms that Japan should promptly ratify both the Hague Convention of 13 January 2000 on the International Protection of Adults and the CRPD. In particular, the latter states that 'persons with disabilities enjoy legal capacity on an equal basis with others' (article 12(2)). Although there is still question over whether Japan's adult guardianship law meets that requirement, the country ratified the CRPD in 2014.

---

[14] The text of the Yokohama Declaration is set out in this chapter's appendix. K. Blankman, 'The Yokohama Declaration and Maximizing Autonomy in the Netherlands', in Arai, Becker and Lipp (eds.), *Adult Guardianship Law for the 21st Century*, n 7, pp. 115–124, is a useful English reference, while M. Arai 'The Yokohama Declaration and reform of the adult guardianship system' (2011) 1415 *Jurist* 2 is a useful Japanese reference.

Second, the Yokohama Declaration makes the three following proposals.

1. Revise the current Japanese guardianship law and improve its operation: Based on the experience of the adult guardianship system following its implementation, it is necessary to revise the law and improve the system's implementation.
2. Create a public support system: Irrespective of the scale of a user's assets or the existence of a petitioner, the system of legal support and protection for adults should be available to everyone. For this reason, it is essential that the government publicly support the entire system. Because a public support system results in the socialisation of protections for adults, the creation of such a system by the government is recommended.
3. Investigate the possibility of a new adult guardianship system: Rather than remain within the framework of the current adult guardianship system, the government should pursue new ideas and investigate possibilities for further development.

Each of these reform proposals is discussed in turn in the next section.

IV   Reform Proposals

A   Creation of a Public Support System

The Yokohama Declaration states that the adult guardianship system should be positioned as a system that anyone can use regardless of his or her assets or the existence of a petitioner. Therefore, it is essential that the government provide public support for the adult guardianship system as a whole. Doing so will achieve the socialisation of adult guardianship. The creation of a governmental support system is also recommended. Furthermore, the Declaration also states that the main purpose of the smooth implementation of a public support system is the further expansion and enhancement of the functions of the judiciary, particularly the functions of family courts in the operation of the system for the legal support and protection of adults. The Declaration adds that establishing such a public support system will expand the support network for the adult in question to his or her family, the general public and specialists in related fields, thereby securing appropriate legal representation for that adult and enhancing the system's advocacy functions to ensure his or her legal support and protection. In fact, the Declaration drafters prioritised the creation of a public support system. What makes an adult guardianship system function is not the letter of the law but, rather, its spirit in conjunction with a system that embodies that spirit, a system that is lacking in Japan's current approach to adult guardianship.

Clearly, the establishment of a public support system is a matter of urgency if the use of Japan's adult guardianship system is to be expanded. Government support for the operation of the courts and the private sector should be institutionalised. The author proposes that the family courts serve only a judicial function in the adult guardianship system, with other institutions assigned other relevant functions within the public system. Such a move would truly constitute the embodiment of the socialisation of adult guardianship.

B   Possibility of a New Adult Guardianship System

The Declaration calls for the constant pursuit of new ideas rather than remaining within the framework of the current adult guardianship system, as well as the investigation of possibilities for further development. This chapter focuses on two mid- to long-term issues with the system.

The first issue is that the current adult guardianship system is based on three types of protection, namely guardianship, curatorship and advisorship. To take into account article 12 of the CRPD, it is necessary to review the suitability of the current protection on offer. Guardianship, despite being the most commonly used of the three types, considerably limits the capacity of the adult concerned, which contradicts the spirit of the CRPD. In addition, guardians are burdened by the duties stipulated in the Act on Mental Health and Welfare for the Mentally Disabled.[15] It is questionable whether the rights of persons with disabilities are excessively constrained under adult guardianship laws and whether the right of rescission conferred on adult guardians truly protects the persons concerned. According to the CRPD, there should be no difference in legal capacity between persons with disabilities and others, and the adult guardianship imposed should be the 'least restrictive' possible. From this perspective, the effects of the current adult guardianship law require a full review. Moreover, the general impression of legal guardianship stems primarily from the types of protection therein. However, advisorship

---

[15] Act no. 123 of 1950.

may also violate the spirit of the CRPD. Originally, continuing power of attorney and advisorship formed the core of the Japanese adult guardianship system. The author believes that we should return to that starting point and seek to expand and encourage the use of advisorship.

The second issue is that the Yokohama Declaration mentions the use of welfare-type trusts in which vulnerable members of society such as the elderly and disabled are the beneficiaries as a means of protection for persons with reduced capacity. As such trusts are not commonly used in Japan, the courts should consider the introduction of a trust system as a substitute for adult guardianship. Although the rights of the persons concerned would be slightly restricted under trusts, as their assets would be transferred to trustees, they would not be as restricted as they are under the adult guardianship system. There are good reasons for introducing trusts as a form of substitute adult guardianship in Japan. For example, trust systems are already functioning as alternatives or complements to the adult guardianship system in the United States and Canada. However, in Japan, trust banks are usually trustees offering financial products, and are unfamiliar with the type of trust needed in the adult guardianship arena. Trusts are a public institution and part of the social infrastructure. Hence, particularly in an ageing society such as Japan, the trust system needs to change as part of the social infrastructure. Trust banks currently convey a rather mercenary impression by focusing on their existing financial products. The author thus believes that a paradigm shift is necessary to move beyond existing frameworks. Court involvement in setting up a trust system that could substitute for the adult guardianship system under management by a new type of trustee would be welcome.

C   Formulation of an Act to Promote the Use of the Adult Guardianship System

1   Cabinet Decision on a Master Plan

On 24 March 2017, a Cabinet decision was made on a master plan for promoting the use of the adult guardianship system ('the Master Plan') based on article 12(1) of the Act for Promoting the Use of the Adult Guardianship System.[16]

---

[16] Act no. 29 of 2018 ('Adult Guardianship Promotion Act').

The process leading to the Cabinet decision on the Master Plan was by no means smooth. Its starting point was the Yokohama Declaration, based on the principles of which the original bill of the Adult Guardianship Promotion Act was formulated. Diet members and political parties sympathetic to the idea of promoting adult guardianship – as well as various government ministries, departments and agencies – came together with professional organisations, and, as a result of their joint efforts, the Adult Guardianship Promotion Act was formulated on 8 April 2016 and took effect on 13 May 2016. The Council for Promoting the Use of the Adult Guardianship System ('the Council') and Commission for Promoting the Use of the Adult Guardianship System ('the Commission') were subsequently launched. The Council asked the Commission to provide input in the form of its views. After the Commission had compiled its views, a public hearing was held. Following all of this, the Council formulated the Master Plan, which was then approved by a Cabinet decision. It should be noted that the Chairman of the Council is the Prime Minister. In no other country has the prime minister him or herself led an initiative to promote the use of adult guardianship. However, it must also be emphasised that it was six and a half long years from the starting point of the Declaration to the Master Plan's approval by the Cabinet.

2   Details of the Master Plan

The Secretariat of the Commission offers three points as constituting the gist of the Master Plan. The first point is the need to improve the system and its management in a way that ensures users can truly experience its benefits. In this connection, the Master Plan lists the following two matters ((a) and (b)) under the heading 'Future Goals of the Plan'.[17]

(a) Managing the programme in close connection with the users
  (i)   creating and managing an adult guardianship system that users can truly be benefited from. This can be achieved by emphasising the importance of detailed consultation on the needs and wishes of adults with senile dementia or disabilities and providing support for them to exercise their right of self-determination on their daily living and financial affairs. It is insufficient for guardians to focus solely on managing the assets of persons concerned;

---

[17] Available from www.cao.go.jp/seinenkouken/keikaku/pdf/keikaku1.pdf (in Japanese).

(ii) in the case of persons with disabilities, guardians should provide support for their decision making, livelihood protection and care on a continuous basis. It is essential to keep improving the support system and removing environmental barriers that hinder their full participation in the society [Preamble (e) of the CRPD]. The care system will be improved when it is switched from a medical to a social model of support. In particular, careful considerations should be given when persons with disabilities are relocating from hospitals into the local community, taking employment and participating in the society. The guardian should play the role of a life escort, making an effort to provide continuous support based on the individual needs of each person with disabilities;

(iii) the family court should take into account the user's living conditions before selecting an appropriate guardian who can safeguardand protect the user's right and interests; and

(iv) in order to determine the type of guardianship required, users' mental capacity have to be assessed by medical doctors. It is important to provide full disclosure of users' circumstances to medical doctors, including their living conditions and the level of support they require, so that the latter can make an accurate assessment of the users' conditions. Further, specific forms of reports should be used by doctors to record their diagnosis of the users' medical and mental conditions in this respect.

(b) Promoting the use of curatorship, advisorship and continuing power of attorney system

(i) in addition to promoting the use of curatorship and advisorship based on the users' mental capacity, which are not widely used in Japan, the Commission also encourages the use of continuing power of attorney system which respects the wishes of users. This would improve the operation of the adult guardianship system as a whole;

(ii) there should be flexible adjustment or switching among curatorship, advisorship and guardianship based on the current mental capacity of senior users with progressive senile dementia. In light of what precedes, the appropriate level of support and care provided will also depend on the current state of the users' physical and mental health; and

(iii) there should be increased marketing of the use of continuing power of attorney system, curatorship and advisorship with sufficient information and consultation services being provided to persons with disabilities from an early stage.[18]

The second point is the need to create local community networks to support the protection of users' rights. In this connection, the Master Plan also lists the following under 'Future Goals of the Program'.

(a) to establish local community cooperative networks and core institutions with a view to support and protect the user's rights;

(b) to establish local community structure to enable those in need to have easy access to the adult guardianship system irrespective of their geographical location;

(c) to establish local community organisations to look out for those in need of the guardianship system and assist them to access appropriate support in each case, in addition to setting up a consultation desk in each district, the Commission is keen;

(d) to establish the adult guardianship system which recognises the importance on protecting the users' livelihood and respects their right of self-determination. It also seeks to set up a system which coordinates relatives and personnel involved in providing welfare, medical care and community support to form a team to look after the users' welfare and to provide appropriate care based on continuous assessments of the users' wishes and health conditions. The system should also involve welfare and legal experts whom would offer professional advice and consultation service in each case. Such teams should build on the existing framework of those who already provide support to the user;

(e) to establish local councils to strengthen the cooperation between professional organisations and related institutions in every district and to promote their cooperation on a voluntary basis;

(f) to establish core institutions as secretariat responsible for coordinating the community networks and securing support from professional bodies; and

(g) to promote the above, based on the circumstances of each local community and to continue the existing initiatives made by local

---

[18] The Secretariat of the Commission for Promoting the Use of the Adult Guardianship System, *Seinenkoukenseido riyou sokushin kihon keikaku ni tsuite (The Master Plan)* (2017), pp. 3–4.

governments, such as adult guardianship support centres and rights protection centres and so on.[19]

In addition, the Master Plan further lists the following under 'Establishment of Core Institutions and Format of Operation'.

(a) Core institution districts
    (i) to establish core institutions at local governmental level which are easily accessible to residents; and
    (ii) to adopt a flexible approach in implementing the structure. Depending on the circumstances of the districts and the prefecture, it could be more convenient to set up a single core institution for several local governments.

(b) Establishing a relevant entity
    (i) local governments should be the entity to establish the core institutions because they possess personal information recorded in the welfare department and they are in a position to coordinate the provision of support from the administrative to the local community members; and
    (ii) as described in (c) below, the establishment of the core institutions must be approached with flexibility based on the circumstances of each district in question. For instance, the operations of the core institution could be commissioned to an institution that is considered suitable for taking on the leading role in a community cooperative network (or in the case of a single core institution commonly established for several local governments, the operations would be jointly commissioned by those governments to this institution). Where there are already existing adult guardianship centres in some districts, they can be utilised for the same purpose.

(c) Operating entity
    (i) Depending on the circumstances of the district in question, the core institutions can either be operated by the local government directly or be commissioned to another entity by the local government;
    (ii) in cases where the local government commissions the management of the institution to another entity, the local government shall choose a corporate entity appropriately (e.g. a social

---

[19] Ibid., pp. 4–5.

welfare council, and NPO, or a public services corporation). The chosen entity should be capable of providing professional services on a consistent basis while maintaining its neutrality and fairness in operations; and

(iii) taking into account of previous experience, the work of the core institutions could be commissioned to multiple institutions if the local government thinks fit.[20]

Finally, the third issue is the prevention of fraud while maintaining the convenience and accessibility of the system. Accordingly, the Master Plan outlines the following under 'Future Goals of the Programme'.

(a) Improving the guardianship system for preventing fraud

(i) it is important to establish a system that will prevent fraud before it occurs so as to minimise the occurrence and damages in this regard; and

(ii) not only are professional organisations to undertake independent and proactive supervision of guardians in performing their duties, the Ministry of Justice and the Supreme Court will also conduct relevant investigations when it is deemed necessary.[21]

3   Executing the Master Plan

The smooth execution of the Master Plan will not be easy. Building local community-based cooperative networks, which lies at the plan's core, is expected to require a tremendous amount of time and effort. However, given the rapid increase in the number of people with senile dementia and other disabilities anticipated in the near future, it is necessary to establish an adult guardianship system as a matter of urgency.

The Council, which holds a prominent position in government administration, has declared the Master Plan a national project under the Adult Guardianship Promotion Act. Thus, relevant ministries, agencies, local governments and family courts are expected to act together to create an environment in which people with disabilities can easily access the adult guardianship system. However, it is vital that not only the administration and judiciary become involved, but also the private sector and professional organisations. In other words, the administration, judiciary and

---

[20] Ibid., pp. 16–17.
[21] Ibid., p. 5.

private sector must pool their expertise and resources to ensure the effective operation of the adult guardianship system.

The implication of widening social disparities in Japan is that senior citizens and persons with disabilities will find it increasingly difficult to fully and effectively participate in society. The challenge ahead is to ensure that these members of society are included on an equal basis with others. Implementation of the Master Plan, which recognises the need for inclusion, is the first step to resolving this social challenge.

V   Conclusion

In Japan, the ageing of the population and nuclearisation of families are proceeding at a rapid rate; the role of adult guardianship laws has therefore become increasingly important, and demand for a sound adult guardianship regime is expected to grow. It is hoped that the reform proposals made in the Yokohama Declaration will render the adult guardianship system easier to utilise. Further, the author strongly believes that the use of trusts and the adult guardianship system in conjunction, continuing power of attorney in particular, would be beneficial to society. The right to self-determination would be better respected if the assets of the persons concerned were managed by the trust system and their livelihoods by the continuing power of attorney system. It is hoped that such a scheme will become a model for the creation of a modern adult guardianship system in Japan.[22]

---

[22] M. Arai, 'Continuing Power of Attorney and Trust' (2015) 8 *Journal of International Aging and Law & Policy* 149.

∽

Appendix

The World Congress on Adult Guardianship Law 2010, held in Yokohama, Japan, from 2 to 4 October 2010, is the first world congress in the field of Adult Guardianship Law, and its hosts and co-hosts decided to issue the Yokohama Declaration to reconfirm the extremely significant implications of the Adult Guardianship Law and the international roles it will play in the years to come, while making a proclamation to the world on the proper use of the adult guardianship system.

This Yokohama Declaration is the result of a three-day congress, as summarised by the participants of the World Congress on Adult Guardianship Law 2010. Part I covers the issues shared by countries around the world, and Part II covers the issues specific to Japan.

The World Congress on Adult Guardianship Law 2010 Organising Committee expresses its gratitude to all participants involved in the drafting of this Yokohama Declaration and hopes that this declaration will contribute to the continued development of the Adult Guardianship Law around the world.

I International Part

1. **WE**, the participants in the World Congress on Adult Guardianship Law 2010, held in Yokohama, Japan, from 2 October to 4 October 2010
     ACKNOWLEDGE that:
(1) throughout the world the number of older people is increasing due to a combination of demographic factors, social changes, medical advances, and improvements in living conditions;
(2) the existence of an ageing population has an enormous impact on resources for health care, pensions, benefits, housing, transport, and social services, and will be a serious socioeconomic issue for decades to come;
(3) mental capacity sometimes deteriorates with age, and the number of older people who are suffering from age-related impairments or disorders of the mind is also increasing;

(4) there is emerging evidence and awareness of the nature and extent of the abuse of vulnerable older people in both family and institutional environments;

(5) although older people are the primary recipients of adult guardianship services, mental incapacity can affect younger people with psychiatric illnesses, learning disabilities, and acquired brain injuries; and

(6) despite an overall improvement in the protection of human rights, in many states the law relating to adult guardianship has been either neglected or not fully developed to take into account modern thinking with regard to anticipatory decision-making, best practices when assessing mental capacity, and establishing the procedures for substituted proxy decision-making on behalf of adults who lack the capacity to make decisions for themselves.

2. **AFFIRM** the guiding principles and provisions of:

(1) the *Hague Convention of 13 January 2000 on the International Protection of Adults*, which entered into force on 1 January 2009, and regulates jurisdiction, applicable law, recognition, enforcement and cooperation; and

(2) the *United Nations Convention of 13 December 2006 on the Rights of Persons with Disabilities*, which requires states who are parties to the convention to reaffirm the universality, indivisibility, interdependence, and interrelatedness of all human rights, and to reaffirm the need for persons with disabilities to be guaranteed full enjoyment of such rights without discrimination.

3. **DECLARE** that in the context of adult guardianship:

(1) a person must be assumed to have the mental capacity to make a particular decision unless it is established that he or she lacks capacity;

(2) a person is not to be treated as unable to make a decision unless all practicable steps to help him or her do so have been taken without success;

(3) legislation should recognise, as far as possible, that capacity is both 'issue specific' and 'time specific' and can vary according to the nature and effect of the decision to be made, and can fluctuate in an individual from time to time; and

(4) measures of protection should not be all-embracing and result in the deprivation of capacity in all areas of decision-making, and any restriction on an adult's capacity to make decisions should only be imposed where it is shown to be necessary for his or her own protection, or in order to protect third parties.

(5) measures of protection should be subject to periodic and regular review by an independent authority wherever appropriate.

4. **FURTHER** DECLARE that every adult who lacks the capacity to make a particular decision at a particular time, and is without any other means of support or representation in the decision-making process, is entitled to have a competent guardian who will:

(1) act with due care and diligence when making any decision on behalf of the adult;
(2) act honestly and in good faith;
(3) act in the best interests of the adult;
(4) respect and follow the adult's wishes, values, and beliefs to the greatest possible extent, where these are known or can be ascertained, and clearly will not result in harm to the adult;
(5) limit interference in the adult's life to the greatest possible extent by choosing the least intrusive, least restrictive, and most normalising course of action;
(6) protect the adult from ill-treatment, neglect, abuse, and exploitation;
(7) respect the adult's civil and human rights, and take action on his or her behalf whenever those rights are threatened;
(8) provide the adult with assistance and support, and actively pursue things to which he or she may be entitled, such as pensions, benefits, or social services;
(9) not take advantage of his or her position as guardian;
(10) be alert to, and seek to avoid, any conflict between his or her interests as guardian and the interests of the adult for whom he or she is acting;
(11) actively assist the adult to resume or assume independent or interdependent living wherever possible;
(12) involve the adult in all decision-making processes to the greatest possible extent;
(13) encourage participation and help the adult to act independently in those areas where he or she is able;
(14) keep accurate accounts records, and be ready to produce them immediately whenever required to do so by the court, tribunal, or public authority that appointed him or her;
(15) act within the scope of the authority conferred upon him or her by the court, tribunal, or public authority that appointed him or her; and
(16) keep under review the continuing need for any form of guardianship.

5. **AND FURTHER DECLARE** that, because adult guardianship can involve a deprivation of liberty, human rights are engaged, and because the work and duties of guardians worldwide are generally based on public intervention:

(1) states should address the development of professional standards, provide appropriate instruments of control, and guarantee a satisfactory infrastructure supported by adequate resources; and

(2) this Yokohama Declaration should be disseminated and communicated to public bodies and national governments to raise awareness of the issues involved, and to obtain the support required to implement the provisions that we have acknowledged, affirmed, and declared herein.

II Japanese Part

After expressing their full accord with the spirit of Part I of this declaration, the Japanese participants of the World Congress on Adult Guardianship Law 2010 urged the Japanese government to ratify at the earliest opportunity the United Nations Convention on the Rights of Persons with Disabilities and the Hague Convention concerning the protection of adult(s), and confirmed the following items to be included in the Yokohama Declaration with the full support of overseas participants:

1. Revision of the current Adult Guardianship Law and improvement in the operation of the law

(1) Mayors around the country should make legislative preparations for a system that further facilitates statements to be made by mayors on guardianship for adult(s), etc.
(2) Public subsidies should be provided to those who have difficulty paying the costs of the adult guardianship system
(3) Given that the commencement of adult guardianship has an aspect of restricting the rights of adults, an appraisal and interview with adults should not be omitted and the current situation – in which the rate of execution of appraisals and interviews with adults remains at a low level – should be improved.
(4) Although the current Adult Guardianship Law specifies that a guardian of an adult must be assigned with power of attorney for the adult's property only, the guardian's power of attorney should not be limited to property management alone and this point should be revised. The guardian should be able to consent to medical treatment for the adult as well.
(5) Disqualifications remaining in the current adult guardianship system should be abolished. There are no rational grounds for disfranchisement on the determination of the commencement of guardianship. Doing so contravenes the principles of the constitutionally guaranteed right to vote and represents a gross violation of basic human rights.
(6) Although the continuing power of attorney system is the most appropriate system in terms of 'respect of the right to self-determination', it has not been widely used. Legislative measures should be taken to promote the use of the continuing power of attorney system and at the same time to prevent abuses.

2. Creation of a public support system

Irrespective of the scale of the user's assets or the existence of the petitioner, the adult guardianship system should be positioned as a system available for everyone, and for this reason it is essential that the government publically support the entire adult guardianship system. Since the public support system results in the 'socialisation of guardianship for adult(s)', a public support system by the government is recommended. The main premise of smooth implementation of a public support system should be further expansion and enhancement of functions of the judiciary, especially functions of the family courts in the operation of the adult guardianship system. The establishment of such a public support system is to expand the network among the adults' families, the general public and the specialists in each field and to contribute to securing appropriate guardians of adults and enhancing the advocacy functions of the adult guardianship system.

3. Potential of the new adult guardianship system

The potential for further development should always be sought after in search of a new philosophy rather than staying within the framework of the current Adult Guardianship Law.

(1) The current adult guardianship system is based on the three types of protection, namely guardianship, curatorship, and advisorship. Guardianship, in particular, considerably limits the capacity of the adult. Considering the effect of article 12 of the United Nations Convention on the Rights of Persons with Disabilities, it is necessary to study appropriateness of the current three types. At the same time it is also necessary to study procedural protections of the adult in the procedures for the guardianship of adult(s).

(2) Although one possible method to protect adults without limiting their capacity is the use of trusteeship, this type of trusteeship is not commonly used in Japan. Courts need to study the introduction of a trusteeship system as a substitute for adult guardianship with respect to the setting of trusteeship.

(3) To improve the present situation, in which victims of traffic accidents with higher brain dysfunction rarely use the adult guardianship system, it is necessary to adopt new legislative measures to encourage people with higher brain dysfunction to use the system.

4

The Use of Trusts in Taiwan's Adult Guardianship System

TAI YU-ZU*

I The Adult Guardianship System in Taiwan: Current Status and Dilemma

Taiwan's Adult Guardianship System (AGS) was established with the objective of helping persons with mental or intellectual disabilities to manage their personal affairs and property. Initially, the AGS focussed primarily on protecting such persons – with guardians acting on their behalf and for their benefit – and regard was rarely paid to their own intent or wishes. However, the situation changed with the enactment of the UN Convention on the Rights of Persons with Disabilities, which promotes respect for the inherent dignity of all persons with disabilities and requires promotion of their right to decide for themselves how to live with respect to various aspects of their lives.[1] Taking into account the abilities and characteristics of individual such persons, it also specifies the provision of assistance to enable them to exercise that right. This shift in approach is particularly meaningful for members of an ageing society who suffer mental or intellectual disabilities by reason of physical degeneration or dementia. As the degree and timing of mental degeneration amongst this group of elderly may vary widely, it is necessary to conduct case-by-case assessments and respect their intent to the greatest extent possible. Accordingly, countries and territories around the world have made efforts to review and revise their respective AGSs by moving from the concept of protecting those with mental or intellectual disabilities to a consideration of how best to enable them to enjoy autonomy and live with dignity notwithstanding their need for care.

---

* Associate Professor, Department of Law, National Taipei University.
[1] V. Lipp, Betreuungsrecht und UN-Behindertenrechtskonvention (Supervision Law and UN Disability Rights Convention) (2012) FamRZ 669, 670.

Taiwan implemented a new AGS on 23 November 2009. Its former 'declaration against dealing with property' was replaced by a two-pronged system comprising a 'declaration of guardianship' (DCG) and 'declaration of assistantship' (DCA). Once a DCG is made, the person at whom it is directed (i.e., the ward) becomes an incapacitated person (Civil Code article 15) who cannot perform juristic acts, including daily transactions, on his or her own, whereas the person at whom a DCA is directed (i.e., the assisted person) retains the capacity to act, although he or she has to obtain the consent of an assistant to validate acts concerning material property matters expressly specified by law. Therefore, in contrast to the previous system, which provided only for a declaration against dealing with property that incapacitated the person subject thereto in all respects, the current two-pronged approach distinguishes different degrees of intellectual disability, thereby showing greater respect for the exercise of personal residual abilities.

Under the new AGS, in addition to retaining the previous provisions that protected wards or assisted persons, provisions have also been added that expressly require respect for a ward's intent. Examples of the former provisions are those that seek to prevent a guardian from infringing a ward's interests in exercising his or her duties as guardian. In managing a ward's property, a guardian is subject to three restrictions: (1) a guardian is not allowed to use, dispose of or consent to the disposal of a ward's property except to serve the ward's interests; (2) a guardian's act of purchasing or disposing of real property for a ward, renting out a building in which the ward resides or is based, making such a building or base available for others to use or terminating a lease on such a building or base is not valid unless permission has been obtained from the courts; and (3) a guardian is not allowed to take a ward's property (Civil Code articles 1101 and 1102). Further, if a guardian does not perform his or her duties in the best interests of the ward, the courts shall, upon petition, elect another guardian (Civil Code article 1106-1). The new provisions specify that in selecting a guardian the courts are required not only to act in the best interests of the ward (Civil Code article 1111-1) but also to consider, as a matter of priority, his or her opinions (Civil Code article 1111-1). Further, the previous provision requiring a guardian to arrange for the treatment of a ward in accordance with the ward's best interests and financial status (old Civil Code article 1112) was amended to stipulate that when performing duties relating to the ward's life, treatment and financial management, the guardian is required to respect the ward's intent and take into account his or her physical health, well-being and living conditions (Civil Code article 1112). It is thus clear that Taiwanese legislators have indeed placed considerable emphasis on respecting the intent of wards.

Nevertheless, several years into the new system's implementation, amendments to the adult guardianship law have revealed a number of inadequacies in relation to both protecting the interests of wards and respecting their intent. Those inadequacies are detailed in the following paragraphs.

A   Protecting the Interests of a Ward

It is true that the AGS emphasises the protection of wards' interests. However, because Taiwan's current law on adult guardianship does not – unlike the laws of Japan and Germany, for example – provide for a guardianship supervisor, Taiwan lacks a mechanism for the effective supervision of the performance of duties by guardians, and the courts are unable to appoint a new guardian immediately upon the discovery of any abuse of power or embezzlement of a ward's property by a guardian. As a result, the ward's interests may be seriously prejudiced. Despite the presence of provisions requiring court permission with respect to significant acts involving property (see previous section), the courts' powers do not extend to dealing with a guardian who fills his or her own pockets by way of managing a ward's property. Therefore, Taiwan's current AGS is unable to effectively guard against such a situation.[2]

B   Respecting a Ward's Intent

Under the statutory guardianship system, which is the only AGS available in Taiwan, when a DCG is made in respect of a person, who then becomes a ward, the court emphasises the opinion of the ward in selecting a guardian and specifying his or her duties. However, by the time a DCG is necessary, the ward in question is usually no longer able to express an opinion. As a result, Taiwan's AGS, which provides for wards' interests as a starting point in the selection of guardians and execution of

[2] S. C. Huang, 'New Directions for the Adult Guardianship System: What Does the Supervision Mechanism under Japanese Law Mean for Taiwan?' (2016) *Japan-Taiwan Exchange Association Business Results Report* 1, available from www.koryu.or.jp/Portals/0/resources/tokyo/ez3_contents_nsf/0/8d95d99465f916b24925812f000e50ee/$FILE/2016huangsiehchuen.pdf.

their duties, is unable in practice to achieve the legislative purpose of according priority to respect for wards' intent. The AGS lacks a mechanism for 'freezing' a ward's wishes when he or she is capable of clearly expressing them and then 'resurrecting' them when he or she is no longer able to do so.

II   The Role of Trusts in the Adult Guardianship System

A   Relevant Provisions under the Taiwan Trust Law

The Trust Law of the Republic of China (Taiwan Trust Law, or TTL) was passed in 1995. Then, in 2009, in light of amendments to the Civil Code regarding the AGS, the relevant wording in the TTL was adjusted, although no changes were made to its substantive content. To date, the major direction of development lies with business trusts and commercial trusts, with emphasis placed on the application of such wealth management tools as mutual funds,[3] albeit with no ability to apply those tools flexibly to various forms of asset management.[4] This situation is clearly inadequate compared with the flexible application of trusts permitted in other countries.[5] The role that the current law plays in Taiwan's AGS is discussed in the proceeding section.

Articles 1 and 2 of the TTL state that a trust is an arrangement by which the trust settlor transfers or disposes, by a contract or will, of a right of property and causes the trustee to administer or dispose of the trust property according to the stated purposes of the trust for the benefit of a beneficiary or for a specified purpose. Therefore, a trust can be established by any person who possesses full legal capacity or, for those with limited legal capacity or who are incapacitated, with the consent of or expression of their wishes by a statutory agent. The settlor may be the trustee (i.e., self-benefit trust), or he or she may designate another person as trustee (i.e., non-self-benefit trust).[6] It thus follows that, for a minor in

---

[3] Y. C. Chen, 'The Trust Law Has Not Been Amended in 21 years. The Association Is Looking to the Ministry of Justice to Speed Up the Pace', *Economic Daily*, 19 September 2017, available from https://money.udn.com/money/index.

[4] See S. C. Pan, *Trusts for Persons with Disabilities: Theory and Practice* (Taipei: Xinxuelin, 2010), p. 1; C.C. Wang, *Trust Law*, 4th edn (Taipei: Wu-Nan Book Inc., 2015), p. 49.

[5] In light of this, Taiwan's Ministry of Justice has established a working group on amendments to the trust law with a view to conducting relevant studies and working on legislative amendments. Some members of the Legislative Yuan have also proposed amendment bills.

[6] Wang, *Trust Law*, n 4, pp. 58–62.

respect of whom a DCG is made by reason of an inborn intellectual deficit, his or her parents can act as the settlor and establish a non-self-benefit trust with a trustee (usually a bank) for his or her benefit. Alternatively, the parents, acting as statutory agents, may enter into a contract that transfers property under the name of the minor to a trustee, thereby establishing a self-benefit trust. For an elderly person subject to a DCG because of a mental or intellectual disability caused by age-related diseases such as dementia, the trust arrangement usually takes the form of a self-benefit trust. The elderly person as settlor (or a guardian acting on his or her behalf in the case of a DCG) enters into a trust contract with a trustee that transfers his or her property to the trustee. The elderly person is designated as the beneficiary, and the trustee administers the trust property for his or her benefit.[7] This arrangement ensures that property intended to be used to take care of children with disabilities or the elderly cannot be invaded by other relatives or third parties, thereby depriving those children or elderly of an opportunity to live in peace and security.[8]

Further, pursuant to articles 9,[9] 24[10] and 35[11] of the TTL, although the trustee acquires the settlor's property rights by virtue of a trust act, such ownership is merely nominal; the actual proprietary rights still rest with the settlor, whereas the substantive trust interests are vested in the beneficiary (TTL article 17). This serves to prevent a trustee from damaging a beneficiary's interests to obtain trust benefits for him or herself.[12] If the trustee disposes of trust property in violation of the stated purposes of the trust, the beneficiary is entitled to apply to the court for the revocation of such disposal (TTL article 18). If the trustee improperly administers the trust property, thereby causing damage to it, the beneficiary may request that the trustee pay pecuniary compensation and may also seek a reduction of the remuneration payable to the trustee

---

[7] S. C. Pan, 'Planning for Trust Products in an Aging Society' (2008) 12 *Financial and Economic Law Review* 4.

[8] Pan, *Trusts for Persons with Disabilities*, n 4, pp. 19–23.

[9] Article 9 of TTL: 'The property rights acquired by a trustee by virtue of a trust act shall be deemed to be a trust property.'

[10] Article 24 of TTL: 'A trustee shall administer a trust property independently of his own property and other trust properties.'

[11] Article 35 of TTL: 'A trustee shall not convert any of the trust property to his own property or create or acquire any right thereto except [in any one of the specified circumstances].'

[12] Pan, 'Planning for Trust Products in an Aging Society', n 7, 5.

(TTL article 23). The TTL further provides for the appointment of trust supervisors. If it is deemed necessary to protect the interests of the beneficiary, the court may, upon the application of an interested party or the prosecutor, appoint one or more trust supervisors unless a trust supervisor or his or her method of appointment is otherwise provided for in the trust act. An appointed trust supervisor may, in his or her own name, perform any trust-related litigious or non-litigious acts for and on behalf of the beneficiary (TTL article 52). Therefore, in terms of protecting a beneficiary's property from invasion or damage by a trustee, the trust mechanism is far more sophisticated than the guardianship system.

Finally, based on the principle of trust subsistence, a trust relationship cannot be extinguished because the settlor or trustee dies, becomes bankrupt or loses his or her legal capacity (TTL article 8(1)). Therefore, once a trust has been created, even if the settlor becomes incapacitated, the trustee may continue to administer the trust property in accordance with the initial purposes of the trust.[13] It thus follows that even if the settlor is made the subject of a DCG and is unable to express his or her intent, his or her original intention to have his or her assets administered by means of a trust still subsists and is unaffected. It can therefore be said that the trust mechanism serves the function of 'freezing' intent.[14]

In summary, the trust mechanism serves not only to preserve property but also to freeze the intent of the subject person. If these trust functions are applied and given full effect, then Taiwan's current AGS will be able to accord greater prominence to the autonomous intent of subject persons and, at the same time, protect their interests.[15]

---

[13] See S. C. Chou, 'The Use of the Trust System in an Aging Society' (2005) 9 *The Journal of Long-term Care* 283; Pan, 'Planning for Trust Products in an Aging Society', n 7, 6.

[14] See M. Arai, *The Law of Trust in Japan*, 3rd edn, (Tokyo: Yuhikaku Publishing Co., 2008), pp. 459–461, quoted in C. J. Li, 'The Aging Society and the Application of the Trust System – Observations on the Japan Experience' (2013) 32 *Financial and Economic Law Review* 107.

[15] A number of academics in Taiwan have advocated the application of the trust system to adult guardianship: see Chou, 'The Use of the Trust System in an Aging Society', n 13, 279–288; S. C. Pan, 'Obstacles and Breakthroughs to the Development of Current Trust Products in Taiwan: A Study from the Perspectives of Will Trusts and Adult Care and Maintenance Trusts' (2009) 17 *Financial and Economic Law Review* 103; S. C. Huang, 'A Preliminary Study of the Combined Operation of Adult Guardianship and Trust in Taiwan' (2014) 193 *FT Law Review* 23; C. Lee, 'Trusts for the Elderly and Persons with Disabilities in Japan' (2016) *Kainan Law Journal* 1.

B   Legal Basis for Application of the Trust Mechanism Under Taiwan's Adult Guardianship System

As discussed in the preceding section, the trust mechanism is an important property management measure and is capable of performing unique functions in the adult guardianship arena. That being the case, does the Taiwanese legal system pertaining to adult guardianship afford the possibility of using that mechanism? To answer this question, it is apposite to further discuss the active and passive uses of trust at law; i.e., those involving mandatory and voluntary trusts, respectively – the former being the compulsory imposition of a trust in accordance with the law, and the latter the creation of a trust over specific property in accordance with a person's intent (or with a guardian acting on his or her behalf).[16]

1   The AGS under the Civil Code

In Taiwan, the AGS is provided for primarily in the Civil Code. As noted, two types of declaration, namely the DCG and DCA, may be made by the courts, depending on the subject person's degree of mental or intellectual disability (Civil Code articles 14 and 15-1). After making a declaration, the court then appoints a guardian or assistant for the subject person (Civil Code article 1111), with the former assisting the ward in managing his or her person and property (Civil Code article 1112) and the latter exercising his or her right to give consent to any material act relating to property performed by the assisted person such that the act becomes valid (Civil Code article 15-2). Further, the court may select several persons as guardians and designate the enforcement scope of their rights jointly or separately (Civil Code article 1112-1). Eligible guardians/assistants are not confined to natural persons. Juristic persons may also fulfil those roles, as long as they do not provide care services to the ward or assisted person or are related to him or her to avoid conflicts of interest (Civil Code article 1112-2). The following is a discussion of whether the aforesaid provisions allow the possibility of trust use.

(a)   **DCA**   If a DCA is made in respect of a person who, by reason of a mental or intellectual disability, lacks sufficient capacity to understand, reason and express intent, although that person possesses full legal capacity, the law provides that to safeguard his or her interests an assistant must consent to material acts expressly relating to property

---

[16] See Chou, 'The Use of the Trust System in an Aging Society', n 13, 283–285.

(Civil Code article 15-2, first part) in order to be valid. One such act is the establishment of a trust (Civil Code article 15-2, paragraph 1, item (2)). Consider the case of an assisted person who intends, as settlor, to establish a self-benefit or non-self-benefit trust using his or her own property. The act of establishing such a trust will not be deemed valid unless the assistant consents to it. If the assistant does not give consent, then the assisted person may request permission directly from the court (Civil Code article 15-2, paragraph 4). It follows that cases involving a DCA allow only for the possibility of a voluntary trust, which must be initiated by the assisted person. Under the Civil Code, the assistant is empowered only to give consent; there is no room for him or her to take the initiative to set up a trust with the property of the assisted person even for the benefit of that person.

(b)   DCG   If a DCG is made in respect of a person who, by reason of mental or intellectual disability, lacks the capacity to understand, reason and express intent, the law considers that person (the ward) to lack the capacity to perform any juristic act (Civil Code article 15), and his or her life, treatment and financial affairs must be managed by a court-appointed guardian (Civil Code article 1112). Given that the court may select several persons as guardians and designate the enforcement scope of their rights separately, and that a juristic person may be selected as guardian, in theory the court may appoint a professional guardian vis-à-vis the administration of the ward's property, and a trust enterprise may act as a professional guardian.[17]

In performing his or her duties with respect to property affairs, the guardian is required to respect the ward's intent and act in the ward's interests, taking into account his or her physical and mental status and living conditions (Civil Code article 1112). Therefore, if a ward has subjected his or her property to a trust prior to a DCG being made, then, out of respect for the ward's intent, the guardian cannot terminate or discharge the trust relationship on his or her own accord unless circumstances contrary to the ward's interests have arisen. The first paragraph of article 1101 of the Civil Code provides that a guardian cannot use, dispose of or consent to the disposal of a ward's property except for the benefit of the ward's interests. The creation of a trust relationship, involving as it does the transfer of property rights to a trustee, constitutes

---

[17] See Pan, *Trusts for Persons with Disabilities*, n 4, p. 37.

an act of property disposal. Hence, a guardian may subject a ward's property to a trust only in the interests of the ward, and only the ward can be the beneficiary. That said, the creation of a trust is not mandatory. It is merely one of the means by which a guardian can manage a ward's property and, hence, falls within the scope of a voluntary trust.

2 People with Disabilities Rights Protection Act and Senior Citizens Welfare Act

Under the Civil Code, the majority of those who require assistance by way of the AGS are people with disabilities and the elderly. Therefore, in addition to the Civil Code, the People with Disabilities Rights Protection Act (PDRPA) and Senior Citizens Welfare Act (SCWA) also contain provisions relevant to adult guardianship.

(a) **PDRPA** Implemented in 1997, the PDRPA incorporates the trust mechanism as a way to manage the property of people with disabilities and combines it with the guardianship system.[18] In 2007, following extensive amendment, the PDRPA's original provisions were revised and became articles 81 and 83. Article 81 requires the central competent authority (i.e., the Ministry of the Interior) to assist in filing an application with the court when a DCG or DCA is needed for a person with a disability. It also imposes duties on that authority when the court appoints a social welfare institution as the person's guardian. To protect the property-related rights and interests of people with disabilities who are incapable of managing their property, article 83 provides that the central competent authority – in conjunction with the competent authority in charge of the trust business (i.e., the Financial Supervisory Commission) – should encourage trust enterprises to provide property trust schemes for the individuals concerned. This provision gives the so-called establishment of a property trust system under the old law more concrete form. In the process, however, the property trust system has been rendered specifically applicable to people with disabilities who are

---

[18] Article 43 of the (Physically and Mentally) Disabled Citizens Protection Act provides as follows: 'to ensure that the disabled can still be taken care of and [their interests] secured when their lineal relatives or supporters are old, the central competent authority shall, together with the related competent authorities in charge of specific business[es], establish a secure maintenance guarding system and property trust system for the disabled.' For the legislative history of the Act, please refer to the legal database of the Legislative Yuan.

incapable of managing their property. There are divergent views on whether the change has had the effect of narrowing the range of people to whom the system applies.[19]

Further, the article 83 provision merely requires the Ministry of the Interior to join hands with the Financial Supervisory Commission in encouraging trust enterprises to provide property trust schemes for people with disabilities. Its effect is no more than declaratory, as there is no provision imposing sanctions on the competent authorities for any failure to comply with their statutory duty.[20]

(b)   SCWA   When enacted in 1980, the SCWA was intended to regulate matters relating to the welfare of the elderly. With the rapid ageing of society, increased emphasis has been placed on elderly-related rights, which has led to several additions and amendments to the SCWA in response to public demands. In 2007, for example, with a view to preventing the elderly from being defrauded and/or their property embezzled by a third party owing to the degeneration of their intellectual capabilities, two new sections, namely articles 13[21] and 14,[22] were added to the SCWA's chapter on financial security. Under article 13, a municipal or city/county government authority may assist an elderly person in need of guardianship or assistantship by applying to the court for a DCG or DCA, the abatement of a DCG or DCA, or a change of guardian or assistant. A duty is also imposed on the authorities to request that the court make the necessary disposal orders and to provide other services necessary to protect the person and property of the elderly. Article 14(1),

---

[19] One view is that, on the strictest interpretation, because this provision is intended to apply to people with disabilities who lack the capacity to make judgments, it should rest on the premise that a person is made subject to a DCG. See Huang, 'A Preliminary Study of the Combined Operation of Adult Guardianship and Trust in Taiwan', n 15, 24. Another view is that this provision excludes cases of physical disabilities and applies only to cases of mental disabilities. See Pan, *Trusts for Persons with Disabilities*, n 4, p. 21.

[20] Lee, 'Trusts for the Elderly and Persons with Disabilities in Japan', n 15, 5.

[21] This provision is a response to practical needs: Elderly people who are of unsound mind or insane, and thus incapable of handling their daily affairs by themselves, are often at risk of having their property invaded and embezzled by others, and yet, in the absence of a legal basis, social workers are unable to immediately intervene and protect that property. Hence, there is a need to modify the provision.

[22] This is a measure in support of article 13 of SCWA. Modelled on article 83 of PDRPA and the relevant provisions of the TTL, the provision provides a legal basis by which municipal and city/county government authorities can promote the property trust business to the elderly to safeguard their financial security.

which is modelled on the relevant provisions of the PDRPA and TTL, states that municipal and city/county authorities should encourage the elderly to subject their property to a trust in order to protect it. This stipulation serves as a legal basis for those authorities to promote the property trust business for the elderly. The second paragraph of article 14 was amended in 2015 by substituting '[i]f the court has declared guardianship or assistantship in respect of an elder who does not have a person under a statutory duty to support the elder, the property of the elder shall be entrusted with a trust enterprise approved by the central authority for management and disposal'[23] with '[the f]inance authority shall encourage trust and financial enterprise to provide property trust and commercial reverse mortgage services', and by adding a new third paragraph that reads '[the h]ousing authority shall provide rental housing related services'.

In summary, the PDRPA and SCWA focus on protecting persons with disabilities and the elderly, respectively. Taiwanese law imposes upon the authorities a duty to help these individuals to apply to the courts for a DCG or DCA to reduce the risk of their property being easily embezzled by others by reason of their mental condition rendering them unable to deal with daily affairs. In enacting the PDRPA and SCWA, legislators further took the view that, given the characteristics of the trust mechanism for preserving assets and segregating funds and their use, greater financial protection could be afforded to persons with disabilities and the elderly if their property could be placed in a trust. However, the relevant provisions merely encourage such trusts rather than imposing any mandatory duty, possibly because the trust industry in Taiwan is focussed primarily on the development of commercial trusts. Disability/elderly care trusts are rarely provided, and are thus in need of robust promotion by the authorities. Another possible reason for the failure to make such trusts mandatory is the protection of property rights under the law, with the concomitant understanding that the state should not compel citizens to subject their assets to trusts. Trusts, therefore, remain voluntary in nature.[24]

---

[23] This provision has been criticised by academics for being uncertain as to who and how to entrust property to a trust. See Huang, 'A Preliminary Study of the Combined Operation of Adult Guardianship and Trust in Taiwan', n 15, 25.

[24] Huang, 'A Preliminary Study of the Combined Operation of Adult Guardianship and Trust in Taiwan', n 15, 25–26.

C   Actual Operation of the AGS in the Courts

As discussed earlier, under the Civil Code, the trust mechanism is only one option available to the courts in specifying the duties of guardians, and is also an alternative available to guardians in managing the property of their wards. Further, although both the PDRPA and SCWA contain express provisions concerning trusts, emphasising their effectiveness as a measure to protect the property of disabled people and the elderly and encouraging competent authorities to promote trusts over assets, the wording of the relevant provisions indicates that the creation of trusts is not mandatory. We now turn to a discussion of the actual application of those provisions to particular cases by the courts to examine the application of the trust mechanism to Taiwan's AGS.

Over the past decade or so, there have been roughly 10 court judgments dealing with the issue of whether a ward's property should be subjected to a trust.[25] These judgments pertain both to cases involving voluntary trusts and those involving court orders subjecting properties to trusts.

1   Voluntary Trusts

In the first case we consider,[26] a guardian applied to the court for permission to dispose of a ward's immovable property and took the initiative to request that the proceeds of that disposal be subjected to a trust. The ward, who was subject to a DCG, suffered from dementia and lived in a nursing home. The guardian wished to dispose of property under the ward's name to help the ward to meet daily expenses and nursing costs. Article 1101 of the Civil Code provides that a guardian is not allowed to dispose of a ward's property for any purpose other than the ward's interests and that any disposal of immovable property by a guardian on behalf of a ward is not legally valid unless permitted by the court (article 1113 states that article 1101 shall apply mutatis mutandis). At the case hearing, the court ascertained both that it was necessary for the ward to meet daily expenses and nursing costs and that the intended disposal by the guardian of the immovable property in question was in

---

[25] Shiling District Court Case No. 64 of 2007; Hualien District Court Case No. 79 of 2008 (Hualien District Court Case No. 9 of 2009); Taichung District Court Case No. 773 of 2013 (Taichung District Court Case No. 105 of 2014, Supreme Court of Taiwan Case No. 117 of 2015); Taipei District Court Case No. 72 of 2015; Yilan District Court Case No. 141 of 2015; Kaohsiung Juvenile and Family Court Case No. 21 of 2015.

[26] Taipei District Court Case No. 72 of 2015.

the ward's interests. Therefore, permission for the disposal was granted. Further, taking into account the opinion of the other persons concerned, namely the daughter and elder sister of the ward, that a trust account should be set up for the proceeds of the disposal, the court held – with the guardian applicant's declaration of consent – that the proceeds should indeed be subjected to a trust.

2   Placing Property in Trust

The second group of cases involves the selection and change of a guardian. In two of these cases, the family members involved were unable to agree on a guardian, whereas in one the persons connected with the case discovered that the guardian in question had embezzled property in performing his or her duties and therefore applied to the court for a change of guardian.

In Yilan District Court Case No. 141 of 2015, the ward was involved in a car accident while fulfilling mandatory military service, and the ensuing brain damage and complications had rendered him unable to understand or reason. Hence, a DCG had been made. Both of the ward's parents were deceased. The applicant was the ward's third elder sister. His other siblings had requested that all of his siblings be appointed as joint guardians. In considering the ward's interests, the court noted that the applicant had been looking after him for 20 years, whilst his other siblings visited him only occasionally, and some had not visited him at all in the past few years. Further, the siblings resided in different locations. The court therefore took the view that it was in the ward's interests to appoint the applicant his sole guardian. However, as the ward's property formed the major source of dispute amongst the siblings, the court held that the applicant should place that property in trust, with the ward named the trust beneficiary. The trust benefits would then be used to meet the ward's daily living expenses and the costs of his care and medical treatment. An account was also to be set up and properly managed to safeguard the ward's interests and prevent further property-related disputes amongst the siblings.

Another case involving a guardian-related dispute amongst siblings was Kaohsiung Juvenile and Family Court Case No. 000021 of 2015. The ward in this case suffered from an inborn intellectual disability and had been looked after by his mother prior to a DCG being made. He had three brothers and two sisters. After their mother had been diagnosed with dementia, the five siblings hired a nurse to care for the ward full time and took turns looking after him (one sibling per week). Their mother had previously authorised one of her daughters (i.e., the defendant) to deal with property matters, an arrangement that held after her dementia diagnosis. The defendant had assisted in selling land under the mother's name and was suspected by her siblings of having embezzled the balance of the proceeds. After the sibling relationship had descended into open hostility, the defendant's elder brother applied to the court for a DCG in respect of the mother and for an order naming him as guardian. The first instance court ruled in favour of the brother. The defendant then filed a defence, contending that she and not her brother was the appropriate guardian because she had been trusted by their mother. The court instructed a competent authority to carry out a visit and inspection, and appointed a guardian ad litem. Then, based on the authority's report, the court dismissed the defence on the grounds that none of the siblings agreed that the defendant should serve as guardian. Hence, further dispute might easily arise amongst the siblings over care of the ward and property planning. However, the judge considered it appropriate to supervise the guardian's administration of the ward's property to prevent further disputes between the two 'camps' and further held that the guardian should place the ward's property in trust to protect his property rights.

The last case considered in this subsection also concerned a change in guardian.[27] After a DCG had been made in respect of the ward in question, the family members involved could not agree on the discharge of duties by the guardians who had been appointed, thus leading to litigation. The first instance court held that because property administration issues had caused the guardians to distrust one other, it was necessary for the court to specify the mode of guardianship to avoid any further delay in the guardians' performance of their statutory duties. Referring to article 13 of the SCWA and article 83 of the PDRPA, the court ruled that it was appropriate for the ward's property to be administered and disposed of by a professional institution, as this would enable the ward to receive benefits and, furthermore, would ensure checks and balances between the ward's carer and the institution entrusted with the property. It would also help to advance the legislative objective of safeguarding property owned by the elderly or disabled. Therefore, the first instance judge issued directions stating that the ward's property

---

[27] Hualien District Court Civil Case No. 79 of 2008; Hualien District Court Case No. 9 of 2009. For a commentary by an academic on this case, see Huang, 'A Preliminary Study of the Combined Operation of Adult Guardianship and Trust in Taiwan', n 15, 26–28.

should, within six months of the issuance of a property inventory, be entrusted in a trust enterprise approved by the central authority for management and disposal. However, at the trial of defence, the defendant contended that that judgment was nugatory and unenforceable because the first instance court had not designated any trust authority or applicant. The court hearing the defence took the view that the 'property trust' mode of guardianship was an obligation imposed by the court on the guardians and not an order to be executed. Hence, there was no question of enforcement. If the guardians did not follow the mode of guardianship specified by the court – that is, did not place the property in trust – they could be deemed to have failed in their obligation to protect and take care of the ward, which could in turn constitute a reason for changing guardians. This case demonstrates that, although property trusts are encouraged rather than mandated by both the SCWA and PDRPA, they can be made indirectly mandatory by the courts. In DCG cases where there is a need to protect or safeguard the property of an elderly or disabled person, the court may specify property trust as a mode of guardianship.

3   A Court Not Being Allowed to Subject Property to a Mandatory Trust

In the final case we consider, in which a social welfare institution had filed a defence,[28] four out of five members of a family, namely a mother and her two sons and one daughter, had been identified as mentally and intellectually disabled. The family's fourth son alone was deemed to be of normal intelligence. The family had been looked after by relatives and friends since the father's death. Given that property embezzlement was suspected, the family was housed by the Taichung City Government Social Affairs Bureau in accordance with the law. Following the third daughter's application for a DCG, a dispute arose over the selection of a guardian. The social welfare institution responsible for the family's daily care took the view that the way the fourth son and a nephew were managing the family's daily life and property was inappropriate and that

---

[28] Taichung District Court Case No. 105 of 2014. For the first instance trial, see Taichung District Court Case No. 773 of 2013. Its defence having been dismissed, the defendant filed another with the Supreme Court of Taiwan, but the Supreme Court held that the case did not involve any error in the applicable law but rather issues of the acceptance/rejection of evidence and findings of fact, and therefore dismissed the defence on the ground of unlawfulness. See Supreme Court of Taiwan Case No. 117 of 2015.

it was necessary for another social welfare institution to intervene and act as joint guardian. The institution even proposed that real estate under the name of the connected person (i.e., the mother and her two sons and one daughter) be placed in trust, although the court rejected that proposition. Based on the extensive interactions and trust that had developed between the nephew and the family over the years, as well as the mother and second son expressing a desire during the trial to be guarded by a relative rather than an outsider, the court designated the nephew and fourth son as joint guardians. The social welfare institution's defence against the decision was dismissed. At the defence hearing, the judge opined that the state should be slow to intervene in family matters because family rights are closely related to human dignity and ethics. Therefore, with respect to the appointment of guardians, the judge ruled that only in exceptional circumstances should competent authorities or social welfare institutions be considered guardian candidates in preference to a ward's relatives. Further, referring to provisions of the Constitution and PDRPA, the judge took the view that the state is required merely to make suitable provisions and render the support necessary to ensure that people with disabilities are able to maintain their human dignity. Although those provisions set out objective obligations that bind the state, they are not intended to be legislative restrictions that form the basis of the rights of disabled people. Therefore, as a matter of law, article 83 of the PDRPA goes no further than encouraging trust enterprises to provide relevant services. As the property trust system is still in an early stage of implementation, its actual operation and effect remain to be seen. Hence, it should be viewed only as a dual welfare measure available to disabled people that is economic in nature. The state is not entitled to place those people's property in mandatory trusts.

4   Summary

It can be seen from the foregoing cases that the Taiwanese courts have not come to a definitive view concerning whether they may require properties to be placed in trust in adult guardianship cases. Although both the PDRPA and SCWA contain express provisions concerning trusts, those provisions use the word 'encourage' and do not have the legal effect of subjecting properties to mandatory trusts. Therefore, even though some of the cases discussed earlier involved heated disputes amongst a ward's relatives over the administration of his or her property, and the courts may have required the guardians in question to place the ward's property in trust, doubts remain over the enforceability of such a requirement or the penalty for not following it. At best, a court could rely on the provision in the Civil Code stipulating that a guardian can be changed if his or her failure to place a ward's property in trust causes obvious harm to the ward's interests. It thus follows that although the trust mechanism has the advantage of preserving a ward's property, under Taiwan's current AGS, that mechanism remains voluntary.

D The Use of Trusts in Taiwan's AGS: Current Status and Dilemma

1 The Use of Trusts: Current Status

Before the trust mechanism was incorporated in the PDRPA in 1997, that mechanism was considered an important measure for preserving the property of people with disabilities, and thus it was thought that the competent authorities should be required to establish a property trust system. The amendments made to the PDRPA in 2007 merely required those authorities to encourage trust enterprises to offer property trust services for disabled people, and the SCWA followed suit. It is thus clear that between 1997 and 2007, Taiwan failed to establish a property trust system designed for the care and maintenance of those in need, and the use of trusts to preserve the property of disabled persons is still uncommon, although the courts may encourage it. Even in the 2014 court judgment discussed earlier, the judge took the view that the trust mechanism was still a newly implemented system whose actual operation and effect remained to be seen. Against this backdrop, what follows is a discussion of the current status of trusts and the dilemma facing their use under Taiwan's AGS.

Pursuant to article 14 of the SCWA, enacted in 2007, municipal and city/county authorities should encourage the elderly to put their property into a trust with a view to safeguarding the security of that property. In 2008, the Parents' Association for Persons with Intellectual Disability, Taiwan, conducted a survey on the trust industry. Of the banks that responded, nine indicated that they did not engage in trust business whose aim was to preserve the property of disabled people or care/maintain such people. Seventeen other responding banks indicated that they lacked relevant operational information but would welcome enquiries from customers in need. Therefore, the greatest difficulty facing the use of trusts within Taiwan's AGS is the question of whether the family members of a disabled person would be willing to entrust his or her property in a professionally managed trust enterprise, with the principal and interest under trust then used to meet that person's daily needs.[29] The Central Trust of China (which merged with the Bank of Taiwan in 2007) has offered care and maintenance (C&M) trusts for the elderly since 1992. Under a C&M trust, the settlor designates the trustee to deal with the entrusted property in accordance with contractual instructions. All proceeds obtained go to the beneficiary, whereas all expenses and any losses or damages that arise are borne solely by the settlor. However, C&M trusts have a strong charitable element, and from the service provider's perspective yield a lower rate of return than other trust products. In addition, the trust concept is not as popular in Taiwan as it is in Europe and North America, and the Taiwanese are reluctant to entrust property to others and to pay trust management/processing fees. For these reasons, the volume of C&M trust business was small for many years.[30] Following the SWCA's incorporation of the trust mechanism in 2008, a few trust enterprises began offering and managing C&M trusts to ensure the preservation and effective use of pensions and other assets. However, these trusts have attracted few users.[31]

---

[29] Pan, *Trusts for Persons with Disabilities*, n 4, p. 5.

[30] For relevant details, see Pan, 'Planning for Trust Products in an Aging Society', n 7, 7–8.

[31] A number of studies and surveys have revealed that the following obstacles lie in the path of subjecting the properties of the elderly to trusts in Taiwan. The first is a psychological factor, in that many elderly people feel safe only when their properties are put in locations to which they have physical access. They do not feel comfortable with handing their properties to persons in the trust industry with whom they are not familiar. They also worry about the potential loss of their hard-earned money as a result of mismanagement by the trust industry. The second obstacle is a family factor: in general, the children of elderly parents agree that their parents' assets should be managed by the parents themselves, subject to the precondition that the parents are physically and mentally sound and capable of managing their wealth. If the parents suffer from physical or mental degeneration and become incapable of managing their assets, children would generally want to assume the management role on behalf of their parents. They generally do not support the idea of subjecting their parents' wealth to a trust because they harbour doubts about the ability of trust industry practitioners and are unwilling to pay trust management/handling fees. For these reasons, the family factor looms large in limiting the feasibility of property trusts, regardless of whether the elderly take the initiative to place their property under trust or a mandatory trust is imposed upon them when incapacitated. The family factor stems largely from an inadequate understanding of property trusts amongst the elderly and their families. Although C&M trusts were launched as long ago as 1992, the trust concept and related knowledge have never been widely promoted in Taiwan. In the absence of knowledge of what a property trust is or what the advantages of subjecting property to a trust are, the elderly and their families are highly unlikely to set up such trusts. See J. K. Lee, 'A Study on the Feasibility of Property Trusts for the Elderly' (1989) *Ministry of the Interior Study Report* 132, quoted in Pan, 'Planning for Trust Products in an Aging Society', n 7, 17–18.

Accordingly, the National Finance Management Committee – the authority in charge of the trust industry – has since late 2015 made considerable effort to promote property trusts. For example, it launched Measures for the Evaluation of and Reward for Trust Enterprises Offering Property Trusts for the Elderly and Persons with Disabilities, under which incentives are awarded to trust enterprises achieving outstanding performance. In March 2017, there were 24 trust enterprises in Taiwan offering products related to C&M trusts. In 2016, the number of beneficiaries of property trusts for the elderly and disabled rose by 7,155, and the total amount of entrusted funds increased by NTD5.3 billion. The number of C&M trust beneficiaries now stands at 6,787, exceeding the late-2015 figure by 5,924, and the trust property principal totals NTD8.636 billion, exceeding the late-2015 figure by NTD4.403 billion.[32] These figures show that the volume of C&M trust business is growing year by year thanks to promotion by the authorities.

2 The Use of Trusts: Dilemma and Doubts

In addition to the limited use of trusts at the community level (for the reasons set out in footnote 31), there are also a number of issues pertaining to the application of the laws and regulations on the use of trusts in the AGS.

(a) **Selection of Trustees** Subjecting the property of the elderly or persons with physical or mental disabilities to trusts serves an important function – namely, achievement of the objective of providing care and maintenance to them by way of managing their property.[33] Given that the trust mechanism primarily involves the administration and disposal of trust property for the benefit of a beneficiary or for a specified purpose (TTL article 1), the scope of a trust does not extend to personal care and protection (PC&P). Therefore, a commonly held view is that it is not possible to use a trust deed to engage a bank to manage a settlor's property and PC&P simultaneously. However, when it comes to meeting the needs of persons with physical or mental disabilities and those of the elderly, one aspect of PC&P is medical care and treatment, which inevitably incur costs and expenses and thus cannot be completely separated

---

[32] The Financial Supervisory Commission, 'Financial Products Offered by the Banking Industry in Response to an Aging Society', 4 May 2017, available from www.fsc.gov.tw.

[33] See Pan, 'Obstacles and Breakthroughs to the Development of Current Trust Products in Taiwan', n 15, 103.

from the management of trust property. To address this issue, a Japanese academic has proposed[34] that a trust deed may also provide for the engagement of a social welfare organisation as a trustee vis-à-vis PC&P. The following paragraphs discuss whether that proposal would be viable in Taiwan.

Article 21 of the TTL prohibits only minors, wards/assisted persons and bankrupts from becoming trustees. Hence, both natural and juristic persons may be named as trustees. Furthermore, the TTL does not restrict the number of trustees (TTL article 28[35]), and – based on the private law principle of autonomy – if a settlor is allowed to designate two or more persons as trustees, then doing so is not prohibited by law.[36] It thus follows that, in Taiwan, social welfare organisations with the status of juristic persons should be qualified to become trustees and act as trustees jointly with trust industry professionals. The next question is this: If social welfare organisations and trust industry professionals act as joint trustees, is it possible to delineate their respective scope of duties as PC&P and property management? According to article 28(2) of the TTL, which expressly states that 'trust affairs other than routine affairs or the preservation of trust property shall be managed by all the trustees unless the trust act provides otherwise', it is not possible to assign different scopes of duties to joint trustees with reference to their respective professions. Doing so would require amendment of the TTL.[37]

The foregoing difficulties with the TTL could be readily resolved if cases were dealt with in accordance with the Civil Code provisions relating to adult guardianship, but then other difficulties would arise. First, upon making a DCG, the court is expected to select a guardian who is in the best interests of the ward, and that guardian may be a natural person or juristic person (Civil Code articles 1111 and 1111-1). Second, the court may select several guardians and designate the scope of the duties they are to perform jointly or separately (Civil Code article 1112-1). In light of these two provisions, it thus appears that it would be more feasible for the court to select multiple guardians, including a trust industry practitioner responsible for property administration and a social

---

[34] See M. Arai, 'Trust in an Aging Society', quoted in Chou, 'The Use of the Trust System in an Aging Society', n 13, 283.

[35] If a trust has multiple trustees, the trust property is jointly owned by all of the trustees.

[36] See Wang, *Trust Law*, n 4, pp. 205–211.

[37] See Pan, 'Obstacles and Breakthroughs to the Development of Current Trust Products in Taiwan', n 15, 108.

welfare organisation responsible for PC&P affairs, than to designate joint trustees by way of a trust.

However, the Civil Code imposes restrictions on guardian eligibility to avoid conflicts of interest, with certain classes of persons prohibited from becoming guardians, including juristic persons or organisations who provide care services to wards or their representatives or persons-in-charge and any persons who have a contract for the hire of services, a mandate or other similar relations with the said juristic persons or organisations (Civil Code article 1111-2). These restrictions limit the potential for the social welfare organisations that take care of wards to also become their guardians. However, if a court simultaneously selects a trust industry practitioner to act as guardian – and entrusts the administration of property matters to that practitioner and appoints a trust supervisor to exercise supervision – with the organisation that provides care services made responsible for PC&P affairs alone, it seems that such an arrangement would alleviate the risks of concern to legislators and should thus be permitted, with the law amended accordingly.

In response to that proposal, the Financial Supervisory Commission has indicated that some banks are actively exploring the possibility of collaborating with organisations that provide care and attention services for the provision of related ancillary services such as hospital treatment and social welfare, as well as the extension of their traditional wealth entrustment and management services to trust products that cater to the actual daily needs of the elderly. These measures would help to enhance the functionality of C&M trusts for addressing those needs,[38] although, from the legal perspective, it is necessary to consider whether corresponding amendments to the relevant law are needed.

(b) **Selection of Trust Supervisors** With a view to preventing trustees from abusing their authority in property administration, protecting the interests of beneficiaries and ensuring achievement of the trust purposes, the TTL provides for a trust supervisor who exercises a supervisory role.[39] According to article 52 of the TTL, if no beneficiary is specified or if protection of the rights and interests of a beneficiary is deemed necessary, then the court may, upon the application of an interested party or the prosecutor, appoint one or more trust

---

[38] The Financial Supervisory Commission, 'Financial Products Offered by the Banking Industry in Response to an Aging Society', n 32.

[39] Wang, *Trust Law*, n 4, p. 272.

supervisors. Accordingly, trust supervisors can be put in place at will in trusts for private benefits. However, in the case of trusts whose beneficiaries are persons with physical or mental disabilities or the elderly, self-benefit trusts in particular, the beneficiaries are very often unable to defend their interests effectively because of incapacity (TTL article 18), and are thus reliant on supervision by trust supervisors.[40] As trust supervisors are generally paid compensation out of the trust property (TTL article 56), the requirement for supervision puts off those of limited financial means. It is also often difficult to find suitable relatives or friends to act as trust supervisors.

To address these issues, the Taichung City Government – joining hands with the Bank of Taiwan and the Family Wellness Association (a social welfare body) – launched the Project for the Provision of Property Trust Services to Persons with Disabilities in Taichung City, which uses surpluses from a charitable lottery to subsidise trust-related charges and expenses. The local Social Affairs Bureau appoints legal professionals or social welfare organisations as trust supervisors and assists disabled persons and elders in need in setting up trusts. However, the project is limited to specific eligible individuals rather than being open to the general public. Looking ahead, therefore, in the short run, city governments will need to train up people to act as trust supervisors; in the long run, trust associations will need to facilitate the passage of legislation to refine the mechanism of public trust supervisors.[41]

(c) **Termination of Trust Deeds**   In a self-benefit trust, where the settlor is also the beneficiary, the settlor or his or her inheritor may terminate the trust at any time (TTL article 63(1)). As the trust benefits are entirely vested in the settlor, termination of the trust relationship by the settlor or his or her inheritor does not prejudice any other person's interests, and it is therefore desirable to recognise such a termination right.[42] In a self-benefit trust set up by a person with a disability or an elderly person, in contrast, the trust relationship is not extinguished because the settlor dies, becomes bankrupt or is incapacitated (TTL article 8), and this is so whether the trust was hitherto the act of the

---

[40] Pan, *Trusts for Persons with Disabilities*, n 4, p. 164.
[41] Q. Y. Wei, 'Public Trust Supervisor seems to be encouraging the enactment of legislations', China Times, 31 August 2017, available from www.chinatimes.com/newspapers/20170831000113-260205.
[42] Wang, *Trust Law*, n 4, p. 309.

settlor's parents as statutory agents or of the settlor him or herself when in possession of full capacity to act. It is thus doubtful that the subsisting trust deed could be terminated at any time by such a person. In the case of a person subject to a DCA, even though he or she still possesses the capacity to act, a trust is expressly stated as an act that requires the consent of the assistant (Civil Code article 15-2, paragraph 1, item (2)), and hence the termination of the trust by the assisted person is also subject to the assistant's consent. In the case of a DCG, as the person concerned has lost the capacity to act, trust termination is carried out by the guardian on his or her behalf. However, regardless of whether it is an assistant giving consent or a guardian acting on the subject person's behalf, any termination must in that person's interests (Civil Code article 1113, applying article 1101 mutatis mutandis). If consent to the termination of a trust causes harm to the interests of a ward or assisted person, the court may thus select another person as guardian or assistant (Civil Code articles 1113 and 1113-1, applying article 1106-1 *j mutandis*).

III Recommendations and the Ways Forward

In 1993, Taiwan became an ageing society according to the World Health Organisation definition. Owing to a declining birth rate and outward migration, its elderly population is predicted to cross the 20 per cent threshold by 2026, thus pushing Taiwan into the hyper-aged society category.[43] Many of the elderly have no family members to look after them. It is therefore essential for everyone in Taiwan to formulate plans for their future care and maintenance while they enjoy the capacity to do so. As explained earlier, the trust mechanism, which serves the function of preserving and freezing assets, can help individuals to achieve the objectives of protecting their own interests and having their wishes respected – the very objectives that the legislative provisions under the Civil Code with respect to the AGS seek to achieve. However, with respect to the question of how to combine the trust mechanism with that system in Taiwan, although a number of suggestions and proposals have been put forward over the years, further work and development

---

[43] Big Data Group, 'With the Society Moving to a "Hyper-Aged Society" in 9 Years, How Can Taiwan Shoulder the Burden of Aging?', Big Data Group, 1 January 2018, available from http://group.dailyview.tw/2017/12/20/.

along the three following three directions are needed at the legal and practical levels.

A   Trust Used in the Statutory Guardianship System: Protecting the Interests of Wards

At present, Taiwan's AGS boasts a statutory guardianship mechanism under which a court shall, upon making a DCG, select one or more guardians from amongst a ward's spouse, relatives within the fourth degree of kinship, other relatives who resided with the ward in the preceding year, competent authorities, social welfare organisations or other proper persons (Civil Code article 1111). As discussed before, both natural and juristic persons are eligible to become guardians, and in selecting guardians, the courts are to take the ward's opinion into consideration (Civil Code article 1111-1). In theory, therefore, a court may, in principle, appoint a trust industry practitioner as guardian if it considers doing so necessary to protect the ward's interests. However, trust industry practitioners are not capable of dealing with PC&P affairs, and hence it is desirable to select other natural or juristic persons as joint guardians. In this regard, it is necessary to consider the possible conflicts between trust law and the adult guardianship provisions in the Civil Code – for example, whether the restrictions on the disposal of property under article 1110 of the Civil Code are applicable to trust industry practitioners acting as guardians in administering the property of a ward. In practice, cases in which the Taiwanese courts have appointed such practitioners as guardians are few and far between. Statistics for the past three years show that in the vast majority of cases, the courts have selected spouses and other relatives as guardians and assistants. Only when a ward or assisted person does not have a spouse or relative, or when there is a serious property-related conflict of interest with a spouse or relative, do the courts appoint a competent authority or social welfare organisation.[44] Also, with respect to the latter, given the constraints set out in Civil Code article 1111-2, only a few such organisations in

---

[44] Take the DCG and DCA cases in 2016 as an example: in 4,014 cases, the spouses/relatives of the wards/assisted persons in question were selected as guardians/assistants, whereas competent authorities were so selected in only 145 cases, and social welfare organisations in only 16. See X. R. Deng, 'A Study on the Support by Social Welfare Organizations to the Adult Guardianship System' (2017) 159 *Community Development Journal* 304.

Taiwan are eligible for selection by the courts.[45] Hence, the common practice in Taiwan is for judges to accord priority to a ward's relatives rather than a trust industry practitioner in selecting a guardian. At most, in cases of property disputes, judges will request that the ward's relatives acting as guardians subject his or her property to a trust to protect his or her interests. However, as shown in the cases discussed in this chapter, such requests exert only an indirectly mandatory effect.

B   Effect of the Voluntary Guardianship System on Trusts: Taking the Ward's Intent into Account

Under the current law on adult guardianship, there are provisions requiring that priority be accorded a ward's intent in appointing guardians or carrying out a guardian's duties. However, it is doubtful that a ward made subject to a DCG is able to express his or her intent. Although the legislative explanation is that 'intent' in this context refers to opinions expressed by the ward before he or she lost his or her mental capacity, or while he or she still possesses it,[46] how does one assess whether a ward still possesses such capacity? Furthermore, it is difficult to determine with any certainty whether opinions he or she expressed in the past reflect his or her true intent today. Therefore, to ensure the actual realisation of the legislative objective of respecting a ward's intent, it is crucial that a voluntary guardianship system (VGS) be introduced. The Ministry of Justice began drafting an amendment bill in 2016, to which six provisions have been added.[47] All six are currently pending deliberation and passage by the Legislative Yuan. Salient features of those provisions are as follows. First, a subject person may, while in possession of cognitive ability, enter into a deed with an appointee whereby the appointee will become that person's guardian when a DCG is made in respect of him or her. Second, there may be one or more appointees, with the deed setting out the duties of each in relation to the subject person's daily life, care and treatment, and property administration affairs. Third, the subject person may, by way of a voluntary guardianship deed, request that the guardian place his

---

[45] For example, the Hondao Senior Citizen's Welfare Foundation in Taichung City.

[46] See the legislative explanation for article 111-1 of the Civil Code on the Legislative Yuan website, https://lis.ly.gov.tw.

[47] For a general explanation of the amendment bill regarding voluntary guardianship under the 'relatives' section of the Civil Code, see www.moj.gov.tw/cp-23-60922-8f448-001.html.

or her property in trust when a DCG is made. Accordingly, voluntary guardianship may serve to 'freeze' the expression of intent and, in combination with the trust mechanism, achieve the objective of preserving the subject person's property in accordance with his or her wishes. Relative to statutory guardianship, the VGS can indeed better respect the wishes of the subject person and also allow for more flexible use of the trust mechanism.

C Use of Voluntary and Mandatory Trusts in the AGS

Under the current legal framework governing Taiwan's AGS, trusts are, by and large, voluntary trusts. Does the state have the power to intervene to protect the interests of persons subject to DCGs, with the courts able to mandate that their assets be placed under trust? The answer is still a matter of debate. Those who are opposed to such power take the view that it would undermine the constitutional protection afforded citizens' property rights, violate the principle of autonomy in private law, interfere with individuals' right to control their own assets and infringe upon freedom of contract,[48] thereby rendering nugatory the guardianship system under civil law.[49] Commentators adopting the public interest perspective, in contrast, take the view that to meet public interest demands, it is necessary for the state to interfere with private law by means of the force of law. Further, in the present context, with a view to safeguarding the interests of incapacitated persons and preventing their relatives or social workers from encroaching upon their property in the course of administering it, it is essential that the law provide for mandatory trusts, with necessary amendments made to provide a legal basis for such trusts.[50] The aforementioned Project for the Provision of Property Trust Services to Persons with Disabilities in Taichung City constitutes an attempt to introduce mandatory trusts, although it is applicable to only a handful of cases.

---

[48] See Pan, *Trusts for Persons with Disabilities*, n 4, p. 247.

[49] See Huang, 'A Preliminary Study of the Combined Operation of Adult Guardianship and Trust in Taiwan', n 15, 30.

[50] It has been suggested that a provision along the following lines may be added to art. 2 of the TTL: 'Based on the interests of the person with no or limited capacity to act, the court may, upon application by the subject person, two social workers or an interested party, order that all or part of the property of the person with no or limited capacity to act be placed on trust, with the trustee(s) and trust supervisor(s) to be elected by the court.' See Pan, 'Planning for Trust Products in an Aging Society', n 7, 16.

In summary, the trust mechanism is not widely used in Taiwan's current AGS, and most cases involving trusts involve voluntary trusts. It remains for potential trust users to acquire a more thorough under-standing of the functions of the trust–AGS combination in preserving assets and 'freezing' intent. At the same time, once the VGS has been approved and is recognised by law, the trust mechanism may, in addition to playing a part in investments and wealth management, also serve the important function of ensuring the financial security of disabled persons and the elderly.

PART II

Lasting/Enduring Power of Attorney

5

Adult Guardianship and Powers of Attorney in England and Wales

DENZIL LUSH*

I   Adult Guardianship

A   Broader Issues

I shall begin with a brief history lesson because, in order to understand adult guardianship systems in the western world today, it helps to know why and how the present structures originated and developed. It also allows us to reflect on some of the broader issues before we become immersed in the current operational aspects of the mental capacity jurisdiction in England and Wales. These broader issues include the following questions:

(1) For whose benefit does the adult guardianship system exist? Is it purely for the benefit of the individual concerned, or does it also exist for the benefit of their family or creditors?[1]

(2) What are the respective roles of the incapacitated adult, their family, the state, the medical profession, the legal profession and the press?

(3) To what extent should the state compel compliance on guardians in a system that relies mainly on volunteers taking on the guardianship of a family member?

---

* Former Senior Judge of the Court of Protection, UK.

[1] The previous legislation in England & Wales, the Mental Health Act 1983, was much clearer on this point than the Mental Capacity Act 2005. Section 96(1) of the 1983 Act provided that: 'The judge may, with respect to the property and affairs of a patient, do or secure the doing of all such things as appear necessary or expedient – (a) for the maintenance or other benefit of the patient; (b) for the maintenance or other benefit of members of the patient's family; (c) for making provision for other persons or purposes for whom or which the patient might be expected to provide if he were not mentally disordered; or (d) otherwise for administering the patient's affairs.' Subsection (2) provided that 'regard shall be had first of all to the requirements of the patient, [but] ... the judge shall, in administering a patient's affairs, have regard to the interests of creditors and also to the desirability of making provision for obligations of the patient notwithstanding that they may not be legally enforceable.'

B   The Roman Origins of Modern Adult Guardianship Law

The ancient Romans developed a comprehensive legal system over a period of almost a thousand years, beginning with the promulgation of the *Twelve Tables* in 451 BC and ending with the publication of Justinian's *Corpus Juris Civilis* in 534 AD. It was one of their greatest achievements and legacies.[2]

In early Roman law, Table V of the Twelve Tables dealt with both inheritance and guardianship, and provided that the closest relative on the male side of the family was responsible for both the property and the person of an incapacitated adult, or *furiosus*. The closest male relative became what was known as the *curator furiosi*, or keeper of the incapacitated adult. There was no involvement on the part of the state whatsoever. It happened automatically. If, however, there was nobody who was willing and able to take on these duties, then a magistrate would appoint a *curator furiosi* from outside the family.

In theory, acting as a curator was an honorary office, but in later Roman law, obligations that had once been an honour and privilege to perform became a matter of compulsion, and the family member had a public duty (*munus publicum*) to act on behalf of a *furiosus*, just as he had a public duty to provide military service, to pay taxes and to maintain the road network. The curator's responsibilities were threefold: to protect the incapacitated adult, to protect their fortune and to protect members of the public from them. Not everyone had the time, the energy or the inclination to take on a task of this nature and, as a result, various grounds for exemption (*excusationes*) arose, whereby a male relative could be excused from acting as a curator. Females, incidentally, played no part in the curatorial scheme.

Roman adult guardianship law appeared in its final form in Justinian's *Corpus Juris Civilis* in the year 534, and the key features of the system were as follows:

(1) there was an inquisitorial public process, whereby a curator for an incapacitated adult was appointed by a public official, who was satisfied that such an appointment was necessary;

(2) family members had a public duty to act as a *curator furiosi*, unless they were specifically exempted;

---

[2] For a more detailed discussion, see D. Lush, 'Roman Origins of Modern Guardianship Law', in A. K. Dayton (ed.), *Comparative Perspectives on Adult Guardianship* (Durham: Carolina Academic Press, 2013), ch. 1, pp. 3–15.

(3) the curator was required to produce an inventory of the incapacitated adult's assets and liabilities;

(4) the curator was obliged to provide accounts;

(5) the curator had to provide security (*satisdatio*) to cover the possibility that he might cause loss to the estate through his incompetence or dishonesty; and

(6) it was expected that curators would act honestly and conscientiously and for the benefit of the incapacitated adult.

That was the position in the sixth century AD and there has been surprisingly little change over the last 1,500 years. Other than the matter of who actually makes the appointment, the three requirements – to draw up an inventory, to give security and to produce accounts – are what distinguish the appointment of a guardian from the appointment of an attorney today.

C   English Common Law

After the Norman Conquest in 1066, England adopted a feudal system, whereby all land ultimately devolved from the king, and anyone who held or occupied land owed specific feudal obligations to the king. These obligations varied in accordance with a chain of tenure descending from the king's tenants-in-chief, through individuals known as mesne lords and eventually down to the vassals, who actually occupied the land.

In about the year 1270, the king, as feudal overlord, assumed direct control of the lands of two kinds of incapacitated adult known as *lunatics* and *idiots*, regardless of the chain of tenure, thereby cutting out the middlemen.[3] This was known as the Royal Prerogative or parens patriae jurisdiction,[4] and it was confirmed by an Act of Parliament, the *Statute de Praerogativa Regis*, in 1324. A *lunatic* was a person with a psychiatric illness, from which he or she might possibly recover and regain capacity. An *idiot* was someone who was mentally handicapped from birth and, so it was believed, would never acquire capacity.

---

[3] See, generally, F. W. Maitland, 'De Praerogativa Regis' (April 1891) *English Historical Review*, 182.

[4] Parens patriae relates to a notion initially invoked by the King's Bench in the sixteenth century in cases of adults who were no compos mentis. Coke refers to it in his report on *Calvin's Case* (1608) 7 Co Rep, 1a, where he stated that 'moral law, *honora patrem* … doubtless doth extend to him that is *pater patriae*'.

English law also developed the jury system, whereby a group of laymen were summoned to decide an issue of fact on the evidence they heard. Thus, after 1270, before the crown could assume control of the estate of an incapacitated adult, a trial, known as an inquisition, was held, in which a jury of up to 23 men decided whether the person concerned was, in fact, a lunatic or an idiot, and whether he was mentally incapable of managing himself or his property and affairs. In these trials, a majority verdict was sufficient.

There was no need for medical evidence. Whether a person lacked capacity or not was, essentially, a matter of common sense and a decision that a layman was competent to make. When considering the capacity of someone with learning difficulties, for instance, the jury would simply apply the following criteria:[5]

> Idiot is he that is a natural fool from his birth, and knows not how to count twenty pence or name his father or mother, nor tell his own age, or such like easy and common matters, so that it appears he hath no manner of understanding, reason or government of himself. But if he can read, or learn to read by the instruction and information of others, or can measure an ell of cloth, or name the days of the week, or beget a child, or such like, whereby it may appear he hath some light of Reason; such a one is no Idiot naturally.

If, at an inquisition, an adult was found to be a lunatic or idiot, then a public official would appoint a person known as a 'committee of the person' to manage his personal welfare or a 'committee of the estate' to manage his property and financial affairs. The role of the committee was similar to that of a curator in the Civil Law jurisdictions based on Roman law.

Unlike the position in Roman law, family members were never automatically entitled to be appointed as committees in England, nor was there a public duty for them to act as a committee, and for that reason English law never developed the elaborate system of excuses that applied in continental Europe. Today, the Court of Protection has a complete discretion as to whom it appoints to manage someone else's affairs – as, indeed, did its antecedents. Nevertheless, the court has traditionally preferred to appoint family members, wherever possible, rather than strangers.[6]

---

[5] J. Rastell, *Les Termes de la Ley* (1671), p. 419. An 'ell of cloth': an 'ell' was an old English measurement equivalent to 18 inches, the approximate length of a man's arm from the elbow to the tip of the middle finger.

[6] See the dicta of Mr Justice Hedley in *Re P* [2010] EHWC 1592 (Fam); [2010] COPLR Con Vol. 922, para. [9]. 'Therefore, the court ought to start from the position that, where family members offer themselves as deputies, then, in the absence of family dispute or other evidence that raises queries as to their willingness or capacity to carry out those functions, the court ought to approach such an application with considerable openness and sympathy.'

As far as lunatics (although not idiots) were concerned, the royal prerogative jurisdiction was an optimistic jurisdiction, because it was based on the assumption that they would regain capacity and would expect their assets to be restored to them intact. Accordingly, committees of the estate, who were entrusted with looking after their property and financial affairs, were required to ensure that the lunatic's property was 'safely kept without waste and destruction'.[7] This meant that the court could not authorise a committee of the estate to dispose of any part of a lunatic's property. This was inconvenient in some cases, and legislation permitting the court to sell, charge or encumber the land of any lunatic was passed in 1830.[8] Sixty years later, in 1890, the court acquired for the first time an unrestricted power to authorise the alienation of any property (not just land) belonging to a lunatic.[9]

Inquisitions were public trials, which the press could attend and report. In February 1823, the editor of *The Times* sent a reporter to cover the inquisition into the alleged lunacy of an English aristocrat, John Charles Wallop, the third Earl of Portsmouth.[10] The case was absolutely sensational, and subsequently *The Times* and many other national and regional newspapers reported on the lunacy inquisitions held throughout the nineteenth century.

Another striking feature of the Portsmouth Inquisition was the number of medical professionals who gave evidence. Physicians specialising in insanity were known as 'mad doctors' in those days. All the heavyweights of the profession turned up to give evidence, but there was no consensus among them. While the majority opinion was that Lord Portsmouth's mind was unsound, three experts believed that his mind was weak but not unsound. Dr Edward Thomas Monro (1789–1856), the physician in charge of Bethlem Hospital ('Bedlam'), the leading lunatic asylum in England, said: 'With respect to insanity, the definitions are always unsatisfactory. It is next to impossible to define insanity clearly, or separate it from weakness of mind. It is as difficult to define as to settle the precise boundaries of day and night.'[11] Understandably, Lord

---

[7] *De Prerogativa Regis*, 17 Edw. II (1324), stat. 1, cap. 10. (salvo custodiantur sine vasto et destructione).

[8] The Infants' Property Act 1830, s. 28.

[9] Lunacy Act 1890, s. 120.

[10] See, E. Foyster, *The Trials of the King of Hampshire: Madness, Secrecy and Betrayal in Georgian England* (London: Oneworld Publications, 2016).

[11] *The Times*, 28 February 1823, p. 3, available from www.newspapers.com/newspage/32868093/.

Portsmouth's defence lawyers asked how, then, can you expect a jury to declare a man to be insane, when the so-called experts are unable to define what insanity is?[12] Throughout the nineteenth century, psychiatry became progressively medicalised, and a tension developed between the medical and legal professions, which lasted for more than 150 years and was reflected in the marked shifts that occurred at each major legislative juncture. Clive Unsworth described this tension as follows:[13]

> Toward the mentally disordered, both medical and legal approaches have traditionally adopted a posture of paternalism. In the legal approach this was the foundation of the jurisdiction over the person and property of lunatics and idiots originating in the medieval period. In medical approaches, it flows from the central contention that psychiatric patients are afflicted by an illness which has the special character of depriving them of the ability to calculate their own best interests. Both legal and medical approaches are founded upon moral positions, albeit opposed. The legal position is one of concern to protect liberty unless there is good justification for its suppression, while the medical position is one of concern to alleviate the mental suffering afflicted by mental disorder.

The role of the medical expert in capacity cases has steadily diminished over the last 40 years and is now confined principally to diagnosis and prognosis. The United Nations Committee on the Rights of Persons with Disabilities has stated that a supported decision-making regime should be based not on mental capacity assessments but, rather, on 'new, non-discriminatory indicators'.[14]

The costs of an inquisition were enormous, and, unless there was an element of bad faith in making or opposing an application, they were generally paid from the estate of the person who allegedly lacked capacity. The significance of this problem was illustrated in the sequel to the *Windham Inquisition*, which had taken place over 34 days during December 1861 and January 1862. It was the longest lunacy trial in English legal history. Forty-eight witnesses were called by the petitioner, and 91 were called by the alleged lunatic, William Windham, a young man aged 21. Fifteen of the 23 members of the jury considered him to be of sound mind and found in his favour. The costs, which by modern standards amounted to several million pounds, were payable by William

---

[12] See Foyster, *The Trials of the King of Hampshire*, n 10, p. xxxi.

[13] C. Unsworth, *The Politics of Mental Health Legislation* (Oxford: Oxford University Press, 1987), pp. 6–7.

[14] UN Committee on the Rights of Persons with Disabilities, *General Comment No. 1 (2014)*, CRPD/C/GC/1, para. 29.

Windham, even though he had been successful in opposing the petition.[15] It ruined him financially, and he died four years later.

After the *Windham* case, Parliament enacted the Lunacy Regulation Act 1862, section 12 of which provided that cases within certain limits could be dealt with in lunacy without an inquisition. Thereafter, inquisitions became obsolescent and ceased to be held entirely after the Mental Health Act 1959 came into force in 1960. One of the consequences of dealing with cases without holding an inquisition was that the proceedings progressively ceased to be held in public, and ultimately it became the general rule that adult guardianship proceedings were private.

These two issues – the costs of proceedings in the court[16] and the role of the press in reporting adult guardianship proceedings[17] – are still live issues today. Because the primary focus of the adult guardianship system is on promoting and safeguarding the rights and interests of vulnerable people, it is important that judicial decisions made within that system are open to scrutiny.

D   The Present Infrastructure

The infrastructure of the mental capacity jurisdiction in England and Wales consists of

(1) a unique, specialist court known as the Court of Protection, which appoints and removes deputies, adjudicates on disputes relating to powers of attorney, and makes other judicial decisions regarding the property and financial affairs or health and welfare of incapacitated adults; and

(2) the Office of the Public Guardian (OPG), whose functions are administrative rather than judicial. The Public Guardian is required to maintain a register of powers of attorney, to supervise deputies appointed by the Court of Protection and to investigate

---

[15] *Re Windham* (1862) 31 LJNS, Ch. 720.

[16] See *A and B (Court of Protection: Delay and Costs)* [2014] EWCOP 48; [2015] COPLR 1. A were B are two young men living semi-independently. In A's case, the proceedings had lasted for 18 months. In round figures, the estimated legal costs were GBP140,000, of which about GBP60,000 fell on the local authority, GBP11,000 on a legally aided family member and GBP69,000 on the young man himself, paid from his personal injury damages award. In B's case, the proceedings had lasted for five years, and the estimated legal costs were GBP530,000.

[17] See Court of Protection Practice Direction PD13, which provides for a pilot scheme for the holding of hearings to be in public with a standard order for restrictions on reporting

complaints about the manner in which a deputy or attorney is exercising his powers.

The origins of the Court of Protection go back to the middle ages. Following the restoration of the monarchy in 1660,[18] the royal prerogative jurisdiction was exercised by the Lord Chancellor, who was the head of the Court of Chancery. He delegated to the Masters in Chancery the function of making orders relating to the estates of lunatics and idiots. In 1842, the Lord Chancellor decided to appoint two Masters in Lunacy,[19] who did nothing other than lunacy work, and their office became known as the Lunacy Office. The number of Masters was reduced from two to one in 1922,[20] and the Lunacy Office was rebranded as the Court of Protection in 1947.[21]

The office of the Public Guardian developed out of the office of the Public Trustee. The Public Trustee Act 1906 provided for the appointment of such an official to act as an executor of wills and as a trustee of wills, trusts and pension funds.[22] In 1987, the Public Trustee took over the administrative functions (though not the judicial functions) of the Court of Protection.[23]

On 1 October 2007, when the Mental Capacity Act 2005 came into force:

(1) the old Court of Protection was replaced with a new Court of Protection,[24] consisting of nominated High Court judges, circuit judges and district judges;[25] and

(2) a public official, known as the Public Guardian, was appointed to handle the administrative aspects of the mental capacity jurisdiction.[26]

---

[18] The Tenures Abolition Act 1660 (12 Car 2 c. 24), sometimes known as the Statute of Tenures, was an Act of the Parliament of England, which changed the nature of feudal land tenure in England. The long title of the Act was 'An act for taking away the Court of Wards and Liveries, and tenures *in capite*, and by knights-service, and purveyance, and for settling a revenue upon his Majesty in lieu thereof'.

[19] The appointment of two Masters in Lunacy had been authorised by s. 1 of the Commissioners in Lunacy Act 1842 (5 & 6 Vict., c. 84). Under this Act, Lord Chancellor Lyndhurst made a general order on 27 October 1842 appointing the first two Masters.

[20] Lunacy Act 1922, s. 1.

[21] Patients' Estates (Naming of Master's Office) Order 1947 (SR&O 1947 No. 1235/L16).

[22] See, generally, P. Polden, 'The Public Trustee in England, 1906–1986: The Failure of an Experiment?' (1989) 10 *Journal of Legal History* 228.

[23] Public Trustee and Administration of Funds Act 1986.

[24] Mental Capacity Act 2005, s. 46.

[25] Ibid., s. 47.

[26] Ibid., s. 57.

The Court of Protection has an administrative staff of just less than 100 civil servants, and more than 200 judges are nominated to adjudicate in Court of Protection proceedings. Only five of these judges are assigned to the court on a full-time basis. The Office of the Public Guardian (OPG) has a staff of more than 1,500.

E   Appointment of a Deputy by the Court of Protection

If someone lacks capacity to make decisions in relation to their property and affairs or health and welfare, and they have not appointed an attorney under a Lasting Power of Attorney to make those decisions for them, it may be necessary to make an application to the Court of Protection to appoint a deputy to act on their behalf.

Deputies must be individuals aged 18 or older, and are usually relatives or close friends of the person who lacks capacity. A trust corporation can act as deputy for property and affairs, but not as a deputy for health and welfare.[27] The court can appoint more than one deputy, and will generally appoint to them to act either 'jointly' (where all deputies must act together) or 'jointly and severally' (where a deputy can make decisions on their own or together with the other deputy).[28]

An applicant applying for the appointment of a deputy has to submit the following completed documents to the court:

(1) two copies of an application form (COP1);
(2) an information form (COP1A in property and affairs cases, and COP1B in health and welfare cases). In property and affairs cases, the COP1A assumes the role of the inventory, which is one of the abiding features of adult guardianship systems generally;
(3) an assessment of capacity form (COP3);
(4) a deputy's declaration (COP4); and
(5) a cheque for the application fee, which is currently GBP385.

These documents should be sent to the central registry of the Court of Protection, at PO Box 70185, First Avenue House, 42–49 High Holborn, London WC1A 9JA. The court will return a stamped copy of the application, signifying that it has received and is considering the application.

---

[27] Ibid., s. 19(1).
[28] Ibid., s. 19(4).

Within 14 days of the application being issued, the applicant must tell ('serve') the following people:

(1) the person to whom the proceedings relate; in other words, the incapacitated adult. They need to be served personally with an acknowledgment of service form (COP5) and a form headed 'Proceedings about you in the Court of Protection' (COP14); and

(2) anyone named in the application as having an interest; usually the person's relatives. They must be served with an acknowledgment of service form (COP5) and a 'Notice that an application form has been issued' (COP15).

Within seven days of serving these people, the applicant must send the court a certificate of service or notification (COP20) stating that he or she has served the persons mentioned above.

The acknowledgment of service form (COP5) states that, 'If you do not wish to take part in the court proceedings, you do not need to complete this form'. If, however, the recipient does wish to take part in the proceedings, they need to complete the form and state whether they:

(1) consent to the application;
(2) oppose the application; or
(3) seek a different order or direction.

The acknowledgment of service must be sent to the court within 28 days of service of the application and, where necessary, should be supported by evidence in the form of a witness statement (COP24). If everyone consents to the application, then the court will make an order appointing a deputy. The order:

(1) makes the appointment;
(2) sets out the scope of the deputy's authority (including their authority to make provision for the incapacitated adult's dependents and a limited authority to make gifts on customary occasions);
(3) sets out the deputy's duty to provide an annual account to the Office of the Public Guardian;
(4) requires the deputy to provide security of a given amount;
(5) specifies whether the deputy may be remunerated for his or her services; and
(6) authorises the costs of the applicant to be assessed and paid from the estate of the incapacitated adult.

If, on the other hand, the court receives an acknowledgment of service objecting to the application, it will fix a time, date and venue for an attended hearing before a judge.

Attended hearings usually only take place if there is a dispute. The Court of Protection operates on a regional basis for hearings in contentious cases, and the matter will be transferred to the regional court which is most convenient for the majority of the litigants concerned. The press is now entitled to attend Court of Protection hearings, unless the judge orders otherwise.

As part of a drive towards greater transparency in order to improve public understanding of the court process and inspire greater confidence in the court system, a practice direction was issued on 16 January 2014, which requires judgments in certain kinds of cases to be published on the database managed by the British and Irish Legal Information Institute (BAILII).[29]

F   Supervision of a Deputy by the Office of the Public Guardian

Generally speaking, the appointment of a deputy is the end of the proceedings as far as the involvement of the Court of Protection is concerned, and the matter is then transferred to the Public Guardian, who has a statutory duty to supervise deputies appointed by the court.[30] The address of the Office of the Public Guardian is PO Box 16185, Birmingham B2 2WH, though the supervision of deputies is generally carried out at its office in Nottingham.

There are five different types of deputy:

(1) lay deputies – who are predominantly family members, rather than friends;
(2) professional deputies – usually solicitors;
(3) public authority deputies – mostly money management teams in county councils and London borough councils;
(4) panel deputies – these are 'deputies last resort', who are appointed to act where no other suitable person is willing or able to act as deputy. There are 66 panel deputies and they are almost entirely solicitors; and
(5) health and welfare deputies.

---

[29] Practice Guidance: *Transparency in the Court of Protection: Publication of Judgments* [2014] EWHC B2 (COP); [2014] COPLR 78.
[30] Mental Capacity Act 2005, s. 58(1)(c).

As at 31 March 2018, the OPG was supervising a total of 59,928 deputies, which was an increase of 3.2 per cent on the 57,702 at the end of March 2017.[31] In December 2015, when the OPG was supervising a total of 56,691 deputies, the breakdown between the types of deputy was as follows:

Lay deputies – family members	26,006	45.87%
Public authority deputies	18,966	33.45%
Professional deputies	10,735	18.94%
Friends	531	0.94%
Panel deputies	453	0.80%
	56,691	100.00%

There are six main elements in the supervision of a deputy – (1) First Contact, (2) Visits, (3) Security, (4) Reports, (5) Guidance, and (6) Investigation of complaints – each of which is briefly considered in the proceding subsections.

1   First Contact

The first contact process involves an introductory and settling-in telephone call with new lay and professional deputies within 35 days of their appointment, which aims to ensure that new deputies are supported at an early stage in their appointment.

2   Visits

The Mental Capacity Act 2005 empowers the Lord Chancellor to appoint a Court of Protection Visitor.[32] There are two types of Visitor:

(1) Special Visitors, who are either registered medical practitioners or persons who appear to the Lord Chancellor to have other suitable qualifications or training; and

(2) General Visitors, who need not have a medical qualification.

---

[31] Office of the Public Guardian, *Annual Report & Accounts 2017/18* (19 July 2018), pp. 7 and 12.

[32] Mental Capacity Act 2005, s. 61(1). The office of Visitor goes back to the Lunatics' Visitors Act 1833, which authorised the Lord Chancellor to appoint two physicians and a barrister to visit patients at least once a year and to superintend, inspect and report on their care and treatment. The panel of General Visitors was introduced with effect from 1 October 1981 by virtue of the Supreme Court Act 1981, s. 144.

Reports by a Special Visitor are usually only commissioned if there is an issue relating to a person's mental capacity at a particular time, and routine supervision visits on behalf of the OPG are carried out by General Visitors. Deputies are visited by a General Visitor to check that they understand their duties, are carrying out their duties properly and have the right level of support from the OPG.

As at 31 March 2018, there were 39 Special Visitors and 88 (9 permanent and 79 contracted) General Visitors. There had been 12,175 visits during the year, of which 654 were Special Visitor commissions.[33]

3   Security

When the Court of Protection appoints a deputy to manage the financial affairs of someone who lacks capacity to manage their own affairs, the deputy must put in place a security bond to cover the assets being managed.[34] This adds to the protection of the person lacking capacity. The scheme is administered by an insurance broker,[35] and the bond is provided by an insurance company (principally AVIVA). The amount of security required is a judicial decision, set by the court, and cannot be varied by the bond provider or the OPG. The court can call in all or part of the bond up to the limit secured. There is no requirement to prove fraud, and the loss may not be quantifiable. The insurer must pay on demand without further investigation. Insurers have the right to recover the amount they have paid out, plus their expenses, from the deputy. The average level of security is just less than GBP100,000, and the annual premium payable is usually 0.2 per cent of the limit secured: so, where security is set at GBP100,000, the annual premium will be GBP200.

4   Reports

Deputies are required to produce reports to the Public Guardian annually on the anniversary of the date of the court order appointing them as deputies, although sometimes the Public Guardian may ask deputies to submit reports more frequently. There are several different report forms:

---

[33] Office of the Public Guardian, *Annual Report & Accounts*, n 31, p. 19.

[34] Mental Capacity Act 2005, s. 19(9)(a).

[35] Office of the Public Guardian, *Annual Report & Accounts*, n 31, p. 15. In October 2016, following a competitive tender, the Court of Protection and the Public Guardian awarded the contract for the security bond scheme to the insurance broker, Howden Group UK Limited.

(1) Deputy report form: property and financial decisions (OPG 102)
(2) Deputy report form for property and financial decisions: minimal or first-year general supervision less than GBP21,000 (OPG 103)
(3) Deputy report form: health and welfare decisions (OPG 104)
(4) Professional deputy fees insert (OPG 105)
(5) Public authority deputy fees insert (OPG 106)

The deputy report form (OPG102) refers to the incapacitated adult as 'the client' and contains eight sections:

(1) Deputy and client information
(2) Decisions made over the reporting period: including details of significant decisions and the client's involvement in the decision-making process
(3) People the deputy consulted
(4) Safeguarding. This includes details of: (a) contact with the client; (b) care arrangements; (c) any benefits and income received by a third party
(5) Bank accounts: the deputy must record money that has gone in and out of the client's bank account during the reporting period
(6) Client's assets and debts. An up-to-date statement is required
(7) Decisions in the next reporting period
(8) Deputy's declaration that the information is correct

Deputies making property and financial decisions can complete their annual report online. More than 10,000 deputies have registered to use this service, and more than 6,000 reports have been submitted online.[36]

5 Guidance

One of the statutory functions of the Public Guardian is to publish any information he thinks appropriate about the discharge of his functions.[37] The following are examples of publications that are designed to support deputies in carrying out their duties:

(1) *How to be a property and affairs deputy*.[38] In this guide, the OPG uses other deputies' stories to show some things to consider when making decisions. These are not final answers but may give deputies ideas about how to act.

---

[36] Office of the Public Guardian, *Annual Report & Accounts*, n 31, p. 13.
[37] Mental Capacity Act 2005, s. 58(1)(i).
[38] Office of the Public Guardian, *How to Be a Deputy: Property and Financial Decisions* (Public Guardian Practice Note SD3, issued on 15 February 2012, updated on 14 August 2017).

(2) *How to be a health and welfare deputy.*[39]

(3) *Giving gifts for someone else,*[40] which gives practical advice on what counts as a gift, who can give gifts for someone else, when you can give gifts, changing the limits on gift giving and what happens with unauthorised gifts.

(4) *Professional deputy standards,*[41] which set outs what is expected of professional and public authority deputies and provides an important checklist of actions and conduct that every deputy should follow. There are five standards:

Standard 1: Secure the client's finances and assets

Standard 2: Gain insight into the client to make decisions in their best interests

Standard 3: Maintain effective internal office processes and organisation

Standard 4: Have the skills and knowledge to carry out the duties of a deputy

Standard 5: Health and welfare standards

(5) *Claiming travel costs as a public authority or professional deputy.*[42]

(6) *Public authority deputyship responsibilities,*[43] which includes information for authorities considering entering into a contractual agreement with an external provider.

(7) *OPG's approach to solicitor client accounts,*[44] which sets out the OPG's approach to the use of client accounts to manage deputyship funds, and how the deputy should act under the Mental Capacity Act 2005, the Mental Capacity Act Code of Practice and the Solicitors Regulation Authority Accounts Rules 2011.

(8) *OPG's approach to family care payments,*[45] which sets out the legal framework and the OPG's view of how Court of Protection deputies

---

[39] Office of the Public Guardian, *How to Be a Deputy: Personal Welfare Decisions* (Public Guardian Practice Note SD4, issued on 15 February 2012, updated on 14 August 2017).

[40] Office of the Public Guardian, *Giving Gifts for Someone Else: A Guide for Attorneys and Deputies* (OPG2, published 15 May 2016, updated 17 January 2017).

[41] Office of the Public Guardian, *Deputy Standards: Professional Deputies* (Public Guardian Practice Note SD5, published 6 July 2015, updated 17 January 2017).

[42] Office of the Public Guardian, *Claiming Travel Costs as a Public Authority or Professional Deputy* (Public Guardian Practice Note PN9, 2017).

[43] Office of the Public Guardian, *Public Authority Deputyship Responsibilities* (Public Guardian Practice Note SD12, issued on 14 January 2016, updated on 31 August 2017).

[44] Office of the Public Guardian, *OPG's Approach to Solicitor Client Accounts* (Public Guardian Practice Note SD13, issued on 15 February 2016, updated on 30 August 2017).

[45] Office of the Public Guardian, *OPG's Approach to Family Care Payments* (Public Guardian Practice Note SD14, issued on 18 May 2016, updated on 31 August 2017).

should approach family care payments, including factors for them to consider when deciding on the level of such payments.

(9) *OPG's approach to surety bonds*,[46] which explains what the OPG expects from a bond provider so that surety bonds are suitable for deputies.

6 Investigation of Complaints

In addition to his duty to supervise deputies appointed by the court, the Public Guardian also has a statutory duty to deal with representations, including complaints about the way in which a deputy or attorney is exercising his or her powers,[47] and he will usually commission a General Visitor to visit that deputy or attorney if the OPG is investigating a complaint about him or her.

During the financial year 2017/18, the OPG received 5,245 safeguarding referrals. These covered deputyships and powers of attorney, and most of them related to Lasting Powers of Attorney. The OPG investigated 1,886 of these cases, of which 459 resulted in an application to the Court of Protection for the removal of a deputy or attorney. Where cases were not investigated by the Public Guardian, the OPG offered advice or directed referrals to the appropriate agency, such as the local authority or police.[48]

II Powers of Attorney

A Introduction

In England and Wales, there are two types of power of attorney which remain in force after the donor has become mentally incapacitated:

(1) Enduring Powers of Attorney, which could be made between 10 March 1986 and 30 September 2007; and

(2) Lasting Powers of Attorney, which were introduced on 1 October 2007.

This part of the chapter focuses on the policy considerations underpinning the legislation on enduring and lasting powers of attorney, how

---

[46] Office of the Public Guardian, *OPG's Approach to Surety Bonds* (Public Guardian Practice Note SD15, issued on 6 December 2012, updated 31 August 2017).

[47] Mental Capacity Act 2005, s. 58(1)(h).

[48] Office of the Public Guardian, *Annual Report & Accounts*, n 31, p. 16.

policy and legislation have changed over the last 35 years and how they may change yet again in the foreseeable future.

B   The Automatic Revocation Rule

A power of attorney is a deed in which one person (known as 'the donor') gives another person (known as 'the attorney') authority to act on the donor's behalf. Traditionally, the area of law known as 'the law of agency' governed the creation and operation of these deeds.

At common law, an ordinary power of attorney is automatically revoked when the donor becomes mentally incapacitated.[49] This automatic revocation of a power of attorney can be highly inconvenient. At the time when the attorney's assistance is not simply desirable, but essential, the attorney no longer has the authority to act on the donor's behalf. In order for someone to be authorised to act on the donor's behalf, an application has to be made to a court for what is commonly referred to by people from other nations as an adult guardianship order. In England and Wales, that court is the Court of Protection, and the person the court appoints to act on behalf of an incapacitated adult is called a 'deputy'.

Some territorial jurisdictions sought to overcome these practical difficulties by simply abolishing the automatic revocation rule. For example, in 1969 in the United States, the National Conference of Commissioners on Uniform State Laws approved and promulgated the Uniform Probate Code, which abolished the automatic revocation rule.[50]

In 1983, the Law Commission[51] in England and Wales published a report called *The Incapacitated Principal*, in which it said:

> In making our detailed recommendations we have been conscious throughout of the necessity to balance two conflicting needs. First, the need to provide a simple, effective and inexpensive method of allowing powers to continue despite the donor's incapacity. Secondly the need to protect the donor's

---

[49] *Drew v. Nunn* (1878) 4QBD 661; [1874–80] All ER Rep 1144.

[50] Uniform Probate Code, ss. 5-501 and 5-502.

[51] The Law Commission is an independent body set up by the Law Commissions Act 1965 to keep the law of England and Wales under review and to recommend reforms. It is based at 52 Queen Anne's Gate, London SW1H 9AG, and it proposes changes that will make the law simpler, more accessible, fairer, modern and more cost-effective. It consults widely on its proposals, and, in the light of the responses to public consultation, it presents recommendations to Parliament which, if legislated upon, implement those recommendations.

interests against exploitation. Both needs are perfectly valid. Unfortunately, they are not easily reconciled. In trying, however, to balance these conflicting needs we have had to bear in mind a number of considerations:

(1) The first consideration is that a capable donor should be entitled to direct his affairs as he wishes without requiring the consent of others.

(2) The second consideration is the need to protect the interests of the donor when he has become incapable. Once that event has happened, the attorney would, in the absence of special safeguards, be able to use the power without any supervision by anybody.

(3) The third consideration is that the introduction of EPAs would be unlikely to increase substantially the risk of donors' being exploited.

(4) The fourth consideration is that an EPA scheme would only be acceptable if it were simple, effective and inexpensive. Otherwise no one would want to use it but would be tempted instead to continue using revoked ordinary powers regardless of the legal niceties.[52]

The Law Commission rejected the abolition of the automatic revocation rule, because it felt there would be insufficient safeguards to protect the donor from financial abuse. Instead, it proposed that it should be possible to make a power of attorney which remained in force, notwithstanding the donor's incapacity, provided that various safeguards were in place. The appendix to the report contained a draft Enduring Powers of Attorney Bill, which received the Royal Assent two years later.

C   The Enduring Powers of Attorney Act 1985

The Enduring Powers of Attorney Act 1985 made it possible for a donor to create a power of attorney (known as an 'enduring power of attorney', or EPA) which would continue to remain in force after the donor had lost mental capacity, subject to the following safeguards:

(1) **A prescribed form**. An EPA had to be in a prescribed form containing explanatory information about the effect of creating an EPA. The form was prescribed by the Lord Chancellor and had to be passed by Parliament in a statutory instrument – the main form of secondary legislation in England and Wales.[53]

(2) **Execution in the prescribed manner**. The EPA had to be executed in the prescribed manner. Basically, it had to be executed by the donor before it was executed by the attorney, and the donor's signature and

---

[52] The Law Commission, *The Incapacitated Principal* (Law Com. No. 122, 1983), pp. 12–13, paras. 3.9–3.13.
[53] Enduring Powers of Attorney Act 1985, s. 2(1)(a); now the Mental Capacity Act 2005, Sch. 4, para. 2(1)(a).

the attorney's signature had to be witnessed. At the time of execution by the donor, the prescribed form must have incorporated prescribed explanatory information, explaining the nature and effect of the transaction.[54]

(3) **A duty to apply for registration.** When the attorney had reason to believe that the donor was, or was becoming, incapable, by reason of mental disorder of managing and administering his property and affairs, the attorney had a duty to apply to the Court of Protection for the registration of the EPA.[55] Since 1 October 2007, when the Mental Capacity Act 2005 came into force, the Office of the Public Guardian has been the registration authority for EPAs, rather than the Court of Protection.

(4) **The donor and the donor's relatives had to be notified of the attorney's intention to apply for registration.** Immediately before applying to the court or the OPG for the registration of the EPA, the attorney was required to give notice of his intention to apply for registration (on prescribed form EP1) to the donor personally, and by post to at least three of the donor's closest relatives.[56]

(5) **The donor and his or her relatives could object to the registration of the EPA.** Within five weeks of receiving a notice of intention to apply for registration (form EP1), the donor or his or her notified relatives could object to the registration of the EPA. The burden of proof was on the objector, who could oppose registration on any one or more of the following prescribed grounds:

   (a) The power is not valid as an enduring power of attorney – usually an objector would claim that the donor lacked the capacity to make an EPA when he or she made it.

   (b) The power no longer subsists – usually an objector would claim that the donor had expressly revoked the EPA, or that the donor had made a subsequent EPA.

   (c) The application is premature because the donor is not yet becoming mentally incapable.

   (d) Fraud or undue pressure was used to induce the donor to create the power; and

---

[54] Enduring Powers of Attorney Act 1985, s. 2(1)(b) and (c); now the Mental Capacity Act 2005, Sch. 4, para. 2(1)(b) and (c).

[55] Enduring Powers of Attorney Act 1985, s. 4; now the Mental Capacity Act 2005, Sch. 4, para. 4.

[56] Enduring Powers of Attorney Act 1985, Sch. 1; now the Mental Capacity Act 2005, Sch. 4, Part 3 (paras. 5–10).

(e) Having regard to all the circumstances, the attorney is unsuitable to be the donor's attorney.

(6) **If there were no objections to registration, the Court of Protection would register the EPA, and if there were objections, the court would consider them at an attended hearing.**

(7) **Limited authority to make gifts.** Under an EPA, the attorney has authority 'to dispose of the property of the donor by way of gift to the following extent but no further:

(a) he may make gifts of a seasonal nature or at a time, or on an anniversary of a birth, marriage or the formation of a civil partnership, to persons (including himself) who are related to or connected with the donor, and

(b) he may make gifts to any charity to whom the donor made or might be expected to make gifts,

provided that the value of each such gift is not unreasonable having regard to all the circumstances and in particular the size of the donor's estate.'[57]

(8) **The ongoing role of the Court of Protection.** In its report, *The Incapacitated Principal*, The Law Commission stated:[58]

> We would envisage that the primary function of the court under our proposed EPA scheme would be to provide support and assistance to the attorney where necessary. Apart from the registration procedure, we would regard court involvement in the running of any given EPA as very much more the exception than the rule. This would underline the essential distinction to be drawn between the court's functions under [the adult guardianship legislation] on the one hand and those under the EPA scheme on the other. Under the former, the court has a continuing responsibility to supervise the [deputy]: under the latter the responsibility would be firmly vested in the attorney and the court would only be involved if a problem arose. Nevertheless, the court would have corrective functions. It would be able to investigate the conduct of an attorneyship and, if necessary, bring it to an end.

(9) **If the EPA is registered, no revocation of it by the donor is valid unless and until the Court of Protection confirms the revocation.**[59]

---

[57] Enduring Powers of Attorney Act 1985, s. 3(5); now the Mental Capacity Act 2005, Sch. 4, para. 3(3).

[58] The Law Commission, *The Incapacitated Principal*, n 53, para. 4.78.

[59] Enduring Powers of Attorney Act 1985, ss. 7(1)(a) and 8(3); now the Mental Capacity Act 2005, Sch. 4, paras. 15 and 16(3).

D   Re K, Re F *(1987)*

The Enduring Powers of Attorney Act 1985 did not specify the level of capacity required in order to make an EPA and this was eventually decided by Mr Justice Hoffmann in the combined cases of *Re K* and *Re F* on 27 October 1987.[60]

The facts of both cases were basically the same. An elderly woman suffering from dementia signed an EPA, and a day or two later the attorney applied to register the power. In both cases, there was evidence that, when she executed the power, the donor understood its nature and effect, but there was also evidence that both of the donors were incapable, by reason of mental disorder, of managing and administering their property and affairs. The question arose as to whether the EPAs were valid.

Mr Justice Hoffmann held that the test of validity of the EPA was whether, at the time of its execution, the donor had the mental capacity, with the assistance of such explanation as she may have been given, to understand the nature and effect of the power, not whether the donor would hypothetically have been able to perform all of the acts authorised by the power. On the facts, both donors had understood the nature and effect of the power, even though they were incapable of managing and administering their property and affairs. Accordingly, both powers were valid and should be registered under the 1985 Act.

At the end of his judgment, the judge considered the degree of understanding involved in understanding the nature and effect of the EPA. He said:

> Plainly, one cannot expect that the donor should have been able to pass an examination on the provisions of the 1985 Act. At the other extreme, I do not think that it would be sufficient if he realised only that it gave the attorney power to look after his property ... I accept the [following summary submitted by counsel] as a statement of the matters which should ordinarily be explained to the donor ... and which the evidence should show he has understood:[61]
>
> (1) first, if such be the terms of the power, that the attorney will be able to assume complete authority over the donor's affairs;
> (2) second, if such be the terms of the power, that the attorney will in general be able to do anything with the donor's property which the donor could have done;

[60] *Re K, Re F* [1988] Ch 310, [1988] 1 All ER 358, [1988] 2 WLR 781.
[61] Ibid., p. 363.

(3) third, that the authority will continue if the donor should be or become mentally incapable; and

(4) fourth, that if he should be or become mentally incapable, the power will be irrevocable without confirmation by the court.

E   Enduring Powers of Attorney: A Report to the Lord Chancellor (1991)

After the Enduring Powers of Attorney Act had been in operation for five years, the Faculty of Law at the University of Bristol conducted some research into EPAs, which was published by the Lord Chancellor's Department in June 1991.[62] Their findings and conclusions were as follows:

(1) **The registration of EPAs should be mandatory.** 'A widespread failure to register renders us somewhat sceptical about the effectiveness of the limited protective mechanism built into the EPA procedure.'[63] 'On the basis of our interviews, the proportion of EPAs created to EPAs registered would seem to be in the order of 20 to 1.'[64]

(2) **Registration should not be linked to supervening incapacity.** 'The timing of the registration process seems something of a lottery and we can hardly be surprised that registration is not effected in many cases where it ought to be.'[65]

(3) **Notification of an application to register the power should be to persons selected by the donor, rather than the donor's nearest relatives.**

(4) **The donor's capacity should be certified at the time of creating the power.** The researchers at the University of Bristol were concerned that the decision of Mr Justice Hoffmann in *Re K, Re F* (1987)[66] had set too low a threshold for the capacity required to create an EPA, and said, 'we believe there is a case for focusing more narrowly upon the question of the donor's capacity when creating the power; and we consider that the interpretation put on the law in *Re K* reinforces the

---

[62] S. Cretney, G. Davis, R. Kerridge and A. Borkowski, *Enduring Powers of Attorney: A Report to the Lord Chancellor* (London: Lord Chancellor's Department, 1991). Professor Stephen Cretney QC had been the Law Commissioner responsible for the 1983 report, *The Incapacitated Principal*, which had recommended the introduction of EPAs.

[63] Ibid., para. 2.19, p. 37.

[64] Ibid., para. 2.19, p. 34.

[65] Ibid., para. 2.38, p. 69.

[66] *Re K, Re F* [1988] Ch 310, [1988] 1 All ER 358, [1988] 2 WLR 781.

view that there is a case for requiring medical evidence of capacity and for requiring registration of the EPA in order for it to become legally effective. These suggestions are, we recognise, far-reaching and we recognise also that the legislation was based on a different philosophy.'[67]

(5) **The administrative, protective and adjudicative roles of the Court of Protection should be separated.**

This report was highly influential. These recommendations were all approved by the Law Commission, which published a report on *Mental Incapacity*, in 1995, containing in the appendix a draft Mental Incapacity Bill.[68] The Law Commission's report was initially shelved by the government but was ultimately enacted as the Mental Capacity Act 2005 (MCA) and came into force on 1 October 2007.

The MCA repealed the Enduring Powers of Attorney Act 1985, and replaced EPAs with Lasting Powers of Attorney (LPAs). It has not been possible for a donor to create an EPA since 1 October 2007, though EPAs which were executed before that date can still be registered, when the attorney has reason to believe that the donor is, or is becoming, mentally incapable.

F   Lasting Powers of Attorney

The characteristics of an LPA are as follows:

(1) **A prescribed form.** An LPA must be in the form prescribed by statutory instrument.[69] There are two separate prescribed forms: one for property and finances, and the other for health and welfare.

(2) **An LPA may contain the names of up to five people who are to be notified of an application to register an LPA.**[70] Unlike an EPA, where the attorney has to notify at least three of the donor's relatives, the donor can choose who (if anyone) should receive notification of an intention to register the power.

---

[67] Cretney et al., *Enduring Powers of Attorney*, n 62, para. 5, p. 76.

[68] Law Commission, *Mental Incapacity* (Law Com. No. 231, 1995).

[69] Mental Capacity Act 2005, Sch. 1, para. 1(1). The current prescribed forms are those set out in The Lasting Powers of Attorney, Enduring Powers of Attorney and Public Guardian (Amendment) Regulations 2015 (Statutory Instrument 2015 No. 899), which came into force on 1 July 2015.

[70] Ibid., Sch. 1, para. 2(1)(c).

(3) **An LPA must contain a certificate of capacity** at the time of the creation of the power. The certificate must be made by a person of a prescribed description, who should state that the donor understands the purpose of the LPA and the scope of the authority conferred under it.[71]

(4) **An LPA cannot be used until it has been registered by the OPG.**[72] Unlike an EPA, where registration has to take place when the attorney has reason to believe that the donor is, or is becoming, mentally incapable, an application for registration of an LPA can be made by the donor or the attorney before the onset of the donor's incapacity.

(5) **Objections to registration.** To a large extent, the objection process has been superseded by complaints to the OPG about the manner in which the attorney is exercising his powers.

(6) **Limited authority to make gifts.**[73] The position is the same as for EPAs.

(7) **Ongoing role of the Court of Protection.** The position is the same as for EPAs.

(8) **The donor can revoke an LPA at any time, provided that he or she has the capacity to do so.**[74] Unlike an EPA, there is no need for the Court of Protection to confirm the revocation.

G   Statistics

The Office of the Public Guardian operates on a financial year beginning on 1 April and ending on 31 March, and publishes its annual report and accounts for the preceding financial year in July. The following table shows the number of applications to the OPG to register LPAs and EPAs since 2009. It reveals a colossal increase in the number of applications to register LPAs and, as one would expect, a gradual decrease in the number of applications to register EPAs.

---

[71] Ibid., Sch. 1, para. 2(1)(e).

[72] Ibid., s. 9(2).

[73] Ibid., s. 12.

[74] Ibid., s. 13(2): 'P may, at any time when he has capacity to do so, revoke the power.'

Year	LPAs	EPAs
2009/10	107,000	18,000
2010/11	171,000	19,000
2011/12	200,000	18,000
2012/13	242,000	17,000
2013/14	295,000	16,000
2014/15	394,079	15,000
2015/16	533,229	13,792
2016/17	635,540	12,778
2017/18	759,976	11,019

As of 31 March 2018, there were 3,142,284 current instruments on the register.[75]

H   Registration Fees

The following fees are payable to the Public Guardian in respect of powers of attorney:

	Amount
Application to register an EPA	GBP82
Application to register an LPA	GBP82
Repeat application to register an LPA	GBP41

These fees came into force on 1 April 2017[76] and represent a fairly substantial reduction on the registration fees of GBP110 and GBP55 payable under the previous fee order of 2013. The fee reduction was made possible because of the high number of applications the OPG is processing and efficiencies which have driven down the cost of providing the service. The OPG has, in fact, admitted that it has been overcharging fees for the last four years and will be refunding customers who were overcharged. The amount owed is estimated at GBP89 million.[77]

---

[75] Office of the Public Guardian, *Annual Report & Accounts*, n 31, p. 7.

[76] The Public Guardian (Fees, etc.)(Amendment) Regulations 2017 (SI 2017 No. 503).

[77] M. Beckford, 'Hundreds of thousands of elderly and vulnerable people are to get a refund after being overcharged £89million in legal fees by government quango', *Daily Mail*, 23 July 2017, available from www.dailymail.co.uk/news/article-4721548/Elderly-refund-89m-legal-fees-rip-off.html.

I   *The Foreword to the Eighth Edition of* Cretney & Lush on Lasting and Enduring Powers of Attorney *(2017)*

In the foreword to the latest edition of *Cretney & Lush on Lasting and Enduring Powers of Attorney*, published in October 2017, I expressed my own personal view on powers of attorney. I wrote:

> I began preparing Enduring Powers of Attorney for clients on Monday 10 March 1986 – the day that the Enduring Powers of Attorney Act 1985 came into force – and must have drawn up hundreds of them while I was still a solicitor in private practice.
>
> In April 1996 I was appointed as Master of the Court of Protection. My job-title changed to Senior Judge when the Mental Capacity Act 2005 ('MCA') was implemented in October 2007, and I retired in July 2016. During those twenty years at the court I adjudicated on issues relating to over a thousand Enduring Powers of Attorney ('EPAs') and over five thousand Lasting Powers of Attorney ('LPAs').
>
> In addition to thirty years' experience of dealing with powers of attorney, both as a practitioner and a judge, I have also been one of the authors of this book, but I have never made an EPA or LPA myself, and I feel that an explanation is both due and overdue.
>
> In a nutshell, I have seen so much of the pathology associated with powers of attorney and the causes and effects when things go pear-shaped, that I find it difficult to recall cases where powers have operated smoothly and to the credit of everyone involved.
>
> During the financial year 2016/17, there were 648,318 applications to the Office of the Public Guardian ('OPG') to register LPAs and EPAs and the year ended with 2,478,758 current instruments on the register.
>
> LPAs are clearly popular. Their popularity is the result of a vigorous and effective campaign by the OPG and the Ministry of Justice to promote them, but I am sorry to say that this crusade has involved demonizing the appointment of deputies by the Court of Protection.
>
> For example, LP9,[78] one of the leaflets published by the OPG, asks the question, 'What could happen if I don't create an LPA?' and gives the following answer:
>
> If you lose mental capacity, through illness or injury, and haven't created an LPA:
>
> - you'll no longer be able to decide who makes decisions for you (you can only make your LPA while you still have mental capacity)
> - people you don't know could end up making crucial decisions for you instead – such as whether to accept medical treatment to keep you alive, or about what you eat and wear and where you live

---

[78] Office of the Public Guardian, *LP9 What Happens When I Can't Make Decisions for Myself?* (London: The Crown, 2017), available from https://assets.publishing.service.gov.uk.

- your family or friends might have to go to court to make decisions on your behalf – which can be a lot more expensive and time-consuming than making an LPA.

If you still have mental capacity, LPAs are a simple and legally robust way of giving someone you trust power to make decisions for you – temporarily or for a longer time.

In mentioning only the problems that can arise if you do not make an LPA, this leaflet is disingenuous because it fails to mention the risks if you do make one, or to inform you that, if something does go wrong, putting it right will be significantly more expensive and time-consuming than applying to the court for the appointment of a deputy in the first place.

One of the reasons why I have not made an LPA personally is that I have greater confidence in deputyship as a means of managing someone's property and financial affairs. I accept that deputyship is more costly, more onerous and more time-consuming than making an LPA, but there are other entries on the balance sheet, which, in my opinion, are factors of magnetic importance.

(1) The autonomy principle whereby 'you decide' who to appoint has consistently been overstated. Unless there is a cogent reason why someone should not be your deputy, it is likely that the Court of Protection will appoint as your deputy the person whom you would have appointed to be your attorney, if you had the capacity to do so. In deciding what is in your best interests, the court has a duty under the MCA to consider your past and present wishes and feelings, beliefs and values, and any other factors that you would be likely to consider. The true beneficiaries of the autonomy principle are the attorneys, who can basically do as they please.

(2) A deputy is required to account annually to the OPG and a deputyship usually starts with the preparation of an inventory of assets and liabilities, which acts as a focal point on which to base and audit all future accounts. Attorneys are also expected to keep accounts, receipts, invoices, bank statements and other financial documents, but generally speaking nobody ever calls for them or routinely scrutinises them, so most attorneys don't bother to maintain proper records. I was astonished how few of them were able to produce accounts when they were asked to do so by the court or the OPG. This is unacceptable.

(3) Deputyship is more structured and disciplined than attorneyship. The Public Guardian has a statutory duty to supervise deputies, but he is under no obligation to supervise attorneys. Supervision involves more than just checking accounts. It includes educating, supporting and visiting deputies and, if necessary, admonishing them. No comparable service exists for attorneys, who have the exactly the same need as deputies for instruction, back-up and the occasional reprimand.

(4) A deputy is generally required to give security to cover the possibility that he or she could act incompetently or dishonestly. A few years ago there was a notorious case, which illustrates this point perfectly. It was widely reported in the national press and also appeared in the formal law reports under the titles *Re GM*[79] and *Re Gladys Meek; Jones v. Parkin and Others.*[80] Gladys Meek was a 94-year-old widow who lived in Heanor, Derbyshire. Her late husband's niece and great niece were appointed as her deputies for property and affairs and they went on a spending spree with her money. They bought themselves a Mini Countryman, a Ford Fiesta, an Apple laptop computer, a Sony laptop, Rolex and Omega watches, handbags by Vivienne Westwood, Alexander McQueen and Mulberry, season tickets to watch Derby County Football Club, and expensive rings and perfume, and then started buying presents for other members of their families. The court was able to call in a security bond for £275,000, which just about covered the extent of their defalcation. This would not have been possible if they had been Gladys Meek's attorneys, because a security bond would neither have been required nor available.

(5) For all the talk of deputyship being costly and time-consuming, the average life-expectancy of a case in the Court of Protection is only 3½ years. The OPG's annual deputy supervision fee is currently £320, so in most cases the expenditure on supervision fees is likely to be around the £1,000 mark, to which should be added, of course, the application fee to the court and the annual premium payable in respect of the security bond. Hence, for a relatively modest outlay over a fairly short period of time, a person's property and financial affairs can be more adequately safeguarded than if he or she made an LPA.

(6) Finally, it has been suggested – and I fully understand why – that the main problem with deputyship is the time it takes to obtain an order appointing a deputy, which can cause difficulties if there is an urgent need to access someone's funds. Judges of the Court of Protection have power to make interim orders instantly in an emergency because the rules allow them to shorten or extend any time limits. The Public Guardian has no comparable powers to reduce the period for registering an LPA, so in theory, at least, obtaining an order from the Court of Protection should be quicker than applying to the OPG register an LPA.

There is another key reason why I have not made an LPA, and that's the devastating effect it can have on family relationships. The lack of transparency and accountability causes suspicions and concerns,

---

[79] [2013] COPLR 290.
[80] [2014] COPLR 535.

which tend to rise in a crescendo and eventually explode. I have seen it happen in a family related to mine by marriage.

In October 2016, Dr Gillian Dalley and her colleagues at Brunel University presented a report to the Dawes Trust on *Financial Abuse of People Lacking Mental Capacity*.[81] In chapter 4 of the report, they analysed 34 of my judgments, which had been published on the BAILII website in 2015, and came up with the following observations:

(1) 'Having to take responsibility for the property and financial affairs of a relative, often a parent, seems to have one or other of two negative aspects – that it poisons pre-existing relationships further, or that it precipitates bad feeling where none existed in the past.'[82]

(2) 'Misuse of a donor's funds did not, it appears, always result from a fraudulent impulse; sometimes it was grounded in naïve incompetence, bitter intra-family disputes, or the pressure of personal problems.'[83]

(3) 'It was striking to see that in a number of cases, attorneys, who had been appointed jointly, or jointly and severally, failed to observe their co-operative responsibilities. The tensions that are shown time and time again to exist within families do not necessarily sit comfortably with their duties to work jointly often imposed by the attorneyship. And those self-same arrangements may exacerbate pre-existing tensions that had not surfaced before.'[84]

(4) 'Reports of cases often included statements from the attorneys involved in tones that ranged through contrition, faux surprise, apparent amazement, brazen self-justification to argumentative contestation of the judge's view.'[85]

(5) 'The assumptions often embedded in public discourse about the "family" – goodwill, mutual support, blood being thicker than water – are often challenged by behaviour and attitudes revealed in court.'[86]

I know precisely whom I would appoint as my attorney, if I had any intention of making an LPA for property and financial affairs. She is a

---

[81] G. Dalley et al., *Financial Abuse of People Lacking Mental Capacity: A Report to the Dawes Trust* (Uxbridge: Brunel University London Institute of Environment, Health and Societies, 2017), available from www.mentalcapacitylawandpolicy.org.uk.

[82] Ibid., p. 85.

[83] Ibid., p. 73.

[84] Ibid., p. 83.

[85] Ibid., p. 73.

[86] Ibid., pp. 84–85.

family member and a practising solicitor and the most honest person I know, but I would rather she acted as my deputy than as my attorney. This would ensure that there is accountability on her part and that she gets all the support she needs from the OPG, but the main advantage is that there is a greater likelihood that her relationship with her siblings will remain cordial, rather than turn sour.

I have not made an LPA for health and welfare because, in most cases, I do not think they are necessary. The people, who, according to LPA9, 'don't know you' and 'could end up making crucial decisions for you, such as whether to accept medical treatment to keep you alive' are usually qualified healthcare professionals who will make these decisions in your best interests after consulting you and your nearest and dearest.

Mr Justice Jonathan Baker expressed this elegantly in *G* v. *E*.[87] When describing health and welfare decision-making, where the issues that need to be addressed are quite different from those relating to the management of someone's property and financial affairs, he said:[88]

> The Act and the Code are therefore constructed on the basis that the vast majority of decisions concerning incapacitated adults are taken informally and collaboratively by individuals or groups of people working together. It is emphatically not part of the scheme underpinning the Act that there should be one individual who as a matter of course is given special legal status to make decisions about incapacitated persons.

I apologise if this has been a rant rather than a heart-warming homily, but I need to voice these concerns, which I suppressed in the past because they were difficult to express while I was in office. I hope that in future, the media, the Ministry of Justice, the OPG, and professional advisors will be more judicious when advising people to make an LPA. There is a perfectly viable alternative, which is by no means as unattractive as they have hitherto portrayed it.

J   *A Gradual Alignment in the Accountability of Attorneys and Deputies*

It is possible that, in future, we may see a gradual alignment in the supervision of attorneys and deputies. The Republic of Ireland has

---

[87] [2010] COPLR Con Vol. 470.
[88] Ibid., para. [57].

recently enacted state-of-the-art capacity legislation, which is compliant with the United Nations Convention on the Rights of Persons with Disabilities (CRPD) and is called the Assisted Decision-Making (Capacity) Act 2015. It still uses the term 'Enduring Power of Attorney', and functions similar to those of the Public Guardian in England and Wales are performed by a public official known as the Director of the Decision Support Service. Section 76 of the Act states that:

(1) An attorney under an enduring power of attorney which confers authority in relation to property and affairs shall, within three months of the registration of the instrument appointing him or her as attorney, submit to the Director a schedule of the donor's assets and liabilities and a projected statement of the donor's income and expenditure.

(2) An attorney under an enduring power of attorney which confers authority in relation to property and affairs shall keep proper accounts and financial records in respect of the donor's income and expenditure and shall (a) submit such accounts and records as part of a report to the Director under this section, and (b) make available for inspection by the Director or by a special visitor, at any reasonable time, such accounts and records.

(3) An attorney shall, within 12 months after registration of the instrument appointing him or her as attorney, and thereafter at intervals of not more than 12 months, prepare and submit to the director a report in writing as to the performance of his or her functions as such attorney during the relevant period.

Article 12.4 of the CRPD requires States Parties to 'ensure that all measures that relate to the exercise of legal capacity provide for appropriate and effective safeguards to prevent abuse in accordance with international human rights law', and article 16.1 requires them to 'take all appropriate legislative and administrative measures to protect persons with disabilities from all forms of exploitation and abuse'.

There is an obvious attraction in having common standards of probity, integrity, accountability, transparency and redress, which apply to anyone who is managing someone else's money, regardless of who actually appointed them: whether it be the Secretary of State in social security appointeeship cases, the donor of a lasting or enduring power of attorney, the Court of Protection in deputyship cases or the trustees of a special needs trust. They are all performing basically the same tasks.

The disadvantage, as the Law Commission hinted in *The Incapacitated Principal* in 1983, is that, if the power of attorney scheme ceases to be simple, effective and inexpensive, people will be deterred from using it, and there is a danger that they will try to circumvent it in various ways, one of which may be to use ordinary powers of attorney and to continue to use them even after they have been automatically revoked by the donor's incapacity – the very mischief that the Enduring Powers of Attorney Act 1985 sought to remedy in the first place.

6

Supported Decision-Making and Enduring Powers

Innovations in Ireland

ÁINE HYNES

I Introduction

The current legislation governing the creation of enduring powers in Ireland is the Powers of Attorney Act 1996 ('the 1996 Act'). Prior to the commencement of the 1996 Act on 1 August 1996,[1] it was not possible for a donor to create an instrument providing for the appointment of an attorney to make decisions for them in the event of a subsequent loss of mental capacity. The only legal mechanism that had previously been available to families in attempting to deal with the affairs of a family member who had lost mental capacity was to make an application to the President of the Irish High Court to have the person made a Ward of Court under the Lunacy Regulations (Ireland) Act 1871 and Section 9 of the Courts (Supplemental Provisions) Act 1961. The 1871 legislation provides for a committee to be appointed to make decisions on behalf of that person with the permission of the President of the High Court.[2]

The Irish State signed up to the United Nations Convention on the Rights of Persons with Disabilities (CRPD) in March 2007. In Ireland, we have a dualist system in respect of international law, which means in practice that even when Ireland signs an international convention and agrees to its principles, the convention does not become legally applicable until a second step has been taken, a process of ratification, within our domestic legal system. This compares to monist systems, whereby once a convention is signed, it is also ratified by that country and becomes applicable in that jurisdiction. Generally, in Ireland, we have ratified

---

[1] Powers of Attorney Act 1996 (Commencement) Order 1996 (SI 1996 No. 195).

[2] It is also possible for applications in wardship to be made to the Circuit Court, although this jurisdiction is very rarely utilised. (Section 22(2) of the Courts (Supplemental Provisions) Act, 1961 as amended by Section 2(3) of the Courts Act, 1971.)

international conventions by including provisions in legislation relevant to the areas covered by the conventions.

Accordingly, as part of its legislative programme to ratify the CRPD, our legislative body, the Oireachtas, passed the Assisted Decision-Making (Capacity) Act 2015 (ADMA) and it was signed by our President on 30 December 2015.

The ADMA is an ambitious piece of legislation – the headnote to the ADMA[3] sets out, inter alia, that it is intended to reform the law relating to persons who require assistance in exercising their decision-making capacity, and it also extends to amending the law relating to enduring powers of attorney. It will serve to repeal our current Wards of Court system, which is regulated by the Lunacy Regulation (Ireland) Act 1871[4] and Section 9 of the Courts (Supplemental Provisions) Act 1961.

Part 7 of the ADMA provides for new arrangements for those who wish to make an enduring power of attorney and sets out legislative provisions for supported decision-making. However, the ADMA will be implemented incrementally by way of a series of commencement orders. There are concerns as to when it will finally be fully implemented, which concerns are set out more fully in Section IV of this chapter.

---

[3] 'An Act to provide for the reform of the law relating to persons who require or may require assistance in exercising their decision-making capacity, whether immediately or IN THE FUTURE, HAVING REGARD, *INTER ALIA*, TO THE PROTECTIONS AFFORDED BY THE CONVENTION FOR THE PROTECTION OF HUMAN RIGHTS AND FUNDA-MENTAL FREEDOMS DONE AT ROME ON THE 4TH DAY OF NOVEMBER 1950 AS IT APPLIES IN THE STATE; to provide for the appointment by such persons of other persons to assist them in decision-making or to make decisions jointly with such persons; to provide for the making of applications to the Circuit Court or High Court in respect of such persons, including seeking the appointment by the Circuit Court of decision-making representatives for such persons; TO PROVIDE FOR THE MAKING OF ADVANCE HEALTHCARE DIRECTIVES BY PERSONS OF THEIR WILL AND PREFERENCES CONCERNING MEDICAL TREATMENT DECISIONS SHOULD SUCH A PERSON SUBSEQUENTLY LACK CAPACITY; TO PROVIDE FOR THE APPOINTMENT IN ADVANCE HEALTHCARE DIRECTIVES OF DESIGNATED HEALTHCARE REPRE-SENTATIVES WITH THE POWER TO, *inter alia*, ENSURE THAT THE ADVANCE HEALTHCARE DIRECTIVES CONCERNED ARE COMPLIED WITH; to provide for the appointment and functions of the Director of the Decision Support Service in respect of persons who require or may shortly require assistance in exercising their decision-making capacity; to provide for the amendment of the law relating to enduring powers of attorney; to provide for the ratification by the State of the Convention on the International Protection of Adults; and to provide for related matters.'

[4] See Assisted Decision-Making (Capacity) Act 2015, s. 7(2):

> 'Subject to the provisions of Part 6, the Lunacy Regulation (Ireland) Act 1871 is repealed.'

While it may be some considerable time before the ADMA is fully implemented, and law and policy are appropriately aligned with the CRPD, as a common-law country, we can take some comfort that our evolving case law is increasingly reflective of many of the principles of the CRPD and, in particular, article 12.[5] Our courts have long since recognised the principle of presumption of capacity[6] and have approved the functional approach to assessing capacity,[7] and our courts apply the subjective test if the person cannot express their wishes.[8] The current President of the High Court, His Honour Mr Justice Peter Kelly, in whom wardship jurisdiction and jurisdiction for enduring powers is vested, now holds the majority of applications in respect of wardship in open court (with appropriate reporting restrictions as to the identity of the person). All wards and persons whose capacity is being examined are invited to attend court at any time and put their views to him, and if they do not attend in person, their views are considered and taken into account by way of appropriate representation.

Mr Justice Peter Kelly has repeatedly indicated in open court that all wards have the right to equal access to the law and cannot be

---

[5] Article 12 – Equal recognition before the law provides as follows:

1. States Parties reaffirm that persons with disabilities have the right to recognition everywhere as persons before the law.
2. States Parties shall recognize that persons with disabilities enjoy legal capacity on an equal basis with others in all aspects of life.
3. States Parties shall take appropriate measures to provide access by persons with disabilities to the support they may require in exercising their legal capacity.
4. States Parties shall ensure that all measures that relate to the exercise of legal capacity provide for appropriate and effective safeguards to prevent abuse in accordance with international human rights law. Such safeguards shall ensure that measures relating to the exercise of legal capacity respect the rights, will and preferences of the person, are free of conflict of interest and undue influence, are proportional and tailored to the person's circumstances, apply for the shortest time possible and are subject to regular review by a competent, independent and impartial authority or judicial body. The safeguards shall be proportional to the degree to which such measures affect the person's rights and interests.
5. Subject to the provisions of this article, States Parties shall take all appropriate and effective measures to ensure the equal right of persons with disabilities to own or inherit property, to control their own financial affairs and to have equal access to bank loans, mortgages and other forms of financial credit, and shall ensure that persons with disabilities are not arbitrarily deprived of their property.

[6] See decision of the Supreme Court *In re Ward of Court (withholding medical treatment) No. 2* [1996] 2 IR 79.

[7] See *Fitzpatrick v. F.K.* [2008] IEHC 104 (Ms Justice Laffoy).

[8] See *Health Service Executive v. J.M. A Ward of Court & Ors* [2017] IEHC 399 (His Honour, Mr Justice Peter Kelly, President of the High Court).

discriminated against on the basis of disability. Previously, wardship was considered to deprive a person of their legal capacity in all aspects of their lives; now, substituted decision-making is more commonly utilised on a matter-specific basis and as a last resort, where the life or health of the person who has lost mental capacity may be at risk. The capacity of the person concerned, along with any restrictive measures, is kept under regular review. In addition, it is more commonly used as a temporary measure, and wards are now regularly discharged from wardship if they recover mental capacity. A ward can apply at any time for discharge and the High Court will facilitate a hearing within days of such application.

Jurisdiction under the current enduring powers legislation is also vested in the President of the High Court, and similar principles are applied in any contentious matters involving an enduring power of attorney.

II   Current Enduring Powers System

The 1989 Law Reform Commission Paper on enduring powers of attorney[9] had highlighted the necessity for the provision of a comprehensive legislative system to introduce enduring powers of attorney to address the increase in life expectancy and the higher incidences of cognitive impairment associated with this increase. As previously noted, the 1996 Act was an important innovation in Ireland as, prior to its introduction, any power of attorney automatically terminated on the loss of capacity of the donor. Previously, the only legal recourse available to deal with decisions in respect of a person who lost mental capacity, or to deal with their assets, was to apply under the Lunacy Regulations (Ireland) Act 1871 ('the 1871 Act').

The 1996 Act sets out that its purpose is to 'provide for powers of attorney to operate when the donor of the power is or is becoming mentally incapable and to amend in other respects the law relating to powers of attorney generally'. There are a number of relevant statutory instruments associated with this primary legislation.[10]

---

[9] The Law Reform Commission, *Report on Land Law and Conveyancing Law: (2) Enduring Powers of Attorney* (Report No. 31, 1989).

[10] Powers of Attorney Act 1996 (Commencement) Order 1996 (SI 1996 No. 195),

   Enduring Powers of Attorney Regulations 1996 (SI 1996 No. 196),

   Enduring Powers of Attorney Regulations (Personal Care Decision) Regulations 1996 (SI 1996 No. 287),

   Rules of the Superior Courts (No. 1) (Powers of Attorney Act 1996) 2000 (SI 2000 No. 66).

Section 5(1) of the 1996 Act deals with the creation of an enduring power of attorney (EPA) and provides that:

> A power of attorney is an enduring power within the meaning of this Act if the instrument creating the power contains a statement by the donor to the effect that the donor intends the power to be effective during any subsequent mental incapacity of the donor and complies with the provisions of this section and regulations made thereunder.

A   Safeguards

The 1996 Act introduced formalities on the creation of an EPA to provide safeguards for the donor and introduced specific statutory provisions for recourse to the High Court in the event of a difficulty in the operation of the EPA when registered. The President of the High Court has jurisdiction to hear all applications pursuant to the 1996 Act.[11]

The formalities on the creation of an EPA include formalities on the prescribed form of the EPA, and these are set out in Enduring Powers of Attorney Regulations 1996.[12] The form includes information to the donor and the attorneys as to the effect of creating or accepting the power. Furthermore, statements are required from a solicitor and a medical practitioner which must be included on the statutory form. A solicitor must confirm 'that, after interviewing the donor and making any necessary enquiries, the solicitor ... (I) is satisfied that the donor understood the effect of creating the power, and (II) has no reason to believe that the document is being executed by the donor as a result of fraud or undue pressure'.[13] The registered medical practitioner must confirm 'that in his or her opinion at the time the document was executed the donor had the mental capacity, with the assistance of such explanations as may have been given to the donor, to understand the effect of creating the power'.[14] These statements reflect the necessity for the solicitor and the registered medical practitioner to perform rudimentary capacity assessments of the donor within a time frame proximate to the creation of the power.

Finally, the statutory form for creating an EPA requires the donor to identify two persons to be notified of the creation of the EPA. Those notice parties are notified in the event that it is intended to register the

---

[11] Rules of the Superior Courts (No. 1) (Powers of Attorney Act 1996) 2000 (SI 2000 No. 66), rule 1.

[12] Enduring Powers of Attorney Regulations 1996 (SI 1996 No. 196).

[13] Powers of Attorney Act 1996, s. 5(d)(ii).

[14] Ibid., s. 5(d)(iii).

EPA (thus making it operative) on the subsequent loss of the donor's mental capacity and may assist the donor in resisting the registration of the EPA if he or she objects to its registration.

B Definition of Mental Incapacity

The 1996 defines mental incapacity in relation to an individual as meaning 'incapacity by reason of a mental condition to manage and administer his or her own property and affairs and cognate expressions shall be construed accordingly'.[15]

C Scope of Authority

The 1996 Act provides that '[a]n enduring power may confer general authority (as defined in subsection (2)) on the attorney to act on the donor's behalf in relation to all or a specified part of the property and affairs of the donor *or* [emphasis added] may confer on the attorney authority to do specified things on the donor's behalf and the authority may, in either case, be conferred subject to conditions and restrictions'.[16] If a general authority is provided without restrictions, then the attorney may do anything which the donor can lawfully do by attorney: 'Where an instrument is expressed to confer general authority on the attorney, it operates to confer, subject to the restriction imposed by subsection (5)[17] in relation to gifts and to any conditions or restrictions contained in the

---

[15] Ibid., s. 4.
[16] Ibid., s. 6(1).
[17] Ibid., s. 6(5) provides that:

'Without prejudice to subsection (4) but subject to any conditions or restrictions contained in the instrument, an attorney under an enduring power, whether general or limited, may, if specific provision to that effect is made in the instrument, dispose of the property of the donor by way of gift to the following extent but no further, that is to say, by making –

(a) gifts of a seasonal nature or at a time, or on an anniversary, of a birth or marriage, to persons (including the attorney) who are related to or connected with the donor, and

(b) gifts to any charity to which the donor made or might be expected to make gifts,

provided that the value of each such gift is not unreasonable having regard to all the circumstances and in particular the extent of the donor's assets.'

instrument, authority to do on behalf of the donor anything which the donor can lawfully do by attorney.'[18]

Crucially, the 1996 Act does not provide authority to attorneys to make medical decisions for donors, and Ireland does not have specific legislation governing advance healthcare directions. This lack of legislative provision regarding decisions for medical care in the event of a loss of mental capacity often necessitates applications to the High Court in wardship, even where the person concerned may have completed an EPA. Many such applications are made when authority is required for medical procedures or to deal with end-of-life care in respect of a person who has lost mental capacity. It is important to note that the 1871 Act was not repealed to any extent by the 1996 Act.

D   Substituted or Supported Decision-Making

The 1996 Act provides for substituted decision-making in relation to the donor's property and affairs, without having any particular regard to the inclusion of the donor in the decision-making process. This can be contrasted with the position in relation to personal care decisions. Section 6 of the 1996 Act provides authority may be given to an attorney to make specified care decisions on the donor's behalf.[19] Any personal care decision made on behalf of a donor must be made in the donor's best interests. In deciding what is in a donor's best interests the attorney must have regard to the following:

(a) so far as ascertainable, the past and present wishes and feelings of the donor and the factors which the donor would consider if he or she were able to do so;

(b) the need to permit and encourage the donor to participate, or to improve the donor's ability to participate, as fully as possible in any decision affecting the donor;

(c) so far as it is practicable and appropriate to consult any of the persons mentioned in the proceeding items, their views as to the

---

[18] Ibid., s. 6(2).

[19] Ibid., s. 2: 'personal care decision', in relation to a donor of an enduring power, means a decision on any one or more of the following matters: (a) where the donor should live, (b) with whom the donor should live; (c) whom the donor should see and not see; (d) what training or rehabilitation the donor should get; (e) the donor's diet and dress; (f) inspection of the donor's personal papers; (g) housing, social welfare and other benefits for the donor.

donor's wishes and feelings and as to what would be in the donor's best interests:

(d) any person named by the donor as someone to be consulted on those matters;

(e) anyone (whether the donor's spouse, a relative, friend or other person) engaged in caring for the donor or interested in the donor's welfare;

(f) whether the purpose for which any decision is required can be as effectively achieved in a manner less restrictive of the donor's freedom of action.[20]

Accordingly, the 1996 Act recognises that where the donor has become mentally incapable, within the meaning of the 1996 Act, the donor should nonetheless be involved in the decision-making process regarding any personal care decisions and encouraged and supported to participate in these decisions. In applying the criteria that the wishes of the donor, both past and present, be ascertained, the 1996 Act applies a subjective test to substituted decision-making for the donor, where it may not be possible to ascertain the donor's wishes or feelings.

E   Procedures for Implementing an EPA

Registration of an EPA in Ireland is made to the Registrar of the Wards of Court,[21] and the procedures and proofs required for registration are set out in section 9 of the 1996 Act. These include the requirement to lodge with the Registrar a medical certificate that the donor is or is becoming incapable of managing their property or affairs.[22] The EPA can only come into force when it has been registered. However, once an

---

[20] Ibid., s. 6 (7)(b).

[21] Ibid., para. 2(2) of Part 1 of Sch. 1.

[22] Ibid., s. 9:

> '(1) If the attorney under an enduring power has reason to believe that the donor is or is becoming mentally incapable, the attorney shall, as soon as practicable, make an application to the court for the registration of the instrument creating the power.
>
> (2) Before making the application the attorney shall comply with the provisions as to notice set out in the First Schedule.
>
> (3) The attorney may, before making the application, refer to the court for its determination any question as to the validity of the power.
>
> (4) A certificate to the effect that the donor is, or is becoming, incapable by reason of a mental condition of managing and administering his or her own property and affairs and purporting to be signed by a registered medical practitioner may be accepted as evidence of the matters contained therein.'

application to register the EPA has been made to the Registrar of the Wards of Court, the attorney may take action under the EPA's powers to maintain the donor and prevent loss to the donor's estate. The attorney may also make any personal care decisions (as are permitted under the EPA) that cannot reasonably be deferred until the application for registration has been determined.[23] In addition, applications can be made to the Court to exercise any power under the EPA prior to its registration, provided the Court is satisfied that the donor may be, or may be becoming, mentally incapable. [24]

Notice of the intention to register the EPA is given to the donor by way of personal service and also to the notice parties five weeks prior to the application to the Registrar of Wards of Court.[25] During this time, the donor or the notice parties are given the opportunity to object to the Registration of the EPA. Objections can be made on specified grounds as set out in section 10(3) of the 1996 Act and include grounds such as the donor is not becoming mentally incapable, or the attorney is not suitable to act.[26] It is notable that the court has no inherent jurisdiction to make a conditional registration or vary the effect of an instrument.[27] Therefore,

---

[23] Ibid., s. 7(2).

[24] Ibid., s. 8.

[25] Ibid., s. 10:

> '(1) On an application for registration being made in compliance with section 9 the Registrar of Wards of Court shall, unless subsection (2) applies, register the instrument to which the application relates
> (2) If, in the case of an application for registration –
> a valid notice of objection to the registration pursuant to subsection (3) from a person to whom an attorney has given notice pursuant to paragraph 2(1) of the First Schedule is received by the court before the expiry of the period of five weeks beginning with the date on which that notice was given ... the court shall neither register the instrument nor refuse the application until it has made or caused to be made such enquiries (if any) as it thinks appropriate in the circumstances of the case.

[26] Ibid., s. 10 (3): 'For the purposes of this Act a notice of objection to the registration of an instrument is valid if the objection is made on one or more of the following grounds, namely:

(a) that the power purported to have been created by the instrument was not valid;
(b) that the power created by the instrument is no longer a valid and subsisting power;
(c) that the donor is not or is not becoming mentally incapable;
(d) that, having regard to all the circumstances, the attorney is unsuitable to be the donor's attorney;
(e) that fraud or undue pressure was used to induce the donor to create the power.'

[27] See ibid., s. 12(2) for limits to the Court's functions and SCR – *Power of Attorney* [2015] IEHC 308 (Ms Justice Baker).

if an EPA fails, the only option available to manage the person's affairs in the event of mental incapacity is to apply in wardship.

The High Court also has a supervisory role in respect of operation of the EPA once registered. Section 12(2) gives the High Court powers to require production of records and to require the attorneys to provide certain information.[28] However, aside from applications to the High Court where a concern arises, EPAs in Ireland are largely unregulated. There is no requirement for the attorneys to file the donor's financial records or accounts with a central authority such as the Wards of Court Office, and there is no system for scrutiny of the management of the donor's affairs. Some of the new legislative oversight and reporting provisions in the ADMA are designed to meet these concerns.

There have been very few reported cases on the 1996 Act. The decision of Ms Justice Baker in the 2015 case of *SCR – Power of Attorney*[29] is one of the more significant recent cases on the legislation. It confirmed the principles to be applied with regard to the test for capacity on the creation of an EPA and also helpfully sets out best practice for solicitors and medical practitioners with regard to the appropriate completion and formalities of the EPA instrument.

---

[28] Ibid., s. 12(2):

'The court may –

(a) determine any question as to the meaning or effect of the instrument;
(b) give directions with respect to –
  (i) the management or disposal by the attorney of the property and affairs of the donor;
  (ii) the rendering of accounts by the attorney and the production of the records kept by the attorney for that purpose;
  (iii) the remuneration or expenses of the attorney, whether or not in default of or in accordance with any provision made by the instrument, including directions for the repayment of excessive, or the payment of additional, remuneration;
  (iv) a personal care decision made or to be made by the attorney;
(c) require the attorney to furnish information or produce documents or things in his or her possession as attorney;
(d) give any consent or authorisation to act which the attorney would have to obtain from a mentally capable donor;
(e) authorise the attorney to act for the attorney's own benefit or that of other persons than the donor otherwise than in accordance with section 6(4) and (5) (but subject to any conditions or restrictions contained in the instrument);
(f) where appropriate, relieve the attorney wholly or partly from any liability incurred or which may have been incurred on account of a breach of duty as attorney.'

[29] *SCR – Power of Attorney*, n 26.

The case concerned a contested application pursuant to section 10 of the Powers of Attorney Act 1996 to register an EPA and concerned the question as to whether the donor, Mr SCR, had the capacity to execute the instrument creating the power made by him on 1 November 2013.

SCR executed an instrument creating an EPA in the statutory form on 1 November 2013 in the presence of his solicitor Anthony F O'Gorman in a nursing home. He appointed his son ER to act as attorney for the purposes of the 1996 Act, and the instrument gave ER general authority to act on his behalf. Notice of the execution of the power was given to his two other children, DR and FR.

Prior to executing the instrument, the donor was diagnosed with suffering from senile dementia – medical staff had noted on 30 August 2013 that SCR was suffering from 'senile dementia + + +'. When his son ER applied to have the EPA registered in early 2014, SCR's other children DR and FR objected to the registration on the grounds that the donor was, at the time of the execution of the instrument, suffering from a cognitive incapacity as a result of a dementia or Alzheimer's condition and that 'his condition was such that he did not understand the nature and import of the document executed by him'.[30]

F   Functional Assessment of Capacity

The Court held that the appropriate date of assessing whether Mr R had the capacity to execute the EPA was the date of execution of the EPA, namely 1 November 2013, and held that the approach should be that as outlined in the case of *Fitzpatrick* v. *F.K.*[31]

The Court accepted submissions made that the test for capacity must be on a functional basis and stated:

> that capacity must be tested having regard to the function being under-taken, and at the time of the execution of the instrument. This is consistent with the test of capacity explained in *Fitzpatrick* v. *F.K.* Thus, the court will ask a broad range of questions in order to assess the capacity of a donor to execute an instrument creating an EPA. There can be circumstances where a person is at the time of the execution of an instrument incapable of managing his or her property and affairs if they are very complex, but capable of understanding the need or desirability to give authority to another person to so manage those affairs, and to choose that

[30]   Ibid.
[31]   *Fitzpatrick* v. *F.K.*, n 6.

person. This is not to say that the creation of an EPA is a simple task, as some complexity is undoubtedly found in the range of the powers and duties imposed on an attorney after a power is registered, but I consider that there are probably many examples where a person understands and appreciates that he or she is suffering from a progressive dementia type condition likely to lead to circumstances where the management of financial affairs is beyond his or her capacity, and may even have come to a position where he or she is unable to actually manage or direct complex financial affairs, but is still in a position to understand and give instructions for the appointment of another person to act on his or her behalf. The cognitive capacity has to be at a level sufficient to understand the effect of giving decision-making authority to another.[32]

The court refused to register the EPA, however, on the grounds that it had not been shown that SCR understood the nature and effect of what he was doing when he executed the EPA.

The court pointed to the issue of medical certification by Dr Doyle, who executed the statutory part of the instrument creating the power on 6 November 2013, specifying that SCR had capacity to execute the instrument. When he did so, he had not personally examined SCR, and in certifying that SCR was capable of executing the document, he did so on reliance of the information provided to him by the solicitor that the donor was lucid when he executed the instrument in the presence of the solicitor on 1 November 2013. The last examination of SCR by Dr Doyle was on 8 October 2013, when he noted that Mr R displayed signs of confusion and agitation.

The Court noted that she accepted 'that a person with senile dementia has a progressive condition, and that within the progression there may be periods of lucidity', but that 'the legislation did not envisage circumstances where a doctor would rely on the opinion of a solicitor with regard to capacity, especially so in the case of a person who was suffering from a progressive dementia condition'. She added that 'the responsibility for the certification cannot depend on the opinion on another non-medical person'.

The court concluded her reasoning as follows:

> I am satisfied on the evidence that Mr R did not have cognitive capacity at the date he executed the instrument creating the EPA. I come to this conclusion on the whole of the evidence before me. The court in the exercise of its statutory power may refuse the application to register on

---

[32] *SCR – Power of Attorney*, n 26.

any of the grounds identified in s. 10(3) one ground being that the power purported to have been created is not valid. While I accept that there is a presumption at law that a person has legal capacity, that presumption is rebuttable. I am satisfied that Mr R was suffering from moderate dementia which impaired his cognitive functions. I am not satisfied that the evidence as a whole shows that he was sufficiently lucid at the time he executed the instrument to understand its nature as a general power, nor am I satisfied that the scope and purpose of the power was fully explained to him or understood by him. In the circumstances the objection to registration is sustained and in the exercise of my statutory power I refuse to order that it be registered.

It is noteworthy in this case that neither the doctor nor the solicitor who certified capacity on the instrument executed by SCR adduced contemporaneous notes at the hearing. Ms Justice Baker stated that she regarded this as less than satisfactory and she expected at the 'very minimum a solicitor and a doctor who have a statutory obligation to certify capacity for the purposes of the creation of an EPA should record their findings and make these available if necessary to a court charged with determining the question of mental capacity in any further dispute'.

III   Assisted Decision-Making (Capacity) Act 2015 and Reform of Enduring Powers

The ADMA provides for the reform of the law relating to persons who require assistance in exercising their decision-making capacity. It will repeal the 1871 Act and introduces reforms to the 1996 Act. It is designed to align our domestic legislation with the CRPD and to give statutory expression to the principles of the CRPD, in order to enhance autonomy and self-determination of persons with disabilities. It will provide a legislative framework for supported decision-making in place of substituted decision-making and give statutory expression to a functional approach to capacity. The ADMA will bring about major changes in relation to Wards of Court as the current Wards of Court system will be abolished in respect of adults. Every adult who is a Ward under the existing regime will have their wardship reviewed under section 54 of the ADMA and will be discharged from wardship, once the operative sections of the legislation are in force.

The statutory provisions governing the creation of EPAs after the commencement of the ADMA are contained in Part 7 of the ADMA. An EPA made after the commencement date must be made in accordance with Part 7 of the ADMA and regulations made pursuant to section

79 of the ADMA. EPAs made prior to the commencement date under the 1996 Act will be subject to the provisions of the 1996 Act, but will also be subject to section 76 of the ADMA, which is a section allowing for complaints to be made to the new Director of Decision Support Services.

A   Guiding Principles

Section 8 of the ADMA sets out Guiding Principles on interventions with relevant persons[33] and applies to all parts of the ADMA, including Part 7 dealing with Enduring Powers of Attorney. In the first instance, the capacity of the relevant person is presumed. Section 8(2) of ADMA provides that it 'shall be presumed that a relevant person . . . has capacity in respect of the matter concerned unless the contrary is shown'.

A relevant person shall not be considered as unable to make a decision in respect of the matter concerned unless all practicable steps have been taken, without success, to help him or her to do so. Section 8(4) provides that a relevant person shall not be considered as unable to make a decision in respect of the matter concerned merely by reason of making, having made or being likely to make an unwise decision. This subsection ensures that an 'outcome approach' is not applied to an assessment of the capacity of the relevant person.

The guiding principles provide that an intervention in respect of a relevant person shall

(a) be made in a manner that minimises
   (i) the restriction of the relevant person's rights, and
   (ii) the restriction of the relevant person's freedom of action,
(b) have due regard to the need to respect the right of the relevant person to dignity, bodily integrity, privacy, autonomy and control over his or her financial affairs and property,
(c) be proportionate to the significance and urgency of the matter the subject of the intervention, and

---

[33] See Assisted Decision-Making (Capacity) Act 2015, s. 2(1):

'"relevant person" means –
(a) a person whose capacity is in question or may shortly be in question in respect of one or more than one matter,
(b) a person who lacks capacity in respect of one or more than one matter, or
(c) a person who falls within paragraphs (a) and (b) at the same time but in respect of different matters, as the case requires'

(d) be as limited in duration in so far as is practicable after taking into account the particular circumstances of the matter the subject of the intervention.[34]

The preceding guiding principles regarding the participation of the relevant person in the decision-making process, while more expansive, are not dissimilar to those set out in section 6(7)(b) of the 1996 Act. The guiding principles then outline the approach that should be taken in assisting a person in making decisions, and provide that the intervener,[35] in making an intervention in respect of a relevant person, shall

(a) permit, encourage and facilitate, in so far as is practicable, the relevant person to participate, or to improve his or her ability to participate, as fully as possible, in the intervention,
(b) give effect, in so far as is practicable, to the past and present will and preferences of the relevant person, in so far as that will and those preferences are reasonably ascertainable,
(c) take into account –
    (i) the beliefs and values of the relevant person (in particular those expressed in writing), in so far as those beliefs and values are reasonably ascertainable, and
    (ii) any other factors which the relevant person would be likely to consider if he or she were able to do so, in so far as those other factors are reasonably ascertainable,
(d) unless the intervener reasonably considers that it is not appropriate or practicable to do so, consider the views of –

---

[34] Ibid., s. 8(6).
[35] Ibid., s. 2(1):

> "'intervener", in relation to an intervention in respect of a relevant person, means the person referred to in paragraph (a), (b), (c), (d) or (e) of the definition of "intervention" making the intervention;
> "intervention", in relation to a relevant person, means an action taken under this Act, orders made under this Act or directions given under this Act in respect of the relevant person by
>
> (a) the court or High Court,
> (b) a decision-making assistant, co-decision-maker, decision-making representative, attorney or designated healthcare representative,
> (c) the Director,
> (d) a special visitor or general visitor, or
> (e) a healthcare professional;'

(i) any person named by the relevant person as a person to be consulted on the matter concerned or any similar matter, and

(ii) any decision-making assistant, co-decision-maker, decision-making representative or attorney for the relevant person,

(e) act at all times in good faith and for the benefit of the relevant person, and

(f) consider all other circumstances of which he or she is aware and which it would be reasonable to regard as relevant.[36]

The intervener, in making an intervention in respect of a relevant person, may also consider the views of any person engaged in caring for the relevant person or any person who has a bona fide interest in the welfare of the relevant person or healthcare professionals.

B Functional Assessment of Capacity

The Law Reform Commission, in its 2005 *Consultation Paper on Vulnerable Adults and the Law: Capacity*, noted that the 'status approach to capacity is evident in the Wards of Court system and in respect of enduring powers of attorney under the Powers of Attorney Act 1996, both of which make a broad assessment of general legal capacity which amounts to making a status decision on capacity'.[37] The test under the 1871 Act is whether the person 'is or is not of unsound mind, and incapable of managing his person or property'.[38] The test under the 1996 Act is 'incapacity by reason of a mental condition to manage and administer his or her own property and affairs and cognate expressions shall be construed accordingly'.[39] This can be contrasted with the ADMA, which applies a functional approach in assessing capacity to make decisions.

The guiding principles of the ADMA provide that 'it shall be presumed that a relevant person ... has capacity in respect of the matter concerned unless the contrary is shown in accordance with the provisions of this Act'.[40] Section 3(1) ADMA provides that a person's capacity is to be construed on a functional basis and it states:

---

[36] Ibid., s. 8(7).
[37] The Law Reform Commission, *Consultation Paper on Vulnerable Adults and The Law: Capacity* (Consultation Paper No. 37, 2005).
[38] See Lunacy Regulation (Ireland) Act 1871, s. 15.
[39] Powers of Attorney Act 1996, s. 4.
[40] See Assisted Decision-Making (Capacity) Act 2015, s. 8(2).

Subject to subsections (2) to (6), for the purposes of this Act, a person's capacity shall be assessed on the basis of his or her ability to understand, at the time that a decision is to be made, the nature and consequences of the decision to be made by him or her in the context of the available choices at that time.

It is important to note that while the ADMA is not yet in force, it gives statutory expression to the common law tests for assessing capacity on a functional basis[41] and the right to legal capacity. While there have been considerable very recent advancements in the wardship court under the jurisdiction of the current President of the High Court, Mr Peter Kelly, as noted before; generally where a person was admitted to wardship, they lost their right to legal capacity in a considerable range of aspects of decision-making. The European Court of Human Rights has held that the complete deprivation of a person's legal capacity is a violation of article 8 (right to respect for private and family life) of the European Convention on Human Rights.[42]

Accordingly, in order to determine whether a person has capacity to make an EPA, a functional approach should be applied. Those persons assessing the capacity of the person to make the EPA should ascertain whether or not the donor understands the provisions of the EPA and be satisfied that the donor has the necessary decision-making ability to create the EPA. Guidance for this functional approach in the creation of an EPA is clearly outlined by Ms Justice Baker in the case of *SCR – Power of Attorney*. The donor must understand that he or she will effectively be passing full control of his or her property and assets to the attorney to make decisions, including selling the property and assets in the event that the donor lacks decision-making capacity to make such decisions for him or herself at a later date. If the authority extends to decisions regarding personal welfare, the donor must understand the specific healthcare matters and the extent of those powers.

The functional approach to capacity will also be applied in respect of determinations as to whether the donor has decision-making capacity to make a relevant decision. For example, where the scope of the authority permits the attorney to decide where the donor may live, the attorney should ascertain whether the donor has the relevant decision-making capacity to decide where he or she wishes to live and if so, the attorney should assist with implementation of those wishes. If the donor has that

---

[41] *Fitzpatrick v. F.K.*, n 6 and *SCR – Power of Attorney*, n 26.
[42] *Shtukaturov v. Russia* Application (Application No. 44009/05) [2008] ECHR 223.

capacity, then there would be no need to apply for registration of the EPA for that purpose.

C   Formalities on the Creation of an EPA

The ADMA has extended the formalities required on the creation of an EPA.

Under section 60 of the ADMA, the instrument creating the EPA must contain the following statements:

- A statement from the donor to confirm that he or she understands the implications of creating the EPA, that or she intends it to be effective at any subsequent time when he or she lacks capacity in relation to one or more relevant decisions which are the subject of the EPA and also that he or she is aware that he or she can vary or revoke the EPA at any time prior to its registration.
- A statement from the solicitor to confirm that after interviewing the donor and making any necessary enquiries he or she is satisfied that the donor understands the implication of creating the EPA, that he or she is satisfied that the donor is aware he or she can vary or revoke the EPA at any time prior to its registration and also that he or she had no reason to believe the EPA was being signed as a result of fraud or undue coercion.
- A statement from a registered medical practitioner to confirm that at the time the EPA was signed the donor had the capacity to understand the implications of creating the EPA.
- A statement from a healthcare professional that in his or her opinion the donor had the capacity to understand the implications of creating the EPA when he or she did so. A Healthcare Professional is defined in the ADMA as 'a member of any health or social care profession whether or not the profession is a designated profession within the meaning of section 3 of the Health and Social Care Professionals Act 2005'.

This final statement from a healthcare professional is an additional requirement to the 1996 Act.

The form must also include a statement by each attorney that he or she understands the implications of undertaking to be an attorney for the donor, has read and understood the information contained in the EPA, understands and undertakes to act in accordance with his or her functions as specified in the instrument creating the EPA, understands and undertakes to act in accordance with the guiding principles and under-stands the requirements in relation to registration of the EPA.[43]

Additional further personal information is required under the ADMA, including the date of birth and contact details of the donor and date of birth and contact details of the attorney.[44]

The execution requirements under section 60(4) of the ADMA differ from the execution requirements under the 1996 Act. The donor and the attorneys will need to sign the EPA in the presence of each other and in the presence of two witnesses who both must witness the signatures of the donor and attorney by signing his or her name. While these require-ments are somewhat similar to those required for a will under the Succession Act 1965,[45] in practice, these requirements are likely to cause considerable difficulties.

Attorneys will invariably be family members who may be abroad. It is good practice to have more than two attorneys, which would require at least six persons, (the donor, three attorneys and two witnesses) apart from the solicitor, to be present on the execution of the EPA. In these circumstances, it may prove impossible to execute an EPA and meet the formality requirements in a timely manner, where capacity may be fluctuating or deteriorating. This formality requirement can only serve to frustrate the intention of the legislature in the creation of an EPA, which is to provide a mechanism for persons to have some control in relation to advance planning and to express a choice in relation to the persons who will assist them in their affairs in the future.

Finally, it should be noted that attorneys can be appointed to make decisions jointly or severally – this is the same position as set out in the 1996 Act.[46]

Once the EPA is executed, the ADMA provides for an extended list of persons who must be given notice. As soon as practicable after the EPA is

---

[43] See Assisted Decision-Making (Capacity) Act 2015, s. 60(1)(e).
[44] Ibid., s. 60(2).
[45] See Succession Act, 1965, s. 78.
[46] See Powers of Attorney Act 1996, s. 14: 'An instrument which appoints more than one person to be an attorney may specify that the attorneys are appointed to act either jointly or jointly and severally. In default, the attorneys shall be deemed to have been appointed to act jointly.' See also Assisted Decision-Making (Capacity Act) 2015, s. 64(1): 'A donor may, in an enduring power of attorney, appoint more than one attorney and may specify that the attorneys shall act – (a) jointly, (b) jointly and severally, or (c) jointly in respect of some matters and jointly and severally in respect of other matters, and, in default of the power so specifying, the attorneys shall be deemed to have authority to act jointly.'

executed, the donor must give notice of the execution of the EPA to the following persons:

(a) the donor's spouse or civil partner,
(b) the cohabitant of the donor,
(c) any children of the donor who have attained the age of 18 years,
(d) any decision-making assistant for the donor,
(e) any co-decision maker for the donor,
(f) any decision-making representative for the donor,
(g) any designated healthcare representative for the donor,
(h) any other attorney for the donor under the Act of 1996 in respect of the donor,
(i) any other person or persons as may be specified by the donor in the instrument creating the enduring power of attorney as a person or persons to whom notice shall be given.[47]

D   Scope of Power

Under the provisions of section 59 of the ADMA a donor is a person who has attained the age of 18 years and has appointed another person who has also attained that age, the attorney, on whom he or she confers either or both of the following:

(a) general authority to act on the donor's behalf in relation to all or specified part of the donor's property and affairs; or
(b) authority to do specified things on the donor's behalf in relation to the donor's personal welfare or property affairs or both.

These powers can be restricted in respect of certain property and can apply to only certain assets of the donor – however, this may mean that a decision-making representative may need to be appointed by the court should it become necessary to take a decision for which authority is not given by the EPA.

The scope of the authority is similar to the 1996 Act with regard to the property and affairs of the donor, but is expanded in relation to personal welfare decisions. Personal welfare is defined as one or more of the following matters:

(a) accommodation, including whether or not the relevant person should live in a designated centre;

---

[47] Assisted Decision-Making (Capacity) Act 2015, s. 61(1).

(b) participation by the relevant person in employment, education or training;
(c) participation by the relevant person in social activities;
(d) decisions on any social services provided or to be provided to the relevant person;
(e) healthcare; and/or
(f) other matters relating to the relevant person's well-being.[48]

This can be contrasted with the 1996 Act definition of 'personal care decision', which included decisions on where the donor should live, with whom the donor should live, whom the donor should see and not see and the donor's diet and dress.[49]

Where an EPA confers authority in relation to personal welfare, section 62(1) of the ADMA permits restraint, including physical or medical restraint, of the donor in exceptional emergency circumstances, where the attorney reasonably believes that it is necessary to do the act in order to prevent an imminent risk of serious harm to the donor or to another person, and the act is a proportionate response to the likelihood of the harm and to the seriousness of such harm.

Personal welfare authority does not extend to a decision relating to refusal of life-sustaining treatment, in respect of which an application may have to be made to the High Court,[50] or a decision which is the subject of an advance healthcare directive. Part 8 of the ADMA provides separate provisions for the making of advance healthcare directives. Section 62(5) of the ADMA stipulates that an attorney will not be empowered to make any form of healthcare decision that is already the subject of an advance healthcare directive of the donor.

E   Eligibility of Attorneys

Section 65 of the ADMA sets out certain persons who are not eligible to be attorneys. These are defined as a person who:

(a) has been convicted of an offence in relation to the person or property of the donor,
(b) has been the subject of a safety or barring order application in relation to the donor,

---

[48] Ibid., s. 2(1).
[49] Powers of Attorney Act 1996, s. 4(1).
[50] Assisted Decision-Making (Capacity) Act 2015, s. 4(3).

(c) is an undischarged bankrupt or is currently in a debt settlement arrangement or personal insolvency arrangement or has been convicted or an offence involving fraud or dishonesty,

(d) is the subject of a disqualification order issued under the provisions of the Companies Act 2014, or

(e) is the owner of the registered provider of a designated centre or mental health facility where the intended donor resides.

Attorneys can also be disqualified from acting in certain circumstances, for example, where the attorney is a spouse, civil partner or cohabitee of the donor, the attorney will be disqualified in the event of the annulment or dissolution of the marriage or the civil partnership, or in the case of cohabitants, if he or she ceases cohabiting for a period of 12 months.[51]

F   Applications to Court

Applications in respect of EPAs will be heard by the Circuit Court, which is the primary court in respect of all applications under the ADMA. Prior to registration of the EPA, application can be made to the Circuit Court. Section 67 provides that, on application to it by any interested party, the court may, where it has reason to believe that the donor of an enduring power of attorney lacks capacity in relation to one or more relevant decisions, exercise any power which would become exercisable under section 77(3) on the registration of the instrument creating an enduring power of attorney and may do so whether or not the attorney concerned has made an application to the Director for registration of the instrument. Section 77(3), therefore, applies both prior to, and after registration of the EPA, and gives the court power to do the following:

(a) determine any question as to the meaning or effect of the power,

(b) give directions with respect to
(i) a relevant decision relating to the personal welfare of the donor made or about to be made by the attorney,
(ii) the management or disposal by the attorney of the property and affairs of the donor, and
(iii) the remuneration or expenses of the attorney, whether or not in default of or in accordance with any provision of the enduring

---

[51] See s. 68 of the Assisted Decision-Making (Capacity) Act 2015 for a full list of persons who may be disqualified.

power, including directions for the repayment of excessive, or the payment of additional, remuneration, and

(c) consent to a disclaimer by the attorney of the enduring power.

Similar to the provisions of the 1996 Act, notwithstanding the fact that the EPA may not comply with the legislative provisions, the Court may nonetheless admit the EPA for registration.

Section 77(1) provides authority for the Director to refer to the court for a determination on whether the instrument may be registered, and the court can register the instrument where it is desirable in the interests of justice to register it, notwithstanding defects in the creation of the power. Section 77 also enables any interested person to apply to court for a determination as to the meaning and effect of the power or to provide directions.

G   Registration of an EPA under the ADMA

There are expanded requirements under the ADMA, in comparison to the requirements under the 1996 Act, for the registration of an EPA, and these are set out in section 68 of the ADMA.

Where an attorney has reason to believe that the donor lacks capacity in relation to one or more relevant decisions which are the subject of the EPA, the attorney must make an application to the Director. The attorney must:

(a) obtain medical certificates from a registered medical practitioner and a healthcare professional that, in their opinion, the donor lacks capacity in relation to one or more relevant decisions, and
(b) arrange to complete the following notices
   (i) notice of intention to apply for registration addressed to the donor and served on the donor;
   (ii) notice of intention to apply for registration addressed to the notice parties being the spouse, civil partner, cohabitant, children over 18 years, other intervenors, if any, and any person specified by the donor; and
   (iii) notice of intention to apply for registration addressed to the Director of Support Services.

The attorneys then will arrange to swear an affidavit and file relevant documentation, including the original EPA, with the Director.

There is a five-week notice period within which the donor or other parties can object.[52] Where there is an objection, and the Director is of the view that the objection is well founded, they can notify the person who made the objection of his or her view and make an application to the Court for a determination on the matter and for a determination as to whether the enduring power should be registered.[53]

The Director, once he or she is satisfied that the EPA has been created in accordance with the legislation, that the attorneys are suitable and eligible for appointment, that proper notice has been given and that there is no objection, can proceed to register the EPA.[54]

H   Reporting Obligations of the Attorney

Section 75 of the ADMA introduces new reporting obligations and imposes obligations on attorneys to report to the Director of the Decision Support Services (DSS). This represents a significant innovation in the operation of EPAs under the ADMA.

Once the EPA is registered, the attorney is obliged to prepare a full inventory of the donor's assets and liabilities for submission to the Director of the DSS within three months of registration and provide a projected statement of the donor's income and expenditure.[55]

Additional reporting is required thereafter every 12 months after registration of the instrument.[56]

Section 75(2) requires the attorney to keep proper accounts and financial records and submit these reports to the Director as part of the reporting obligation and to make available for inspection by the Director or by a special visitor, at any reasonable time, such accounts and records. Regulations will provide for the form of the reports to be made and will include details of all costs, expenses and remuneration paid to and claimed by the attorney in the relevant period together with such other matters as are prescribed.[57]

Additionally, if the attorney has restrained the donor at any time during the relevant period, he or she must include in the report details

---

[52] See Assisted Decision-Making (Capacity) Act 2015, s. 71.
[53] Ibid., s. 71(3)(c)(ii).
[54] Ibid., s. 69.
[55] Ibid., s. 75(1.
[56] Ibid., s. 75(3).
[57] Ibid., s. 75(4).

of each such restraint, including the date and place where such restraint occurred.[58]

If an attorney does not submit a report or submits an incomplete report, the Director will notify him or her of this and give them a period of time to submit a report – if the attorney does not comply with the notification, the Director can make an application to court and the court may determine that an attorney who has not complied with this section would no longer act as attorney for the donor concerned.

I Complaints to the Director

Section 76 of the ADMA deals with new provisions which provide a complaints mechanism to the Director, in relation to attorneys, concerning any of the following matters:

(a) that an attorney has acted, is acting, or is proposing to act outside the scope of his or her functions as specified in the instrument creating the enduring power of attorney;
(b) that an attorney is not a suitable person;
(c) that fraud, coercion or undue pressure was used to induce a donor to appoint an attorney.

Section 76 applies also to EPAs created under the 1996 Act and is the only section of the legislation that applies to such EPAs. It stipulates that a person may make a complaint in writing to the Director in relation to attorneys concerning any of the following matters:

(a) that an attorney under the Act of 1996, is acting or is proposing to act outside the scope of the enduring power under the Act of 1996;
(b) that an attorney under the Act of 1996 is unable, for whatever reason, to perform his or her duties and obligations as construed in accordance with that Act; or
(c) that fraud, coercion or undue pressure was used to induce a donor under the Act of 1996 to appoint an attorney under the Act of 1996.[59]

The Director is then entitled to carry out an investigation of the matter, and where he or she is of the view that the complaint is well founded, the Director can then make an application to the court for a

---

[58] Ibid., s. 75(5).
[59] Ibid., s. 76(2).

determination in relation to a matter specified in the complaint.[60] The court has powers to determine that an attorney shall no longer act as such in relation to the donor concerned. Where the Director notifies a complainant that the complaint is not well founded, he or she may, within 21 days after issue of that notification, appeal this decision to the court.

J   Register of EPAs

Section 72(1) of the ADMA entitles the Director to establish and maintain a register of instruments creating an enduring power of attorney. The Register shall be in such form as the Director considers appropriate, and the Director shall make the Register available for inspection by a body or class of persons prescribed by regulations made under section 79 for this purpose and any person who satisfies the Director that he or she has a legitimate interest in inspecting the Register.

IV   Innovations and Conclusions

The primary innovations that the ADMA will bring to the operation of enduring powers in Ireland will be to provide a statutory basis for the functional approach to capacity and to provide specific statutory mechanisms designed to enhance the participation of the donor in any interventions that may happen before and after the registration of the EPA. The guiding principles of the ADMA reflect the requirements of article 12 of the CRPD to ensure that persons with disabilities can enjoy legal capacity on an equal basis with others in all aspects of life and that there are appropriate measures to provide access by persons with disabilities to the support they may require in exercising their legal capacity. The ADMA provides appropriate measures relating to the exercise of legal capacity to respect the rights, will and preferences of the person.

Section 75 of the ADMA, providing new reporting requirements, is very welcome. Currently, there are no specific reporting requirements, meaning that the operation of the EPA and actions of attorneys are largely unregulated. The Register of EPAs created under the ADMA will be maintained by the Director rather than the Office of the Wards of Court.

A significant innovation is that the ADMA allows for complaints in relation to an attorney to be made directly to the Director. The Director

---

[60] Ibid., s. 71(3)(c)(ii).

will initially investigate the complaints. It is significant that the referral will be made by the Director to the Circuit Court where he or she upholds the complaint. The court can then exercise its powers, making such directions as appropriate. This can be contrasted with the current position whereby families need to apply to the High Court if there is a difficulty relating to the exercise of the powers of the attorneys. There is also provision for the Director to apply to court under section 77 of the Act for a determination on a question affecting the EPA.

Finally, the ADMA widens significantly the scope of the powers of the attorneys in relation to healthcare and also gives statutory effect to the creation of Advance Healthcare Directives.

However, while the ADMA will bring about these innovations, it is an inescapable fact that at the time of writing, only a limited number of the provisions of the ADMA have been commenced. This is despite the fact that Ireland was the last European state to ratify the CRPD and in the face of considerable pressure on Government to fully implement the ADMA.

The former Minister for Justice and Equality, Frances Fitzgerald, had indicated in response to a Parliamentary question in Dáil Éireann (17 January 2017) that it was her intention that the new decision-making support options provided for in the ADMA 2015 would be substantially implemented during 2017. She advised that 'new administrative processes and support measures, including the setting up of the Decision Support Service within the mental health commission must be put in place before the substantive provisions of the ADMA 2015 come into force'.

To date, however, there have only been two commencement orders made since the ADMA 2015 was signed. These orders commenced some of the sections of the ADMA on 17 October 2016. Minister Fitzgerald, by SI 2016 No. 515 Assisted Decision-Making (Capacity) Act 2015 (Commencement Of Certain Provisions) Order 2016, appointed 17 October 2016 as the day for the coming into operation of the following parts of the Act:

- Part 1, other than sections 3, 4 and 7; and
- Part 9, other than sections 96 and 102 and chapter 3.

The sections of Part 1 that have become operative deal with interpretation and expenses and do not deal with the substantive elements of Part 1 of the ADMA with the guiding principles of the ADMA 2015 and the functional approach to capacity. Part 9 deals with the establishment of the new role of the Director of the DSS. The Mental Health Commission is statutorily charged with the appointment of the Director and Áine Flynn, Solicitor was appointed Director and commenced her role in October 2017.

The DSS will require considerable resources in order to manage the extremely wide range of functions of the Director, including promoting awareness of the ADMA; registering and monitoring complaints in respect of EPAs; establishing a register of advance healthcare directives; registering and monitoring co-decision-making agreements; conducting investigations; providing codes of practice to professionals and the healthcare sector on the operation of the ADMA and its principles; and establishing panels of general and medical visitors, decision-making representatives and court friends.

The second commencement order was signed by Minister for Health Mr Simon Harris. By SI 2016 No. 517 Assisted Decision-Making (Capacity) Act 2015 (Commencement of Certain Provisions) (No. 2) Order 2016, he appointed 17 October 2016 as the day for the coming into operation of the definition of 'Minister' in section 82 and the definitions of 'code of practice' and 'working group' in sections 91(1) and 91(2).

This order provides for the commencement of section 91(2), and relevant definitions, of the Assisted Decision-Making (Capacity) Act 2015 for the establishment, by the Minister for Health, of a multidisciplinary working group of suitable persons willing and able to make recommendations to the Director of the DSS in relation to codes of practice pertaining to the advance healthcare directive provisions of the Assisted Decision-Making (Capacity) Act 2015. This is a very limited provision.

A further Part 13 of the ADMA Act is being drafted to deal with Deprivation of Liberty Safeguards, and it is proposed that this will be inserted into the ADMA prior to its being commenced. The Department of Health issued draft heads of a bill for public consultation on 8 December 2017. The draft legislative provisions outline proposed safeguards for older people and persons with a disability to ensure that they are not unlawfully deprived of their liberty in residential facilities. The public consultation process was extended and concluded in May 2018. The final text of the legislation is awaited, and it will then be presented to the Dail by the Minister and progress through the normal legislative process.

The Department of Justice has indicated that no further parts of the ADMA will be commenced on a piecemeal basis and stated that the rest of the legislation will commence concurrently. Given that the text of Part

13 of the ADMA has not yet been finalised and in view of the sheer scale of work required to establish fully the structures required to support the DSS, it would appear that the commencement of the entirety of the ADMA is some way off.

On 7 March 2018, despite the fact the ADMA has not commenced to any significant extent, the Government passed a motion to ratify the UNCRPD. Ireland was the last state in the European Union to do so. However, it did not ratify the Optional Protocol, which is a separate instrument which allows individuals and groups of individuals to take a complaint to the CRPD in the case of an alleged violation of their rights. While it had previously been indicated that the Optional Protocol would be ratified at the same time as the ratification of the CRPD, the Department of Justice has confirmed that it will not ratify the Optional Protocol to the Convention at this time. The Disability Federation of Ireland has expressed deep disappointment at the Department's stance, noting that it renders the ratification of the CRPD toothless.[61]

As noted at the outset, while the ADMA is not commenced, Irish case law has very usefully delineated a set of principles, not dissimilar to those in the guiding principles of the ADMA, reflecting the principles of the CRPD. The cases, some of which are described in this chapter, establish precedents for the functional approach to capacity. The approach of the President of the High Court in operating the wardship jurisdiction has also been described in this chapter.

A very recent case has established principles that should apply to deprivation of liberty of persons who have lost decision-making capacity. On 2 July 2018, the Court of Appeal in the case of *A.C.* v. *Cork University Hospital & Ors*,[62] held that a person cannot be deprived of their liberty in a hospital (and indeed other facilities) without attendant deprivation of liberty safeguards and found that the detention of an elderly woman in a

---

[61] See K. Holland, 'Ratifying UN Laws on Disability without Appeal Option "Ridiculous"', *The Irish Times*, 13 March 2018.

[62] See the decision of Mr Justice Hogan in *A.C* v. *Clare & Ors* [2018] IECA 217 where he notes:-

> 'Article 40.4.1 provides that all detention must be in accordance with law. The reasons and motives of the detainer are not relevant to any consideration of this issue of law. Since no power to detain Ms A.C. in these circumstances has been identified, it follows, therefore, that I am not satisfied that CUH acted lawfully in restraining and preventing her leaving the hospital in the company of her son and daughter on the 23rd June 2016. I would, therefore, to that extent allow the appeal.'

hospital against her will, without some form of legal process, was unconstitutional. Deprivation of liberty safeguards, as noted before, are due to be included in the ADMA as an additional Part 13. In the meantime, the deprivation of liberty of persons, who have been found to meet the capacity threshold under the 1871 Act, is regulated by the President of the High Court under the wardship jurisdiction and is subject to regular review.

7

Developments in Enduring Powers of Attorney Law in Australia

TREVOR RYAN*

I Introduction

An enduring power of attorney is a legal instrument by which one person, the 'principal', may delegate decision-making authority to a second person, the 'representative' or 'enduring attorney', to the effect that this delegation continues even where the principal suffers an impairment in decision-making capacity. There is variation across jurisdictions in form, terminology and content. For the most part, in Australia, an enduring power of attorney relates to financial and legal transactions and is distinguished from enduring power of guardianship, which relates to personal decisions, such as where to live and with whom to associate.[1] Enduring power of attorney is also distinguished from 'advanced care directives', which relate to health and medical decisions. Enduring powers of attorney in Australia date back to the 1980s, when all jurisdictions clarified that an enduring power of attorney could, unlike a general power of attorney, survive the principal's loss of capacity. They are widely used in Australia. In one estimate, 11 per cent of Australians have an enduring power of attorney.[2]

Enduring power of attorney is considered a form of agency, which brings with it fiduciary obligations.[3] Since their inception, enduring powers have also undergone a series of statutory reforms towards more intensive regulation, such as the possibility of review by state or territory courts and guardianship tribunals of their validity and operation. This

---

* Associate Professor, University of Canberra, Faculty of Business, Government & Law.
[1] This mirrors the distinction between appointed 'adult guardians' and 'financial managers'.
[2] House of Representatives Standing Committee on Legal and Constitutional Affairs, *Older People and the Law* (Canberra: The Parliament of the Commonwealth of Australia, 2007), p. 71, citing Office of the Public Advocate Queensland, *Submission No. 76*, p. 7.
[3] N. O'Neill and C. Peisah, *Capacity and the Law*, 2nd edn (Sydney: Sydney University Press, 2017), ch. 10.2.

regulation seeks a balance between the convenience and utility of enduring powers for enabling important transactions and preventing predatory
behaviours on the one hand and protection from abuse by attorneys
themselves on the other. While this abuse includes cases where enduring
powers have been granted by principals without capacity to do so, it is
also apparent that validly created powers of attorney have been widely
abused in Australia.[4] This is reflected in the phrase 'early inheritance
syndrome', where impatient relatives in an overheated property market
dip into their inheritance prematurely by gifting the principal's assets to
themselves or others inconsistent with any intent of the principal.

Calls to reform the law of enduring powers have gathered strength in
the context of an ageing society, increased prevalence of dementia and
Australia's ratification of the Convention on the Rights of Persons with
Disabilities (CRPD).[5] Article 12 ('Equal Recognition before the Law')
enshrines the right of persons with disabilities to legal capacity 'on an
equal basis with others in all aspects of life'. The Committee on the Rights
of Persons with Disabilities takes the view that substitute decision-
making of the type that has characterised decisions made under enduring
powers in the past should be instead replaced by 'supported' decision-
making frameworks, which provide the context for principals to exercise
their capacity and autonomy.[6] Though more attention has been placed
on court- or tribunal-appointed administrators and adult guardians than
enduring attorneys, each shares similar challenges in implementing this
paradigm shift. Enduring powers and newer innovations such as 'supportive attorneys' potentially align with the ideals of the CRPD given the
principal-driven nature of the relationship. There is, however, dispute
about the precise implications of a supported decision-making model.
For example, Sullivan attempts to reconcile the vision of the CRPD with
what protective or even coercive features of the model, if any, remain.[7]
He notes that, in some cases, the absence of decision substitution may
compromise human rights – for example, where housing or medical

---

[4] Parliament of Victoria Law Reform Committee, Inquiry into Powers of Attorney (Parliamentary Paper No. 352, 2010), pp. 26–27.
[5] Convention on the Rights of Persons with Disabilities, New York, 30 March 2007, in force
3 May 2008, 2015 UNTS 3.
[6] UN Committee on the Rights of Persons with Disabilities, *General Comment No. 1 (2014)*,
CRPD/C/GC/1, paras. 26–27.
[7] D. Sullivan, 'A New Ball Game: The United Nations Convention on the Rights of Persons
with Disabilities and Assumptions in Care for People with Dementia' (2012) 20 *Journal of
Law and Medicine* 12, 31.

treatment must be paid for or where financial abuse would otherwise occur.[8] As explored in this chapter, Australia has grappled with these issues in considering how to regulate enduring powers of attorney.

This chapter describes the state of enduring powers of attorney law in Australian jurisdictions, actual and proposed reforms, and argues that regulation of conflict transactions is a key area that can contribute to reducing elder financial abuse and, moreover, reveals deeper lessons about the nature and significance of enduring powers of attorney today. It does not consider the separate questions of capacity to make gifts, the status of gifts to secure care 'contracts'[9] or other forms of substituted or supported decision-making.

II   The Legal Framework for Enduring Powers of Attorney in Australia

In the absence of any overriding Commonwealth law, the regulation of enduring powers of attorney is a state and territory matter, and each of these jurisdictions has its own dedicated Act.[10] Australia also saw a shift in the 1980s from courts to tribunals in overseeing substituted decision-making generally,[11] though courts retain inherent parens patriae jurisdiction developed historically by English courts to protect members of society without capacity.[12] Each state and territory now has a general civil and administrative tribunal, some of which have a guardianship division. All states and territories except South Australia recognise enduring powers of attorney created in another jurisdiction in Australia.[13] Only in Tasmania must enduring powers of attorney be registered before being

---

[8]   Ibid.
[9]   See M. Hall, 'Equitable Fraud: Material Exploitation in Domestic Settings' (2006) 4 *Elder Law Review* 7.
[10]   Powers of Attorney Act 2003 (NSW); Powers of Attorney Act 2014 (Vic); Powers of Attorney Act 1998 (Qld); Powers of Attorney and Agency Act 1984 (SA); Guardianship and Administration Act 1990 (WA); Powers of Attorney Act 2000 (Tas); Advance Personal Planning Act 2013 (NT); Powers of Attorney Act 2006 (ACT).
[11]   See T. Carney, 'Challenges to the Australian Guardianship and Administration Model?' (2003) 2 *Elder Law Journal* 11.
[12]   See J. Seymour, 'Parens Patriae and Wardship Powers: Their Nature and Origins' (1994) 14(2) *Oxford Journal of Legal Studies* 159.
[13]   Powers of Attorney Act 2003 (NSW), s. 25, Powers of Attorney Act 1998 (Qld), s. 34, Powers of Attorney Act 2000 (Tas), s. 42, Powers of Attorney Act 2014 (Vic), s. 138, Guardianship and Administration Act 1990 (WA), s. 104A, Powers of Attorney Act 2000 (ACT), s. 89 and Advance Personal Planning Act (NT), s. 88 and Advance Personal Planning Regulation (NT), reg. 8 and the Schedule.

used by the attorney,[14] yet all jurisdictions require registration for dealings with land.[15] The following describes the common features of these regimes, except where there are anomalies worthy of note.

An enduring power of attorney in Australia may be granted by a principal or 'donor' to single or multiple representatives, to both adult individuals and legal persons including a public body such as a state trustee and, in most states, a private corporation. Some persons are disqualified, such as (in Victoria) those who are bankrupt; convicted of a fraud offence; or providers of care, health services, or accommodation to the principal.[16] The disqualification is generally less strict for enduring guardians (an adult with capacity in the case of Western Australia).[17] In Victoria, there is a further restriction on 'a care worker, a health provider or an accommodation provider for the principal'.[18] The rationale for this is evidently that enduring guardians have less ability to inflict financial harm yet, at least for professional caregivers, have a conflict of interest as a service provider. In principle, as discussed later, the scope of authority that can be granted is limited only by the scope of authority of the principal. However, some matters are excluded under legislation such as relating to wills or consent to marriage and adoption.[19] Other legislative restrictions imposed upon enduring attorneys relate to the giving of gifts and other benefits, which will be considered in greater detail later in this chapter.

A   Capacity

The principal is presumed to have capacity to make the enduring power.[20] However, this can be challenged before a court or tribunal in an application for the enduring power to be revoked. The tests for capacity are found in the common law for some states and in legislation for others. A general principle for capacity is stated in *Gibbons* v. *Wright*:

---

[14] Powers of Attorney Act 2000 (Tas), ss. 4, 9 and 30.
[15] Powers of Attorney Act 2003 (NSW), ss. 51, 52; Land Title Act 1994 (Qld), s. 132; Land Titles Act 1925 (ACT), s. 130(2); Real Property Act 1886 (SA), ss. 155–156.
[16] Powers of Attorney Act 2014 (Vic), s. 28(1).
[17] Guardianship and Administration Act 1990 (WA), s. 110D.
[18] Powers of Attorney Act 2014 (Vic), s. 91(d).
[19] Powers of Attorney Act 2014 (Vic), s. 26.
[20] *Scott* v. *Scott* [2012] NSWSC 1541, para. 233. This principle is also codified, for example in Powers of Attorney Act 2014 (Vic), s. 4(2).

[T]he mental capacity required by the law in respect of any instrument is relative to the particular transaction which is being effected by means of the instrument, and may be described as the capacity to understand the nature of that transaction when it is explained.[21]

This test was developed in *Ranclaud* v. *Cabban,* in which Young J held that the principal must understand not only the fact of authorisation but also the sort of things the attorney could do without consulting the principal – for example, selling real estate.[22] Subsequent case law has provided more specific guidance about the degree of understanding required of a principal regarding the enduring powers arrangement. On the standard and burden of proof of capacity, Forrest J in *Ghosn* v. *Principle Focus Pty Ltd*[23] held that the applicable principles are those that apply to testamentary capacity formulated in *Banks* v. *Goodfellow.*[24] Accordingly, if there is sufficient doubt about the capacity, a tribunal must invalidate the enduring power unless it is satisfied that the principal was capable of understanding the document.[25]

Those jurisdictions that have codified matters relating to capacity vary in the formulation used. The most recent is that of Victoria, which stipulates that a person has decision-making capacity if they are able to:

(a) understand the information relevant to the decision and the effect of the decision;
(b) retain that information to the extent necessary to make the decision;
(c) use or weigh that information as part of the process of making the decision; and
(d) communicate the decision and the person's views and needs as to the decision in some way, including by speech, gestures or other means.[26]

The legislation also stipulates the wider support context in which capacity is to be assessed:

(a) a person may have decision-making capacity for some matters and not others;

---

[21] (1954) 91 CLR 423, 438.
[22] (1988) NSW Conv R 55–385.
[23] [2008] VSC 574, para. 76.
[24] (1870) LR 5 QB 549, 565.
[25] Ibid.
[26] Powers of Attorney Act 2014 (Vic), s. 4.

(b) if a person does not have decision-making capacity for a matter, it may be temporary and not permanent;

(c) it should not be assumed that a person does not have decision-making capacity for a matter on the basis of the person's appearance;

(d) it should not be assumed that a person does not have decision-making capacity for a matter merely because the person makes a decision that is, in the opinion of others, unwise;

(e) a person has decision-making capacity for a matter if it is possible for the person to make a decision in the matter with practicable and appropriate support.

The Act also requires that upon making or revoking the enduring power, the principal understand certain matters including:

(a) that the principal may, in the power of attorney, place conditions on the power given to the attorney and give instructions to the attorney about the exercise of the power given to the attorney;

(b) when the power of attorney commences;

(c) that once the power of attorney is exercisable in relation to a matter, the attorney has the same powers the principal has, when the principal has decision-making capacity for that matter, to do anything for which the power for that matter is given;

(d) that the principal may revoke the power of attorney at any time when the principal has decision-making capacity in relation to making the power of attorney;

(e) that the power of attorney continues even if the principal subsequently becomes a person who does not have decision-making capacity for a matter in the power of attorney;

(f) that at any time when the principal does not have decision-making capacity in relation to revoking the power of attorney, the principal is unable to effectively oversee the use of the power. These principles also apply to capacity to revoke enduring powers of attorney.[27]

B   Representatives

For an enduring power of attorney to take effect, it must be accepted and signed by the representative. There is flexibility in the timing of the activation of the enduring powers – in other words, when a representative may begin to make decisions and transactions under the power. For

---

[27] Ibid., s. 23(2).

example, in Victoria, the legislation specifies that the power can take effect immediately or when decision-making capacity for a specific matter is impaired, or when some other activating event occurs.[28] The default position is for the power to come into effect immediately.[29]

A representative has a number of responsibilities. Perhaps the most important is the fiduciary duty not to obtain an advantage for themselves or act contrary to the interests of the principal. This principle was endorsed in *Watson* v. *Watson*,[30] quoting Thomas J in the New Zealand case of *Powell* v. *Thompson*:

> The powers of attorney are specifically directed at the management of the principal's affairs: it is not open to attorneys to either obtain an advantage for themselves or to act in a way which is contrary to the interests of their principals.[31]

There is statutory reinforcement of this duty in Queensland, Victoria and the Australian Capital Territory, which impose a duty to avoid conflict transactions.[32] The significance of this duty is explored further later. A state or territory Supreme Court has jurisdiction to determine such breaches and grant relief by setting aside the transaction or awarding equitable damages.[33]

A second responsibility is fidelity to the document itself. Instructions and limitations made by the principal must be followed for a general power of attorney. Yet once the principal has lost the particular decision-making capacity, these instructions become merely one consideration to be balanced with other obligations – for example, to act with reasonable diligence. This is because attorneys are required to consider the views and wishes of the principal, yet balance these against protection. This balance can be seen in the Victoria legislation, which stipulates that representatives must, in making a decision:

(a) give all practicable and appropriate effect to the maker's wishes; and
(b) take any steps that are reasonably available to encourage the maker to participate in decision-making, even though they do not have decision-making capacity; and

---

[28] Ibid., s. 39(1).
[29] Ibid., s. 39(2).
[30] [2002] NSWSC 919, para. 49.
[31] [1991] 1 NZLR 597, 605 (Master Berecry).
[32] Powers of Attorney Act 1998 (Qld), s. 73; Powers of Attorney Act 2014 (Vic), ss. 64, 65 and Powers of Attorney Act 2006 (ACT), s. 42.
[33] See discussion later in the chapter.

(c) act in a way that promotes the personal and social wellbeing of the
maker, including by
   (i) recognising the maker's inherent dignity; and
   (ii) having regard to maker's existing supportive relationships,
        religion, values and cultural and linguistic environment; and
   (iii) respecting the confidentiality of confidential information relat-
        ing to the maker.[34]

Third, a representative is obliged to act honestly and with reasonable
diligence. In Queensland, this is both a cause of action and grounds for
criminal sanctions.[35] Where there is no such statutory duty, such as in
New South Wales and the Australian Capital Territory, the duties are
inherently part of the fiduciary relationship.[36] Fourth, enduring attorneys
have a duty to not resign after the principal has lost capacity. If an
attorney wishes to resign, generally they must apply to the Supreme
Court or guardianship tribunal of the state or territory.[37]

Fifth, enduring attorneys also have several powers and responsibilities
surrounding the exercise of their administrative powers, such as to
execute documents.[38] Some jurisdictions require enduring attorneys to
keep records of dealings[39] and to keep their own property separate from
the principal's property.[40] Some jurisdictions codify an enduring attorney's power to seek information.[41] This circumvents the problem that
some service providers refuse to provide information to an enduring
attorney regarding matters such as electricity bills or healthcare. The

---

[34] Powers of Attorney Act 2014 (Vic), s. 21(2).
[35] Powers of Attorney Act 1998 (Qld), s. 66.
[36] O'Neill and Peisah, *Capacity and the Law*, n 3, para. [10.1.6.2].
[37] Powers of Attorney Act 1998 (Qld), ss. 82 and 109A; Powers of Attorney and Agency Act
    1984 (SA), s. 9; Powers of Attorney Act 2006 (ACT), s. 53(2); Guardianship and
    Administration Act 1990 (WA), ss. 107(1)(c) and 109.
[38] Powers of Attorney Act 1998 (Qld), s. 69, Powers of Attorney Act 2014 (Vic), s. 27
    and Powers of Attorney Act 1980 (NT), s. 10. For examples of such implication
    see, Powers of Attorney and Agency Act 1984 (SA), s. 13 and Advance Personal Planning
    Act (NT), s. 20(1).
[39] Powers of Attorney Act 1998 (Qld), s. 85; Powers of Attorney Act 2014 (Vic), s. 66;
    Powers of Attorney Act 2006 (ACT), s. 47; Guardianship and Administration Act 1990
    (WA), s. 107(1)(b).
[40] Powers of Attorney Act 1998 (Qld), s. 86; Powers of Attorney Act 2006 (ACT), s. 48. The
    exception is if the property is jointly owned.
[41] Powers of Attorney Act 2006 (ACT), ss. 45(2) and (3); Powers of Attorney Act 1998
    (Qld), s. 81.

enduring attorney is, however, required to maintain the confidentiality of this information.[42]

C   Tribunal and Court Oversight

In principle, a tribunal will defer to an enduring power of attorney where it is made validly because it is a less restrictive alternative.[43] Yet, if a tribunal does make an order for financial management, this generally suspends or modifies the enduring power of attorney.[44] This supervisory role will typically be activated upon an application by a family member or other interested party for the tribunal to make an administration order.[45] Some tribunals – for example, that of the Australian Capital Territory – are able to act on their own initiative.[46] This supervisory function extends over both the validity of enduring powers and their continuing operation. Remedies that the tribunal or court may order include varying the power of attorney, removing an attorney, appointing a substitute attorney or requiring an attorney to furnish accounts.[47] The supervisory role of tribunals and courts also extends to providing advice or directions upon the enduring attorney's request.[48] There is considerable variation across jurisdictions with regard to the supervisory role of courts and tribunals. For example, in Victoria, the threshold for the guardianship tribunal to revoke the appointment of attorney is somewhat higher, requiring clear evidence that the attorney is not complying with the provisions of the Act and that the principal does not have decision-making capacity in relation to making an enduring power of attorney.[49]

Long considered a deficiency in the supervisory role of courts and tribunals was the absence of the ability for these authorities to order compensation for a loss resulting from a contravention by an attorney of legislation regulating the power. This was remedied by legislation in Victoria, which enables either VCAT or the Victorian Supreme Court

---

[42] See, e.g., Powers of Attorney Act 1998 (Qld), s. 74A.
[43] O'Neill and Peisah, *Capacity and the Law*, n 3, para. [10.10].
[44] See, e.g., Powers of Attorney Act (Vic), s. 83(1).
[45] See, e.g., Powers of Attorney Act 2003 (NSW), s. 35(1).
[46] Powers of Attorney Act 2006 (ACT), ss. 62(2) and (4).
[47] See, e.g., Powers of Attorney Act (Vic), s. 116.
[48] See, e.g., ibid., s. 121.
[49] Ibid., s. 120(2).

to order an attorney to compensate the principal to no upper limit.[50] Furthermore, the Court may impose criminal sanctions on a person who dishonestly obtains, uses or brings about a revocation of an enduring power of attorney for financial gain or to cause loss to the principal or another person.[51] There are defences in the Act of acting honestly and reasonably.[52]

D   Supportive Attorneys

In 2015, Victoria introduced a new form of enduring attorney called a 'supportive attorney' in a deliberate departure from a substituted decision-making model. In line with the philosophy of the CRPD, a supportive attorney assists a principal (an 'appointor') in making and giving effect to decisions. This innovation lends a degree of formality to hitherto informal supportive relationships in a way that may engender respect and compliance from third parties such as service providers.[53] The Victorian Government's design was that principals would have considerable autonomy over choosing the identity of the supportive attorney, the types of decisions for which support will be given and the types of support.[54] An exception is that, for conflict of interest reasons, a care worker, health provider or accommodation provider for the principal may not be appointed.[55] Nor may a corporate person, presumably because of the personal and practical nature of the role.[56] The supportive attorney must avoid conflict transactions and may not be remunerated.[57] The supportive relationship may commence at a time specified by the principal or, by default, at the time that it is made. Several criteria must be met for a supportive attorney to be appointed. First, the principal must understand certain matters:

(a) that the appointment enables the appointor to make and give effect to their own decisions with support;

---

[50] Ibid., ss. 77–80.
[51] Ibid., s. 135.
[52] Ibid., s. 74.
[53] Parliament of Victoria, Parliamentary Debates (Hansard), Legislative Assembly, 57th Parliament, First Session, 26 June 2014, 2394.
[54] Ibid.
[55] Powers of Attorney Act 2014 (Vic), s. 91(d).
[56] Ibid., s. 91; See Parliament of Victoria, Parliamentary Debates (Hansard), n 53.
[57] Powers of Attorney Act 2014 (Vic), s. 90(2).

(b) that the appointment allows the appointor to choose a person to support them to make and give effect to their own decisions;

(c) that supported decisions are decisions of the appointor and not the supportive attorney;

(d) when the appointment commences; and

(e) that the appointor may revoke the appointment at any time when they have decision-making capacity in relation to making the supportive attorney appointment.[58]

There are safeguards in the legislation against coercion, intimidation or undue influence on the part of a supportive attorney or other person.[59] When activated, the supportive attorney has authority in relation to financial or personal matters, as described in the appointment form. Yet, unlike general enduring powers, the powers of the supportive attorney are narrow in scope, and each must be expressly granted. These powers are as follows. The 'information power' allows the supportive attorney to access, collect or obtain personal information about the principal or support the principal in doing this.[60] However, the information must be related to a supported decision authorised by the appointment. The 'communication power' authorises the supportive attorney to communicate information about the principal required to give effect to a supported decision.[61] The appointment may also include a power to give effect to decisions, which includes any reasonable action to give effect to a supported decision, albeit not in relation to significant financial transactions.[62] The obligations of supportive attorneys mirror those of enduring attorneys – such as the duty to act honestly, diligently and in good faith; to exercise reasonable skill and care; to refrain from using the position for profit and to avoid conflict of interest; and, uniquely to this arrangement, to discuss matters relating to a supported decision in a manner understandable and assistive to the principal.[63] Furthermore, the Victorian Civil and Administrative Tribunal has regulatory powers over supportive attorneys – for example, finding undue influence, giving advisory opinions or other orders relating to capacity.[64]

---

[58] Ibid., s 86.
[59] Ibid., s. 85.
[60] Ibid., s. 87.
[61] Ibid., s. 88.
[62] Ibid., s. 89.
[63] Ibid., s. 90.
[64] Ibid., s. 116(2).

The Tribunal may revoke or suspend the appointment or make any other order it deems necessary. Criminal offences apply, but supportive attorneys cannot be ordered to pay compensation if they cause loss by infringing the legislation.[65]

It is too early to comment on the success of the new system, but critics point to teething problems such as an alleged increased risk of undue influence.[66] Uncertainties remain: for example, O'Neill and Peisah argue that the decision to appoint a supportive attorney should itself be able to be supported, else persons who may benefit from supported decision-making be excluded from the arrangement.[67] This suggests that the level of uptake may disappoint reformers, though until a registration system is introduced, it is difficult to assess success on this score. Nevertheless, not only in nomenclature, but also in the nature and extent of the powers of the supportive attorney, the innovation can be seen as a substantial step towards compliance with article 12 of the CRPD.

III   Reform of Enduring Powers of Attorney

A number of parliamentary commissions and law reform commissions have explored reform of enduring powers of attorney in Australian jurisdictions and measures to combat elder abuse generally.[68] The most recent and comprehensive review was conducted by the Australian Law Reform Commission (ALRC) in the 2017 Final Report of its inquiry Elder Abuse – A National Legal Response.[69] Its main recommendations

---

[65]   Ibid., ss. 135–136.
[66]   C. Bigby, M. Whiteside and M. Douglas, *Supporting People with Cognitive Disabilities in Decision Making – Processes and Dilemmas* (Melbourne: Living with Disability Research Centre, La Trobe University, 2015).
[67]   O'Neill and Peisah, *Capacity and the Law*, n 3, para. [10.13.2].
[68]   See, for example, Parliament of Victoria Law Reform Committee, Inquiry into Powers of Attorney, n 4; Australian Law Reform Commission, *Equality, Capacity and Disability in Commonwealth Laws: Report* (ALRC Report 124, 2014); House of Representatives Standing Committee on Legal and Constitutional Affairs, *Older People and the Law* (Canberra: The Parliament of the Commonwealth of Australia, 2007); Victorian Law Reform Commission, *Guardianship* (Report No. 24, 2012); Communities, Disability Services and Domestic and Family Violence Prevention Committee, Parliament of Queensland, *Inquiry into the Adequacy of Existing Financial Protections for Queensland's Seniors* (Report No. 2, 2015); and Legislative Council General Purpose Standing Committee No. 2, Parliament of New South Wales, *Elder Abuse in New South Wales: Report* (Report No. 44, 2016).
[69]   Australian Law Reform Commission, *Elder Abuse – A National Legal Response: Final Report* (ALRC Report 131, 2017).

were (1) a nationally consistent set of safeguards that minimise abuse of enduring documents; (2) the diffusion of the compensation model adopted by Victoria; and (3) the establishment of a national online registration scheme for enduring documents.

A Safeguards

One of the safeguards recommended by the Commission was to restrict conflict transactions, which will be discussed in further detail later. Other recommendations include the following. First, the Commission recommended changes to laws – for example, those relating to land transactions – that demand enduring power appointments to be plenary. Instead, by removing such obstacles, principals should have the choice to tailor their appointments to their needs by limiting the scope of the representative's authority.

Second, the Commission recommended replacing the 'best interests' standard for substituted decision-makers with a Commonwealth decision-making model. This model focusses on what the principal's will and preferences would likely be where they cannot be determined in the moment and, as a further underlying standard where this assessment cannot be made, a duty to uphold the person's human rights and act in a manner that is least restrictive to those rights.

Third, the Commission made several recommendations for improving the witnessing of the document creating enduring powers. The Commission observed a trend towards tightening such requirements in Australian jurisdictions – for example, stipulating which professionals may witness enduring documents and what they are required to satisfy, namely the presence of legal capacity and voluntariness. In justifying its recommendation for a second witness, the Commission noted that the second witness can provide further confirmation that the parties understand the document and an additional opportunity to identify duress or coercion. In its earlier Discussion Paper, the ALRC proposed that one of these witnesses should be (a) a legal practitioner, (b) a medical practitioner, (c) a justice of the peace; (d) a registrar of the Local/Magistrates Court or (e) a police officer holding the rank of sergeant or above.[70] In response to criticisms that this list of prescribed professionals was too narrow, the Commission instead settled on a more flexible formulation,

---

[70] Ibid., para. [5.29].

namely that one of the witnesses must be a 'professional whose licence to practise is dependent on the ongoing integrity and honesty and who is required to regularly undertake a course of continuing professional education the covers the skills and expertise necessary to witness and enduring document'.[71]

As to the content of the declaration, the ALRC had proposed certifying that: '(a) the principal appeared to freely and voluntarily sign in their presence; (b) the principal appeared to understand the nature of the document; and (c) the enduring attorney or enduring guardian appeared to freely and voluntarily sign in their presence.'[72] The Commission noted the educative function of this step in the process in addition to its evidentiary value, but was cautious not to recommend requirements so onerous as to dissuade principals from making enduring documents. The Commission eventually endorsed the submission of the Law Council of Australia: that 'the witness is not aware of anything that causes them to believe that the principal did not freely and voluntarily sign the document; the principal did not understand the nature of the document; or the enduring attorney did not freely and voluntarily sign the document'.[73] The Commission commended this approach for not expecting of witnesses any legal or medical expertise in assessing legal capacity.[74]

Finally, the Commission argued that the attorney's signature should also be witnessed. In this case, the witness should certify that the attorney understood the document and was signing voluntarily. The purpose of this was to provide an opportunity for formal discussion with the representative as an additional measure to address the problem that some enduring powers are abused through ignorance rather than ill intent. This educative role takes primary importance because the undertakings an attorney made with this signature do not appear to have any independent legal force.[75]

The Commission recommended that there be a nationally consistent position that a person who is, or has been, a care worker, a health provider or an accommodation provider for the principal should be ineligible to be an enduring attorney. The Commission was, however,

---

[71] Ibid., para. [5.44].

[72] Australian Law Reform Commission, *Elder Abuse: Discussion Paper No. 83* (DP83, 2016), proposal 5-4.

[73] Australian Law Reform Commission, *Elder Abuse – A National Legal Response*, n 69, para. [5.46].

[74] Ibid., para. [5.47].

[75] *Daunt v. Daunt* [2013] VSC 706.

responsive to a concern in some submissions that further clarification should be provided to ensure that family members and other informal carers should not be excluded on this basis, as with informal providers of accommodation and health services. The Commission's initial position was to retain restrictions upon persons convicted of an offence involving fraud or dishonesty. However, in its Final Report, it concluded that the autonomy of a principal who wishes to appoint a representative of this status with notice can be balanced with protection by allowing tribunal approval of such persons and requiring notification of any subsequent convictions.[76]

Fifth, the Commission argued that a nationally consistent list of prohibited decisions building on case law should be adopted, namely:

(a) making or revoking the principal's will;
(b) making or revoking an enduring document on behalf of the principal;
(c) voting in elections on behalf of the principal;
(d) consenting to adoption of a child by the principal;
(e) consenting to marriage or divorce of the principal; or
(f) consenting to the principal entering into a sexual relationship.[77]

The Commission considered that this should be a non-exhaustive list which allows the common law to supplement it with types of decisions, such as in relation to superannuation, that should also be prohibited, at least without specific authorisation in the enduring document.

Sixth, the Commission recommended that, where this had not already been codified, enduring attorneys should be required to keep records and keep their own property separate from that of the principal. The Commission noted that this can have an educative function and can protect representatives in the face of aspersions cast upon their conduct.

Another set of recommendations made by the Commission relates to redress for financial abuse suffered at the hands of enduring attorneys. The Commission recommended that all state and territory civil and administrative tribunals be vested with

---

[76] Australian Law Reform Commission, *Elder Abuse – A National Legal Response*, n 69, para. [5.69].

[77] Australian Law Reform Commission, *Elder Abuse: Discussion Paper No. 83*, n 72, proposal 5–8.

(a) jurisdiction in relation to any cause of action, or claim for equitable relief, that is available against a substitute decision-maker in the Supreme Court for abuse, or misuse of power, or failure to perform their duties; and

(b) the power to order any remedy available to the Supreme Court.[78]

This would be a deterrent to wrongdoing even where the victim does not wish to jeopardise a personal relationship through criminal sanctions or expensive and adversarial litigation.[79] The Commission's position was that this power should be used with the 'discretion to excuse [enduring attorneys for] breaches that are inadvertent or otherwise in good faith' (given the onerous nature of the undertaking.[80] It did not specify how this discretion would apply to the duty to act honestly and with reasonable diligence, but because these duties overlap with good faith, breaches of this nature would presumably be less excusable. The Commission did note, however, some uncertainty about the legality of the provisions and their scope of application, not having come before the Supreme Court for clarification. In this sense, tribunals may be less well-positioned to grant relief relative to Supreme Courts, which have inherent jurisdiction, which may have a bearing on remedies. This difference is further explored later in relation to conflict transactions. The Commission also took the view that Commonwealth legislation would need to be amended for state and territory tribunals to have jurisdiction over interstate disputes, but that the constitutional validity of this is questionable.[81]

B   Registration

The Commission recommended the establishment of a national online register of enduring documents and guardianship and administration appointments. Necessary preconditions for this, it argued, are nationally consistent laws and template documents on enduring powers of attorney and guardianship and other personally appointed substitute decision-makers. The Commission determined that any possible disincentive to

---

[78] Australian Law Reform Commission, *Elder Abuse – A National Legal Response*, n 69, p. 177, Recommendation 5-2.

[79] Ibid., para. [5.83].

[80] Ibid., para. [5.89].

[81] Ibid., para. [5.97]. *Burns v. Corbett* [2017] NSWCA 3 found that states may not under the Constitution confer jurisdictions on tribunals to exercise judicial power in cases in interstate matters.

create enduring powers posed by the registration scheme should be minimised by making it user-friendly and affordable by respecting privacy and adopting efficiencies that contribute to its supervisory potential. These include automatic notifications to the principal and designated persons or a 'personal monitor' upon registration and activation of powers, with the potential for customisation. The effect of registration of enduring powers would be to revoke earlier registered or unregistered powers. The scheme would replace the current state regimes, most of which only require registration for land transactions. The Commission took the view that educational transitional arrangements would be required.

The primary purpose of this register would be to reduce financial abuse. First, the register would provide certainty about which document of potentially multiple documents is current and valid. Second, it provides a vehicle for identifying documents that have been activated because the entry in the register indicates whether the powers commence immediately or upon some other event. Where this event is loss of decision-making capacity, this can be confirmed through a notification scheme. Third, the information on the register can clarify the authority of the representative. The Commission also contends that a register would prevent a principal from being encouraged to create a new enduring power after an initial power has been activated on the basis of impaired decision-making capacity. The Commission noted submissions to the inquiry that the very existence of a register signals to representatives that they are subject to a degree of official oversight. A register would also have utility to third parties who may otherwise be reluctant to accept the validity of documents carried by the representative. This in turn may prevent financial abuse by ensuring that desirable transactions occur in a timely fashion. Indeed, registration would obviate the need for institutions such as banks issuing their own documentation demonstrating authority, which are typically less strict in their witnessing requirements than those recommended by the Commission.

The Commission cited some evidence from overseas jurisdictions to the effect that registration has reduced the number of cases in which a representative has abused an enduring power to commit financial abuse. The Commission pointed to the United Kingdom as a case study for the educative role of a register and the importance of ease of use and affordability to ensure that it does not have a chilling effect on the uptake of enduring powers. The Commission considered that customisable automatic notifications upon registration and activation of enduring powers was a reasonable alternative to the more burdensome option of linking activation to a formal assessment of capacity, although this could be required by the principal if they chose to include it in the arrangement.

The Commission summarised counterarguments as follows. First, the burden of a register may not outweigh any tangible benefit or reduction in financial abuse. Second, a register may have a chilling effect on the uptake of enduring powers. Third, similarly, a register entails issues of affordability and privacy independent of any chilling effect. The Commission found that each of these risks could be addressed. For example, for those senior citizens unfamiliar with the Internet, face-to-face support could be given to complete the procedures to create the documents, or this process could be managed by a solicitor or other professional. With regard to cost, the Commission provides the example of the Personal Property Securities Register introduced in 2012 as an example of a national online register that is user-friendly and affordable.

With regard to privacy, the Commission was responsive to suggestions by Australia's Privacy Commissioner and other privacy experts that information on the register be tightly controlled and subject to rigorous data protection including criminal offences. The Commission supported the introduction of licensing arrangements for institutional users such as hospitals, banks, government agencies and lawyers. The Commission recommended that accessibility to the register be customisable by the principal. Its view was that registration of enduring powers should not, like Torrens land registration, be evidence of the authority of the document. In other words, a registered document could be found to be invalid on the grounds of incapacity, which would then resurrect prior valid enduring powers. Nevertheless, the Commission recommended that third parties who rely in good faith on information on the register should be protected from liability.

The Commission explored the possibility of using the information on the register to conduct random checks on representatives, but noted a range of views in submissions to the inquiry and advocated a hybrid model whereby checks would only proceed on the basis of a reasonable ground for suspicion, the provision of reasonable notice and opportunities to rectify potential breaches of duties.[82]

---

[82] Australian Law Reform Commission, *Elder Abuse – A National Legal Response*, n 69, para. [5.176].

C   Terminology

Finally, the Commission expressed its view that as part of a shift towards a national model for the enduring document, the model that should be adopted throughout the Commonwealth is one of 'representative agreements'. The Commission contends that this model complies with the CRPD by placing the principal's preferences and rights at the centre of the agreement. As part of this model, any assessments of capacity would proceed pursuant to the Commonwealth decision-making model, which eschews a binary approach to capacity and instead shifts the question to one context: the degree of support required to enable a principal to express his or her will and preferences:

(a) All adults must be presumed to have ability to make decisions that affect their lives.
(b) A person must not be assumed to lack decision-making ability on the basis of having a disability.
(c) A person's decision-making ability must be considered in the context of available supports.
(d) A person's decision-making ability is to be assessed, not the outcome of the decision they want to make.
(e) A person's decision-making ability will depend on the kind of decisions to be made.
(f) A person's decision-making ability may evolve or fluctuate over time.[83]

The Commission justifies the term 'representatives' as superior to 'attorney', which conveys legalism and its commercial origin and also terms such as voluntary 'guardianship', which carry connotations of paternalism.[84] Furthermore, according to the Commission, the term 'agreement' signals to third parties that the arrangement has not been imposed upon the principal. This may reduce instances whereby third parties defer to a representative even where that representative does not seek to reflect the wishes of the principal. However, the Commission does note that the term 'agreement' is not synonymous with 'contract', given

---

[83] Australian Law Reform Commission, *Equality, Capacity and Disability in Commonwealth Laws: Final Report* n 68, p. 70.
[84] Australian Law Reform Commission, *Elder Abuse – A National Legal Response*, n 69, p. 201.

that in Australian law contract requires consideration, which is not necessarily the case for enduring powers of attorney.

Disputes over terminology are not merely cosmetic. They reflect differing views on the essence of enduring powers. The following section turns to conflict transactions as a means of shedding further light on these deeper issues.

IV Conflict Transactions

To reiterate, there are fiduciary and statutory rules in Australia to the effect that representatives must avoid conflict transactions and, more generally, any act that promotes their own interests rather than those of the principal.[85] Indeed, article 12(4) of the CRPD requires that: 'measures relating to the exercise of legal capacity . . . are free of conflict of interest'. This is a principle with roots in antiquity.[86] Examples of conflict transactions include where the principal's property is leased by the representative, perhaps having been a business partner, or where the representative uses a family holiday home.[87] Other examples are where the representative uses the principal's property as a residence or to fund personal expenditure or debt or to guarantee loans. Benefits to third parties such as a relative, business associate or close friend of the representative are also conflict transactions.[88] Evidence suggests that the rules against conflict transactions are often infringed either intentionally or through ignorance, which has been identified as a key challenge in the fight against elder abuse.[89] In one study, financial abuse in families through sharing assets was indicated in 47 of 127 interviews, which included pressure to give or lend money or property.[90] The study also

---

[85] *Watson v. Watson* [2002] NSWSC 919, para. [49]; Powers of Attorney Act 1998 (Qld), s. 73; Powers of Attorney Act 2014 (Vic), ss. 64, 65 and Powers of Attorney Act 2006 (ACT), s. 42.

[86] A. Johns, 'Ten Years After: Where Is the Constitutional Crisis with Procedural Safeguards and Due Process in Guardianship Adjudication?' (1999) 7 *Elder Law Journal* 47.

[87] Australian Law Reform Commission, *Elder Abuse – A National Legal Response*, n 69, para. [5.52].

[88] See, for example, Powers of Attorney Act 2014 (Vic), s. 64.

[89] Law Reform Committee, Parliament of Victoria, Inquiry into Powers of Attorney, n 4, p. 175; Hall, 'Material Exploitation in Domestic Settings', n 9.

[90] D. Setterlund, J. Wilson, C. Tilse, G. Robinson and L. Rosenman, 'Financial Abuse within Families: Views from Family Members and Professionals', p. 3, conference paper, 8th Australian Institute of Family Studies Conference, Melbourne, 12–14 February 2003, available from www.researchgate.net/publication/237514099.

identified as an abusive behaviour 'asset managers being overly generous with an older person's money – for example, by using a gifting option excessively'.[91]

Alongside a conceptual shift from paternalism to supported decision-making, exceptions to rules against conflict transactions (discussed in further detail later) have developed in state law to enable principals to continue with altruistic behaviours such as sharing a residence, gift giving, donations and other transfers to third parties and even to representatives themselves. As wealth accumulates in older investors, gifting could be an aspect of estate planning and tax minimisation, though not to reduce inheritance taxes, which were abolished in Australia in 1979.[92] It could be a supported decision or otherwise pursuant to wishes expressed in the enduring document or inferred from past conduct. Without these exceptions, gift giving and other altruistic acts would be liberties foregone in the 'civil death' that once characterised substituted decision-making through a loss of capacity.[93] An order of adult guardianship (defined broadly) in the past was either premised on the notion that the interests of the 'ward' did not include altruism or even that the property should be preserved for the family in succession from 'spendthrift' behaviour. While the new exceptions are a worthy development, there is a risk that they merely encourage rather than pre-empt exploitative gift giving known as 'early inheritance syndrome'. There is also potential confusion between gifts and remuneration for the services of a representative: 'the difference between self-gifting and self-dealing can be difficult to differentiate and can also include built in adverse tax, estate planning and self-support problems'.[94] For example, there are complications that may arise in relation to ademption, namely where a transaction depletes property left in a will.[95]

Fiduciary law can provide guiding principles and thus regulate these risks to some extent. There have been numerous cases in Australia that

---

[91] Ibid., p. 2.

[92] See US Army The Judge Advocate General's School, 'Gifts Made under a Durable Power of Attorney' (Nov 2000) *Army Lawyer* 38, for a description of such reduction arrangements in the USA making the point that taxation authorities do not always recognise such gifts when granted pursuant to an enduring power of attorney.

[93] M. Andrews, 'The Elderly in Guardianship: A Crisis of Constitutional Proportions' (1997) 5(1) *The Elder Law Journal* 93.

[94] J. Pietsch, 'Becoming a "Dementia-Capable" Attorney - Representing Individuals with Dementia' (2015) 19 *Hawaii Bar Journal* 1, footnote 180.

[95] See, e.g., *RJL* [2011] NSWSC 200, overruled by *RL* [2012] NSWCA 39.

have established that representatives may not advantage themselves.[96] The caveat to this is that the fiduciary rules of equity will not necessarily override the text of the enduring document, which may expressly permit the representative to make conflict transactions to their own advantage, though requiring unambiguous language.[97] Yet even with this caveat, courts have invoked what they regard as the essence of the enduring powers relationship to impose limits upon the express words of the document, mirroring a similar trend in consumer and contract law.

A recent example of this is the New South Wales Supreme Court decision of *Cohen* v. *Cohen*.[98] In this case, the 92-year-old plaintiff's 'tutor'[99] sued the plaintiff's son, who had in 2013 transferred to himself for minimal consideration real estate bought by his mother 12 years earlier for AUD245,000. The transaction was made pursuant to a power of attorney granted in 2000 under the Conveyancing Act 1919 (NSW) using the Act's statutory form.[100] The document retained two key optional provisions of the statutory form. One provided that the appointment would be an enduring one. The other granted the representative express authority to 'execute any assurance or other document, or do any other act, whereby a benefit is conferred on him'. Because the document was made before the legislative amendments on conflict transactions discussed later, it was governed by the now repealed sections 163B(1) and (3), which provided that the attorney held authority coterminous with that of the principal, unless otherwise provided in the instrument. Section 163B(2)(b) of the Conveyancing Act 1919 (NSW) allowed as an exception express authorisation of conflict transactions in similar wording to that found in the statutory form. The instrument was duly registered to allow for transactions in real estate. The point at which the plaintiff lost 'capacity through unsoundness of mind' (in the language of the Act[101]) is unclear, but around the time of the transfer of property in

---

[96] *Watson* v. *Watson* [2002] NSWSC 919, para. [49], *Greenland* v. *Intellectually Disabled Citizens of Queensland* [2000] QSC 84, para. [30]; *Re KJS* [2003] QGAAT 27, para. [61] and *Klotz & Klotz* v. *Neubauer & Klotz* [2001] SASC 454, paras. [33]–[37].

[97] *Tobin* v. *Broadbent* [1947] 75 CLR 378, 401 (Dixon J).

[98] [2016] NSWSC 336.

[99] A person appointed by a court or tribunal to represent a person without capacity in litigation.

[100] In Schedule 7. The instrument was given continuing validity by the transitional provisions of the Powers of Attorney Act 2003, s. 6(3) and Schedule 1. The plaintiff also appointed the defendant as her enduring guardian in 2008. He resigned both positions soon after the transfer in 2013.

[101] Conveyancing Act 1919 (NSW), s. 163F.

2014, the plaintiff was found to suffer from significant hearing and sight loss and dementia.

The only reason the transfer came to light was the fact that the plaintiff was in arrears to her aged care facility over AUD8,000, reflecting the fact that her social security payments were unable to cover her aged care costs. This shortfall resulted from the government department responsible for administering the welfare system having deemed the property a gift to her son, whereas a family home would otherwise be exempt from social security assessments. This prompted the manager of the facility to apply successfully for the appointment of a financial manager to the New South Wales Civil and Administrative Tribunal. The defendant was unresponsive to the Tribunal's investigations so it lodged a caveat on the title of the property, and proceeded to liquidate the property to satisfy the debt. The Supreme Court agreed that procedural justice such as notice had been afforded to the defendant. On the substantive point, the Court endorsed the Tribunal's actions. The reasons for this are as follows.

Hallen J examined the precedents, which mainly consider the same provisions and statutory form of the Conveyancing Act, albeit as applied to general, non-enduring powers. Quoting *Taheri* v. *Vitek*, Hallen J conceded that the terms of a contractual agreement between principal and agent ordinarily override the fiduciary duty for a representative to obtain informed consent before making a conflict transaction: 'An instrument ... may empower an attorney to do "anything" the principal may lawfully authorise an attorney to do, even if there is a benefit to the attorney and no benefit to the principal.'[102] Yet in *Cohen*, the plaintiff's argument was that despite this authority, 'by reason of the Power of Attorney, the Plaintiff's then condition and the Defendant's relationship with her, the Defendant, whilst authorised to transfer the property to himself, should not have done so' due to the continuing operation of the principal's fiduciary obligations.[103] The plaintiff cited *Ward* v. *Ward*, in which Brereton J made precisely this point: power or authority 'does not exonerate the attorney from fiduciary obligations by which an attorney under power is bound'. Hallen J also quoted at length *Spina* v. *Permanent Custodians Ltd*, in which Hammerschlag J explained why the agency relationship is a fiduciary one:

> An agent may be in a special position to exercise a power or discretion given to him by his principal to the detriment of the principal, who is

---

[102] *Taheri* v. *Vitek* [2014] NSWCA 209, para. [130] quoted in *Cohen*, para. [61].
[103] [2016] NSWSC 336, paras. [62]–[63].

accordingly vulnerable to abuse by his agent. For this reason equity
imposes on such an agent obligations or duties called fiduciary obligations
or duties which regulate the manner in which the agent may exercise
powers or discretions given by the principal.[104]

Fiduciary obligations are not, however, binary in nature: 'the scope
and extent of fiduciary obligations imposed will depend on the nature of
the relationship.'[105] As to the role a power of attorney instrument has on
defining this scope, Hammerschlag J quoted Mason J in *Hospital Products Ltd* v. *United States Surgical Corp* in reference to the comparable
situation where a fiduciary relationship springs from a contractual one:

> the terms of the contract will affect the scope and extent of the fiduciary
> obligations between the parties, not the other way round. The ambit of the
> authority conferred by a principal on an agent pursuant to a power of
> attorney is derived by properly construing the terms of the instrument in
> accordance with accepted canons of construction.[106]

Mason J extended this reasoning to powers of attorney: 'The terms of a
power of attorney will circumscribe the extent of the power.' Yet here,
too, Mason J draws a distinction between the scope of authority and the
question of how this is to be used: '[there is] an important difference
between lacking power and abusing it'.

Applying this distinction, in *Cohen*, Hallen J held that, despite the
broad authority in the instrument and express authorisation of conflict
transactions, the circumstances were such that it was an abuse of this
authority. Matters that contributed to this conclusion included the fact
that the property was the plaintiff's only property and the defendant
made no attempt to inform her of the transfer. Hallen J also noted that
the transfer placed the plaintiff in a position of significant disadvantage.

While *Cohen* is a valuable precedent in clarifying the relationship
between fiduciary principles and freedom of contract (and, by extension,
to enduring powers), it is not entirely helpful in sketching the fiduciary
limits of clauses in enduring documents that expressly permit conflict
transactions. There is perhaps the influence of a support paradigm in
Hallen J's criticism for not consulting the plaintiff. Yet *Cohen* suggests
that mild cognitive impairment combined with significant disadvantage
to the principal will likely attract fiduciary limitations on conflict

---

[104] [2008] NSWSC 561, paras. [113]–[121].
[105] citing *Kelly* v. *CA & L Bell Commodities Corporation Pty Limited* (1989) 18 NSWLR 248,
256–258.
[106] (1984) 156 CLR 41, 97.

transactions under a power of attorney, regardless of whether the impairment is significant enough to warrant activation of the enduring powers (under the former regime, the principal's 'unsoundness of mind'). This will often overlap with the existence of a 'special disadvantage' rendering the transaction also void for unconscionability (as held in *Cohen*) or increasingly undue influence irrespective of any threshold level of incapacity.[107]

At the heart of Mason J's somewhat artificial attempts to reconcile the plain language of instruments with fiduciary law through the concept of 'abuse of rights' is the vexed balance between protection and autonomy. A legal realist may be sceptical whether the principles applied in *Cohen* give much guidance beyond general notions of justice. Similarly, the earlier case of *Smith* v. *Glegg* was resolved by an equally artificial interpretation of a broad authorisation of conflict transactions: securing ownership of the principal's house through an attorney's undue influence could not be regarded as a decision 'on behalf of' the principal.[108] This evokes Mendelson's scepticism whether a substituted decision can ever be anything other than a subjective decision – often driven by self-interest – rather than a true decision made standing in the shoes of the principal: 'where there is a conflict of interests, the competent decision-maker may well – consciously or unconsciously – disregard such conflict when deciding that the incompetent person would have wished to consent or to refuse a particular treatment, including life-saving treatment'.[109]

In recognition of the limits of fiduciary law in regulating financial abuse, some jurisdictions, like the United Kingdom,[110] have codified principles relating to conflict transactions.[111] In Australia, the Victorian legislation is the most developed and provides as follows:

> 64. Conflict transactions
>
> (1) An attorney for financial matters under an enduring power of attorney has a duty not to enter into a transaction in that capacity

---

[107] See F. Burns, 'The Elderly and Undue Influence Inter Vivos' (2003) 23(2) *Legal Studies* 251; See also *Thorn* v. *Boyd* [2014] NSWSC 1159; *Trevenar* v. *Ussfeller* [2005] NSWSC 582; T. Cockburn, 'Elder Financial Abuse by Attorneys: Relief under Statute and in Equity' (June 2005) *Proctor* 22.

[108] *Smith* v. *Glegg* 2004 QSC 443 (McMurdo J).

[109] D. Mendelson, 'Substituted Consent: From Lunatics to Corpses' (2007) 14(4) *Journal of Law and Medicine* 458.

[110] Mental Capacity Act 2005 (UK), s. 12.

[111] Powers of Attorney Act 1998 (Qld), s. 73; Powers of Attorney Act 2014 (Vic), ss. 64, 65; and Powers of Attorney Act 2006 (ACT), s. 42.

if the transaction is one in which there is or may be a conflict
between –
(a) the duty of the attorney to the principal; and
(b) the interests of the attorney, or a relative, business associate or
    close friend of the attorney.

Subsection (2) provides exceptions for permitted gifts, the maintenance of dependants and transactions relating to property already held
jointly. Section 65 lists other exceptions. First, a principal may before-
hand authorise a transaction, the kind of transaction or conflict transactions generally.[112] While this should be interpreted to mean authorised at
a time when the principal had the capacity to understand this authorisation, this is not expressly stipulated. Conversely, capacity with regard to
the specific transaction is required for another exception whereby the
principal may validate an incomplete or completed transaction.[113] VCAT
may also provide the same authorisation or validation.[114]

Section 67 regulates gifts, including those to the representative or a
relative or close friend of the representative or an organisation with
whom the representative has a connection.[115] If there are no words of
limitation in the instrument, a representative may gift the principal's
property if

(1) (a) the gift is reasonable, having regard to all the circumstances and, in
        particular, the principal's financial circumstances; and
    (b) the gift is
        (i) to a relative or a close friend of the principal and is of a seasonal
            nature or for a special event, or
        (ii) a type of donation that the principal made when the principal had
             decision making capacity for the matter or that the principal might
             reasonably be expected to make.[116]

Other than the limiting words of section 67(1)(a), there is no limit on
the amount of a gift, but the representative must keep a written record if
the gift is a conflict transaction over AUD100.[117] The provisions
regarding 'supportive attorneys' are silent on gifts, stipulating only that
supportive attorney must 'avoid acting where there is or may be a conflict

---

[112] Powers of Attorney Act 2014 (Vic), s. 65(1).
[113] Ibid., ss. 65(2),(3).
[114] Ibid., ss. 65(4),(5).
[115] Ibid., ss. 67(1),(2).
[116] Ibid., s. 67(1).
[117] Ibid., s. 67(3), or any other future amount prescribed by regulations.

of interest and, if acting where there is a conflict of interest, must ensure that the interests of the principal are the primary consideration'.[118] Presumably, given the less invasive nature of this arrangement, the scope for altruistic acts such as gift giving is larger.

Queensland and ACT legislation have provisions prohibiting conflict transactions with some exceptions.[119] The Queensland legislation has similar gift-giving provisions as Victoria, albeit clarifying that the gift's value must be reasonable in the circumstances.[120] NSW legislation prohibits gifts and conflict transactions unless expressly provided, but also contains boilerplate clauses that provide default rules should a principal choose to authorise these in the enduring document.[121] For example, using the prescribed expression, 'reasonable living and medical expenses', a principal authorises benefits to representatives or third parties that relate to housing, food, education, transportation, medical care and medication.[122] For gifts, the prescribed expression authorises seasonal gifts to close friends and relatives, which do not explicitly include the representative.[123]

It is likely that fiduciary obligations, the concept of 'abuse of rights' in *Cohen* and other equitable rules on unconscionability, undue influence and the duty to act 'honestly and with reasonable diligence to protect the interests of the donor'[124] will continue to place supplementary limits on conflict transactions that a representative may otherwise legally undertake.[125] Indeed, these statutes do not purport to displace fiduciary duties.[126] Nor does codification dispense with the need for interpretation. Particularly where family is involved, there is a large area of uncertainty. In *Holt & Anor* v. *Protective Commissioner*, Kirby P observed that 'interrelated property interests in a family situation, where a conflict of interest may be "more apparent than real", should not necessarily present an absolute bar to appointment of a family member who is otherwise

---

[118] Ibid., s. 90.
[119] Powers of Attorney Act 1998 (Qld) s. 73; Powers of Attorney Act 2006 (ACT) ss. 38, 42.
[120] Powers of Attorney Act 1998 (Qld) s. 88.
[121] Powers of Attorney Act 2003 (NSW), ss. 11, 12; Schedule 3.
[122] Ibid., s. 12; Schedule 3.
[123] Ibid., s. 11; Schedule 3.
[124] See, for example, *Moylan* v. *Rickard* [2010] QSC 327, where this duty was codified in s. 66 of the Powers of Attorney Act 1998 (Qld).
[125] Some argue that this is the case unless fiduciary rules are displaced by statute: O'Neill and Peisah, *Capacity and the Law*, n 3, para. [10.6]. See also Australian Law Reform Commission, *Elder Abuse – A National Legal Response* , n 69, p. 173.
[126] Powers of Attorney Act 2003 (NSW), s. 11 indicates expressly that the section does not displace common law or equity.

appropriate'.[127] Young J in *Re R* also held that such conflicts of interest can be monitored and managed: 'it is a question of fact and degree as to whether in all the circumstances it is in the best interests of the incapable person that that situation continue'.[128] This apparent lenience was not consistently applied even under the pre-2003 broad boilerplate provisions authorising conflict transactions. In *Re MCQ*, the NSW Civil and Administrative Tribunal replaced an enduring attorney – the wife of the principal – with a financial manager on the basis of the conflict of interest (her own maintenance) and family conflict (with children of a former marriage of the principal).[129] The Tribunal preferred to appoint a financial manager with professional credentials as a chartered accountant, despite his own apparent conflict of interest as a family friend.

Nor do the stricter boilerplate provisions of the Powers of Attorney Act 2003 necessarily lead to stricter outcomes in family situations. As an example of this grey area, the NSW Civil and Administrative Tribunal in *ZBC* v. *ZBD* revoked an order by its Guardianship Division that an enduring power be replaced by a management order on the grounds that the enduring attorney had engaged in conflict transactions, which the enduring document had not authorised. The superior tribunal found that the Guardianship Division provided insufficient reasons for demonstrating the conflict, primarily an enduring attorney (an adult daughter) living rent-free in the principal's house while the principal, with dementia, resided in a nursing home. In particular, the lower tribunal did not consider the appellant's evidence that the premises were unlettable, that she had contributed to its maintenance, that her residence was temporary and that she did not obtain rental income from another property in which she could have lived. The Tribunal cited the principle in *Siahos & Anor* v. *J P Morgan Trust Australia Limited* that what constitutes a 'benefit' is itself a finding of fact.[130]

While it is impossible to eradicate all uncertainty, the Australian Law Reform Commission seeks to provide even greater clarity by recommending that conflict transactions be prohibited unless 'the principal foresaw the particular type of conflict and gave express authorisation in the enduring power of attorney document; or a tribunal has authorised the transaction before it is entered into'.[131] The Commission's view was

[127] *Holt & Anor* v. *Protective Commissioner* (1993) 31 NSWLR 227.
[128] [2000] NSWSC 886.
[129] [2014] NSWCATGD 29.
[130] [2009] NSWCA 20, paras. [24]–[25]
[131] Australian Law Reform Commission, *Elder Abuse: Discussion Paper No. 83*, n 72, proposal 5–6.

that an express prohibition on conflict of interest transactions without prior authorisation requires the autonomous principal to turn their mind ahead of time to what conflicts may occur and which are acceptable to them. In certain cases, the Commission contends, such as where a spouse is the representative, it may be appropriate for a principal to authorise all conflict transactions. The Commission also contends that the prohibition requires representatives to identify conflict transactions and manage them by either avoiding them or seeking tribunal permission. The Commission notes that specific authorisations of conflict transactions also protect the representative from accusations that their decisions are improper. Noting that gifts and donations constitute potential conflict transactions, the Commission advises that the scope of these be clearly specified in the enduring powers document and otherwise in type and nature guided by wishes or intent of the principle expressly stated in the document more generally. The Commission detected consensus among stakeholders for the requirement to regulate conflict transactions. It noted, however, that some submissions were concerned about a lack of understanding about conflicts of interest. To this end, the model national enduring document proposed by the Commission would include guidance on identifying and managing conflicts of interest. These recommendations recognise that even clear rules through codification have limits in alleviating the dilemma faced by courts in balancing protection and autonomy. The solution is preventative, requiring the parties themselves to plan for the future.

The NSW decision of *Smith* v. *Smith*[132] lends some weight to this argument. The plaintiffs sought an order that the defendant compensate a deceased estate for breaching her fiduciary duties as an attorney. The enduring document replaced an earlier document and deleted the boilerplate text authorising benefits to the attorney for 'reasonable living and medical expenses'. The Court duly interpreted the document to prohibit conflict transactions said by the plaintiff to be permitted by a separate authority to trade in shares[133] and ordered the defendant to return more than AUD1.5 million to the estate. Of course, as section 11 of the Act stipulates, a prohibition on conflicts and the equitable remedy in this case were possible without codification. The case does suggest, however, the utility to principals and their lawyers of a choice of 'prescribed powers' in template form. The case is also notable for the Court's interpretation, in obiter, of these prescribed powers (both gifting and benefits to self) as

[132] [2017] NSWSC 408.
[133] Ibid., para. [232].

'much more modest in their reach than the first defendant's assumption that she could deal with the deceased's property as her own', even had they been present as they were in the superseded enduring document.

Of course, as the case also demonstrates, the system relies on attorneys being guided by the legislation. There is still therefore a key role for courts and tribunals and regulatory bodies to monitor, compensate and punish abuses of enduring powers. Egregious cases that come to light may be prosecuted, such as in *R* v. *Naidu*,[134] a case in Queensland, where financial abuse amounted to the offence of fraud.[135] In these cases, like *Cohen*, abuse is detected when a public authority such as a tribunal or the Office of the Public Advocate investigates accumulating nursing home debt. Many cases will still go undetected, hence the importance of a national register of enduring powers – which, as previously discussed, has the potential to play a deterrent and monitoring function. To this end, reformers may wish to reconsider whether the register should be used to conduct random audits and be used as a means of screening capacity at the creation and activation stages of enduring powers as it in in Japan, for example.[136] Of course, lawyers and other professionals have a professional and reputational interest in playing a gatekeeper role too.[137]

While many cases will come to light through applications by interested parties for tribunal appointments to replace enduring attorneys, legislative provision for compensation is also a driver of legal accountability, particularly where a broad range of parties are given standing. In *Alcazar-Stevens* v. *Stevens*, the ACT Court of Appeal granted standing to a non-beneficiary to a deceased estate to apply for an order that the appellant compensate the estate, having – during the life of the deceased – contravened the conflict transactions provisions of the Powers of Attorney Act 2006 (ACT), in part because the validity of the will was also in question.[138] At the same time, expanded avenues for litigation bring risks of overzealous applicants and plaintiffs. A case in point is *Re NXO*, where an applicant's accusation that the enduring attorney, who was authorised to make reasonable gifts under NSW legislation, was funnelling large

---

[134] [2008] QCA 130.

[135] Criminal Code 1899 (QLD), s. 408C(1)(d).

[136] See T. Ryan, B. Arnold and W. Bonython, 'Protecting the Rights of Those with Dementia through Mandatory Registration of Enduring Powers? A Comparative Analysis' (2015) 36(2) *Adelaide Law Review* 355.

[137] L. Willmott and B. White, 'Solicitors and Enduring Documents: Current Practice and Best Practice' (2008) 16 *Journal of Law and Medicine* 466.

[138] [2017] ACTCA 12.

amounts of money to overseas relatives was not borne out by the evidence.[139] This might be remedied by public education about both the risks of financial abuse and also the rules that permit conflict transactions in some circumstances. Other reforms – such as the appointment of personal monitors, and the accounting and audits that registration may entail – might instil trust in the system.

As discussed earlier, some commentators are hesitant to subject volunteer enduring attorneys to the full range of monitoring that a register would allow.[140] The Commission's conclusion that there should first be grounds for an audit aligns with current practice. In *Re Sei*, the NSW Civil and Administrative Tribunal resisted a third party's demand for an enduring attorney to furnish accounts to the Tribunal due to an unfounded suspicion of abuse linked primarily to the authorisation to gift per se rather than any particular transaction: 'An attorney is not required to keep third parties informed of his or her decisions or provide information.' Citing an earlier authority of the NSW Supreme Court, the Tribunal observed that the attorney has a duty in common law to account to the principal only.[141] There is a problem with this reasoning if the principal does not have the capacity to request or understand these accounts. While random audits may have a deterrent effect and tribunal oversight is a powerful tool for discovery, a better means of detecting abuse is a default provision in the prescribed form for the appointment of a personal monitor, who may be in a better position to detect abuse through continuing informal contact with the parties and formal roles such as representing the principal as against the attorney (i.e., in transactions between the principal and representative or in litigation),[142] including a right to request accounts. This role could also be shared with others through mandatory reporting rules for lawyers, financial institutions, care institutions and other stakeholders who may be best placed to detect financial abuse.[143]

Providing templates or tribunal orders that allow for reasonable remuneration for the services of attorneys might be one way of preventing

---

[139] [2015] NSWCATGD 53.

[140] For example, Submission of Bruce Baer Arnold and Wendy Bonython to Australian Law Reform Commission, *Elder Abuse – A National Legal Response, Final Report*.

[141] *Susan Elizabeth Parker* v. *Margaret Catherine Higgins & Ors* [2012] NSWSC 1516 (Slattery J).

[142] This is the case in the Japanese system: A. Kobayashi and I. Otaka, *Understanding the New Adult Guardianship System (wakariyasui shin seinen kouken seido)* (Tokyo: Yuhikaku, 2000), p. 45.

[143] Cockburn, 'Elder Financial Abuse by Attorneys', n 107, 24.

'moral licensing', namely where the vice of self-dealing is justified by the virtue of volunteering for a potentially time-consuming and long-term commitment. At present, this is contrary to, for example, section 70 of the Victorian legislation, which does not permit remuneration unless specified in the enduring powers document.[144] Furthermore, despite the Commission's position against formal carers acting as attorneys, the flexibility of the courts over conflicts of interests by family members could be extended to non-family, remunerated attorneys. Invoking the 'social welfare' model of guardianship prevalent in the United States, Carney observes that permitting such arrangements can capitalise on the expertise of professional carers in sustaining those with dementia in the community rather than in aged care.[145] A former ALRC report notes that managers of institutions sometimes manage small amounts of money for residents, including pension payments and bills.[146] Indeed, Arai is just as concerned about conflicts of interest and potential for abuse from family-member enduring attorneys.[147] Perhaps non-family enduring attorneys can assist in breaking from the paternalism and entitlement that has plagued substitute decision-making in the past despite the added cost this brings. There are problems with commercialising a socially beneficial behaviour,[148] but many members of a generation of ageing investors may be able to bear this cost. Nor is the government and non-profit sector immune to scandal.[149] A compromise would be multiple representatives with a division of roles. A professional attorney or trustee such as a solicitor might be well suited to assess objectively the principal's intent to

---

[144] Supportive attorneys may not be remunerated: Powers of Attorney Act 2014 (Vic), s. 90 (2).

[145] T. Carney, 'Supported Decision-Making for People with Cognitive Impairments: An Australian Perspective?' (2015) 4(1) *Laws* 37, 48.

[146] Australian Law Reform Commission, *Guardianship and Management of Property: Report* (ALRC Report 52, 1989), para. [4.28].

[147] M. Arai, 'Present Situation and Issues Regarding the Adult Guardianship System (seinen kouken seido no genjou to kadai)' (2005) 58(6) *Houritsu no hiroba* 4.

[148] See K. Fukui, 'Can Commercial Guardianship and Asset Management Suffice? A Report on Victoria, Australia's State Trustees Company (seinen kouken zaisan kanri wa eiri jigyou tariuruka? Ousutoraria bikutoria shuu no State Trustees sha no chousa houkoku)' (2007) 28 *Shintaku kenkyuu shoureikin ronshuu* 110.

[149] See, e.g., K. Lawson, 'Two Public Trustee Staff Colluded with Contractors to Take $1.65 Million from Vulnerable Canberrans', *The Canberra Times*, 14 October 2014; N. Harmsen, 'ICAC Recommends Overhaul of SA's Public Trustee Office to Prevent Further Cases of Corruption' ABC, 26 September 2017, available from www.abc.net.au/news/2017-09-26/icac-recommends-overhaul-of-sa-public-trustee-office/8989976.

gift, whereas a family co-attorney might offset conflicts of interests of formal care providers.[150]

V   Conclusion

The most recent round of reforms to enduring powers of attorney to implement the support paradigm of the CRPD in Australia has coincided with widespread media attention on financial abuse of the elderly, who may have accumulated significant wealth over a period of sustained economic growth. Reformers have properly targeted transparency through registration and regulation of conflict transactions. The latter recognises that some financial abuse is committed by well-meaning family members and volunteers who are either ignorant of or disinterested in the legal complexities of conflict transactions such as gifts and other benefits. The analysis here of conflict transactions focusses attention on technical legal issues such as the relative merits of codification and equitable principles. Yet it also reveals deeper issues, such as the vexed and evolving balance between the values of autonomy and protection. This may, in an intuitive sense, have just as much impact on behaviour and legal outcomes as the doctrines and statutes that attempt to capture this balance in law.

---

[150] This is as aspect of the Japanese system: Kobayashi and Otaka, n 142.

8

Financial Planning Mechanisms Available to Persons with Special Needs in Singapore

TANG HANG WU[*]

I Introduction

A woefully underinvestigated area of the law is the management of property rights of persons with special needs. In this chapter, the term 'special needs' is defined widely to include people who are incapable of managing their daily financial affairs. The scope of people within this group may include persons with dementia, schizophrenia and intellectual disability as well as vulnerable elders. It should be noted that persons with special needs may have accumulated substantial property before becoming incapable of managing their financial affairs by reason of illness, old age or dementia. Alternatively, they could have inherited or stand to inherit property from their parents and caregivers. Such wealth places them in an extremely vulnerable position where they are potentially subject to financial abuse by rogues.

A preliminary objection might be raised with the terminology used in this chapter – i.e., 'special needs' to include vulnerable elders. It could be said that by grouping elders together with persons with special needs, this chapter is perpetuating stereotypical ageist assumptions of elders as being weak and incapable. While the author acknowledges that there is some force in this criticism, it should be made clear that the term 'special needs' used in this chapter is out of convenience and not disrespect. The

[*] Professor and Director of Centre for Cross-Border Commercial Law in Asia, School of Law, Singapore Management University. For purposes of full disclosure, I am a director of the Special Needs Trust Company, was a member of a subcommittee in the Office of the Public Guardian and have collaborated with the Pro Bono Services of Singapore's Law Society on the issue of persons with special needs. I am grateful to Julia Abrey, Esther Tan, Simone Wong, Tan Sook Yee, Geraldine Kuah, Kate Galloway, Chan Wing Cheong and Tan Choog Ing for their perceptive comments on earlier drafts. Thanks are also due to Carolyn Wee from NUS's CJ Koh Law Library and Elizabeth Naumczyk and Chai Yee Xin from SMU's Kwa Geok Choo Library for assistance in locating some of the material relied on in this chapter. The usual disclaimers apply and the views expressed are my own.

term is meant to include not all elderly people but only elders who are unable to manage their daily financial affairs. Also, there are two distinct advantages with using a wide definition of 'special needs' in this context. First, it is easier to persuade policymakers to tackle this problem if the class of persons under consideration is a wider cross section of society. Every member of society may become a person with special needs at some point of his or her lifetime. Thus, it would be easier to attract political support and public funding if various schemes were developed to cater to a larger class of persons. Furthermore, if the policymakers decide to do something about this issue, there is the benefit of economies of scale in devising a regime for a larger class of people to include elders who are unable to manage their daily financial affairs. The common feature of persons with special needs as defined in this chapter is their vulnerability to abuse by rogues with regard to their property. Second, the wide definition of 'special needs' highlights the urgency of the issues discussed in this chapter. The scale of the problem considered in this chapter cannot be overstated. With human beings having longer life spans, it is inevitable that most of us will one day become a person with special needs, as functional decline in old age is a common condition.[1] There will be a period of years during a person's life whereby the person will suffer from some disability. By 2030, people older than 60 years old in Singapore are expected to make up 25 per cent of the total population.[2] Such a rapidly ageing demographic is not unique to Singapore and is a global phenomenon found in many developed nations.[3] As Professor Wendy Lacey points out, 'the phenomenon of global ageing is that there is a corresponding increase in the number of older persons living in vulnerable and dependent circumstances, making them particularly vulnerable to abuse and neglect'.[4]

Drawing from the Singaporean experience, this chapter explores the financial planning mechanisms available for persons with special needs within the current framework of legislation and government and non-profit initiatives. Next, this chapter will consider several case studies

---

[1] R. Hébert, 'Functional Decline in Old Age', (1997) 157(8) *Canadian Medical Association Journal* 1037.

[2] L. Williams, K. Mehta and H. S. Lin, 'Intergenerational Influence in Singapore and Taiwan: The Role of the Elderly in Family Decisions' (1999) 14 *Journal of Cross-Cultural Gerontology* 291.

[3] W. Lacey, 'Neglectful to the Point of Cruelty? Elder Abuse and the Rights of Older Persons in Australia' (2014) 14 *Sydney Law Review* 99.

[4] Ibid.

whereby financial abuse is perpetrated on persons with special needs. Through this study, this chapter will highlight gaps in the law and in the pre-existing schemes where the needs of persons with special needs, with respect to their property ownership, are not served. The aims of this chapter are twofold. First, the descriptive account of the various schemes available in Singapore may provide a useful starting point to policy-makers and non-governmental organisations from other jurisdictions which do not have any such schemes catering for persons with special needs. While the Singapore system in this regard is far from perfect and definitely could be improved, there are other jurisdictions which have not begun to implement laws and schemes to help persons with special needs to manage their property. The second aim of the chapter is to fulfil an avowedly advocacy role; the chapter seeks to provoke a conversation on how societies can do better in enacting laws and implementing schemes to prevent the financial abuse of persons with special needs. It is hoped that this will, in turn, lead governments and non-profit organisations to set up new initiatives and laws to address this problem.

II   Laws and Schemes Governing Property Rights of Persons with Special Needs in Singapore

In order to understand Singapore's social welfare landscape, it is neces-sary to sketch out the government's philosophy in relation to designing social structures and policies in relation to social welfare. In Singapore, the government's overarching aim is to cultivate a culture of self-reliance.[5] Braema Mathi and Sharifah Mohamed succinctly describe the Singapore government's philosophy as follows:

> Securing a good job is the most effective way of ensuring one's needs are sustainably met. The family is the next layer of support, followed by the community and lastly, the government.[6]

In modern times, it has become difficult to apply this approach universally, especially with the Singaporean family becoming less extended over time. This difficulty is compounded by the fact that

---

[5] See B. Mahti and S. Mohamed, *Unmet Social Needs in Singapore: Singapore's Social Structures and Policies, and Their Impact on Six Vulnerable Communities* (Singapore: Lien Centre for Social Innovation, 2011), p. 26; I. Ng, 'Social Welfare in Singapore: Rediscovering Poverty and Reshaping' (2013) 23(1) *Asia Pacific Journal of Social Work* 35.
[6] Mahti and Mohamed, *Unmet Social Needs in Singapore*, ibid., p. 26.

modern families are smaller in size and less close to each other beyond the nuclear family. Furthermore, there is a sizeable single population in Singapore.[7] Therefore, it is unrealistic to expect relatives to be the main provider of social and financial support. Unsurprisingly, the government has increasingly been called on to provide more comprehensive support for social welfare.

With regard to the social infrastructure provided by the government, the government appears to refrain from being a direct provider of welfare services. Instead, the government enables, through capacity-building bodies,[8] and funds various Voluntary Welfare Organisations (VWOs) to provide welfare services. In other words, the government acts as the coordinator, facilitator and regulator of the providers of social services through such VWOs. The resultant effect of this approach is a complex network of providers of social services which is known as the 'Many Helping Hands Approach' to social welfare.[9] Thus, social services in Singapore are usually provided through a network of religious- or ethnic-based or non-religious VWOs.

A   The Mental Capacity Act

The Mental Capacity Act[10] passed in 2010 is the centrepiece legislation governing persons with special needs in Singapore. The new Act was largely borrowed from the Mental Capacity Act in England with some modifications and omissions. Prior to the Mental Capacity Act, matters were governed by the Mental Disorders and Treatment Act.[11] Under the old Act, a Committee of Person or Estate was appointed by the High Court to manage the personal welfare and financial matters of a person with 'unsound mind' and who were deemed to be incapable of managing their affairs. The drawbacks to this previous law were that the legislation

---

[7] G. W. Jones, Y. Zhang and P. Chia, 'Understanding High Levels of Singlehood in Singapore' (2012) 43(5) *Journal of Comparative Family Studies* 731.

[8] Examples of these organisations include the Community Chest, National Council of Social Services, Charity Council, Commissioner of Charities and the National Volunteer and Philanthropy Centre. See N. T. Tan, 'Regulating Philanthropy: The Legal and Accountability Framework for Singapore Charities' (2007) 17(1) *Asia Pacific Journal of Social Work and Development* 69.

[9] P. A. Rozario and A. L. Rosetti, '"Many Helping Hands": A Review and Analysis of Long-Term Care Policies, Programs, and Practices in Singapore' (2012) 55(7) *Journal of Gerontological Social Work* 641.

[10] Cap. 177A, 2010 Revised Edition.

[11] Cap. 178, 1985 Revised Edition.

only allowed for the appointment of the Committee of Person or Estate after the individual person had lost his or her mental capacity. Thus, a person could not plan his or her affairs in advance. Singapore's Mental Capacity Act changes this position and allows pre-planning by introducing the lasting power of attorney, which may be executed by a person before he or she loses mental capacity. Furthermore, the old Act relies on the archaic concept of a person of 'unsound mind', which is totally out of line with modern medical views of mental capacity.

Like its English counterparts, Singapore's Mental Capacity Act sets out the following guiding principles in assessing mental capacity and assisting individuals who are adjudged to have lost it.[12] First, a person must be assumed to have capacity unless it is established that he or she lacks capacity. Second, a person is not treated as unable to make a decision unless all practicable steps to help him or her to do so have been taken without success. Third, a person is not to be treated as unable to make a decision merely because he or she makes an unwise decision. Fourth, any act or decision for and on behalf of a person who lacks capacity must be done in his or her best interests.[13] Finally, before an act is done or a decision is made, regard must be had to whether the purpose for which it is needed can be as effectively achieved in a way that is less restrictive of the person's rights and freedom of action.

The Mental Capacity Act envisages that a person (P' would make a lasting power of attorney before he or she loses capacity conferring certain powers on another called the donee(s). The donee may be appointed to act on behalf of P with respect to P's personal welfare and/or P's property and affairs. Under orthodox agency law, a power of attorney usually comes to an end when the principal loses capacity.

---

[12] See Mental Capacity Act (Cap. 177A, 2010 Revised Edition), s. 3. See also S. Menon, 'The Mental Capacity Act: Implications for Patients and Doctors Faced with Difficult Choices' (2013) 42 *Annals of the Academy of Medicine Singapore* 200.

[13] There is uncertainty as to whether Singapore's Mental Capacity Act is consistent with article 12 of the United Nation Convention on the Rights of Persons with Disabilities. The Singapore Government's position is that the Mental Capacity Act is compliant with the Convention. See Committee on the Rights of Persons with Disabilities, *Implementation of the Convention on the Rights of Persons with Disabilities: Initial Report Submitted by States Parties under Article 35 of the Convention – Singapore* (Report No. CRPD/C/SGP/1, 2016), pp. 45–47, available from https://tbinternet.ohchr.org. However, this view is contentious given that the Mental Capacity Act operates on a substituted decision making model instead of a supported decision making model. See generally P. Bartlett, 'The United Nations Convention on the Rights of Persons with Disabilities and Mental Health Law' (2018) 75 *MLR* 752.

However, a lasting power of attorney under the Mental Capacity Act is unique because the power of attorney will only operate when the principal loses capacity.[14] As Jennifer Rhein pointedly observed:

> In the hands of the wrong person . . . a durable power of attorney can be a weapon used to financially abuse elders by stripping them of their life savings.[15]

Therefore, there are onerous formalities associated with the signing of a lasting power of attorney meant to prevent fraud. The creation of a valid lasting power of attorney under the Mental Capacity Act is a two-stage process. First, the instrument must be completed in a form complying with certain prescribed formalities. Crucially, a valid lasting power of attorney must be accompanied with a certificate provided by an accredited medical practitioner or a psychiatrist or a practicing lawyer that the donor understands the scope and purpose of the authority conferred and that no fraud or undue pressure was used to induce the creation of the lasting power of attorney. Second, once the lasting power of attorney is completed, it must be registered.

For individuals who have not made a lasting power of attorney, the process becomes more complicated when such individuals lose capacity. A deputy has to be appointed to act for P. An application must be made to court whereby the court may make a decision on P's behalf in relation to matters or appoint another person called a deputy to make decisions on P's behalf.[16] This process also applies to a person with congenital disabilities who lacks mental capacity from the onset. Between the period of 1 April 2015 to March 2016, there were 8,478 lasting power of attorney applications and 263 court orders for deputies.[17]

In order to oversee donees and deputies, the Mental Capacity Act created a position in the form of an officer known as the Public Guardian. The Public Guardian has inter alia the following functions: (a) establishing and maintaining a register of lasting powers of attorney; (b) establishing and maintaining a register of orders appointing deputies; (c) supervising deputies appointed by the court; (d) dealing with

---

[14] See Mental Capacity Act (Cap. 177A, 2010 Revised Edition), s. 13.

[15] J. L. Rhein, 'No One in Charge: Durable Powers of Attorney and the Failure to Protect Incapacitated Principals' (2009) 17 *Elder Law Journal* 165, 165.

[16] For an extremely contentious application to appoint a deputy, see *Re BKR* [2013] 4 SLR 1257.

[17] Office of Public Guardian, *2015/2016 Annual Report of the Office of Public Guardian* (Singapore: Office of Public Guardian, 2016), pp. 18, 21 (on file with the author).

representations including complaints about the way a donee or a deputy is exercising his or her powers; and (e) investigating any contravention of the Mental Capacity Act. The Mental Capacity Act presupposes that a Public Guardian may apply to court for the exercise of any of its powers under the Mental Capacity Act in situations where (a) a person lacks capacity; (b) no application has been made or is likely to be made for an order under the Mental Capacity Act; and (c) such an order is necessary for the protection of the personal welfare, property or affairs of the person.[18] In addition to this, the Office of the Public Guardian publishes a Code of Practice which is now in its third edition to provide further guidelines and illustrations on the implementation of the Mental Capacity Act.

Singapore's Mental Capacity Act is a work in progress. In 2016, the Mental Capacity Act was further amended to provide for the creation of professional donees and deputies. These new amendments allow those without family or close friends who can act as donees and deputies to engage paid professionals to exercise that duty. Prior to the amendments, there was a small number of lawyers who acted on a pro bono basis as panel deputies for persons without anyone willing to act as deputies.[19] The amendments envisaged creating a new market for professional deputies and donees. In terms of regulations, the professional deputies must be registered with the Public Guardian and must satisfy the Public Guardian's prescribed criteria. Many of the minutiae of the regulation are still currently being considered and worked out by the Public Guardian and not released to the public. Curiously, professional donees are not so tightly regulated by the Public Guardian. One might speculate the reason for this omission is that professional donees, unlike professional deputies, are chosen by the person before he or she loses capacity, and there is less need for regulation in this sphere. The reasoning seems to be based on the assumption that it is for the person to assess the reliability of the professional donee before appointment, and it is not for the Public Guardian to interfere with a person's freedom of choice. If this is indeed the rationale, then it is respectfully suggested that a reconsideration of the omission is due by the legislators and policymakers.[20] Both professional

---

[18] See Mental Capacity Act (Cap. 177A, 2010 Revised Edition), s. 38(1)(e). See also Office of Public Guardian, *2015/2016 Annual Report*, ibid., p. 26.

[19] Office of Public Guardian, *2015/2016 Annual Report*, ibid., p. 17.

[20] This point was also made by T. Tan, 'More Checks Needed on Professionals Who Decide for the Mentally Incapable', *The Straits Times*, 7 June 2018, available on Factiva.

deputies and professional donees ought to be regulated in the same manner by the Public Guardian. Free market forces cannot properly regulate the contract between members of the public and professional donees because of the unique vulnerability of former. When a person loses capacity, he or she will not be able to protect himself or herself vis-à-vis the professional donees. The idea of freedom of contract is lost when the client loses capacity, especially when it comes to revision of the fees payable. It is conceivable that an unscrupulous professional donee might financially exploit a person who loses mental capacity by charging exorbitant professional fees by way of a unilateral revision of the contract. Without the benefit of regulatory oversight, there will be no one to prevent such financial abuse. It is hoped that legislation would move to plug this loophole before any such financial abuse occurs. However, it should be pointed out that there is room even in the current statute to provide for some safeguards against financial abuse. Under the current statute, a professional donee is defined as 'a professional deputy or is within a class of persons prescribed as qualified to be a professional donee'.[21] In the Parliamentary debates, the then Minister for Social and Family Affairs, Mr Tan Chuan Jin, said that it is envisaged that prescribed donees will be licensed trust companies.[22] As a matter of background, licensed trust companies are regulated by the Monetary Authority of Singapore. If this is carried through in the subsidiary legislation, then this might minimise the danger of financial abuse since it is hoped that licensed trust companies will not engage in financial abuse.

The other area of amendment to the Mental Capacity Act is the conferment of wide powers on the court to revoke a lasting power of attorney. This is in response to a case of a well-known abuse of a lasting power of attorney in Singapore.[23] The court is now given the power to revoke the lasting power of attorney in respect of all or such of the matters to which the lasting power of attorney relates as the court thinks fit.[24] This provision allows the court to pre-emptively revoke or suspend the authority of donees even before the conclusion of legal proceedings against donees. For example, if a donee is charged with a crime involving

---

[21] Mental Capacity Act (Cap. 177A, 2010 Revised Edition), s. 2.

[22] Speech of Minister of Family and Social Affairs, Mr Tan Chuan Jin in the Second Reading of the Mental Capacity (Amendment) Bill, Vol. 94, 14 March 2016.

[23] This case has spawned many newspaper articles and case law. See *TDA* v. *TCZ* [2016] 3 SLR 329; *Public Prosecutor* v. *Yang Yin* [2015] 2 SLR 78; *Chung Kin Chun K* v. *Yang Yin* [2015] 5 SLR 467.

[24] Mental Capacity Act (Cap. 177A, 2010 Revised Edition), s. 17(5A).

fraud or dishonesty, a court may suspend the lasting power of attorney even before the conclusion of the criminal trial.

B   Special Needs Trust Company

One of the major innovations in Singapore in managing the property of persons with special needs is the incorporation of the non-profit Special Needs Trust Company (SNTC) in 2009.[25] The idea for this scheme was first floated by the Movement for the Intellectually Disabled of Singapore; parents with children with special needs were worried that money entrusted to relatives for the care of their children might be frittered away when they are no longer around. As a parent puts it:

> When it comes to money, it is tricky. If I die and will my money to a relative to take care of my daughter, what happens if they fail to do so? You can't depend on people, as people may change.[26]

While a trust for the benefit of persons with special needs may be set up with a professional trustee, the cost of setting up and maintaining such a trust is frequently prohibitive. Typically, a professional trustee will not accept a trust where the assets are less than SGD2 million.[27]

In this regard, this scheme is able to plug the gap for those who cannot afford the services of a professional trustee. SNTC charges minimal fees because it is funded by the government, and its schemes are heavily subsidized.[28] The following table lists the fees chargeable as of 6 August 2018 in Singapore dollars.

SNTC Type of Fees	Fee before Subsidy	Subsidy by MSF(%)	Fee after Subsidy
One-time Setup	1,500	90	150
Annual Preactivation	250	100	0
One-time Activation	400	90	40
Annual Post-Activation	400	90	40

[25] T. Tan, 'Govt-Backed Trust to Help Care for Children with Disabilities', *The Straits Times*, 30 October 2009, available on Factiva.

[26] Ibid.

[27] M. Ng, 'Planning for an Uncertain Future', *The Straits Times*, 13 November 2011, available on Factiva.

[28] J. Tai, 'Govt Subsidy for Trusts for Special Needs Kids', *The Straits Times*, 14 June 2013, available on Factiva.

It is important to note that SNTC only handles cash assets. How does it work? The basic idea is that the parents will develop a care plan and letter of intent before settling a trust account with SNTC. Money settled into the trust account would be deposited with the Public Trustee who will manage the fund. The Public Trustee's Office is a pre-existing office created by statute.[29] Hence, SNTC does not manage the investment aspects of the trust fund. When the parents are no longer around, the trust is then activated. In the care plan and letter of intent, the parents would have stipulated how the money ought to be disbursed. For example, SNTC would disburse stipulated sums to the caregiver of persons with special needs, fees for their home (if they are staying in a home) and perhaps a monthly stipend to the persons with special needs if they are high-functioning individuals. Of course, the letter of intent is stated to be non-binding on SNTC, and SNTC is able to depart from the letter of intent if it is in the beneficiary's best interest to do so.[30] An illustration of this would be if the beneficiary requires funds for a medical emergency which is not provided in the letter of intent. In these circumstances, SNTC may depart from the letter of intent if SNTC is of the opinion that such medical treatment is in the best interest of the beneficiary. The scheme is represented pictorially in Figure 8.1.

Legally, this structure is easily achieved through settling a fixed trust where the person with special needs is named as the life beneficiary of the trust. With regard to potential surplus of the trust fund, the settlor would name people to whom the surplus funds are to be distributed after the life beneficiary passes on. It is made clear in the trust deed that the persons entitled to the surplus are not regarded as beneficiaries of the trust. This alleviates SNTC from the burden of having to manage the trust fund while balancing the interest of a life interest and remainderman. Also, by stating explicitly that the funds are to be placed with the Public Trustee, SNTC is also freed from the tricky task of managing the investment of trust assets, especially in a volatile and complex financial environment. These points are important because they lessen SNTC's litigation risk.

As a matter of planning, there is no need for the parents to settle all their assets into the trust from the onset. After settling a trust with SNTC,

---

[29] Public's Trustee Act (Cap. 260, 1985 Revised Edition). See also Sir E. J. Trevelyan, 'The Public Trustee in India, New Zealand, Australia, and England' (1916) *Journal of the Society of Comparative Legislation* 100.

[30] The letter of intent is similar to a letter of wishes. On letter of wishes, see *Breakspear v. Ackland* [2008] EWHC 220 (Ch), [2009] ch 32.

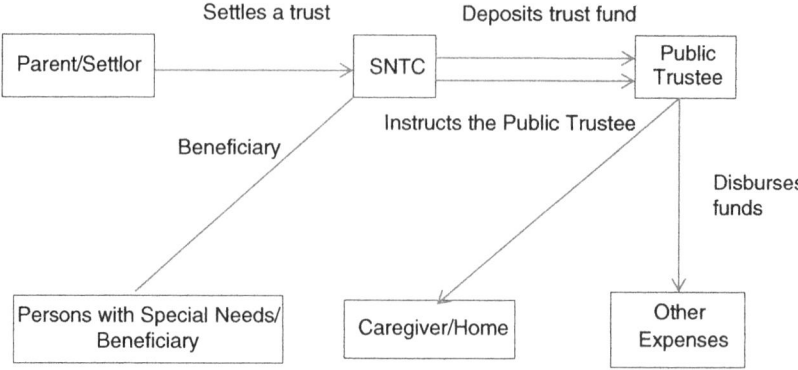

Figure 8.1 Special Needs Trust Company Scheme

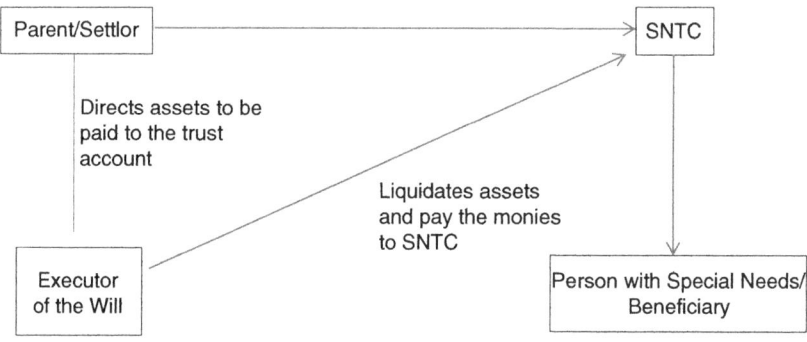

Figure 8.2 Using the Special Needs Trust Company

the parents may provide the necessary bequest by will to the relevant trust account. It is envisaged that the executor of the will would then liquidate the assets and pay the money to SNTC on the parent's demise. Thus, the parents may use and invest their assets during their lifetime and yet have peace of mind that their dependent with special needs would be protected financially when they are no longer around. An example of how the special needs trust may be used is represented pictorially in Figure 8.2.

It is interesting how parents are beginning to use the special needs trust to plan for the future of their dependents. The case of Sarah-Jane Joseph provides a noteworthy illustration.[31] Sarah-Jane has autism, and

---

[31] M. Ng, 'Planning for an Uncertain Future', n 27.

her primary caregiver is a Filipino domestic housekeeper, Mailyn Dulay, who has been taking care of her since she was a baby. Sarah-Jane's father, Dr Sunil Joseph, is a medical practitioner and a single father. Dr Joseph purchased several insurance policies and is the owner of a Housing and Development Board (HDB)[32] flat. Dr Joseph settled a special needs trust for Sarah-Jane because he wanted SNTC to receive the insurance pay out and the proceeds of sales from his properties for the benefit of Sarah-Jane. While Dr Joseph is comfortable financially, he does not have SGD2 million typically required by professional trustees. Dr Joseph's hope is that Ms Dulay would be able to continue caring for Sarah-Jane should something happen to him. Dr Joseph was reported to have told Ms Dulay that '[t]here will be enough money to pay you for the next 30 years. So I hope you can take care of her'.[33] Anecdotally, parents with more than one child are also using the special needs trust. The case of David Tan provides such an example. David is a teenager with Down's syndrome. David has an older brother, Daniel. David's father, Mr Tan Beng San, settled a trust with SNTC to relieve David's eventual caregiver from having to manage a large sum of money. Mr Tan Beng San was reported as saying: 'Let's say I leave $500,000 for David, and I appoint my sister or my older son, Daniel, to take care of him. What should they do with the money? It is a big responsibility.'[34] Mr Tan was mindful that Daniel would have to live his own life.

C   Special Needs Savings Scheme

Another scheme which caters to the special needs community is the Special Needs Savings Scheme (SNSS).[35] The SNSS was developed by the Ministry of Social and Family Development in partnership with the Central Provident Fund Board (CFPB) to enable parents to set aside Central Provident Fund (CPF) savings for the long-term care of children with special needs. Under the SNSS, parents may nominate their children with special needs to receive a regular stream of income upon the parent's demise. The CPF is the predominant form of compulsory

---

[32] This is the predominant public housing scheme in Singapore.

[33] M. Ng, 'Planning for an Uncertain Future', n 27.

[34] M. Ng, 'Trust in Planning for a Rainy Day', *The Straits Times*, 13 November 2011, available on Factiva. See also C. Tilse et al., 'Minding the Money: A Growing Responsibility for Informal Carers' (2005) 25 *Ageing and Society* 215.

[35] Editorial, 'Savings Scheme Starts Today', *The Straits Times*, 6 February 2012, available on Factiva.

retirement fund in Singapore. Under the CPF scheme, it is mandatory for the employer to pay a certain percentage of the employee's salary to the CPF. This sum comprises two legally prescribed percentages representing (a) a contribution from the employer, and (b) a form of compulsory savings by the employee. Save for certain exceptions, the CPF fund cannot be drawn down by the employee until he or she reaches the age of retirement.

How does the SNSS work?

- At the point of nomination, parents can decide the amount of monthly payouts.
- Without the SNSS nomination, a deceased person's CPF savings are distributed to their nominated beneficiaries as a once-off lump sum payment.
- At the point of SNSS nomination, the nominating parent determines the payouts the child with special needs will receive upon their demise.

When the parent passes away, the nominated person with special needs who qualifies for SNSS will receive these predetermined monthly payouts until the deceased parent's savings are exhausted.

In short, the SNSS is seen to complement SNTC as it serves parents with modest savings, i.e., parents who only have their retirement fund as their main asset. Some parents believe that it is better for the special needs person to get a fixed amount to live by rather than have access to all the CPF monies, which may be squandered away.[36] Furthermore, the SNSS scheme is attractive because the interest paid on CPF monies has traditionally been higher than the interest paid out by the Public Trustee.

D   Adult Protection Team, Adult Protective Service and Community Kin Service

In Singapore, there is an Adult Protection Team which considers cases of elder abuse, including financial abuse. The Adult Protection Team comprises professionals from geriatrics, psychiatry, psychology, occupational therapy, social work and law and is situated at several Family Service Centres such as the Trans Family Services. Originally convened as the Elder Protection Team by the Ministry of Community Development, Youth and Sports in 2003, the Adult Protection Team meets every month

---

[36] J. Tai, 'Special-Needs Kids Plan: 98 Sign Up: Children Get Monthly Payout from CPF after Parents' Death', *The Straits Times*, 4 May 2012, available on Factiva.

to discuss all cases referred to it by social workers.[37] The Adult Protection Team does not have any statutory powers and works with the police, public authorities and various VWOs to resolve problems of elder abuse. The government is also in the process of introducing a Vulnerable Adults Act. An Adult Protective Service has also been formed by the Ministry of Social and Family Development. However, it is interesting that the current definition of 'abuse' under the Vulnerable Adults Act does not include financial abuse. Therefore, it is unlikely that the Adult Protective Services will investigate matters of financial abuse. The Ministry of Social and Family Development has also introduced the Community Kin Service pilot project where social workers with VWOs may apply to court to manage the finances of seniors under their care.[38] This scheme is meant to cater for elders who do not have family support and are declining in their abilities to take care of themselves. The scheme is meant for social workers to assist the elders to make regular payments for their healthcare needs and household expenses. The VWOs involved in this scheme will come under the supervision of the Office of Public Guardian.

III   Four Case Studies of Financial Abuse of Persons with Special Needs

Having set out the framework of how the property of persons with special needs may be managed in Singapore, this part considers four case studies of financial abuse of persons with special needs. These case studies highlight the manner in which rogues might take advantage of persons with special needs. In other words, a close examination of these cases will reveal how financial abuse is perpetrated on persons with special needs in Singapore. More importantly, these case studies will reveal the modus operandi of the fraudsters. Hence, a close analysis of the cases will be useful in highlighting the gaps and weaknesses of the various laws and schemes. Due to the fact that financial abuse is often an

---

[37] Trans Family Service Centre, *2011 Annual Report of Trans Family Service Centre*, found at www.transfamilyservices.org.sg/pdf/AR2011.pdf.

[38] Y. C. Toh, 'New Scheme to Allow Social Workers to Manage Finances for Mentally Incapacitated Seniors under Their Care', *The Straits Times*, 29 November 2017, available on Factiva.

unreported and invisible problem,[39] some of these cases are drawn from anecdotal stories told to the author in his work as a director of a non-profit company.[40]

A   The Case of Madam Chiang and Her Lawyer, James Wan ('Madam Chiang's Case')

Madam Chiang became the owner of 18 Maria Avenue, Singapore, in 1961.[41] Years later, she was found wandering in the streets aimlessly in a schizophrenic state. As a result, she was admitted to a home for the aged ('the home') in 1980. In 1999, the Singapore Land Registry managed to track Madam Chiang down because the Registry was converting the land from the deeds system to the Torrens system. The superintendent of the home where Madam Chiang stayed asked his church mate, a lawyer called James Wan, to act for Madam Chiang. By now, Madam Chiang's house was occupied by unauthorised occupiers who initially intended to claim adverse possession against Madam Chiang. Wan managed to evict the unauthorised occupiers.

Wan then got Madam Chiang to sign a power of attorney giving him the authority to manage her affairs even though Madam Chiang had children. A will was also executed by Madam Chiang naming Wan as the sole beneficiary and excluding Madam Chiang's children from any inheritance. Wan got Madam Chiang to sign documents, which enabled him to sell her property in 2002. Madam Chiang also signed a letter drafted by Wan that she only wished to keep SGD500,000 from the sale proceeds, and Wan could keep the excess of the sale price. As a result, Wan pocketed SGD460,000 from the sale price of SGD960,000. All this came to light in 2009, when the Auditor General's Office audited the books of the home and found that Madam Chiang only received SGD500,000. This led the Law Society to begin disciplinary proceedings against Wan, and he was eventually disbarred.

---

[39] W. C. Chan, 'Protect the Elderly from Financial Abuse', *The Straits Times*, 29 August 2012, available on Factiva.

[40] Save for cases reported in the law reports or media, the names in the case studies are changed.

[41] The facts of the case is found in the decision of *Law Society of Singapore* v. *Wan Hui Hong James* [2013] 3 SLR 221.

B The Case of Mr Chan and His Property Agent, Terence Yan ('Mr Chan's Case')

Mr Chan was 89 years old, was confined to a wheelchair, was blind in one eye and had poor vision in the remaining eye.[42] He lived with his intellectually disabled daughter, Siu Lin, who was in her 60s, and his Indonesian helper, Ms Sarina. Mr Chan got to know a property agent, Terence Yan, and they became friends. Terence would occasionally give car rides to Mr Chan and Siu Lin to the hospital for their medical check-ups. Subsequently, Mr Chan asked Terence to sell his flat and help him buy a smaller flat nearby. Terence helped Mr Chan buy a smaller flat, and Mr Chan paid Terence 7 per cent of the purchase price as commission.[43] Mr Chan bought the smaller flat in cash without a bank loan. Terence was subsequently charged for criminal misappropriation of SGD559,000 belonging to Mr Chan.

The alleged criminal offence came to light when Mr Chan's bank detected irregularity in Mr Chan's signature on a SGD200,000 cheque issued by Mr Chan to Terence. Upon reviewing Mr Chan's account, the bank discovered another cheque of SGD150,000 which was issued by Mr Chan to Terence. The bank's representative, Mr Simon Quek, visited Mr Chan to discuss these payments. After the meeting, Mr Chan gave the bank the go-ahead to call the police. During his trial, Terence's defence was that Mr Chan gave him the money as a reward for his work. Terence also claimed that he had lost all the money in the casino. At trial, there was some evidence that Terence asked Ms Sarina to request SGD50,000 from Mr Chan on the pretext that her elder brother in Indonesia was ill and that her house in Indonesia was damaged. Ms Sarina told Mr Chan that she would go home and not take care of Siu Lin unless she got the money. Mr Chan gave Ms Sarina the money. In turn, Ms Sarina passed the money to Terence. Terence promised Ms Sarina a job.

---

[42] E. Chong, 'Ex-Housing Agent Denies Taking $559k from Client', *The Straits Times*, 5 February 2014, available on Factiva; E. Chong, 'Maid Says Employer's Property Agent Offered Her Job and Money to Be His Witness', *The Straits Times*, 27 February 2014, available on Factiva; E. Chong, 'Ex-Property Agent Gambled Away over $500,000 of Client's Money', *The Straits Times*, 12 April 2014, available on Factiva.

[43] This is an unusually large commission in the context of Singaporean real estate practice.

C   The Case of Choo Seng and His friend, Beng ('Choo Seng's Case')

Choo Seng is a high-functioning person with special needs, and he works at a fast-food restaurant.[44] He lives with his single mother, Madam Lim, who works as a secretary. Madam Lim is not close to any of her relatives and often worries what will happen to Choo Seng when she is not around. Madam Lim asked her church friend, Mary, to be the executor of her will. One day, Madam Lim passed away quite suddenly due to a stroke. When Mary began to administer the estate, she discovered that Choo Seng had a joint bank account with Madam Lim where Madam Lim deposited her life savings. Before Madam Lim passed away, there was SGD200,000 in the bank account. The bank account is now depleted. When Mary asked Choo Seng what happened to the money, Choo Seng told Mary that his good friend, Robert, had asked him to withdraw SGD2,000 from the account every day. Choo Seng gave the money to Robert because Robert showered Choo Seng with gifts.

D   The Case of Ali Who Is Abandoned ('Ali's Case')

Ali is an elderly widower who lives alone in his Housing and Development Board flat. He has three estranged children.[45] One day, he suffered a bad fall in his flat and could not get up. Ali was discovered by his neighbour after two days. Upon admission to the hospital, Ali was found to have lost mental capacity. The social workers working on Ali's case discovered that he has SGD50,000 in his bank account. While Ali was in the hospital, squatters took possession of the flat and caused a nuisance to his neighbours. The Housing and Development Board is threatening to re-enter the flat due to Ali's non-occupation of the flat.[46] In the meantime, the hospital is keen to discharge Ali into a nursing home because the hospital is facing a severe bed crunch. However, the nursing home is unwilling to admit Ali because there is no way to secure the nursing home's fees. Ali's children do not want to have anything to do with their father.

---

[44] This case is based on an anecdotal story related to the author. The names of the parties are fictitious, and the details of the facts have been changed slightly.

[45] This case is based on an anecdotal story related to the author. The names of the parties are fictitious, and the details of the facts have been changed slightly.

[46] The Housing and Development Board has very wide powers of re-entry, which includes non-occupation of the flat. See, for example, Housing and Development Act (Cap. 129, 2004 Revised Edition), s. 56.

IV   Unpacking the Problem: Plugging the Gaps

Looking at the case studies, the following points may be made about property rights of persons with special needs:

(a) Persons with special needs are particularly vulnerable to financial abuse when they have valuable assets or stand to inherit substantial assets.

(b) The vulnerability to abuse is compounded when real property is involved. Since real property is worth a lot of money, especially in land-scarce Singapore, there are fraudsters who will scheme to sell their property and pocket the sale proceeds.

(c) A power of attorney may be used by rogues to perpetrate financial abuse. A reported modus operandi is the rogue procuring the person with special needs to sign a power of attorney conferring on the rogue extremely wide powers. This power of attorney enables the rogue to sell the property.

(d) In cases where the person with special needs is no longer living in his or her real property, it is likely that trespassers would have taken over the property. If the property is a HDB flat, HDB might invoke or threaten to invoke its right to compulsorily acquire the property.

(e) Some persons with special needs are stuck in 'no man's land'. They might have assets, but these assets cannot be liquidated to pay for their care because there is no one ready, willing and able to liquidate the assets.

(f) Persons with special needs might have relatives, but these relatives may not be willing to help them. As illustrated in Ali's case, some of them may have estranged children or a spouse. This complicates matters for social workers because any action concerning the person with special needs would require consent from his or her immediate family members who are not willing to step forward.

(g) Persons with special needs depend on the goodwill of people around them – e.g., friends, lawyers, social workers, bank managers, real estate agents, domestic helpers, etc. However, some of these people behave in an unscrupulous manner and hatch audacious schemes to cheat them of their property. For example, in Madam Chiang's case, the lawyer, James Wan, was the rogue who cheated Madam Chiang. In Mr Chan's case, the alleged perpetrator of the fraud was Mr Chan's real estate agent acting in concert with Mr Chan's long-time domestic helper, Ms Sarina. And in Choo Seng's case, it was his 'friend' Robert who took advantage of Choo Seng.

(h) Even though there are many unscrupulous professionals, financial abuse is often uncovered by other professionals who go out of their way when they notice that something has gone awry. In Mr Chan's case, the fraud was uncovered because the bank manager, Mr Simon Quek, had taken the trouble to visit him and asked him about the large payments to the alleged fraudsters. The fraud in Madam Chiang's case was exposed after the Accountant General's Office had taken a close look at the home's accounts.

Many of the case studies discussed occurred prior to the enactment of the Mental Capacity Act and the formation of the Special Needs Trust Company. In order to minimise financial abuse, it is critical that carers of persons with special needs embark on careful pre-planning. It is important to appoint trustworthy persons to act as a deputy for the persons with special needs. Also, the underlying philosophy of pre-planning is to put in place requisite checks and balances, especially when bequeathing large sums of money or property to persons with special needs. For example, if the carer is setting up a private trust for the benefit of a person with special needs whereby the carer intends to use relatives as trustees, it would be better to designate at least two persons as trustees. For good measure, the carer may also consider appointing another relative as a protector of the trust. A clause stipulating that any real property held on trust may not be sold unless an order of court is obtained would also make it harder for financial abuse to be perpetrated. In a situation whereby a person is planning for the day in which he or she may become a person with special needs in future due to old age, it is imperative that the person makes a lasting power of attorney pursuant to the Mental Capacity Act naming donee(s) who may act on his or her behalf. As a matter of prudence, it is better to have more than one donee in a lasting power of attorney. In addition, it would be wise to settle a Special Needs Trust with respect to cash assets. With regard to real property, it would be better not to grant the donees the power to sell, charge or mortgage real property without an order of court.

However, even with the most careful pre-planning, more can be done to strengthen the pre-existing legislation and schemes to prevent financial abuse. The time has come to seriously consider implementing some form of mandatory reporting of suspected financial abuse of persons with special needs.[47] Such mandatory reporting ought to apply to

---

[47] Otherwise, some professionals might struggle with reporting of suspected abuse to the authorities. See R. Landau, 'Ethical Dilemmas in Treating Cases of Abuse of Older People in the Family' (1998) 12(3) *International Journal of Law, Policy and the Family* 345.

professionals such as bankers, lawyers and real estate agents because most financial abuse of persons with special needs often involves these professionals. If professionals are under a mandatory obligation to report suspected financial abuse, the relevant authorities could thwart schemes to cheat persons with special needs of their property. As an author observed in the context of elder abuse:

> The characteristics of exploitation suggest why banks could play a crucial role in combating this very prevalent financial abuse. It is often difficult for the victim to recognize that financial abuse has occurred; they are unlikely to report the abuse, and are generally confused – they need help to protect themselves (sometimes even from themselves). Banks often play a central role when the assets of an elderly person are targeted, so they are a first line of defense in protecting elders from financial abuse. Prevention of financial abuse and prevention of pollution have a striking similarity: just as pollution is best nipped at the point of production, so is much financial abuse – the point of production is at the active bank operations level. Early action can greatly mitigate the effects of financial abuse.[48]

A common argument against implementing a mandatory reporting scheme is that it places too onerous obligations on busy professionals in carrying out their duties. Ultimately, this objection is unconvincing. In Singapore and other major financial centres, there are already a myriad of laws and regulations which impose all sorts of obligations on professionals and institutions such as banks, lawyers, insurance companies, real estate agents, auditors and licensed trust companies to report on suspected transactions involving money laundering and terrorist activities.[49] Since such an obligation to report on suspicious transactions already exists, then it is equally feasible to subject such professionals to an obligation to report suspected financial abuse of persons with special needs. Furthermore, mandatory reporting of elder abuse including financial abuse already exists in some states in the United States[50] and there is simply no evidence that the banks in these states have been unduly

---

[48] C. Pratt, 'Banks' Effectiveness at Reporting Financial Abuse of Elders: An Assessment and Recommendations for Improvements in California' (2003) 40 *California Western Law Review* 195.

[49] See Corruption, Drug Trafficking and Other Serious Crimes (Confiscation of Benefits) Act (Cap. 65A, 2000 Revised Edition) and Terrorism (Suppression of Financing) Act (Cap. 325, 2003 Revised Edition). See also P. Singh, 'Confronting Economic Crime – Singapore's Experience' (2007) 28(3) *Company Lawyer* 78.

[50] C. Pratt, 'Banks' Effectiveness at Reporting Financial Abuse of Elders', n 48; Z. H. Loy and P. Soh, 'Reforming the Law: Protecting the Elderly in Singapore' (2013) 31 *Singapore Law Review* 253.

restricted in their activities. Therefore, the objection that such a mandatory reporting will paralyse commercial activities is unpersuasive.

A further objection against mandatory reporting is that it is very difficult to define circumstances which might properly be characterised as giving rise to suspected financial abuse. As such, it is impractical to insist on mandatory reporting. Upon reflection, this objection is unconvincing. The banking industry has long been aware of cases of elder abuse, and various bodies have issued guidelines on identifying features of elder financial abuse. This literature was cited in the case of *Hsu Ann Mei Amy (personal representative of the estate of Hwang Cheng Tsu Hsu, deceased)* v. *Oversea-Chinese Banking Corp Ltd.*[51] Chan Sek Keong CJ helpfully summarised the principles as follows:

> Some examples of such red flags, as gleaned from the various guidelines, are
>
> (a) where an elderly person is accompanied by a new acquaintance to make a large or unusual withdrawal of cash;
> (b) where an elderly person is accompanied by a family member or other person who seems to coerce them into making transactions;
> (c) where an elderly person is not allowed to speak for him or herself, or where the party accompanying the elderly person does all the talking;
> (d) where an elderly person starts to appear fearful (particularly of the person accompanying him or her) or withdrawn;
> (e) where the elderly person is physically absent when the instructions are given to the bank;
> (f) where there are withdrawal slips presented by a third party, with the elderly person's signature on it but the rest of the slip is filled out in a different handwriting;
> (g) where there are significant withdrawals or transfers suddenly made by or on behalf of an elderly person, especially where the elderly person obtains no apparent benefit from such transactions;
> (h) where the elderly person does not appear to understand or be aware of recently completed transactions;
> (i) where the elderly person signs documents without appearing to understand what the documents mean;
> (j) where the elderly person gives implausible explanations about or appear confused about what he or she is doing with the money;
> (k) where the elderly person engages in banking activity that is unusual, erratic or uncharacteristic; and

---

[51] [2011] 2 SLR 178.

(l) where there is creation of joint accounts with another person or sudden inclusion of new names on the elderly person's account.

The existence of one or more red flags may be sufficient to put a bank on notice of potential financial abuse of the elderly customer.[52]

Thus, even without legislative intervention, banks are already under a common law obligation to verify their clients' instructions if the red flags are present. It is suggested that we should go one step further to mandate professionals to report suspected financial abuse of persons with special needs to the relevant authorities.

If legislation is indeed enacted to mandate certain professionals to report suspected financial abuse of persons with special needs, the next question is this: who should be in charge of receiving these reports? It is envisaged that such reports might become increasingly common, and it is therefore preferable to have a dedicated agency in the form of an Adult Protection Service to look thoroughly into such reports. The case studies on financial abuse also highlight the urgency of setting up an Adult Protection Service which is given substantial powers to investigate, intervene and act in cases of suspected financial abuse of persons with special needs. The current scheme of having an Adult Protection Team which is convened to discuss cases of financial abuse is far from satisfactory because the Adult Protection Team does not have any statutory powers. Hence, the Adult Protection Team has no real 'teeth' to protect the person with special needs. A dedicated Adult Protection Service would be more equipped to deal with the inevitable increase of financial abuse due to a rapidly ageing population. The current Adult Protection Service does not seem to be concerned with the issue of financial abuse. The setting up of an Adult of Protection Service with the responsibility of dealing with financial abuse is not a new idea, as two students from the Singapore Management University had made a similar suggestion in their prize-winning entry to the Attorney General's Chambers Law Reform Essay Competition.[53] Then-Attorney-General Steven Chong had praised the essay at that time saying, 'The policymakers in the ministries might find them useful when they next undertake a review of the

---

[52] Ibid., at [29].
[53] Z. H. Loy and P. Soh, 'Reforming the Law: Protecting the Elderly in Singapore', n 50.

legislation.'[54] The current proposed Vulnerable Adult Act which limits 'abuse' to physical abuse and not financial abuse is too restrictive.

Serious thought should also be given to difficulty posed by the scenario where the person with special needs may have close relatives who are unwilling to act on their behalf. This problem is especially acute in the context of a person with special needs who has some assets but has lost mental capacity. Currently, the Mental Capacity Act does not deal explicitly with this issue. In such cases, it is likely that the person with special needs is stuck in a hospital with mounting medical bills. As mentioned before, the best solution would be to liquidate his or her assets and to let him or her stay in a home. However, this apparently simple solution raises a whole host of practical questions[55] which include: (a) who initiates the process of the appointment of a deputy?; (b) who will apply to court for the appointment of a deputy?; (c) what is the process which the applicant must establish in order for the court to be satisfied that the relatives of the person with special needs do not want to take part in the process?; (d) who will pay for the disbursements of the court application?; (e) what is the legal liability of persons involved in the application?; (f) what safeguards can be built in the application for the appointment of a deputy? (g) who will act as the deputy?; and (h) if there is a need to liquidate the property of the person with special needs, what safeguards can be built into the process? While this list of questions presents a formidable challenge, they are not insurmountable if the relevant policymakers, VWOs and stakeholders sit down to work through these questions. It would be preferable to clarify the procedure through relevant laws and regulations to deal with this increasingly common problem.

V   Conclusion

In this chapter, I have outlined the laws and schemes in Singapore regulating the financial planning mechanisms available to persons with special needs. While much progress has been made in recent years with the enactment of the Mental Capacity Act and the setting up of schemes such as the Special Needs Trust Company and the Special Needs Savings Scheme, it is suggested that more can be done. This chapter has proposed

---

[54] M. Zaccheus, 'A-G Hails SMU Duo's Idea for Protecting Elders', *The Straits Times*, 1 September 2012, available on Factiva.

[55] T. Harrop-Griffiths et al. (eds.), *Dementia and the Law* (Bristol: Jordan Publishing Limited, 2014), paras. [9.40]–[9.44].

the following to further protect persons with special needs from financial abuse: (a) the setting up of a dedicated Adult Protective Service with statutory powers to act and intervene in cases of financial abuse and not just physical abuse; (b) mandatory reporting of suspect abuse of persons with special needs by the relevant professionals; and (c) streamlining the process of appointment of deputies in cases of abandoned persons with special needs. The issues surrounding the financial planning mechanisms available to persons with special needs are complex and require a multi-faceted approach. Much thought and effort is required to unpack and solve these difficulties. Ideally, this issue should be tackled jointly by policymakers and legislators, non-profit organisations, social workers and lawyers. However, we must confront these concerns sooner rather than later, especially in the context of a rapidly ageing population. Otherwise, such problems will become more acute in time to come.

PART III

Special Needs Trust

9

What Will Happen When I'm Gone?

DANA KATHERINE BIRKES*

I Introduction

In 1970, a beautiful baby boy Jeffrey was born in St Louis, Missouri. He was welcomed by two loving parents, father Jerry Zafft and mother Judy Zafft, who soon came to realise that Jeffrey had profound mental limitations. As Jeffrey grew, each birthday brought greater concern for his long-term well-being. Mr Zafft, an attorney, knew only too well that there were state and federal laws limiting the value of the assets that Jeffrey could have readily available to him without risking the loss of crucial assistance. Additionally, Mr Zafft had represented a disabled minor whose grandmother, by leaving USD10,000 to him, had unwittingly made the child ineligible for critical services and benefits. He and his wife struggled with how to accumulate the necessary resources to meet Jeffrey's needs and care without jeopardising his public services and without depleting their own resources for themselves and their other children.

Prior to 1989, households in Missouri and throughout the United States faced this same dilemma. As families thought about the future of their disabled child or grandchild, they quickly learned that distributions from their estate or other sources could jeopardise their loved one's eligibility for state and federal benefits and maybe even irreplaceable services. While parents were struggling to save for their own needs in retirement, provide for their other children and plan ahead for a special needs child unable to fend for themselves, grandparents and other relatives with nothing but best interests at heart were unintentionally leaving resources to disabled individuals, causing them to lose important supports.

For some, the dilemma meant designating a particular family member to receive the resources and be held responsible for the needs of the loved

---

* Executive Director, Midwest Special Needs Trust, USA.

one. Sometimes that worked out, but other times the best-laid plans held challenges. Sometime families were even advised to disinherit their loved one. For other families, no viable options were available at all. And the question repeated over and over was 'What will happen when I'm gone?'

Enter the Midwest Special Needs Trust (MSNT). As an extension of the efforts of Jerry Zafft to find a way to provide financial security for his disabled son, in 1989 by action of the Missouri legislature, the Missouri Family Trust was established and subsequently incorporated as a non-profit pooled trust.[1] A pooled trust creates a separate trust account for each life beneficiary but manages and invests the 'pooled' resources for maximum return. A pooled trust must be established and administered by a non-profit organisation. Initially, pooled trusts were the only vehicle for an individual to create a special needs trust with the individual's own resources. Because these non-profit organisations often serve middle- to lower-income-level families, the pooling of resources can sometimes improve their investment or earning capacity.

The creation of MSNT predated an important federal law by four years. The Omnibus Budget Reconciliation Act of 1993 created pooled special needs trusts on a national level.[2] Missouri was on the cutting edge of the groundswell, stepping out individually before the national option was in place. With minor amendments to the state statute, trust agreements and other documentation, MSNT was in compliance with the 1993 Act and at the forefront of the national movement.

MSNT was originally named Missouri Family Trust (MFT) because in the beginning it only served the residents of the state of Missouri. However, in 2004, services were expanded to permit MSNT to establish trusts for the benefit of the residents in the surrounding Midwest states of Arkansas, Oklahoma, Kansas, Nebraska, Iowa, Illinois, Kentucky and Tennessee, thus the name was changed to Midwest Special Needs Trust. It is also alternatively called 'Missouri Family Trust d/b/a [doing business as] Midwest Special Needs Trust'.

What follows is an account of the history, nature and operation of the MSNT, as well as the creation, administration and termination of MSNT accounts. The chapter concludes with thoughts on the future of the MSNT. To illustrate the practical operation of the trust, I will include staff members' first-hand reflections and case studies.

---

[1] RSMo 402.199–402.208 (2017).
[2] Omnibus Budget Reconciliation Act of 1993, P.L. 103–66, 107 Stat. 312.

II Origin of the Midwest Special Needs Trust

In 1987, Jerry Zafft in his role as the chairman of the Missouri Mental Health Commission began a conversation with the director of the Missouri Department of Mental Health, Keith Schaefer, about the needs of families with a member who is disabled. The Mental Health Commission and Director Shafer went on to assist Governor John Ashcroft in appointing a 19-member Family Trust Fund Task Force to focus on ways to provide for disabled persons without jeopardising their eligibility for public entitlement programmes. The Task Force consisted of four state legislators, including two state senators (one from each political party) and two state representatives (one from each political party); three persons with a family member with mental illness; three persons with a family member with a developmental disability; three persons with a family member with chemical dependency; three individuals who were appointed by the governor to represent the general public interest; one representative from the Department of Mental Health; one representative from the Department of Social Services; and one representative of the Mental Health Commission who served as Chairperson of the Task Force, namely Jerry Zafft.

His vision was that there should be a vehicle through which families with moderate and low incomes could help their disabled child financially without threatening the child's public benefit eligibility. As important, families would be able to do estate planning as well – something readily available to wealthy families through attorneys and financial advisors, but difficult for families of moderate means. This potential organisation could assist families in opening a trust, administering the trust for the life beneficiary's lifetime and terminating the trust when appropriate. This trust, the Missouri Family Trust (MFT), would also receive the assets of the life beneficiary to invest and disburse for the life beneficiary's sole benefit, but the assets would not be included in a public benefit resource test for eligibility. Additionally, this organisation would operate a charitable trust fund for the benefit of indigent, disabled Missourians; the charitable trust would provide individual grants for supplemental needs not covered elsewhere. Under the original plan, interest earned on contributions to the trust would go to the charitable trust; and if a beneficiary died without using all the trust funds, up to 50 per cent of the remaining amount would be contributed to the charitable trust fund.[3]

---

[3] After several amendments, MSNT subsequently decided on a 25 per cent charitable contribution from a closing trust account.

After holding four meetings around the state of Missouri and taking
into consideration what was being done in other states, the task force
prepared a memorandum outlining a proposed trust by which parents
and grandparents could leave assets for a disabled loved one without
jeopardising their eligibility for public benefits. Jerry Zafft's passion,
Keith Schafer's experience and the knowledge of supporters drove forward this innovative idea to allow families a venue to save and invest for
their disabled relatives. Moreover, after meeting with various constitu-
ents, organisations and legislators, that momentum took on a life of its
own. The task force adopted the idea and proposed legislation as a means
of enacting the idea in Missouri law.

State Representative Carol Roper Park sponsored the legislation,
House Bill 318, in the Missouri House and State Senator Henry
Panethiere sponsored the legislation in the Missouri Senate. Missouri
currently has more than six million residents and ranks as the 18th most
populous of the 50 states in the United States. The bicameral Missouri
General Assembly is composed of the 34-member Senate and the 163-
member House of Representatives. It was no small feat to get this
legislation proposed, sponsored, debated and voted on in its first year
of introduction to the General Assembly. The proposed legislation creating the Missouri Family Trust was overwhelmingly adopted. Former
Missouri Department of Mental Health Director Keith Shafer remembers
the process:

> Clearly, Jerry Zafft was the driving inspiration behind the creation of the
> trust. He proposed it and led the creation of the substance of the legisla-
> tion. He provided eloquent testimony at legislative hearings in both the
> House and Senate. This was one of those unusual pieces of legislation that
> passed in the first year of its introduction as a bill. This was quickly
> followed by the support of the Missouri Bar Association. The Missouri
> Bar sponsored the bill because of Jerry's influence in that organisation.[4]

Finally, in June 1989, House Bill 318 was signed into law by Governor
Ashcroft, with Messrs Zafft and Schafer standing by his side.

One important aspect of the enacted legislation was the composition of
the governing Board of Trustees for MFT. The nine-member Board is
divided into three categories. Three of the trustees must be members
of the immediate family of people with mental illness, and three
trustees must be members of the immediate family of people who are

---

[4] K. Shafer, 'Re: Midwest Special Needs Trust', email to K. Birkes, 6 September 2017.

developmentally disabled. Those trustees are chosen from panels recommended to the governor by state advisory councils on mental illness and developmental disability, the State Advisory Council for Comprehensive Psychiatric Services and the Missouri Planning Council for Developmental Disabilities, respectively. The third category of trustee consists of three people who are also selected and appointed by the governor. The only restriction or qualification for these trustees is that they are 'recognised for their expertise in general business matters and procedures'.[5]

All nine of the appointees are subject to confirmation by the Missouri Senate. Six of the nine trustees are people who have a sensitivity to those eligible to be beneficiaries of the MSNT trust, and three of the trustees represent, in effect, the public sector. The original appointments were for one, two and three years. Thereafter, appointment terms were all for three years, thereby ensuring staggered appointments and making certain that 'veteran' members would always be available for purposes of institutional knowledge, consistency and continuity of policies and programmes of the Board.

Passing the legislation required a lot of time and energy from Jerry Zafft, but it was far from over. The real work had only just begun!

With a USD50,000 grant from the Missouri Department of Mental Health (DMH), MFT hired a part time executive director and accepted free office space from DMH. Jerry Zafft gave seminars all over the state to whomever would listen, including regional offices of DMH and advisory councils. He also prepared documents – getting the organisation incorporated within the State of Missouri, securing tax-exempt status from the Internal Revenue Service (IRS) and documenting exemption from registration by the Securities and Exchange Commission. According to Mr Zafft:

> To a large extent, we had control over these items. The biggest obstacle we had to overcome was one we had no control over – getting people to turn their money over to us on our promise to hold and invest it and, at some future date, use it for the benefit of their loved one, when we had no record of performance to show them. It was a difficult 'sell'.[6]

As Keith Schafer shared, 'Jerry continued to be the dynamic force behind the development of the administrative operation of the trust, and did so for many, many years subsequently'.[7]

---

[5] RSMO 402.201(2017).
[6] G. J. Zafft, personal telephone conversations with K. Birkes, 7–14 September 2017.
[7] See n 4.

III MSNT Special Needs Trust

Getting the organisation itself established and open for business was one thing; organising and beginning to do business was another. It was important to have very specific definitions, requirements, roles and responsibilities, practices, and policies and procedures.

A What Is a Special Needs Trust?

A special needs trust is a method for managing assets under which ownership of the assets is transferred by the trust creator, or settlor, to a named trustee. The trustee then owns the assets and is under a duty to use the assets solely for the benefit of the life beneficiary named by the settlor. When properly drafted and administered, special needs trusts protect government benefits for the beneficiary with a disability.

This is a very useful concept for persons with disabilities[8] who are receiving means-tested benefits such as Supplemental Security Income (SSI) or Medicaid. These public benefits have an income and resource limit. Someone who earns over the income limit or has accumulated assets over the resource limit will not be eligible for benefits or, if already receiving them, will have their benefits reduced or eliminated. By transferring ownership of assets (funds) into a special needs trust, the funds are obligated to be used for the sole benefit of the person with a disability without counting as income to the life beneficiary or affecting their eligibility for public benefit programmes.

As such, special needs trusts are an important financial planning tool for family members who wish to use their assets either during their lifetime or at their death for a family member with a disability. In the United States, the special needs trust must be established for the sole benefit of the individual with a disability; disability is determined by the federal Social Security Administration (SSA) for either the Supplemental Security income (SSI) or Social Security Disability Insurance (SSDI) programme. Proper administration of these special needs trusts require that the trust document and all authorised trust distributions must

---

[8] Under Social Security rules, a person is disabled if they have a mental or physical impairment that (a) makes it impossible for them to work and (b) is expected either to last continuously for at least a year or to result in death. See www.ssa.gov/redbook/eng/definedisability.htm.

comply with federal statute and regulations for special needs trusts as set forth in the SSA Program Operation Manual System (POMS).[9]

B   What Types of Special Needs Trusts Will MSNT Open?

1   First-Party Trusts

First-party special needs trusts, also called self-settled or Medicaid pay-back trusts, are funded with assets or resources belonging to the person with a disability. Self-settled trusts are funded with personal injury settlements, inheritances paid directly to the person with a disability, retroactive or back payments from the Social Security Administration, or conserved funds of the life beneficiary. This type of trust is *irrevocable*. At the death of the life beneficiary, self-settled trusts are subject to a 25 per cent contribution of the remainder balance to the MSNT Charitable Trust and a required reimbursement to Medicaid. What does this mean? First, the trust terms cannot be changed or revoked by the settlor. Second, at the death of the life beneficiary, there will be a 25 per cent contribution to the MSNT charitable trust fund (what had originally been proposed as a 50 per cent contribution, now halved).[10] This contribution is only taken if the trust has been used, meaning it has made a distribution for the benefit of the life beneficiary. Third, MSNT must notify the Medicaid programme and ascertain whether they have any claims for services which MSNT must pay back. If the life beneficiary received Medicaid in more than one state, MSNT will contact all as appropriate and prorate any Medicaid paybacks.

2   Third-Party Trusts

Third-party special needs trusts are funded with assets or resources from someone other than the life beneficiary. The parent, grandparent or another relative or friend of an individual with a disability may use their own resources to establish a third-party trust. Third-party trusts are

---

[9] The primary POMS resource is Social Security Administration, *Exceptions to Counting Trusts Established on or after 1/1/00* (POMS SI 01120.203, 2013), available from https://secure.ssa.gov/poms.nsf/lnx/0501120203. For trusts established before that date, see Social Security Administration, *Information on Trusts, Including Trusts Established Prior to January 01, 2000, Trusts Established with the Assets of Third Parties, and Trusts Not Subject to Section 1613(e) of the Social Security Act* (POMS SI 01120.200, 2018), available from https://secure.ssa.gov/poms.nsf/lnx/0501120200, which also includes information regarding the treatment of third-party trusts.

[10] See Section V(D) for a description of the grant program.

usually revocable unless the settlor waives the right to revoke the trust. Upon the settlor's death, the trust becomes irrevocable. At the death of the life beneficiary, third-party trusts do *not* have a Medicaid payback requirement. Any remainder balance in the trust – after payment of allowable fees, expenses and the charitable trust fund contribution of 25 per cent – will be distributed to the remainder beneficiaries designated in the trust agreement.

C   What Are the Requirements for Establishing a Special Needs Trust with MSNT?

Establishing a trust with MSNT requires meeting two initial eligibility standards. First, the life beneficiary must have a disability as determined by the SSA.[11] Second, the person establishing the trust must be a permissible settlor. There are no restrictions on who can create a third-party trust, but care must be taken when opening a first-party special needs trust.

Prior to 13 December 2016, only a parent, grandparent, guardian or court could establish a first-party trust for a named life beneficiary – that is, a trust using the beneficiary's own funds. With the passage of the 21st Century Cures Act, also known as the Special Needs Trust Fairness and Medicaid Improvement Act, the disabled individual themselves became eligible to establish their own trust.[12] Pooled trusts like MSNT have always been able to work with the individual in establishing a special needs trust for themselves. MSNT will work with an individual who has an SSA-determined disability, a parent, grandparent, guardian or court in establishing a trust for the individual with a disability.

A secondary threshold for establishing a first-party special needs trust with MSNT is meeting the age requirement. According to federal law, there is no age limit for who can establish a first-party special needs trust with a pooled trust organisation. However, the states have the option to impose a penalty on funds transferred for less than fair market value if the beneficiary is age 65 or older. Missouri is one of the states which impose a transfer penalty. The penalty is often the amount the individual wants to deposit into the special needs trust. This essentially disqualifies anyone 65 and older from creating a special needs trust.

---

[11] Social Security Administration, *Definitions of Disability* (POMS DI 00115.015, 2012), available from https://secure.ssa.gov/poms.nsf/lnx/0400115015.
[12] 21st Century Cures Act of 2016, Pub.L. 114–255, 130 Stat. 1033.

A recent Kansas state court of appeals decision holds some hope that fair market value will be defined in such a way as to improve other opportunities for opening a trust for those 65 and older.[13] The court rejected the argument that the plaintiff merely exchanged legal title for equitable title. The case was remanded to the lower court where a decision seems to turn on placing a market value on the investment and management services provided by the trustee.

After meeting the two requirements of disability and age, MSNT will open a first-party special needs trust with as little as USD1,000.

D   What Are the Roles and Responsibilities in the Oversight of the Special Needs Trust?

1   Trustee

MSNT always serves as the trustee for all MSNT trusts. The trustee is responsible for properly administering the trust for the sole benefit of the life beneficiary. State law imposes responsibilities on trustees called fiduciary duties. Examples of fiduciary duties include:

- Acting in the best interests of the life beneficiary
- Making prudent investment and distribution decisions
- Keeping records of trust transactions
- Providing accounting statements to the co-trustee

As trustee, MSNT must review requests for distributions from the trust and either approve or deny the request based on applicable state and federal laws and regulations and the terms outlined in the MSNT trust agreement. MSNT has the authority to make the final decision regarding distribution requests.

2   Co-Trustee

While the trust agreements are being prepared, the settlor may designate co-trustee(s) and successor co-trustee(s). The co-trustee may be a legal guardian, relative, trusted friend or other service professional who is willing and capable to perform the duties of a co-trustee. The necessary qualities for a co-trustee include: available time, organizational skills and knowledge for trust correspondence, trust tax reporting and trust

---

[13] *Hutson v. Mosier*, 401 P.3d 673 (Kan App 2017).

distribution requests. The role of the co-trustee is to work with the life beneficiary to identify needs, and with MSNT to ensure the trust is used for supplemental services and needs consistent with applicable state and federal law and the terms of the trust agreement. The co-trustee requests distributions by signing each MSNT Request for Funds form. The co-trustee must provide receipts, invoices and written documentation, as well as coordinate third-party vendors to provide services or goods for the life beneficiary.

Co-trustees who are guardians and/or conservators are advised that the trust has a separate tax identification number and is not part of the life beneficiary's estate for tax purposes. In the United States, uses of guardianship and conservatorship and public administrator systems vary from state to state. In general terms, guardianship and/or conservatorship is used when a person has been deemed incapacitated or disabled. The guardian is charged with making decisions like medical and mental health treatment, residential placement, entering into contracts and generally exercising the rights of the individual. However, there are limited guardianships whose roles are specific to the needs of the individual where the individual may retain certain rights like the right to vote or drive. The conservator is charged with overseeing the financial aspects of the incapacitated/disabled person including all bank accounts and other assets.

Missouri public administrators, mostly elected county office-holders, serve as court appointed personal representatives in decedents' estates, and as guardians and/or conservators for individuals who are unable to care for themselves or their property in cases when there is no one else to serve. Out of 1,254 trusts currently administered by MSNT, 484 have a public administrator serving as the co-trustee.

3   MSNT as Sole Trustee

MSNT will serve as sole trustee for trusts without a designated co-trustee or when the co-trustee dies, resigns or is otherwise no longer able or willing to serve. As sole trustee, MSNT will communicate directly with the life beneficiary, their service provider or their legal representative to identify the life beneficiary's needs, document expenses and complete Request for Funds forms. With this increased responsibility, an additional sole trustee fee will be charged. Currently, MSNT serves 247 trust accounts as sole trustee. This represents 20 per cent of the total number.

E   How Is the MSNT Special Needs Trust Used?

When coordinated with public benefits and other community resources, a special needs trust may be helpful to improve the quality of life of the life beneficiary. Special needs trusts are important to help meet those supplemental needs of the life beneficiary that are not covered by their monthly cash benefit, Medicaid, Medicare or other health insurance.

The co-trustee and/or the life beneficiary share responsibility with MSNT to preserve the assets of the trust for as long as practicable for the sole benefit of the life beneficiary. That responsibility includes using the funds wisely, setting priorities, identifying cost-effective options and maximising the benefit of each distribution. Each distribution request will be reviewed in relation to past use of the trust and current and future needs of the life beneficiary. When the co-trustee signs the Request for Funds form, they are verifying:

- The distribution is for the sole benefit of the life beneficiary;
- The documentation is accurate and complete; and
- The issued distribution will be used as represented in the request.

If MSNT is advised of misrepresentation, misuse or misappropriation by the co-trustee, life beneficiary or other involved parties, MSNT will take appropriate action to protect the assets of the trust.

IV   MSNT Administration

Between 1989 and 1991, start-up activities continued until MSNT was open and ready for business. Not only did MSNT get all the official paperwork, insurance and bonding in place, but MSNT found an office location, hired a part time executive director and secured contract partners. These partners included a financial institution capable of receiving deposits, holding the money, investing and making disbursements and an accounting partner capable of performing tax reporting and audit duties. It is important to note that although MSNT was set up by state statute, it is not part of state government and receives no state appropriations. The plan from the very beginning was for MSNT to be a stand-alone, self-sustaining entity independent of state government appropriations.

On 2 February 1991, the very first trust account opened with MSNT. It was a third-party trust opened by Jerry and Judy Zafft for the benefit of their son, Jeffrey.

By February 1992, there were 21 open trust accounts. Approximately one year later, there were 42. The number had more than doubled again with 109 by February 1995. By 2000, there were 286 trusts; by 2005, 480; by 2010, 885. By July 2017, what had started as a USD1,000 deposit into a single trust account for Jeffrey Zafft had swelled to 1,248 active trust accounts with a total market value of over USD38 million.

Additional staff had to be hired, office space needs grew, and adjustments in policy and even in the statute were required to stay abreast of changing government requirements. Here are a few key areas to keep in mind when considering the administration of a special needs trust:

A   Qualified Staff

The best staff for administering special needs trusts have a unique mix of social services/human services delivery knowledge and/or experience and business/banking/finance knowledge and/or experience. MSNT has trust specialists with social work, banking and business backgrounds. All are required to be certified benefits specialists – allowing them to offer helpful information related to Social Security, Medicare, Medicaid, health insurance and other public and private benefits for people with disabilities. Personal experience with having a family member with a disability is extremely valuable. As Jen Homer, MSNT administrative assistant, shares:

> Having had a family member with a disability, I know first-hand how challenging it can be to provide for their special needs while looking after their financial well-being. Working at MSNT allows me to use my talents to support an organisation that has the expertise and caring needed to help individuals and their families navigate the financial intricacies of disability.[14]

B   Fees

Often the first question asked of trustees is about the administrative fees charged. It is important to know what the fees are and what services the life beneficiary is getting. The benefit from having an experienced and knowledgeable trustee may far outweigh the fees being charged. Often greater trustee experience and expertise may yield better outcomes in terms of investment performance or continuity of public benefit eligibility. Having a professional trustee handle trust taxes, supervise

---

[14] J. Homer, 'Re Requested Quote', message to K. Birkes, 29 September 2017.

investments and communicate with public benefit agencies to protect public benefit eligibility during a review is an added benefit. In some cases, investment income and earnings may help offset administrative fees or taxes.

MSNT administration of trust accounts is performed in partnership with a financial institution which serves as the custodian of special needs trust account funds held for life beneficiaries. To pay for the administrative costs for establishing trusts, processing distributions and deposits, account statements and check production, investment management and other trustee and banking functions, administrative fees are necessary. Administrative fee types and rates are included in the trust agreement when the trust is established. Fees are subject to change, although MSNT has not adjusted any fees in more than six years. MSNT strives to be as transparent as possible regarding fees. All fees are outlined on the MSNT website.[15]

The three main areas of the administrative fee structure for MSNT are the enrolment fee, the asset value fee, and the sole trustee fee:

1   Enrolment Fee

The one-time enrolment fee is an initial fee for establishing and opening the trust account. Discounted enrolment fees are available for low-income settlors.

2   Asset Value Fee

The asset value fee covers the cost for the administration and maintenance of the trust account. MSNT utilises an asset value fee based on the individual trust account balance. This fee is charged monthly as a percentage of the market value, and the rate varies for accounts greater or lesser than USD10,000. The asset value fee is also prorated during the opening and closing months. The life beneficiary or their co-trustee or guardian may choose to receive paper copies of the account statements, or they may have access to electronic statements and other account information by secure internet with reporting, lookup and export capacity.

3   Sole Trustee Fee

When MSNT serves as sole trustee, an annual fee is charged on a monthly basis for the increased level of support and assistance provided to the beneficiary by MSNT.

---

[15] Available from http://midwestspecialneedstrust.org/resources/fees/.

Other fees include the following.

4   Disbursement Processing Fee

The disbursement processing fee is a minimal charge for receiving a request for funds, reviewing for public benefit compliance, processing and disbursing funds from the trust.

5   Closing Fee

When a trust account is terminated, a closing fee is charged for closing the account. The fees vary depending on whether the termination is due to death, low balance or revoked third party.

6   Extraordinary Services Fee

Extraordinary services fees may be charged where MSNT as trustee has provided services well beyond usual and customary fiduciary services.

C   *Other Trust Account Expenses*

Responsibility for tax preparation and payment of taxes is dependent on whether the trust account is considered a grantor trust under the federal tax code.[16] Generally speaking, first-party trusts are considered grantor trusts because the settlor receives a benefit of ownership, namely the right to receive the interest on the account. The fact that the interest can be spent only in a manner which preserves the individual's means-tested government benefits is not relevant to the tax status. Similarly, third-party revocable trusts are, in whole or part, deemed grantor trusts because some or all of the corpus may revert back to the settlor. The settlor of a grantor trust is responsible for accounting for the trust income and deductions on their personal tax returns. Required information for tax reporting is sent to the settlor after the end of the calendar year.

For all accounts not deemed to be grantor trusts, generally including all irrevocable third-party trusts, MSNT contracts with an accounting firm to prepare and file state and federal trust tax returns annually and at closing of the account. Charges for preparation of tax returns vary based on the complexity of the return. Tax return preparation charges and any taxes owed will be deducted from the trust account and will be reflected on the quarterly account statement.

---

[16] 26 USC § 671 et seq. (2018).

D   Data Collection and Evaluation

As Midwest Special Needs Trust's growth accelerated, it was recognised that managing, securing and having rapid access to the varied information associated with each trust administered is vital. After evaluating commercial options, it was determined that a custom database would serve MSNT's specific needs most efficiently and completely. This custom database allows MSNT to maintain consistent electronic records and automates access to trust account information for reporting, planning and customer service purposes.

Many important processes are handled in an end-to-end fashion through the Individual Trust Account (ITA) database. Opening and closing trusts, processing distributions and deposits, managing the various individual needs associated with the trust, changing investment directives and other functions are processed, stored and reported through the ITA database.

Each special needs trust involves important permanent information such as trust name, beneficiary information, original investment directive, tax identification numbers (TIN) and trust type. Many other modifiable data points are involved such as trust associates, investment portfolio preference, account balances and beneficiary benefits. This data is collected by input from trust specialists through custom forms as well as direct import from the banking institution. All this information is retained in the database which has local and remote backups to ensure its safety and security.

Another valuable component of the database is its ability to facilitate the scanning, recognising and electronic filing of paper documents related to each trust. The optical character recognition (OCR) turns the image into actual text for searching and changing. This functionality has reduced the footprint of paper file storage as well as improved the ease of access to the history of a trust.

Reporting on the activity and history of MSNT trusts has become a vital function of the database. Reports can be generated and stored for individual trusts, subsets of trusts or all trusts. The system can provide information on a trust's disbursement and deposit history, portfolio preference changes, market value history and other information used internally or to communicate with MSNT banking and accounting partners. Other data is used to report on organisational trends, administrative fees collected, regional growth patterns, cumulative market values, historical numbers of open trusts and other financial information used by the executive director and board of directors to make vital decisions.

E   Investment Policy

MSNT contracts with a financial institution for banking and investment services for MSNT individual trust accounts (ITA). At the direction of MSNT, the depository manages investments for ITA accounts under the terms of the contract. The depository has established mutual fund portfolios as model investment accounts for ITA investment. The depository has full responsibility for all investment management activities and performance as described and agreed to by both parties in the service contract.

Each ITA is invested according to the Investment Agreement contained in the declaration of trust. The settlor must select at opening whether the account will be invested as directed by the settlor or as directed by MSNT. By MSNT directive and trust agreement, irrevocable trust accounts less than USD10,000 are placed in the capital preservation fund portfolio unless the settlor directs the money market fund be selected. All irrevocable trust accounts of USD10,000 or more are invested consistent with the settlor's directive as specified in the trust agreement or, if MSNT directed, by pre-established investment policy approved by the Board of Trustees. The settlor of a revocable trust, in contrast, may exercise more control over managing the funds in their account. No more than once each quarter a settlor may change the investment directive by written notice to MSNT.

MSNT provides investment instructions to the depository at the following times:

- Approximately 30 days after opening of an individual trust account;
- When the settlor requests changes in the investment directive for a settlor-directed account of USD10,000 or more;
- When MSNT identifies as part of its periodic review that any account has fallen to less than USD10,000 and is expected to remain less than USD10,000 for the subsequent quarter;
- When MSNT identifies as part of its periodic review that any account has grown to USD10,000 and is expected to remain at or more than USD10,000 for the subsequent quarter; or
- Under any other circumstances that warrant a change in investment instruction.

Either the co-trustee or the life beneficiary receives quarterly statements, keeping them current on their investment portfolio performance. Quarterly, MSNT posts on its website the aggregate investment portfolio performance.

Because the investment policy, practices and oversight are so important, the MSNT Board of Trustees has a specific Investment Committee. This committee meets every six months to have the financial institution report on performance and any market trends. They review the policy and any unique assets held in the trusts.

V   MSNT Trust Procedures

MSNT administers special needs trusts in such a way as to protect important public benefits for the person with a disability. MSNT has established processes and procedures consistent with applicable federal and state requirements. Laws, rules and regulations change from time to time, so MSNT requirements can be subject to change without notice. Through reference guide updates and notices, MSNT keeps co-trustees, life beneficiaries and their families current on any changes.

A   Opening a Trust

All activity starts with a phone call, an email or a meeting. MSNT trust specialists have conversations with attorneys, families and individuals about the future of their clients and loved ones with disabilities. They discuss the disabled person's special circumstances and considerations that may make a special needs trust a good option or not. As Trust Specialist Mary Lou Hughes explains:

> Each time I meet with a trust prospect my primary goal is to inform them about who MSNT is and what a special needs trust is and is not. My goal is to learn everything I can about their needs now and in the foreseeable future and offer options and alternatives to address them. Sometimes difficult conversations and decisions are made after several calls or meetings. The decision is life changing and must always be carefully considered; the counsel and advice of an attorney or accountant may be necessary.[17]

The following are some real-life third-party trust examples (using fictitious names) from Ms Hughes:

> Joanna Jones, an 84-year-old woman with kidney cancer, is currently working with Ms Hughes to open two third party trusts for her son and daughter, both of whom have MS (multiple sclerosis). Joanna was referred to MSNT by her investment advisor at Edward Jones (an investment

---

[17] M. L. Hughes, 'RE: HK Paper', email to Kathy Birkes, 12 September 2017.

company). The trusts will be funded at Joanna's death with her investments. Her greatest concern is for her son and daughter to receive the benefit of their inheritance without interrupting their benefits and to have a knowledgeable, caring organisation administer the trust and communicate with their cousin, the designated co-trustee.

In August, Ms Hughes met with Teresa Miller, whose mother and sister are co-guardians for her disabled sister. Teresa found MSNT's website and made an appointment for the family to meet and discuss a special needs trust. Several years ago, Teresa's mother bought a home for her disabled daughter and two other friends with disabilities. The friends pay rent and the mother deposits the funds into an account used for property taxes and maintenance of the home. Over the years, the plan has worked well. As mother and sister have aged, it has become increasingly difficult for them to manage the home and daily needs of their disabled family member and friends. Teresa, who does not live near them, is concerned they have been so involved in her disabled sister's daily care that they have not adequately planned for her future. They are considering selling the home to fund a third party trust and moving the sister to a group home.

In Ms Hughes' first year at MSNT, she met with James Milligan. He holds power of attorney for his elderly mother, who was being used by her mentally ill daughter, Sandra, as a source of income. James was referred to MSNT by a local attorney who told him about the third party trust and how it could be funded for his sister at his mother's death. James was anxious about how sister Sandra would use the funds and how she may try to manipulate people into giving her money as she had done with her mother. Ms Hughes assured James that MSNT is trustee, and only allowable disbursements can be made from a special needs trust. James was still not sure this would work with his sister's abusive personality but felt a third party trust might be the best option for their needs and circumstances. James and his trust specialist discussed the option to open the trust and fund it with the money his mother would otherwise give to his sister; he could designate himself co-trustee to approve the use of funds. James's main concern was to help alleviate stress for his mother. No option is ever without challenges, but this worked well for James. James' mother's estate will fully fund the third party trust; James now has the option to continue as co-trustee or resign and make MSNT the sole trustee. In either case, his sister is already familiar with MSNT, her special needs trust's disbursement process, and allowable expenditures.[18]

Here are some first party trust examples from Ms Hughes:

Recently, Ms Hughes spoke with Shari Ferguson, who has been notified she will receive a small back payment from Social Security of USD8,000. Missouri Medicaid asset limit is USD2,000 as of 1 July 2017. Shari said she

[18] Ibid.

was referred to MSNT by her case manager, and she needed the money to buy a new bed and other things for which she has not had the funds prior to receiving this back payment. Ms Hughes asked her about her immediate needs and if she had purchased a pre-paid burial plan, which she had not. During their conversation, Shari decided to use the funds from the back payment to purchase her bed, furniture and pre-paid burial plan and document her purchases with receipts to use for benefit reviews. Opening a special needs trust is not always in the best interests of the disabled person, especially when they have immediate needs for the funds.

Randall Johnson, a disabled gentleman from Paducah, Kentucky, has both a first party trust and a third party trust opened in August 2014. He received an unplanned inheritance from his grandfather which funded his first party trust. Randall's mother, also disabled and receiving public benefits, likewise received an unplanned bequest. She used her inheritance to fund a third party trust for Randall. Randall's aunt who lives in Columbia, Missouri, is the co-trustee for both trusts. It is often advisable to first make disbursements from the first party trust assets because leftover funds in those trusts may have to be repaid to Medicaid, whereas funds left in a third party trust will go to designated remainder beneficiaries as identified in the trust agreement.[19]

B   Making Distributions from a Trust

Once a trust is in place, the uses are as varied as the needs of the individual beneficiary's requirements. Approved requests for funds permit disbursements that can be used for various purposes; examples include a modified vehicle, an irrevocable prepaid burial policy or supplemental household needs. The disbursement process includes MSNT's receipt of the request, reviewing the request for compliance and issuing checks from the trust account. Trust Specialist Casie Stephens has seen more than 25,000 disbursement requests in her six years with MSNT. The following three disbursement stories provide a small insight into the process and how MSNT is making an impact in the lives of MSNT life beneficiaries:

> One of Ms Stephens's first disbursement requests was for hearing aids. Sally's trust opened in the same month Ms Stephens joined MSNT. Ms Stephens got to learn about Sally, a 43-year-old with a developmental disability, and her family got to learn about MSNT. Sally was in desperate need for hearing aids, which are not covered by public benefits for individuals over the age of 21. The family submitted a request for funds to purchase two hearing aids. With the request for funds they also

---

[19] See n 16.

submitted additional verification of her need with a physician's recommendation. Two hearing aids were requested because Sally tended to
break things easily. Repairing a hearing aid can take almost two weeks,
which would leave Sally without a set. The backup set provided family the
assurance Sally would not be 'left without'. The purchase of the hearing
aids improved Sally's behaviours, increased Sally's participation in groups,
and helped Sally express her needs.

Shortly after the hearing aids were purchased, Sally's family submitted a
request for funds to pay for Sally's portion of a family vacation. As the
trust specialist, Ms Stephens was able to authorise a disbursement for
Sally's first real vacation to Disney World. Sally's family called a few weeks
later to report she had fully enjoyed the experience, and they loved seeing
her joy and excitement. When Ms Stephens educates families about
MSNT, she often uses this example of how special needs trusts can have
significant impact on a life beneficiary's life. What may have been considered a simple payment for durable medical equipment had a lifetime
effect on Sally.

Special needs trusts are sometimes used to purchase vehicles with
modifications. These modifications may be required to meet the needs
of the disabled individual to drive themselves or to be driven by others.
Most of the vehicles MSNT has approved are modified for the disabled
individual to ride in. The approved modifications specifically meet their
medical needs. In the case of Elliott, a [teenager with paraplegia] who is
wheelchair dependent, a Request for Funds form was submitted for
modifications to allow him to drive. Months before Elliott turned 16
(the minimum age for a driver's license in Missouri), his mother called
to talk about a potential request for funds. She explained Elliott did not
like riding the bus to and from school each day and as a result did not
want to go to school. He wanted to be like his classmates and drive to
school each morning. His mom thought being able to drive would
increase Elliott's self-esteem and provide him with some independence.
As a trust specialist, Ms Stephens explained this would be an allowable
expenditure from a special needs trust and told her what information
would be needed to review the request. She never promises that a request
for funds will be approved but, rather, confirms that each request for
funds will be reviewed.

When Elliott turned 16, [his] mother submitted a request for funds to
make further modifications to an already modified van. The request
included adding hand controls and a specialised camera. Verification of
Elliott's ability and steps to achieve his goals included a physician's
statement that Elliott, with training by an occupational therapist, could
safely operate a vehicle. The new modifications would allow Elliott to have
full visibility to compensate for limited range of motion. Ms Stephens was
able to authorise a disbursement for the modifications and payment to the
occupational therapist. Shortly thereafter, Elliott's mom reported that he
passed his driver's test and loved his independence. His special needs trust

provided him an opportunity to gain the necessary skills and equipment to become independent for his lifetime.

Some requests for funds are more complex and require additional information, such as a physician's recommendation, ownership information, or additional bids for the price of services. Other requests for funds are very easily approved. If there are sufficient funds in the trust and it meets all applicable provisions as an allowable disbursement from a special needs trust, the request for funds can be approved. Simple requests, like attending camp, are uncontroversial. Brandon, a 26-year-old with a developmental disability, is a great example of someone who uses their trust for just this purpose.

Since his trust was opened in 2007, he has attended at least one camp a year. These camps, specifically designed for individuals with disabilities, provide a summer camp experience while still meeting all medical needs of the individual. Brandon has attended camps all over the country and loves the experience. He and his dad had 'road trips' to these different camps. One summer day, Brandon and his dad called Ms Stephens on their way to camp to express his appreciation to MSNT and thanked Ms Stephens for authorising the disbursement. In terms of quality time and family traditions, this simple authorisation had a huge impact on the trust beneficiary and his family.[20]

Ms Stephens has seen many kinds of requests over the years, small to large, simple to complex, and she knows they are each important:

I know that I play an important role in the lives of MSNT life beneficiaries. The daily struggle of many individuals with disabilities can be eased with approved disbursements from a special needs trust. I am honoured to be a part of their lives.[21]

C   Terminating or Closing a Trust

MSNT will initiate the termination of a trust for any of the following reasons: low balance, death or the revocation of a third party.

1   Low-Balance Termination

MSNT requires a minimum balance of USD500 in each trust. Once the trust balance approaches USD500, the settlor, co-trustee or life beneficiary is notified, and additional funds may be deposited. If additional funds are not available, MSNT initiates termination procedures.

---

[20] C. Stephens, 'HK Paper Disbursement Examples', email to K. Birkes, 14 September 2017.
[21] Ibid.

First-party trust: MSNT notifies the co-trustee, banking institution, tax preparers and the Medicaid Cost Recovery Unit in each state from which the life beneficiary has received benefits. Federal regulation allows payment of administrative fees, tax preparation expenses and any trust taxes due (if applicable) before Medicaid payback claims are paid. If the Medicaid Cost Recovery Unit does not make a claim or claims less than the full balance, the remainder funds are paid to the life beneficiary.

Third-party trust: MSNT notifies the co-trustee, banking institution and tax preparers that the trust is being terminated due to low balance. Federal regulation allows payment of administrative fees, tax preparation expenses, any trust taxes due (if applicable) and the distribution to the MSNT Charitable Trust. MSNT distributes the remainder funds in accordance with the trust agreement.

2 Termination upon Life Beneficiary's Death

The co-trustee is responsible for notifying MSNT of the death of the life beneficiary as soon as possible. MSNT requires a copy of the life beneficiary's death certificate to initiate termination procedures and cannot approve distribution requests received after the death of the life beneficiary.

First-party trust: MSNT notifies the co-trustee, banking institution, tax preparers, and the Medicaid Cost Recovery Unit in each state from which the life beneficiary has received benefits. Federal regulation allows payment of administrative fees, tax preparation expenses, any trust taxes due (if applicable), and the distribution to the MSNT Charitable Trust. MSNT processes Medicaid payback to all states on a prorated basis. Once all fees and claims are paid, MSNT distributes any remainder balance to remainder beneficiaries in accordance with the terms of the trust agreement.

Third-party trust: MSNT notifies the co-trustee, banking institution and the tax preparers of the life beneficiary's death. Federal regulation allows payment of administrative fees, tax preparation expenses, trust taxes due (if applicable), and the distribution to the MSNT Charitable Trust. Once all fees and claims are paid, MSNT distributes any remainder balance to remainder beneficiaries in accordance with the terms of the trust agreement.

3 Revocable Third-Party Termination

The settlor of a revocable third-party trust has the option of revoking and terminating the trust. Once notified, MSNT notifies the banking institution that the trust is being terminated. Federal regulation allows payment of administrative fees and the distribution to the MSNT Charitable Trust.

D   Midwest Special Needs Trust Charitable Trust Programme

Both the 1989 state statute creating MSNT[22] and the federal law in 1993 authorising the creation of pooled trusts[23] included provisions to support not-for-profit trustees in their charitable missions. Consistent with federal law, Social Security[24] and, by extension, Medicaid, allow non-profit organisations to retain at the death of the life beneficiary some or all of a trust account balance to be used by the trustee for its charitable mission. The portion is calculated *before* Medicaid payback, meaning some organisations make no reimbursement to state Medicaid. The Third Circuit Court of Appeals has concluded that such a result was, in fact, the intent of Congress:

> Retaining the residual enables the trust to cover administrative fees and other overhead without increasing charges on accounts of living beneficiaries. At the same time, should the trust attempt to pass the money to the deceased's estate, this provision acts as a safeguard to ensure that the State gets repaid.[25]

MSNT created a charitable trust grant programme. With the contributions from terminated trust account balances, generous contributions by the MSNT Board of Trustees from their operating funds and any charitable contributions that are made on an individual basis outside the trust account administration, the MSNT Charitable Trust grant programme provides small financial assistance grants to impoverished residents of Missouri with an SSA-determined disability. The maximum grant award is USD1,500. Grants may be requested for medical and dental care, rehabilitative services or equipment, educational assistance, specialised transportation and other needs not covered by public benefits or available through other community programmes.

The eligibility requirements for the charitable trust include the same SSA-verified disability standard and a new standard of low income. The low-income standard is measured by federal poverty guidelines published

---

[22] RSMo 402.202, 402.204 and 402.208 (2017).

[23] Omnibus Budget Reconciliation Act of 1993, P.L. 103–66, 107 Stat. 312.

[24] Social Security Administration, *Exceptions to Counting Trusts Established on or after 1/1/00*, n 9.

[25] *Lewis v. Alexander*, 685 F 3d 325, 348 (3rd Cir. 2012).

each year. Depending on the number of persons in a household, maximum income levels guide the definition of 'impoverished' and meeting the eligibility criteria. Additionally, awardees must not have other funding sources available, and they may not receive more than one grant in a 12-month period.

Two types of grants are available. First, General Grants are available to supplement basic needs by providing disability-related goods and services which are beyond the financial means of the individual. These are awarded by the Board of Trustees on a quarterly basis. Second, Urgent Grants are available for urgent medical and healthcare needs which require immediate intervention. These applications are accepted on an ongoing basis and grant awards are made twice each month. The executive director reviews and approves the Urgent Grants.

Charitable Trust Specialist Heather Allen is responsible for soliciting and reviewing grant applications in preparation for approvals. As she explains:

> During the review process, MSNT takes great care in determining which applicants should be provided a grant. No matter how much funding MSNT has available, the need is always greater. The MSNT Board of Trustees has compiled a list of considerations that are used when grant decisions are being made for both the General Grant and Urgent Grant awards. Some of these considerations are:
>
> . if the grant award will cover the full cost of the request;
> . if the applicant has saved money to partially cover the cost of the request;
> . if the provider offers a discount; and
> . if the requested service or item is a one-time cost that does not require ongoing expenditures.
>
> Each grant decision is ultimately made by the board of trustees or executive director. A lot of time goes in to reviewing applications and making grant decisions. I've enjoyed seeing the huge impact that these grants have made to more than 700 people in just the short time that I've been here.[26]

Ms Allen offers the following examples of charitable grant requests:

> Sarah is 32 years old and has cerebral palsy. Sarah lives alone and has an agency that provides a few hours of support for her each day. Sarah has very limited range of motion in her hand making her physically unable to turn the lock on the inside of her house or insert and turn a key on the

---

[26] H. Allen, 'Hong Kong Paper', email to K. Birkes, 14 September 2017.

outside. Sarah had no other option but to leave her home unlocked when staff was not available to assist her. Because of Sarah's limited income and housing expenses, she did not have the funds to purchase a more appropriate lock for her home. MSNT's charitable programme provided Sarah with a grant for USD106 to purchase an electronic deadbolt and remote control that increased her independence and her safety.

Brian is 3½ years old, blind, and has Down Syndrome. He lives with his mom next to a very busy intersection. Brian is very inquisitive and loves to be outside, but he does not have any understanding of safety. For him to be outside safely, his mother had to be next to him watching his every move. Brian's mother requested a grant to pay for a fenced-in area outside of their home so Brian could run freely. For USD1,000, MSNT provided a grant to pay for fencing supplies to do just that. Brian's mother wrote us to say, 'I want to thank you with all my heart for providing Brian with the fenced in area to explore the outdoors. It has helped him so much. He loves it and so do I because I can let him run safely as I sit by and enjoy watching him play and explore.' Not only did MSNT provide needed safety for Brian, but also peace of mind for his mother as she works tirelessly to provide for his needs.

Linda is 61 years old and lives in a very rural part of Missouri. Linda's dental needs were extensive, but she did not have the funds to pay for the extractions that she desperately needed. Linda felt that she had no options and began pulling her teeth herself. Thankfully a check-up with her physician led her to our charitable grant programme. Linda and her doctor's office found a clinic in Linda's area that agreed to perform her extractions at no cost, and MSNT was able to provide a grant for USD985 to pay for her dentures.[27]

VI   The Future of MSNT

No one has a crystal ball to know the future; by collecting and reviewing data, monitoring the legal and political landscapes and staying in touch with the needs of its constituencies, MSNT can make good-faith efforts in planning ahead.

A   ABLE Accounts

The most recent history in the United States has shown an increased awareness and greater appreciation for supporting persons with disabilities, including the passage of the Achieving a Better Life Experience (ABLE) Act of 2014.[28] This federal legislation amended a section of the

---

[27] Ibid.
[28] 26 USC § 529A (2018).

Internal Revenue Code to create tax-free savings accounts for individuals with disabilities. Similar to irrevocable first-party trusts, the accounts are subject to Medicaid payback requirements, but they are different in several ways: there is a limit on the amount of money that can be deposited annually into the account; there is a maximum or cap on how large the balance can grow; the earnings in the account are tax-free; and disbursements can be made for room and board. As predicted, these accounts do not compete with special needs trusts but, rather, can be used alternatively when a special needs trust is not a good fit, or concurrently in a coordinated fashion for maximum support and benefit to the life beneficiary. Individual states are rolling these ABLE accounts out; some only serve their individual state citizens, while others offer enrolment to out-of-state residents. At last count, about 30 states, including Missouri, have set up their programmes.

MSNT has enhanced its educational outreach to include information related to the ABLE accounts. MSNT considers this one more way the disabled population can be assisted in enhancing their lives through finance strategies.

B Disbursements and Technology

Currently, MSNT processes disbursements the same way it has for almost 30 years – with a paper check. This year, MSNT is advancing in its use of a customised debit card for some life beneficiaries. This option will not be available to all trust accounts, but for those meeting certain criteria, MSNT will be able to process their disbursements quicker and with fewer opportunities for lost, misplaced or stale-dated checks.

C Additional Service Opportunities

From the beginning, MSNT has been seen as a strong organisation available to consider add-on programme opportunities to serve the disabled population. Many years ago, the Missouri Department of Mental Health contracted with an insurance company to cover the cost of burials of clients. Almost at the same time MSNT was established, this insurance company filed for bankruptcy. Within a year, the Missouri State Attorney General's Office filed a lawsuit to force the coverage of the remaining policies. A settlement was reached, and as a result, MSNT was provided the funds to establish a separate account to administer burial expense payments. At the direction of the Missouri Department of Mental Health

(DMH), MSNT processes payments from the fund for the burial expenses of deceased DMH clients.

Many pooled trust organisations provide representative payee services. With authorisation, a representative payee is appointed by the Social Security Administration to receive the social security benefits for anyone who cannot manage or direct the management of their benefits. MSNT is considering adding this service opportunity for the benefit of its life beneficiaries.

Much debate is going on in the United States with regard to mainstreaming people with intellectual disabilities in the workplace. Previously, the concept of sheltered workshops allowed individuals with disabilities to work under careful supervision doing menial tasks at less than the national minimum wage. Allowing these individuals to work for less than minimum wage raised questions about fairness and exploitation. The sheltered workshops were also criticised for not providing advancement or more challenging opportunities. Others countered that not all individuals with disabilities are capable of integrating into the open market and approaching the workplace competitively. As this conversation continues to unfold, it has identified a needed service in assisting and advising individuals with disabilities in their decision-making. Many decisions about employment – number of hours, salary rates, potential benefits – could jeopardise state and federal benefits and maybe even irreplaceable services. MSNT is considering adding this service opportunity with certified benefit specialists available to counsel individuals with disabilities in understanding the options and outcomes of their potential employment decisions.

D Public Service

Looking back at the growth in MSNT trust accounts over the years reminds one that liability laws can change and tort reform can occur, but, unfortunately, circumstances remain the same nonetheless: mistakes occur, accidents happen and people are born with or may acquire developmental limitations. The average annual rate of growth in MSNT trust accounts over the last 13 years has been 9 per cent. One year it was as much as 25 per cent, and one year as low as 3 per cent, but always there has been a consistent, steady growth.

MSNT has established a good reputation. MSNT works closely with co-trustees to preserve the assets of the trust accounts for as long as practicable, to use the funds wisely, to set priorities and assist in identifying cost-effective options and to maximise the benefit of each and every distribution. MSNT trust specialists are certified benefit specialists who understand the life beneficiary's benefit programmes, Medicaid, Medicare and other health insurance programmes and provide a coordinated approach to help improve the quality of life for the life beneficiary. Some growth is due to increased awareness of MSNT and its success in administration and investment.

The demand for expertise in special needs trusts continues to grow. According to the United States Census Bureau, nearly one in five people in the United States has a disability.[29] Additionally, half of all working-age American adults who are experiencing income poverty have a disability.[30]

For large amounts of money, whether conserved by the life beneficiary or awarded in some fashion through a personal injury settlement or insurance payout or inheritance, private sources are available to establish trusts and, in some cases, even administer them. MSNT is available for anyone, but its public service is in being specifically available to the moderate- and low-income disabled persons and their families. Many banking institutions in the United States will not open a trust for less than USD250,000, and some require USD500,000. MSNT will open a trust for as little as USD1,000. MSNT will administer a trust as long as a minimum balance of USD500 is maintained. Without a resource like MSNT, many moderate- and low-income families would have no ability to open and utilise a special needs trust.

This brings us back to the make-up of the MSNT Board of Trustees. The composition of the Board includes individuals with family members with disabilities, both mental illness and developmental disabilities. The genius behind this requirement is that the individuals determining policy and making investment decisions are the very ones caring for a loved one living with a disability. Aware of circumstances and conditions, programmes and services, political discourse and public perception, these Board members are making decisions for all MSNT life beneficiaries just like they would want for their own loved ones. In fact, three current

---

[29] US Census Bureau Press Release, 25 July 2012, available from www.census.gov/news room/releases/archives/miscellaneous/cb12-134.html.

[30] S. Fremstad, *Half in Ten: Why Taking Disability into Account Is Essential to Reducing Income Poverty and Expanding Economic Inclusion*, (Washington: Center for Economic and Policy Research, 2009), p. 10, available from http://cepr.net/documents/publications/poverty-disability-2009–09.pdf.

Board members have special needs trusts in place for their loved ones with MSNT.

One Board member has a sister with mental illness. She resides in a group home setting. A MSNT trust account was established in 2008 with her conserved funds. She is now 71 years old. Her trust has primarily been used for medical, dental and personal care expenses. One Board member has a brother with a developmental disability. He resides with one of his sisters, who is also his legal guardian. Two MSNT trust accounts have been established for him: a third-party trust in 2007 and a first-party trust in 2012. He is now 42 years old. His trust has primarily been used for therapeutic riding lessons, other activities, eyeglasses and dental expenses.

As MSNT approaches its 30th anniversary in 2019, we have the following amazing Board of Trustees: President Cathy Steele, an attorney specialising in wills, trusts and real estate in St Louis, Missouri; Vice-President Tish Thomas, an experienced consultant in the areas of mental illness, developmental disabilities and ageing in Rushville, Missouri; treasurer Angela Dalton, a retired financial services executive in St Louis, Missouri; Sarah Giboney, an attorney specialising in estate planning and special needs trusts in Columbia, Missouri; Stephanie Briscoe, an education specialist for individuals with disabilities in Lathrop, Missouri; and Jerry Zafft – yes, that Jerry Zafft, the original visionary who worked tirelessly in creating the Midwest Special Needs Trust – a retired attorney in St Louis who has donated his time for almost 30 years as an active Board member and who has served as an officer on many occasions.

And that third Board member with an MSNT trust account for their relative? That would be Jerry Zafft, with the very first MSNT trust account established in 1991. Once the legislation had passed, once the organisation had been established, once all of the policies and procedures were in place, MSNT Trust #0001 was established for Jeffrey Zafft. Jeffrey resides in a group setting. He is now 47 years old.

And his father has been able to answer the question, 'What will happen when I'm gone?'

10

The Wispact Trusts: Making a Difference in a Means-Tested Support System

ROY FROEMMING*

I Public Benefits Programmes and US Supplemental Needs Trusts

A Introduction

The primary purpose of an account in one of the Wispact trusts is to hold and manage assets for future use to improve the life of a person with a disability. In the United States (US), however, many individuals with disabilities and their families are motivated to establish accounts in community trusts by the fact that a trust is often the only way to set aside substantial assets for the person's future benefit and to give the person influence over decisions affecting major assets, while at the same time maintaining eligibility for public benefits on which he or she depends for basic needs and supports. The design and operation of trusts for people with disabilities in the United States reflect a tension between the promotion of the interests and autonomy of beneficiaries and the need to live within programme rules in order to avoid unduly reducing essential benefits. Accordingly, to understand the environment within which Wispact trusts must operate, this chapter begins with an overview of US public benefits programmes, as they are implemented in Wispact's home state of Wisconsin.

Accounts in the two Wispact trusts are *supplemental needs trusts* (referred to in this chapter as SNTs), designed to wrap around, but not replace, benefits from US public benefits programmes. With few exceptions, Wispact beneficiaries are people with disabilities who have a basic source of income for food, clothing and shelter from a public benefits programme. These payments are based on proof of advanced age or severe, long-term disability and are from either the Social Security

---

* Consulting Attorney to Wispact, Inc., USA.

Retirement, Survivors and Disability Insurance (RSDI) programme (based on employment taxes paid by the person or by a spouse or parent) or the Supplemental Security Income (SSI) programme (based on meeting resources and income tests). Almost all Wispact beneficiaries rely on Medicaid, which is a means-tested entitlement programme for people who are elderly or disabled that not only pays for medical, healthcare and therapies, but is also the primary source of public funding for long-term residential and vocational support services.

Most family caregivers in the United States expect that, when they die or become unable to provide continued care, RSDI or SSI will provide a basic income, and the Medicaid-funded service system will provide support services, including services the family had been providing. They fund SNTs to enhance the quality of life of beneficiaries and to fill often substantial gaps in public programmes, but the intent is rarely for the SNT to be the primary funding source for basic supports or services.

It is essential to start with an understanding of Medicaid and SSI, and their policies on treatment of trusts, in order to understand the structure and operation of the Wispact trusts. Wispact devotes substantial time, expertise and energy to ensuring that its structure, documents and distribution methods comply with often-shifting SSI and Medicaid policies that govern when trust assets are considered assets of the beneficiary, and when distributions from a trust are counted as income.[1] Sometimes, this means that Wispact cannot give the respect it would wish to the autonomy and personal goals of its beneficiaries (see Section IX.B).

B   Supplemental Security Income

Supplemental Security Income (SSI) is a nationwide programme that pays cash benefits to people with disabilities and people age 65 or older. SSI pays an SSI recipient the difference between (1) the national payment level and (2) the amount of income the person gets in a month that the programme considers 'countable'. The national payment level (USD750 per month in 2018 for a single person) is substantially lower than the

---

[1] For more information on how RSDI, SSI and Medicaid work in Wisconsin, see R. Froemming, *One Step Ahead: Resource Planning for People with Disabilities Who Rely on Supplemental Security Income and Medical Assistance* (Madison: Wisconsin Board For People with Developmental Disabilities, 2009).

national poverty level (USD1,012 per month in 2018).[2] Wisconsin makes an additional monthly payment to each person who receives a federal payment, which is higher for people with substantial support needs. A person on SSI is automatically eligible for Medicaid (discussed later). For many people, access to Medicaid is more important than the SSI payment.

To get SSI, a person must demonstrate that he or she meets both a test for *countable income* and a test for *countable resources*. *Income* is money, food or housing-related assistance that the person (1) receives during the month and (2) can use to pay for his or her food and shelter.[3] *Resources* are money or things the person (1) owns on the first moment of the month and (2) can use to pay for his or her food and shelter.[4] The income limit on monthly countable income is the national payment level. The resource test requires that countable assets at the beginning of the month be less than USD2,000. The asset test is not indexed for inflation, and has not changed since 1986, so it has become more important each year for people to have a way of setting aside assets in a way that will not be counted. (If it had been indexed for inflation, the limit would have been more than USD8,000 in 2018.)

As use of the word *countable* suggests, not all income and resources are considered when evaluating eligibility for SSI and the amount of the payment. People (and trusts) that want to help a person on SSI will therefore look for ways to provide help that do not result in countable income in the month received, or countable resource in future months.

In addition to the financial tests, an applicant for SSI who is younger than age 65 must demonstrate that he or she is *permanently and totally disabled.*[5] This means that the person must not be working in *substantial gainful activity* when he or she applies, and that he or she must have an impairment (identified by a doctor) which – considering the person's age,

---

[2] US Department of Health and Humans Services, *U.S. Federal Poverty Guidelines Used to Determine Financial Eligibility for Certain Federal Programs.*

[3] 20 CFR § 416.1102; Social Security Administration, *What Is Income* (POMS SI 00810.005, 2013), available from http://policy.ssa.gov/poms.nsf/lnx/0500810005; Wisconsin Department of Health Services, *Medicaid Eligibility Handbook* (2018), § 15.1.1 (MEH). The POMS and MEH contain program policy used by line workers in administering SSI and Medicaid.

[4] Social Security Administration, *Factors That Make Property a Resource* (POMS SI 01120.010, 2014), available from http://policy.ssa.gov/poms.nsf/lnx/0501120010; MEH, ibid., § 16.2.1.

[5] 42 USC § 1382c(a)(3).

education and work experience – makes it impossible for the person to do his or her previous work or to find other work that exists in substantial numbers in the national economy. In 2018, earnings of USD1,180 in a month indicate engagement in substantial gainful activity for a person with a disability other than blindness. Once a person is on SSI, he or she will not lose disability status because of work in substantial gainful activity, as long as his or her condition does not change.

SSI is often confused with Social Security Retirement, Survivors and Disability Insurance (RSDI). RSDI benefits are based on whether the person is an insured worker (a person who paid RSDI payroll taxes for a sufficient period of time) or is the spouse, ex-spouse, minor child or disabled adult child of an insured worker who is now retired, disabled or deceased. Most people with severe developmental disabilities who were disabled before age 22 will eventually get RSDI from a parent's account when a parent retires or dies. RSDI is not means-tested, and trusts do not affect RSDI benefits. If the RSDI benefit is less than the SSI payment level, the recipient may also receive SSI.

In September 2017, about 31 per cent of beneficiaries of funded Wispact accounts were receiving SSI.[6] The need to protect those beneficiaries means that SSI policy controls the provisions of the Wispact trusts for all beneficiaries.

C Medicaid

Medicaid is a national US programme that provides healthcare to people with low incomes. This chapter will only look at the Medicaid programme that is specifically for people who are elderly (older than age 64), blind or severely disabled ('EBD Medicaid'), as administered in the state of Wisconsin.

Each state in the United States operates its own EBD Medicaid programme. Typically, the federal government reimburses the state for roughly 60 per cent of what it spends on EBD Medicaid services, if the state has followed federal rules and policies on how the programme must be operated. In Wisconsin (and the majority of other states), the state follows SSI policy on how income and resources are counted.

Medicaid is often confused with Medicare, which provides health insurance for people with disabilities and people older than age 64 who

---

[6] All data on beneficiary numbers and characteristics were provided by Wispact, Inc., from its database, in response to the author's request.

receive (or could receive) RSDI. Premiums, copayments and deductibles for Medicare are substantial, and Medicare coverage of long-term care is limited. Medicare is not means-tested, and trusts have no effect on eligibility for Medicare.

1   Medicaid Coverage: Why Medicaid Is Essential for Many People

Medicaid provides broad medical and dental care coverage, and requires minimal copayments. More importantly, Medicaid covers therapy and support services for people who have long-term support needs. This means that eligibility for Medicaid is essential if a person has a long-term need for nursing care (in or out of a residential facility), long-term therapies or home health services, support services to remain in his or her home or in a community-based residential facility, vocational support, or community-based treatment for mental illness.

Rules governing Medicaid have created complex policies to prevent people from meeting the resource test by making transfers to other people or to trusts.[7] These involve three major components:

- **Divestment penalties**. People who have transferred title to assets for less than market value within the past five years are subject to a period of ineligibility for Medicaid long-term support.
- **Estate recovery**. The state has a claim for amounts it has spent on certain long-term support services, which it can impose on property that the person owns at the time of his or her death.
- **Restrictions on trusts**. Punitive restrictions are placed on Medicaid eligibility for people who put funds into trusts for their own future benefit, unless the trust fits very specific exceptions. See Section I.D.

2   Who Is Eligible for EBD Medicaid?

To receive EBD Medicaid, a person must be older than 65, be blind or have a disability.[8] The test for disability is the same as the one for SSI, but work incentives in Wisconsin are more generous.

In general, the *income* test is the same as for SSI. A few major differences in Wisconsin are the following:

---

[7]   42 USC § 1396p(b), (c) and (d).
[8]   MEH, n 3, § 4.1.

- **Medicaid Deductible**. A person can offset income that is over SSI limits by deducting out-of-pocket health insurance and healthcare costs.
- **Long-Term Support Programs**. People who have a functional need for long-term support will generally be eligible if their cost of care, plus a basic living allowance, exceeds their income.
- **Disabled Adult Children**. Medicaid eligibility for people who were disabled before age 22 and who lose SSI because of Social Security payments received from a parent's account is generally protected.
- **Medicaid Purchase Plan (MAPP)**. In Wisconsin, a person who has a disability of a type that would meet the SSI test if he or she were not working can buy in to Medicaid by paying a premium, even if he or she is earning at a middle-income level.

In general, the *resource* test for Wisconsin Medicaid is the same as for SSI (USD2,000). However, the resource test for the MAPP programme is USD15,000.

D   How Are Assets in SNTs Treated by the SSI and Medicaid Programs?

All SNTs must be written so that assets of the trust do not meet the ordinary definition of whether something is a *resource*. An asset in a trust will count as a resource for Medicaid and SSI if the beneficiary can (1) require the trustee to give the value of the property directly to him or her, (2) require the trustee to pay for his or her food or shelter or (3) get money by selling his or her interest in the trust to someone else. Because all distributions from a properly drafted SNT are *discretionary* and the interests of the beneficiary are *non-assignable*, assets are not available resources for Medicaid and SSI. In Wisconsin and most states, an SNT can *permit* the trustee to use funds for food and shelter, as long as the beneficiary has no power to *require* the trustee to do so.

In most situations, it is also necessary for the trustee or trust manager **to make distributions in ways that are not counted as income**. Most distributions from SNTs are made by direct payment by the trustee to suppliers of goods and services so that the beneficiary receives in-kind benefits, rather than cash. See Section VI.D.

Third-Party SNT. For a third-party funded trust in Wisconsin, trust assets will not be countable for SSI and Medicaid if the trust is discretionary and non-assignable – i.e., the person has no legal power to compel a distribution.

Self-Funded SNT (SF-SNT). Under special rules that apply to self-funded trusts, SSI and Medicaid count property that a person has put into a trust for his or her own benefit as a countable resource, regardless of whether the trust is discretionary, and count payments made from the trust for the person's benefit as income.[9] However, there are two exceptions[10] that allow property of a person to be put into a self-funded trust or trust account that can then be used for his or her benefit:

- A *Medicaid Payback Trust* can be established by the beneficiary, a parent, a grandparent, a guardian or a court. The beneficiary must be a person who, at the time of funding, is younger than age 65 and meets the SSI disability test. The trust must be a 'sole benefit' trust – i.e., it must provide that the property in the trust will be used only to benefit the person during his or her lifetime. Any property that remains in the trust when the person dies must go first to repay any state that has provided Medicaid benefits, up to the total amount of Medicaid benefits the person has received during his or her life, before or after the trust is established. Remaining assets can go to named remainder beneficiaries only after all state claims have been paid in full.
- A *Pooled Trust* must be established and managed by a non-profit organisation. A separate account must be maintained for each individual beneficiary, but assets must be pooled for investment. Each account must be established by the beneficiary, a parent, a grandparent, a guardian or a court for the sole benefit of a beneficiary with a disability, as that is defined for SSI. However, the trust can be set up so that all or part of funds remaining in the trust at the person's death can be retained in the trust, to be used by the non-profit organisation for the benefit of other people with disabilities. If not retained in this way, funds must first be used to repay Medicaid benefits, as for a Medicaid payback trust.

E   Other US Public Benefits

The United States has a patchwork of other public benefit programmes on which people with disabilities (of any age) may rely for various needs,

---

[9] 42 USC §§ 1396p(d) and 1382b(e).
[10] 42 USC § 1396p(d)(4)(A) and (C); Social Security Administration, *Exceptions to Counting Trusts Established on or after January 1, 2000* (POMS SI 01120.203, 2018) §§ B1 and 2, available from http://policy.ssa.gov/poms.nsf/lnx/0501120203; MEH, n 3, §§ 16.6.5 &.6.

including basic income, medical care, long-term support, vocational support, help with purchase of food, housing subsidies, assistance to veterans and their families, etc. Some depend on age or disability status, some are means-tested, and some are a combination of the two. Treatment of trust assets and distributions varies widely among programs and is not coordinated with SSI/Medicaid rules. This lack of coordination means that it is not always possible for Wispact to avoid affecting public benefits programmes other than SSI and Medicaid. For example, Medicaid payback and pooled trusts do not provide protection for means-tested veterans' benefits and may not be fully effective in protecting housing subsidy payments. These programmes are not discussed in greater detail in this chapter because Wispact's focus is on protection of the SSI and Medicaid benefits that are essential to most beneficiaries.

F   Why Should Public Policy Encourage the Creation and Funding of SNTs?

It is much easier for the service system to support a person with disabilities, and the person with disabilities is much more likely to be able to avoid dependence, abuse and exploitation, if he or she has a source of funding that can fill gaps in public service funding – e.g., by helping the person get safer or more appropriate housing, needed equipment, good dental care, specialised diets and access to services and activities that make life interesting and enjoyable. For this reason, agencies that arrange or provide long-term support often encourage clients to establish SNTs. It is not unusual for support service agencies and employees to suggest ideas for trust distributions, and in some cases they have been appointed as advisors to Wispact trust accounts.

Only rarely do US families and individuals have enough private resources to be able to refuse public benefits for a child or young adult with long-term support needs. Before there were effective SNT options in the United States, parents and family members were advised to disinherit people with disabilities so that access to public benefits would not be affected. Families might informally give a sibling a larger inheritance with the non-binding wish that the funds be used to assist the person, but the funds were not legally set aside for that purpose, and informal promises are easily forgotten. Similarly, if people reliant on public benefits received a windfall, they were often advised to spend it quickly or to convert it into resources that are not countable (like furniture, vehicles, televisions, etc.) so that they could retain eligibility. Policies that discouraged SNTs pushed resources away from the people served so that they were kept in enforced poverty and had no resources to fall back on in emergencies or to fill service system gaps.

II   Wispact: Basic Structure and Trusts

A   Administrative Structure and Division of Responsibility

Wispact, Inc. ('Wispact'), is a non-profit charitable corporation that was established in 2002 for the specific purpose of creating and managing pooled and community supplemental needs trusts (SNTs) for people with disabilities in Wisconsin. It is not a government agency but must operate under trust law and the government-created policies described in Section I.

The work of administering Wispact's trusts is divided between Wispact, a trustee and an investment company:

- Wispact is the **establisher** of the Master Trusts that govern all accounts and is **trust manager** of its two trusts. The Wispact trusts are **directed trusts,** meaning that the trustee must follow the decisions of Wispact on specified issues. Wispact as **directing party** chooses the trustee, sets policy for the trust and makes all decisions related to distribution of trust assets to benefit the individual beneficiaries during their lives, and for charitable use of other funds held outside of individual accounts. Wispact is also a **trust protector,** and in that role, Wispact can terminate the trustee and appoint a new one, and can amend the trusts, to ensure that they continue to meet legal requirements and carry out the purposes of the trusts. Wispact has had to use its authority to amend several times, as public benefits rules and policies have shifted. It also changed the trustee on one occasion, primarily to obtain more comprehensive and efficient accounting and investment of trust accounts.

  Most beneficiary, family and representative contact is with Wispact. Questions on account creation and distributions are all handled by Wispact, and all creation documents and distribution requests are initially submitted to Wispact.

- Wispact appoints a bank or Trust Company to act as trustee.[11] From 2003 to September 2015, the trustee was Associated Bank. The current trustee is Chemical Bank, appointed in October 2015. The trustee

---

[11] In some states, the non-profit agency that manages the pooled and community trusts is also trustee. This is not an option in Wisconsin.

receives and holds the trust funds and other property, provides accounting services, files the various income tax documents required by United States and Wisconsin tax law and distributes remaining assets in an account when the primary beneficiary dies.

B   Wispact Trusts I and II

Wispact has established two trusts, Wispact Trust I and Wispact Trust II. Both are **community trusts**, in which many individuals can have individual accounts, each administered for the sole benefit of that individual. Each trust is governed by its Master Trust. Each individual account is governed by the Master Trust and by a **contribution agreement** between the **creator** (settlor) of the account, Wispact and the trustee. The two trusts are the following.

- **Wispact Trust I**, established 1 July 2004, is designed exclusively to hold accounts that are funded with assets that belonged to the beneficiary before being placed in the trust (a 'self-funded' or 'first-party' trust). Trust I is recognised as a **pooled trust** for both SSI and Medicaid (see Section I.D.

  As of 31 March 2018, there were 2,197 funded Trust I accounts,[12] with total assets of over USD86.8 million.[13]

  A pooled trust may elect to retain some or all of the funds that remain in an account when the primary beneficiary dies.[14] Wispact retains 100 per cent of remaining account assets if the assets are insufficient to fully pay the state claim for Medicaid benefits that would otherwise apply. In most cases, the state claim exceeds remaining assets, and the remaining assets are retained and transferred to a charitable account called the **Retained Fund** (See Section VII).

- **Wispact Trust II**, established 1 October 2003, is designed primarily to hold accounts that are funded with property that belonged to people other than the beneficiary, usually family members ('third-party' SNT accounts). Third-party accounts can be created by anyone, and there is no requirement that the beneficiary's disability be severe. Accounts are not subject to a Medicaid payback claim or to retention in the trust at the death of the primary beneficiary. The creator of the account can

---

[12] See n 6.

[13] SEI, *Wispact, Inc., Quarterly Investment Review, First Quarter, 2018.*

[14] 42 USC § 1396p(d)(4)(C), made applicable to SSI by 42 USC § 1382b(e)(5).

direct the remainder to any person(s) or organisation(s) he or she chooses.

Some Trust II accounts are funded immediately by current gifts from family members, but the majority are unfunded at the time of creation, to be funded at a future time, either at the death of the family member or when there is some other threat to the ability of the family member to provide direct financial support. All unfunded accounts must be named as a beneficiary in a will, trust, life insurance designation or other remainder designation.

There are some circumstances under which Trust II holds accounts funded with assets of the beneficiary, subject to the requirements for Medicaid payback trusts (see Section I.D). Most of these accounts were established before Trust I was created.

As of 31 March 2018, there were 583 funded Trust II accounts, with total assets of USD30.7 million, and 882 unfunded accounts.[15] Of the funded accounts, 115 were self-funded.

C Investment and Accounting

With only a few exceptions, all assets of individual accounts in each Wispact trust are invested in a single pool, with each person owning a share of the pool, much as accounts are held in a mutual fund. Each beneficiary and advisor receives an individual **Account Statement**, showing the beginning and ending balances, contributions, earnings, gain (or loss) in market value of assets and distributions, including administrative fees.

Wispact and Chemical Bank have arranged for the trust assets to be invested under direction of a separate investment advisory firm, SEI Investments Management Corporation. Investments are in a diversified, growth-oriented portfolio of US and international stock and bond markets, with a preference for stock, and international stock in particular. From 30 September 2015 through 31 December 2017, average annual earnings before fees were 12.5 per cent.[16]

Up to now, Wispact has not offered choices of investment options, because of the added costs of managing and accounting for multiple pools. The strategy chosen has produced substantial growth in accounts, after investment, trustee and trust manager fees, in all years except 2008.

---

[15] See n 6 and 13.
[16] SEI, *Wispact, Inc., Quarterly Investment Review, Fourth Quarter, 2017.*

However, it also exposes accounts to risk of loss of principal, as occurred temporarily in 2008–2009. Some potential settlors have wanted to direct investments, while others would have preferred to be able to choose a strategy that would prioritise protection of principal.

Wispact does allow for exceptions to pooled investment, where there is a clear reason for holding a specific asset to benefit the individual. Some examples are

- **Homes**. Wispact will accept ownership of a home in an individual account, if it will be used by the individual, if it is affordable considering its condition, future costs, and overall assets of the account, and if there is a clear plan for managing and maintaining the home and protecting the trust from undue risk.
- **Liens on homes and cars**. Where the trust uses funds to purchase a home or vehicle for the beneficiary, it may do so as a loan secured by a lien, as a way of protecting the equity from loss, and ensuring that it is returned to the trust if the asset is sold (See Section VI.C).
- **Annuities**. Some people own annuities that cannot be converted to cash without substantial loss of value. Where the annuity is assignable, ownership can be given to the trust.

III Purposes of the Wispact Trusts

A   *Nature, Types and Purposes of US Supplemental Needs Trusts*

A **supplemental needs trust in the United States (US-SNT)** is a trust designed for a beneficiary who is a person with disabilities and may need to rely on public benefits. A properly drafted SNT is written (1) so that the trust will not count as an asset of the person, for purposes of SSI and Medicaid and (2) so that distributions from the trust can supplement what the person receives from public benefits, without causing an undue reduction in what the person would otherwise have received from public benefits. SNTs in the United States share certain basic characteristics:

- US-SNTs are always *discretionary trusts*, meaning that the trustee or trust manager has authority to decide whether to make distributions, what to buy and what form the distributions should take. US-SNTs are not mandatory support trusts, do not provide for mandatory distributions of cash and do not require the trustee to pay for basic support (food and shelter) for the beneficiary. Some SNTs (like the Wispact trusts) allow cash distributions and distributions for basic support, but this is not permitted in all states.

- US-SNTs will usually contain language saying that the trust is intended to **supplement rather than replace public benefits**. Some SNTs, including the Wispact trusts, give the trustee discretion to make a distribution that replaces or reduces a public benefit, if necessary to provide the person with a more appropriate or higher quality service or item, or where the result is an overall improvement in the person's quality of life.

Wispact operates community trusts (see Section II.B), in which accounts for many people are governed by a single master trust. Many SNTs in the United States are established as separate trusts – each with its own terms and named trustee(s), who may be family members, a bank and/or a professional trustee. This kind of trust is referred to in this paper as a *free-standing SNT*. Like the community trust accounts administered by Wispact, free-standing SNTs can be *third-party trusts,* funded from family resources, or *self-funded trusts*, which must be Medicaid payback trusts (see Section I.D).

An SNT, as a discretionary trust, can serve important planning and financial management needs for people with disabilities and their families that are not directly connected with preserving public benefits. These include

- **Property management**. An SNT can provide support to manage and invest property and to make decisions on its utilisation for a beneficiary who is not skilled in financial decision-making. Although a financial guardian serves a similar role, the SNT has advantages, in that it does not require a court finding of incompetence, and it enables the grantor to choose the trustee and to give the trustee greater discretion (or direction) than a guardian would have in managing and using the property.
- **Carrying out intent of the settlor**. An SNT can help ensure that property is only used in the way intended by the settlor. If he or she wishes, a settlor can specify purposes for which funds may and may not be used. Even if the SNT is purely discretionary, the settlor can write a **letter of intent** (see Section VI.A) outlining the beneficiary's needs and the set-tlor's vision of how SNT assets will be used. The settlor can also control who will get the distributable assets after the primary beneficiary dies.
- **Protecting assets from loss due to poor decision-making or exploit-ation by others, and from claims by creditors, spouses and the state.**

The individual beneficiary does not own trust assets, so he or she cannot give them away and they are not subject to claims of creditors. The trust can monitor whether items that the trust pays for are taken or used by others after receipt by the beneficiary. SNTs typically make it impossible for the beneficiary to sell, mortgage or give away an interest in trust property; exempt account assets from liability to the beneficiary's creditors; and exempt account assets from state claims for the cost of care and services. Under Wisconsin law, even a self-funded SNT can be immune from creditors' claims and can continue to make distributions for the benefit of the individual without having the distributions seized by creditors before they reach the beneficiary.[17] A spouse has no claim on trust assets of a third-party trust, and they are not subject to claims for spousal support or division at divorce or death. The only potential spousal claim on a first-party trust would be a case in which the spouse had an ownership interest in assets and did not consent to the transfer to the trust.

B   Specific Reasons for Creation of the Wispact Trusts

Starting in 2001, Wispact was initially planned by a group of attorneys who regularly worked on asset planning for elderly people and people with disabilities in need of long-term support, and with family members who want to assist them. Later in the process, the attorney committee expanded to include people from advocacy agencies serving the same populations. The gaps in options for SNTs in Wisconsin that the committee hoped to fill with the new entity and trusts included:

- **Creation of a trust managed by a non-profit agency primarily concerned with the welfare of people with disabilities**. The experience with the bank that was trustee of the existing Wisconsin community trust was that it lacked expertise in the situations of people with disabilities and public benefits requirements, and it did not reach out to find out what people needed and how trust assets could be used. As a result, trust assets often sat unused if beneficiaries could not speak for themselves and did not have an active advocate.

---

[17] For this purpose, Wisconsin Trust Code, Wisconsin Statutes Ch. 701, refers to an SNT as a 'trust for an individual with a disability'. The Wisconsin Statutes are abbreviated Wis. Stat.. The provisions on effectiveness of spendthrift clauses for SNTs are in Wis. Stat. §§ 701.0502(1)(b) and 701.0505(1)(a)2.

- **Allowing individual people with disabilities to be the creators of their own accounts.** The Medicaid exception at the time did not allow beneficiary creation of free-standing Medicaid payback SNTs but did allow beneficiary creation of pooled trust accounts. The law was changed in 2016 to allow beneficiary creation of free-standing SNTs.[18]
- **Providing a competent, affordable option for trust management for individuals and families who do not have family members or friends to act as trustees of free-standing SNTs.** Many people with disabilities are isolated, and there may be no obvious candidates to appoint as trustee. Parents may not have other children, may feel that their other children lack the expertise to be trustee, may not want to burden other children or may be concerned about conflicts of interest. It can be destructive of family relationships to put a sibling in charge of whether and how funds in a trust will get used for the beneficiary.
- **Allowing accounts in the pooled trust to be established for people age 65 or older.** Wisconsin Medicaid does not count assets in pooed trust accounts transferred by people 65 or older and does not penalise the transfer. Assets transferred to other self-funded SNTs after age 65 continue to count as assets of the individual.
- **Allowing remaining assets at the death of primary beneficiaries to be used for the benefit of other people with disabilities,** through the Retained Fund (see Section VII).

IV   Eligibility Of Beneficiaries

A   Residence in Wisconsin

While neither Trust I nor Trust II requires that a beneficiary be a Wisconsin resident, Wispact generally will not accept an application for an account for a beneficiary who resides in another state. If a person with a funded account moves to another state, or if funding is submitted for an unfunded account for a beneficiary who lives in another state, Wispact will make every effort to arrange for establishment of an account in a community or pooled trust in the beneficiary's state of residence, and to make a trustee-to-trustee transfer of assets from the Wispact trust account to the new account.

The primary reason for this policy is that Wispact does not have expertise in the Medicaid and other public benefits rules of other states

---

[18]   42 USC § 1396p(d)(4)(A).

and would need to use sub-account resources to find and pay for that expertise. In addition, the Wispact trust documents themselves may not comply with state requirements for SNTs and pooled trusts in the new state.

B Disability Status

Wispact, Inc., is a charitable organisation whose purpose is to establish and manage trusts for people with long-term disabilities. Wispact requires that all beneficiaries of its trusts have some level of disability. Wispact was founded by a broad coalition of advocacy groups for people with disabilities and people who are elderly, and serves people regardless of the form of disability or age of onset. One of its most important roles has been its effectiveness in working with people with mental illness and people with challenging behaviors, who may not be served effectively by private banks or by funds controlled by family members. The ability to shift management of funds to an agency has in many cases helped reduce tension and restore the ability of family members to take other roles in the person's life.

1 Disability Status for Beneficiaries of Self-Funded accounts

An account in a self-funded trust or account must be established solely for the benefit of an individual who is disabled, as 'disabled' is defined for eligibility for SSI[19] (See Section I.B). SSI policy reads this to mean that the beneficiary must establish that he or she had the required level of disability **at the time the account was established**.[20] Wispact will only accept accounts in Trusts I or self-funded accounts in Trust II if one of the following is established:

. The proposed beneficiary has an existing, current disability determination for purposes of Social Security, Medicaid or SSI.
. The person has submitted (or will submit in the near future) an application for a disability determination by the state agency that makes determinations of disability for both SSI and Medicaid. This is necessary for new applicants for Medicaid and SSI, and for people who qualify for benefits based on being age 65 or older, and therefore do not have current disability determinations.

---

[19] 42 USC § 1396p(d)(4)(C)(iii).
[20] Social Security Administration, *Exceptions to Counting Trusts Established on or after January 1, 2000*, n 10, §.D.2.

Accounts for people without disability determinations are accepted on a provisional basis. Beneficiaries can enter into agreements under which distributions are made as loans against the assets of the provisional account. This allows access to trust assets to assist the beneficiary while the disability application is pending, but avoids the income-counting rules that would apply if the person is found not to have a disability. In practice, DDB has never found that a Wispact applicant older than age 65 did not meet the disability test.

• The beneficiary has no disability determination and is not receiving or applying for Medicaid or SSI, but the applicant submits evidence to establish that the beneficiary meets the SSI disability test.

SSI policy requires that the beneficiary must meet the disability test at the time of account creation.[21] This means that pre-planning to set aside resources for an expected future disability must be done in other ways, e.g., by empowering an agent under a durable power of attorney to create and fund the account.

2   Disability Status for Third-Party Trust II Accounts

Wispact requires that beneficiaries of third-party accounts in Trust II have a determinable mental or physical disability, but does not impose a severity test. Wispact accepts a statement in the application for a third-party-funded account that the beneficiary has a disability that impairs the person in carrying out one or more major life activities or is expected to have such a disability in future.

V   Contribution Agreement and Funding

A   Who Can Establish and Fund an Account?

All Trust I accounts and self-funded Trust II accounts must be established by the beneficiary, a parent, a grandparent, a guardian or a court. An agent may act for the beneficiary to create an account, but only if he or she has specific authority from the beneficiary to create and fund the account. In Wisconsin, a guardian can establish and fund an account only with a specific order from the court that grants the guardian that authority.[22] Any person who transfers the beneficiary's property to the account must have specific authority to do so. For example, a parent can

---

[21] Ibid.
[22] Wis. Stat. § 54.20(2)(c).

create an account but would not have legal authority to put the child's money into a trust and would need, e.g., to obtain that authority through a guardianship proceeding.

Anyone can establish a third-party-funded account and fund it with assets that he or she controls. The account is established if it is funded or if there is a designation that directs property to the account on the happening of a future event.

B   What Is the Purpose of the Contribution Agreement and Application?

The Contribution Agreement, Application and Asset Transfer forms for Trust I and II are on the Wispact website. The purposes of the forms are to

- Identify the creator of the account and ensure that he or she has authority to create the account.
- Identify the person transferring funds and ensure that he or she has authority to make the transfer.
- Establish that the individual meets the disability requirement for the type of account or that a process for establishing disability is in process.
- Appoint an advisor to the account.
- Provide basic information about the trust to the creator and beneficiary (or representative) and obtain acknowledgment that notice has been given.
- Provide direction to the trustee on distribution of remaining assets at the death of the beneficiary. (A continuing issue is the extent to which creators other than the beneficiary can create remainder designations, without a clear delegation of authority from a competent beneficiary.)
- Ensure that the creator has been advised by an attorney, who must also sign the agreement and agree to make any needed reports of the creation and funding of the account to public benefits agencies.

VI   Distributions

A   Distribution Planning and Counseling; Role of Advisor

Wispact in 2018 employed four **beneficiary specialists**.[23] A beneficiary can consult with his or her designated beneficiary specialist about

---

[23] More detail on Wispact distribution purposes, methods and forms is provided in the Wispact, Inc., *Wispact Handbook: Guidelines for Beneficiaries and Advisors* (Madison: Wispact, Inc., 2017), subsequently referred to as the *Wispact Handbook*.

whether a distribution is permitted, how to request the distribution and the best way to facilitate payment to prevent undue effects on public benefits. Larger distributions (as for cars or homes) require more data gathering and counseling.

Wispact seeks to use funds in ways that will make the beneficiary's life better but does not necessarily seek a 'best possible' or 'best interests' use of funds. The wishes and preferences of the beneficiary are given great weight. This respect for individual choice and autonomy can be seen as a good in itself and as maximising beneficiaries' control of their interest in their accounts.

Wispact strongly recommends that each account have an **advisor**, whose job includes keeping in contact with the beneficiary; informing Wispact about the beneficiary's situation, needs and wants; suggesting ways of using account assets; and responding to requests from Wispact for advice on requests or ideas for distributions. The advisor should be a person familiar with the beneficiary and his or her situation – such as a guardian, family member, friend or support service provider. Either the advisor or beneficiary can ask for review of a Wispact decision by the Distribution Review Committee.

The advisor is initially appointed in the Contribution Agreement (CA). If there is a vacancy, and the CA does not appoint a successor, Wispact will help the creator or beneficiary find a successor advisor and in some cases may appoint a paid advisor. Wispact does accept accounts where no advisor is appointed, usually because the beneficiary does not have a family member or friend he or she trusts to take on the role.

If they wish, account creators can submit a **letter of intent** that describes the situation and needs of the person, and the creator's ideas for how and when account assets will be used. This can be used by the beneficiary, advisor and beneficiary specialist in planning use of account assets.

Wispact encourages (but does not require) use of trust assets to create an **overall long-term plan and budget** that integrates use of account assets with use of other available resources. This can help ensure that account assets are preserved for future priority needs. A barrier to this planning has been a lack of skilled counselors in some parts of the state.

B   Sole Benefit Requirement

The Medicaid laws that govern self-funded SNTs, as interpreted by the administering agencies, require that all distributions from Wispact Trust I accounts, and from all self-funded accounts in Trust II, must be for the *sole benefit* of the primary beneficiary. This applies to a third-party-funded account in Trust II if the settlor is reducing his or her assets so that the settlor can apply for Medicaid long-term support.

The sole benefit requirement that applies to self-funded SNTs prohibits payments that primarily benefit family members, even where there is a support obligation to a spouse or minor children. The inability to use funds to benefit family members (especially minor children), or to fund small gifts to friends and family on special occasions, is an important issue that should be discussed before an account is funded. In addition, the Social Security Administration (SSA) has adopted policies that distributions for certain purposes are never for the person's sole benefit. SSA has enforced its policies by denying SSI eligibility to beneficiaries if trust documents mention the disfavored purposes. Due to backlogs in hearing requests, appeals of individual denials can leave beneficiaries without SSI for periods of up to two years. Successful appeals do not change policy for the next case. The result is that SSA effectively dictates what trusts may and may not include. For example:

- From 2014 to April 2018, SSA enforced a policy of counting assets of SF-SNTs that provided for **payment of travel expenses for a travel companion**, unless necessary to enable the beneficiary to travel to receive medical care. SSA then denied or terminated SSI to Wispact Trust I beneficiaries whose trust were reviewed until the Wispact trusts were amended to remove references to such payments. In May 2018, the policy was reversed so that SSA again recognizes payment for travel and other companionship services as legitimate uses of trust assets.[24]
- SSA continues to count trust as assets if they allow **travel expenses for a friend or relative to visit the beneficiary**, unless the beneficiary is in an institution or residential facility, the beneficiary is receiving paid support services from people other than family members or the visitor is a trustee travelling to carry out his or her fiduciary responsibilities.[25]

SSA's blanket restrictions prevent individual determinations of individual needs. For example, isolation and lack of strong relationships are frequent experiences for people with disabilities outside of institutions and are associated with increased risk of abuse, neglect and exploitation.

---

[24] Social Security Administration, *Trusts Established with the Assets of an Individual on or after 01/01/00* (POMS SI 01120.201, 2018) §§ F3a and b, available from http://policy.ssa.gov/poms.nsf/lnx/0501120201.
[25] Ibid., § F3c.

Visits by family members or friends can be an essential need of such individuals.

C Examples of Distribution Purposes

The Wispact Master Trusts contain few restrictions on how Wispact can use its discretion over distributions. Some restrictions are imposed by the impact on public benefits, e.g., if an item is treated as countable income. As noted earlier, sole-benefit accounts are subject to greater restrictions. The following are some examples of appropriate uses of trust assets for items that SSI and Medicaid do not treat as countable income when received or countable assets when owned:

- **Healthcare treatment, therapy, medications, supplies and medical equipment, etc.,** including items which are not covered by public benefits, or are only covered in an inadequate or inappropriate way.
- **Educational, vocational, case management, advocacy, social, supportive and other services**, whether or not related to alleviating the effects of the person's disability.
- **Travel, vacations, transportation and entertainment**.
- **Appliances, furniture, household goods, electronics, clothing and other personal items** for use by the beneficiary.
- **Purchase of a vehicle,** if it is for transportation of the beneficiary and is the only vehicle he or she owns.
- **Resources to be used in a trade or business** or that are part of a **plan to achieve self-support**.
- **Income taxes** owed by the beneficiary or Wispact account.
- **Funeral and burial or cremation expenses,** with the limitation that, for self-funded accounts, the state Medicaid payback claim has priority for account assets at the person's death, so these expenses must be prepaid while the person is still living. The Retained Fund can also be a source for payment.
- **Food and shelter**.

   For a **beneficiary who is not receiving SSI**, payments for food and shelter can be made in the same way as other payments for goods and services. The ability to help people obtain safe, appropriate and affordable housing is particularly important, and one that can reduce support-service costs.

   For a **beneficiary who is receiving SSI,** in-kind food and shelter payments reduce SSI on a dollar-for-dollar basis, but only up to an amount called the presumed maximum value, or PMV[26] (USD270 per month in 2018). After the PMV reduction is reached, further distributions for in-kind food and shelter have no effect on the SSI payment, so it is sometimes worth it for the individual to accept the limited reduction.[27]

- **Purchase of an interest in a home in the beneficiary's name** is treated in the same way as other shelter expense payments – i.e., there is a reduction of the PMV amount in SSI, in the month the interest is received. A home is an exempt resource, except that equity of more than USD750,000 may count as a resource for Medicaid long-term support.

  Wispact requires a special request form and process for purchase of a home, to ensure that the costs of owning the home will be affordable. To protect equity from being lost through sale or mortgage of the home by the beneficiary, or from becoming a countable resource if the person moves out of the home, Wispact typically makes its distribution in the form of a loan secured by a lien on the home. This creates an unusual asset for the account, as the trustee ends up holding a note and mortgage as an asset. Wispact and Chemical Bank are currently working on ways to hold homes and liens while minimising trustee costs and potential liability.

- **Ownership of a home in the name of the trust account, for the benefit of the beneficiary**. A Wispact account may receive a home for use of the beneficiary as part of the funding of the account, or may purchase a home for use of the beneficiary. Payments by the trust of ownership costs of the home are treated for SSI as in-kind food and shelter (see above). A home is not part of pooled investment, and requires special management to ensure expenses are paid and that the home is repaired and maintained. To make this affordable, it works

---

[26] Social Security Administration, *Presumed Maximum Value (PMV) Rule* (POMS SI 00835.300, 2012), available from http://policy.ssa.gov/poms.nsf/lnx/0500835300. Under Social Security Administration, *ISM and Households – Household Costs* (POMS SI 00835.465), not all expenses connected with owning or renting a home count as 'shelter' costs, available from http://policy.ssa.gov/poms.nsf/lnx/0500835465. For example, costs of repairs and maintenance are not considered shelter costs, and an SNT can pay those costs without affecting SSI.

[27] The *Wispact Handbook* is confusing on this issue, but in practice, Wispact will make distributions of food and shelter to an SSI recipient who understands and accepts the reduction in the SSI benefit.

best where there are family, friends or service providers who can provide oversight and property management for free or at a low cost.

D   Facilitating Distributions

Medicaid and SSI count **cash payments to beneficiaries** as income unless they are small, occasional gifts or are distributions under USD20 per month to a person with no other outside income. For SSI, countable cash distributions result in a dollar-for-dollar payment reduction. For Medicaid, a cash distribution may affect eligibility, increase the cost-share the person must pay for long-term support or increase the premium paid by a working person who buys in to Medicaid. Wispact's policy is that it does not make cash distributions, but exceptions can be made if it shown that the effect on public benefits is acceptable. SSI and Medicaid treat **cash reimbursements to beneficiaries** and distributions for **prepaid credit cards owned by the beneficiary** as payments of cash. In theory, a beneficiary who does not rely on public benefits at the time of the distribution(s) could receive a cash distribution or a regular cash allowance. This is more likely to arise under Trust II, where a beneficiary may not have a disability that qualifies him or her for Medicaid and SSI.

Given the need to work within these restrictions, Wispact makes distributions in one of the following ways:

- **Direct payment to providers of goods and services, in response to request for distribution.** Wispact has a request for distribution form[28] that can be used to request payment to their provider. Direct payment to providers presents the practical problem of how to get the money from the trust to the provider in a timely way, without running the money through the hands of the beneficiary or an account belonging to the beneficiary or a guardian. Where the provider is willing to deliver the good or service and wait for payment, the person requesting reimbursement can submit the bill to Wispact for payment to the provider, with Wispact's request for distribution form.

  For a **store purchase**, such as purchase of clothing or furniture, stores will not release items without payment, unless they have an established relationship with Wispact. Similarly, **service providers** may want an upfront payment. This may mean that the person has to find the item he or she wants to buy – or make a contract for a

---

[28] See Forms, at www.wispact.org, and in the *Wispact Handbook,* p. 17.

service – get the price or estimated cost, and then request a distribution from the trust to pay the provider. This process is cumbersome and is not a practical solution to, e.g., purchase of petrol for a vehicle, purchases of groceries and household supplies or payment of hotel and meal expenses when the person is travelling.

. Wispact can set up **direct payment of regular bills**, such as phone bills, Internet and cable connections, utilities, etc.

. **Payment of credit card bills**. If the beneficiary is able to get a credit card in his or her own name, the beneficiary can charge items and submit the credit card bill, along with receipts for purchases. Wispact will pay the portion of the bill that it decides to allow as a trust distribution. It will typically not pay for charges for cash or for food or shelter for an SSI recipient. This may necessitate separate payments by Wispact and the beneficiary. To make this work, credit card bills need to be submitted in a timely way, to allow for Wispact's 7-to-10-day turnaround time.

. **Appointment of disbursement agent**. Wispact can appoint a person (other than the beneficiary) as an agent authorised to make disbursements.[29] That person can then make purchases from a list of approved items using his or her funds and get reimbursed by submitting a request for distribution form and receipts. This works well if the beneficiary has a person in his life who is willing to make the cash advances or credit card purchases on his or her own account, and who is willing to assist the person in making purchases, e.g., by accompanying him or her to the provider. Finally, the agent must have the judgement to know what Wispact will or will not pay for with trust funds. Receipts are required.

. **Payment to individual support or chore service providers**. Wispact requires that individuals being paid for work from the trust either (1) have bona fide status as independent contractors, under US employment law criteria, or (2) are in an employment relationship with someone other than Wispact, so that payments are made for payroll taxes, unemployment compensation insurance and worker's compensation insurance. A number of agencies exist in Wisconsin which will provide **fiscal intermediary services** which can provide payroll-management services to enable people with disabilities to be employers.

---

[29] See Wispact Agent Agreement Option, www.wispact.org, under Forms, or the *Wispact Handbook,* pp. 18–19.

• **Loans** (even of cash) are not counted as income if there is an obligation and realistic plan to repay the loan. Loans can be used to pay larger recurring expenses (such as real estate taxes or home repairs), which are then paid back over time, so that a loan can be made again when needed.

The SSI/Medicaid limits on distributions of cash and in-kind food and shelter have imposed artificial barriers to providing timely assistance to beneficiaries, significantly added to Wispact's administrative costs and required beneficiaries to identify themselves as trust recipients instead of ordinary shoppers. Two new developments may moderate the effect of these barriers:

• **ABLE accounts** can be funded from a trust account and can then function very much the same as any other bank account held by the individual or guardian (See Section VI.E).
• In May 2018, SSA announced a new policy under which it would not count the balance on a **prepaid administrator-managed credit card** as a resource, where the beneficiary is the cardholder, if the trust is the owner of the card.[30]

E   Use of ABLE Accounts to Meet Beneficiary Needs and Goals

In 2014, the US Congress passed legislation[31] authorising states to establish ABLE account systems to facilitate saving by and for people with disabilities. An ABLE account can be funded with assets of the person with a disability, or of third parties. An ABLE account is not a trust: funds in the account belong directly to the person with a disability, who can draw on them as on a bank account. However: ABLE accounts are not counted towards the resource limit for SSI and Medicaid; third-party deposits to an account are not counted as income; and withdrawals of funds from an ABLE account are not counted as income, even if taken in cash or to pay for food and shelter. Income earned on accounts is exempt from taxation.

---

[30] Social Security Administration, *Trusts Established with the Assets of an Individual on or after 01/01/00*, n 24, § IIf.

[31] Codified at 26 U SC § 529A. SSI policy is in Social Security Administration, *Achieving a Better Life Experience (ABLE) Accounts* (POMS SI 01130.740, 2018), available from http://policy.ssa.gov/poms.nsf/lnx/0501130740, and Wisconsin Medicaid policy is in MEH , n 3, § 16.7.30. A comparison of the plans in different states is available online at www.ablenrc.org.

ABLE accounts are not available to all people who can have SNTs, cannot be funded at unlimited levels and may not meet full range of needs and wants that an SNT can serve. ABLE accounts are only available to people who became disabled before turning 26 years of age. Total deposits to an ABLE account from all donors may not exceed USD15,000 per year. For SSI, total funding of the account cannot exceed USD100,000. State Medicaid limits may be higher, up to USD300,000 (depending on state policy). To come within ABLE account protections, withdrawals must be used for 'qualified disability expenses'. While these are broadly defined,[32] an ABLE account cannot, e.g., pay for entertainment expenses. Finally, there is no trustee, so management and withdrawal decisions are made by the individual or his or her legal representative.

Trusts may be contributors to ABLE accounts, and a self-funded SNT will be treated as a third-party contributor.[33] While its experience to date with ABLE accounts is limited, **Wispact could potentially make cash distributions to ABLE accounts**, which the person could then draw on as he or she wishes to pay qualified disability expenses. This would (1) increase beneficiary autonomy over the transferred funds, and (2) include the potential for a beneficiary who is an SSI recipient to use funds from the ABLE account to pay for food and shelter expenses, which would have been counted as in-kind income if they had paid directly from the Wispact account.

VII Making Wispact Accounts Affordable; Use of the Retained Fund

A Why Is Wispact Committed to Making Small Accounts Affordable?

It often happens that a person has a relatively small amount of money, but this is his or her only resource, and he or she is not likely to have access to additional resources in future. Some sources of one-time assets include the following:

- The person's lifetime savings, which may never have been large or may have been reduced to a small amount.

---

[32] 26 U SC § 529A(e)(5).

[33] Social Security Administration, *Achieving a Better Life Experience (ABLE) Accounts*, n 31, § C1b.

- A retirement account funded by an employer, which becomes available to the person as a lump-sum when he or she stops working for that employer.
- A gift, bequest or inheritance.
- A backpayment of Social Security or SSI benefits, which often occurs because there is a delay between application date and establishment of status as a person with a disability.
- A recovery for damages.

The ability to retain even a small reserve for special expenses can make an enormous difference to a person with disabilities who is otherwise dependent on the government for everything, often living on an income below poverty and forced to hold his or her countable resources under USD2,000.

Where the person does not have a reliable friend or family member to act as a trustee, a Wispact trust may be the only option. US banks typically charge minimum fees of USD3,000 or more per year for acting as trustees of trusts with assets less than USD200,000, and a USD2,000 fee when the account closes is not unusual. The incentive for these accounts is to spend the assets before they are wiped out by the fees. A pooled or community trust with a commitment to small accounts is the only option, and acting in this role is a core part of Wispact's purpose and mission.

B   Administration Fees and Application Fees

The Wispact administrative fee schedule[34] varies with size of account. It is intended to favor small accounts, with no minimum fee. Fees cover both the trustee fee and the fee for the management services of Wispact, Inc. Fees combine a monthly dollar amount with an annual percentage fee based on account assets, which makes comparison difficult. Illustrative fees for accounts of the following sizes in May 2018, as a percentage of trust assets, were

USD10,000	0.46% of account value	USD460 annual fee
USD20,000	2.76% of account value	USD552 annual fee
USD50,000	2.16% of account value	USD1,080 annual fee
USD100,000	1.76% of account value	USD1,760 annual fee
USD250,000	1.13% of account value	USD2,829 annual fee

---

[34] Available at www.wispact.org, under Forms, or in the *Wispact Handbook*, p. 30.

There is an annual fee of USD225 per account for tax preparation (see Section VIII.B), but this fee is covered by the Wispact Retained Fund.

SEI Investments Management Corporation charges a 0.5 per cent annual fee on the pooled investment accounts for its investment advisory services. Reported investment returns are net of that fee. In all years except 2008, account income has more than covered all fees.

An application fee of USD250 is charged for each funded account. The fee for an unfunded account is USD150, with the USD100 balance owed when the account is funded.

C   Large Accounts Help Pay Overall Administrative Costs; Empty Accounts Are Cost-Free

The average value of a funded Wispact sub-account in September 2017 was just less than USD41,000.[35] However, that number hid a wide range:

USD0.00–USD10,000	1,293 sub-accounts
USD10,000–USD30,000	738 sub-accounts
USD30,000–USD100,000	625 sub-accounts
USD100,000–USD150,000	128 sub-accounts
USD150,000–USD250,000	78 sub-accounts
USD250,000+	73 sub-accounts

Wispact is able to attract large accounts because it is seen as providing a stable, long-term source of management, with a commitment to serve people with disabilities. The ability to attract larger accounts has helped Wispact to establish a funding base for administrative costs, and to be able to charge lower fees for smaller accounts, so that people do not see principal being eaten away by fees.

As of 31 March 2018, 882 of the 1,350 third-party Trust II accounts were unfunded, but were designated as beneficiaries in wills, remainder designations on investments or life insurance, etc. Wispact incurs no costs for maintaining these accounts. Families retain responsibility for managing assets and ensuring eventual funding. While this may increase risk of loss, it avoids tying up funds and incurring administrative fees for long periods when no distributions are needed.

---

[35] Information provided from Wispact's database in response to author's query, October 2017.

D   Use of the Retained Fund

A little more than USD1.1 million was spent from the Retained Fund in 2017. The primary use of the Retained Fund has been to offset the expense of establishing and maintaining smaller accounts. This is done by

- **Creation grants**. As of May 2018, the Retained Fund provides creation grants to offset cost of establishing a funded account in Trust I with USD75,000 or less, or an account in Trust II with USD90,000 or less. The grant reimbursed the account for Wispact's application fee and for the attorney fee, up to no more than USD2,000.
- **Tax preparation fees**. The Retained Fund will spend about USD500,000 this year on tax preparation fees that would otherwise be charged to individual accounts.

In 2018, Wispact created and filled the position of Retained Fund coordinator, as part of its effort to increase grants to Trust I and Trust II beneficiaries for other purposes, including general living expenses, funeral costs for deceased beneficiaries, assistive devices, dental care (which is poorly covered by Medicaid in Wisconsin) and advocacy services. These grants are made on a case-by-case basis in response to requests or needs identified by staff, and are often for individuals who have exhausted funding in their accounts.

VIII   Taxation Issues

There is very little coordination between treatment of SNTs for purposes of US public benefits and treatment of trusts for purposes of income taxes. This results in a risk that beneficiaries may pay much higher taxes because of the need to hold assets in a trust, and it results in substantial administrative costs for completing tax returns on smaller accounts, even where minimal or no taxes are owed.

A   Income Taxation of Income Taxable to Third-Party Trust II Accounts

Trusts pay much higher income tax rates than individuals on income that is accumulated in a trust, i.e., not distributed for the person's benefit in the same year that it is earned. The marginal tax rate for trusts hits 35 per cent at USD12,500 in annual income that is taxable to the trust.[36]

---

[36] K. P. Erb, 'What the 2018 Tax Brackets, Standard Deductions and More Look Like under Tax Reform', Forbes, 17 December 2017, available from www.forbes.com.

The high income tax rates that apply to accumulated income are intended to prevent individuals from avoiding tax by voluntarily shifting income to a trust. However, they present a problem for family members establishing SNTs who either:

- want to put away substantial assets in an SNT, and have those trusts earn income and grow over time, during a period when the person is not in need of substantial distributions; or
- are in a situation where they need to fund the SNT with assets that will be taxable income when they go into the trust. Many people now hold substantial assets in retirement accounts that are funded from earnings from work not taxed at the time the money is earned. These accounts are only taxed at the time the funds are distributed from the retirement account. If these are directed to an SNT at the death of the owner, they can result in high taxable income if the funds cannot be usefully distributed in the year received.

US income tax law partially addresses this problem by creating a tax exemption for the first USD4,150 in income otherwise taxable to a *qualified disability trust*.[37] This exemption alleviates the income tax problem for relatively small accounts, but the punitive income tax rates on trusts are a continuing problem for larger accounts in the accumulation phase and for families who plan to fund accounts with substantial pre-tax retirement assets.

B Income Taxation of Income Distributed for Beneficiaries of Self-Funded Accounts

All income of self-funded Wispact accounts is taxed as income of the beneficiary, whether or not the income is distributed. Because beneficiaries typically are in low-income tax brackets, this tax treatment is generally favourable. However, the need to account for and report the earnings for tax purposes creates substantial administrative costs for the Wispact trusts and for beneficiaries.

All Wispact accounts, regardless of size, are invested and earn at least a small amount of income, and the trustee files an income tax return for every account. The return shows types of income; deductions; income distributed, if any; and income retained, if any. The trustee then sends each beneficiary a statement of income that is taxable to the beneficiary,

---

[37] J. McCarten, *The Impact of Tax Reform on Special Needs Planning* (Special Needs Alliance, 2018), available from www.specialneedsalliance.org.

broken down by type of income. The trustee in 2017 charged a uniform fee of USD225 for each tax return. The Retained Fund reimburses all funded accounts for the tax preparation fees.

A beneficiary must show income earned on a Wispact account on his or her personal tax return. This often triggers an income tax filing requirement for a person who might not otherwise have one and complicates the tax returns of beneficiaries whose income situation is otherwise simple. This may mean that a person who was getting free or low-cost help must pay a professional to complete a tax return.

IX   Closing Comments

A   Relevance of the Wispact Experience to the Planned Hong Kong Special Needs Trust

Wispact's role in the lives of its beneficiaries is very different from the role envisioned for the special needs trust that the Hong Kong government has agreed to establish (discussed in Chapter 13 of this book, and referred to here as the HK-SNT). While income maintenance programmes in Hong Kong are somewhat parallel to those in the United States, and present similar issues of how trust assets will be treated to avoid disincentives to saving, Hong Kong does not have a needs-based long-term support programme equivalent to US Medicaid. Hong Kong's residential and vocational support programmes are not needs-based entitlements, and have long waiting lists. Family caregivers cannot expect that public programmes will meet basic support needs, when they are no longer able to provide care. Culturally, also, there is a strong expectation in Hong Kong that families will provide long-term care for family members throughout their lifetimes.

Because of the public benefits and cultural context, the purpose of the HK-SNT is almost the exact reverse of a US-SNT like Wispact: it is intended to be a *basic support and care* trust. It is expected that family members (usually parents) will fund the HK-SNT during their lives, and that the account will make periodic transfers of cash to the people who become caregivers after the primary family members are no longer able to provide care. Future caregivers will be designated by the family in the plan for use of trust assets. Use of trust assets will be largely determined by the family plan. Surveys of potential users indicate that they have greater trust in government agencies to operate the trust and invest assets (rather than a private corporation and bank trustee), and that they value preservation of principal over investment for growth that might put principal at risk.[38]

The HK-SNT is a governmental program to facilitate voluntary saving for future basic needs, and continued care by caregivers. The HK government will have little reason to look to the government policies that affect US-SNTs. As examples:

. Hong Kong will want to encourage savings from all possible sources and will have no reason to place special restrictions on self-funding.
. The HK-SNT is explicitly intended to make cash payments and payments for food and shelter.
. Payments that produce incidental benefit to caregivers will be consistent with encouraging caregivers to continue in their role.
. Administrative burdens will need to be minimised, including accounting on the form and purpose of expenditures.

Despite these differences, Wispact and the HK-SNT share the goal of providing an asset manager and substitute decision maker that understands the needs, experiences and goals of people with disabilities and their families. Some aspects of Wispact's approach that may be relevant, as Hong Kong develops and implements its plans, include the following:

. Wispact emphasises respect for beneficiary preferences, in making decision on use of funds, and of having a disinterested advisor to each account (See Section VI.A).
. Wispact is available to serve beneficiaries with any type of disability, at any age, which has provided a wide funding base and has delivered a valuable public service.
. Wispact's growth-oriented investments have more than covered management fees and might be considered as at least an option that some Hong Kong families might choose.
. Wispact's recognised commitment and expertise and its promise of stable, ongoing management have attracted larger accounts to help build its funding base. The HK-SNT might have similar attractions to larger donors if it decides to seek them.
. Wispact is willing to maintain empty accounts for future funding, at no current cost.

---

[38] See L. Ho and R. Lee, 'Reforming Enduring Powers and Launching a Special Needs Trust in Hong Kong', in Chapter 13 of this volume.

- Wisconsin state law exempts SNTs from almost all creditor's claims. Hong Kong may want to promote saving in the HK-SNT by providing similar protections.
- The Retained Fund allows Wispact to continue distributions after account assets are exhausted, although there is no commitment to maintain the same level of distributions. The question of what will happen to beneficiaries of depleted accounts will be of great concern in Hong Kong, where the account will be the source of basic support.

B Does Wispact Contribute to Rights to Financial Self-Determination?

Article 12 of the United Nations' Convention on the Rights of Persons with Disabilities (CRPD) calls on states to ensure that people with disabilities have equal rights to own and inherit property and control their financial affairs. Measures related to incapacity that restrict independence must meet standards for respect of human rights, protection from abuse and proportionality to the need for protection, in terms of both level and duration of restrictive measures.

Wispact is a non-governmental organization, and is not directly subject to the CRPD. As discussed in Section III, there are good reasons why an individual or family could appropriately choose a Wispact SNT to protect funds for the sole benefit of a person with impaired ability to manage finances, as a way to prevent exploitation, to ensure that funds are preserved for priority needs and wants, and to ensure that unmet needs and wants are identified and addressed. This decision-making support is less restrictive and more flexible than guardianship, and Wispact makes it accessible to individuals and families who could not otherwise afford a corporate trustee.

In the context of SSI/Medicaid policies, Wispact plays a positive role in making it possible for people to own beneficial interests in property they could not own directly, and to receive gifts or inheritances of beneficial interests, when SSI/Medicaid policies would otherwise lead to disinheritance. However, SSI/Medicaid policies penalizing direct ownership of property mean that many Wispact accounts are funded as a direct result of government policy. It is fair to ask to what extent the Wispact trusts carry out the values of the CRPD in administering those funds.

As SNTs, the Wispact trusts cannot give a beneficiary power to dictate distributions, and accounts cannot be revocable. As a result, the legal restriction on beneficiaries is not proportional to level of incapacity, and the duration restrictions on management do not relate to duration of incapacity. Whether or not funds continue to be held in trust is not subject to independent review, although a beneficiary could bring a court action to challenge a failure to act in the beneficiary's interests. Within this legal framework, Wispact and its trustee have discretion to administer the trust to promote beneficiary autonomy and choice and reduce the risk of abuse and exploitation. In practice:

- Wispact gives primary weight to the person's preferences on use of funds (see Section VI.A). Wispact recognises beneficiary autonomy and choice as central to its determination of whether it is acting in the person's interests. Wispact is a fiduciary and can sometimes overrule the beneficiary's wishes, but does so rarely, to protect the person's essential interests (see Section VI). Wispact has discretion to give weight to beneficiary preference and changing conditions over time. Settlors' guidance in a letter of intent, and advisors' recommendations, are advisory only. Wispact will hold accounts with no advisor, where the beneficiary is able to fill that role. Wispact lacks resources to be in regular direct contact with beneficiaries, except by telephone or written communication, which may create a barrier to the ability of some beneficiaries to understand and communicate their choices.
- Distributions, discussed in Section VI.D, must be approved by Wispact, and the process can be cumbersome. Wispact uses methods that allow people to make purchases independently and without being labelled (e.g., through use of credit card reimbursement), but these are not practical for everyone, and can be restricted if Wispact's rules are not followed. The new options of prepaid debit cards and ABLE accounts will increase ability to give beneficiaries similar-to-cash access to funds.
- While Wispact accounts are not time limited or subject to outside review, Wispact has discretion to make direct cash distributions to beneficiaries, and/or to spend down the account to zero, as long as sole-benefit rules are followed. This discretion can be used, e.g., for people who no longer receive public benefits.
- Largely for cost reasons, as well as avoidance of risk, Wispact trusts do not give beneficiaries control over investment of funds (see Section II.C). They do allow some flexibility for unique investments and for trust ownership of homes that are then managed and maintained by the individual, family or other supports.
- Some conflict of interest is built in, as Wispact benefits financially from fees on accounts, and the Retained Fund, managed by Wispact, is a

remainder beneficiary of most Trust I accounts (see Section VII). Internal active board oversight is the primary check on conflict of interest. The board has consciously worked to establish strong consumer and advocate representation, and to prevent control of the board by persons who receive payments from trust funds. Both beneficiaries and advisors have complete and timely access to information on income and expenditures from accounts.

11

SNTC's Operational Experience as Singapore's First Non-Profit Trust Company

ESTHER TAN* AND AMELIA LEO[†]

I Introduction

A How SNTC Started

In the early 2000s, a group of parents whose children were attending special education schools set up by the Movement of the Intellectually Disabled in Singapore (MINDS) realised that there was a gap in the local disability services landscape. While there were many social services and programmes available for persons with special needs (PSNs), no organisation was looking into how the financial security of adults with special needs could be ensured, particularly after their parents' demise. As a result, these individuals with special needs were at risk of financial mismanagement and even financial exploitation by others. The parents thus began advocating for the government to look into this issue. Several years later, in 2008, the Special Needs Trust Company Ltd (SNTC) was set up with the support of the Ministry of Social & Family Development (MSF), the National Council of Social Service (NCSS) and the Public Trustee (PT) as the first – and, to date, only – non-profit trust company in Singapore. SNTC officially launched its trust services in October 2009.

To date, SNTC has been serving the special needs community for 10 years, by providing affordable trust services to PSNs who are widely defined in SNTC's Constitution as

> those whose prospects of securing, retaining places and advancing in education and training institutions, employment and recreation as equal members of the community are substantially reduced as a result of physical, sensory, intellectual and/or developmental impairments. This may also include persons with mental disabilities.

* General Manager, Special Needs Trust Company Ltd, Singapore.
† Manager (Special Projects), Special Needs Trust Company Ltd, Singapore.

In addition, the PSN must be a Singapore citizen or permanent resident residing in Singapore; and the settlor must: (i) be 21 years of age or older; (ii) have mental capacity to set up a trust; and (iii) not be an undischarged bankrupt.

While all PSNs (and settlors) who meet the criteria can sign up for SNTC's service, SNTC specifically targets to serve low- to middle-income families caring for PSNs. This is because such families are in greatest need of affordable trust services. As a non-profit organisation, SNTC also believes that its limited resources should be reserved for those who genuinely need them and cannot afford the other available options.

Parents, caregivers or legal representatives of a PSN can choose to enhance the financial security of the PSN by appointing SNTC as trustee over a sum of money that is to be managed for the benefit of the PSN, who is referred to as the 'life beneficiary' (LB). The money is held and invested by the PT, and the principal sum is guaranteed by the government. Upon the demise of certain individuals designated by the settlor (who could include the settlor him or herself), SNTC will administer the funds to meet the needs of the LB. The funds may be disbursed to individuals identified by the settlor as the LB's caregiver (i.e., the 'appointed caregiver'), or to organisations providing services to the LB. Upon the LB's demise, the trust balance (if any) will be distributed to the residual beneficiaries named by the settlor.

The following diagram summarises how the various parties to the trust arrangement interact with one another:

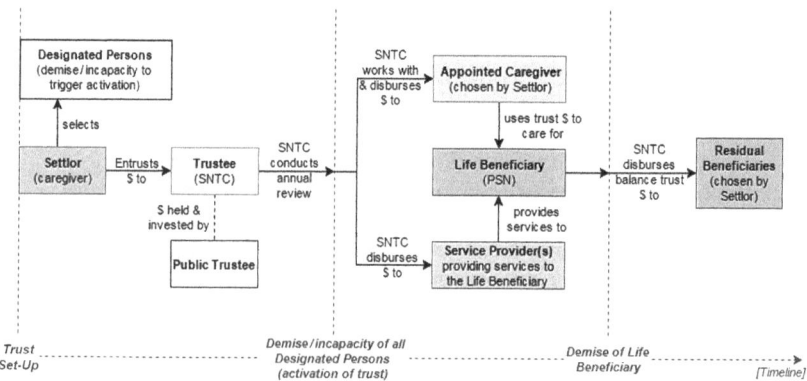

Figure 11.1 Overview of SNTC Trust and the Parties Involved

B SNTC at a Glance

As of SNTC's financial year ending March 2018, 539 trust accounts have been set up with SNTC. A cumulative year-on-year breakdown (based on financial year) is provided in Table 11.1 to indicate the significant widening of SNTC's client base over the years:

The profile of SNTC's beneficiaries is summarised in the two diagrams in Figure 11.2. A large majority of beneficiaries have intellectual or mental disabilities that render many of them mentally incapable of managing their financial matters independently.

C Organisational Structure

SNTC is a company limited by guarantee that has been granted charity status under the Charities Act. Due to the non-profit nature of its business, it has been exempted from licensing under the Trust Companies Act. Nonetheless, the SNTC is regulated by several legislative instruments (e.g., Trustees Act, Charities Act, Companies Act) as well as by the funding agreement it has with the MSF.

SNTC is led by a Board of Directors comprising well-regarded professionals from the legal, financial, public service, medical, business and IT sectors as well as parents of PSNs. All 12 directors are volunteers.

In terms of staff count, SNTC is a small setup. It commenced operations in 2009 with only five staff members,[1] and has since grown to 14 staff and five departments – i.e. (i) Finance, General Administration & Human Resource, (ii) Planning & Operations, (iii) Case Management, (iv) Trust Administration and (v) Community Engagement. The department heads report to the general manager, who in turn reports to the board of directors. There is no Investment Department because the PT is tasked with holding and investing the trust funds. All SNTC's case managers are social work trained, and so have a deep understanding of the social and caregiving needs of PSNs and their families. This sets SNTC apart from other trust companies in the private sector.

---

[1] There was one general manager, one Finance & Administration staff, one Trust Administration staff, and two case managers.

Table 11.1 *Year-on-Year Breakdown on the Number of Trust Accounts*

	FY09	FY10	FY11	FY12	FY13	FY14	FY15	FY16	FY 17
No. of trust accounts	37	95	140	156	236	317	388	460	539
No. of activated accounts	0	1	3	5	6	11	18	22	23
No. of terminated accounts	0	0	2	5	6	9	10	11	15

AGE OF BENEFICIARIES (AS OF FY17)

■ ≤10 years   ■ 11–20 years   ■ 21–30 years   ■ 31–40 years   ■ 41–50 years
■ 51–60 years   ■ 61–70 years   ■ 71–80 years   ■ 81–90 years   ■ ≥91 years

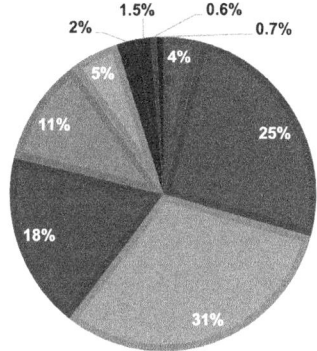

TYPE OF DISABILITY (AS OF FY17)

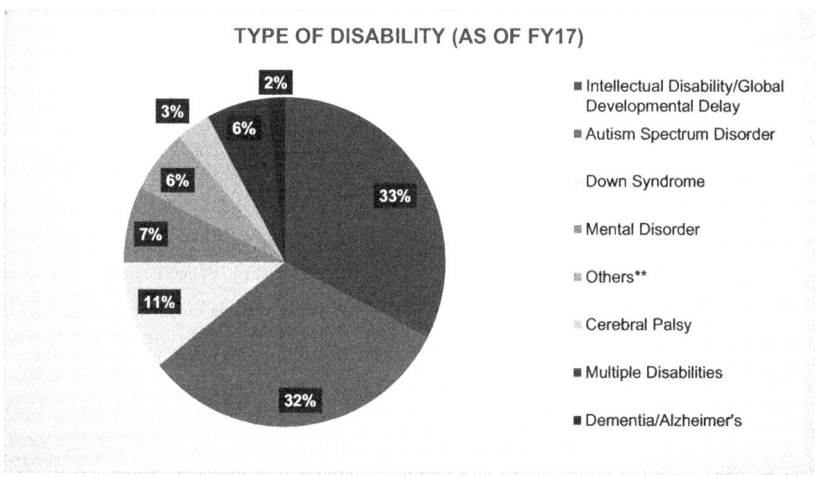

Figure 11.2   Profile of SNTC's Beneficiaries
**Includes physical disabilities, learning disabilities, and rare disorders (Rett Syndrome, Prader-Willi Syndrome, Williams Syndrome, etc.)

Figure 11.3 summarises SNTC's current organisational structure:

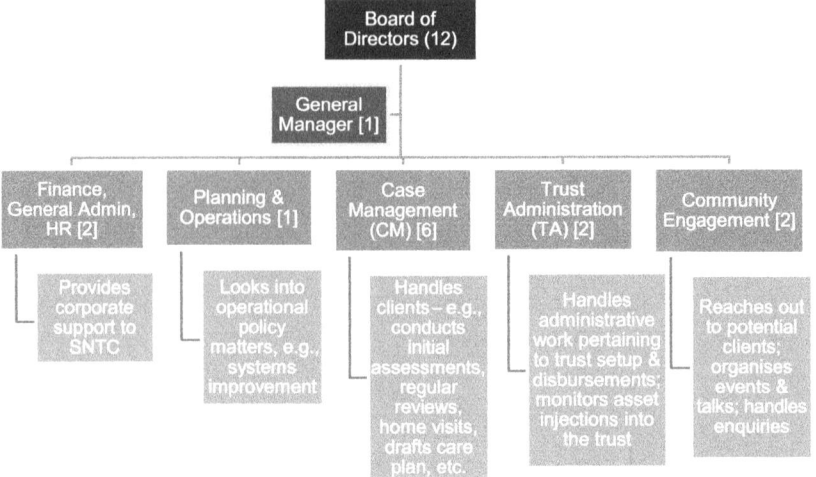

Figure 11.3   SNTC's Organisational Structure

D   *Funding Arrangements*

Currently, SNTC's overall operating and manpower expenditures are fully funded by the MSF, subject to the fulfilment of two key performance indicators: (i) the number of care plans drafted, and (ii) the number of trust accounts set up in the given financial year. Previously, SNTC's funding was based solely on the number of trust accounts established. However, that funding approach was not sustainable as the expense required to maintain the existing trust accounts would increase over time even if there was no concurrent increase in the number of new trust accounts. This approach also led to overemphasis on setting up trust accounts, even if this was not beneficial for the potential client (e.g., due to low trust potential[2]).

To keep the fees affordable, SNTC uses part of the funding provided by the MSF to offset 90–100 per cent of the fees payable to SNTC as illustrated in Table 11.2:

---

[2] A case could have low trust potential if the settlor has hardly any assets to inject or bequeath to the trust if one is set up for the PSN. Financial assistance might be more appropriate for such clients.

Table 11.2 *Funding Arrangements at Different Stages of the Trust Accounts*

	Trust Setup	Pre-Activation	Activation	Post-Activation
Fees payable	SGD1,500	SGD250	SGD400	SGD400
Frequency	One-time	Annual	One-time	Annual
% offset by MSF funding	90	100	90	90
Fees paid by client	SGD150	SGD0	SGD40	SGD40

II   SNTC's Operational Experiences

Over the past 10 years, SNTC has encountered many challenges in several areas of its operations, such as the take-up rate, service delivery, capability building, outreach, and IT systems. Some of these issues have been resolved while others remain a work in progress. The following sections describe SNTC's experience in the more pertinent aspects of its operations.

A   Take-Up Rate

As can be seen from Figure 11.4 (which is derived from the Table 11.2), the sign-up rate during the initial years, FY09 to FY12, was low. Even today, the take-up rate remains relatively low at 539 accounts (as of FY17).

Based on interactions with potential clients at various outreach events, there appeared to be several reasons for the relatively low take-up rates, as follows.

1   High Fees

When SNTC was first set up, the fees were not subsidised by the MSF. This was because the ministry felt that the fees were already significantly lower than the private trust services that existed in the market.

However, many families belonging to SNTC's target group (i.e., the lower- and middle-income families) still found the fees largely unaffordable. For instance, many such families would struggle to pay the SGD1,500 setup fee upfront, in addition to the SGD5,000 required as the minimum capital to set up the trust. To some of these families, the

No. of Trust Accounts

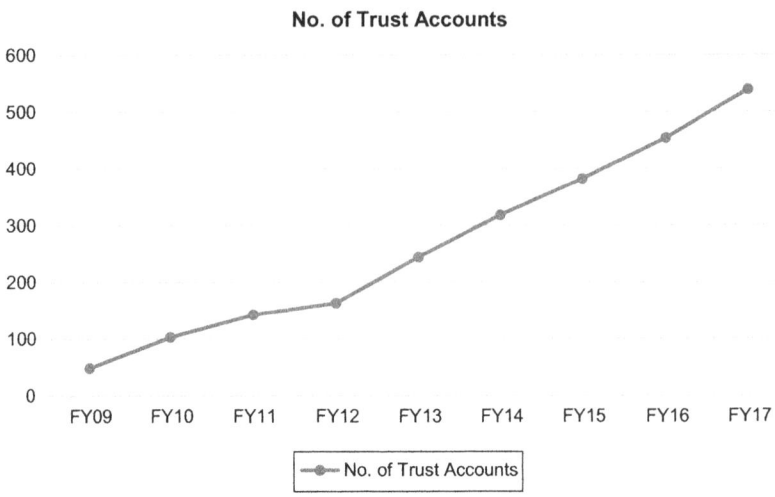

Figure 11.4   **Number of Trust Accounts Set Up over the Years**

combined sum of SGD6,500 would require them to draw down on a significant part of their savings. The annual deductions during the later stages of the trust service (i.e., pre-activation, activation and post-activation) also appeared unreasonable to these families, as they could not understand why some part of the trust fund (which is meant for the LB's benefit) had to be used to pay for SNTC's services.

Furthermore, clients also had to pay for PT's asset management and investment services. The fees payable to PT are shown in Table 11.3.

While such fees may appear reasonable to those familiar with the going rates in the private sector, many lower- and middle-income families considered them to be unreasonable. They were especially concerned that the beneficiary's trust balance could be depleted by the annual pre-activation fees (SGD250) alone, if no top-ups were made during the settlor's lifetime. This was because the financial circumstances of many lower- and middle-income settlors made it impossible for them to contribute to the trust during their lifetime (they could only contribute after their demise via their will and/or insurance nominations). As a result, the fees were considered unaffordable by this group even though they were already less than the market rate.

To address these perceptions, at its outreach events, SNTC attempted to explain the rationale for its fees and highlighted the amount of work

Table 11.3 *Fees Payable to the Public Trustee (PT)*

Acceptance Fees (computed on the sum of initial and subsequent capital injection at the following rates)	
First SGD5,000	6.5%
Next SGD2,000	6.00%
Next SGD3,000	4.25%
Next SGD10,000	2.75%
Next SGD30,000	2.25%
Next SGD200,000	1.70%
Next SGD250,000	1.40%
Next SGD250,000	1.15%
> SGD750,000	0.85%
Fees on Interest Earned	
First SGD1,000 earned	5.50%
Next SGD1,000 earned	4.50%
Next SGD1,000 earned	3.50%
> SGD3,000 earned	2.25%

done by SNTC and the PT for each case (which would justify the fees charged). SNTC also emphasised that the fees were reasonable compared to those for private-sector trust services. Nonetheless, many potential clients in the target group were not convinced. This was not totally unexpected, because lower- to middle-income families typically faced many day-to-day struggles, both in terms of caregiving and financial matters. Many simply lacked the bandwidth to appreciate the importance of long-term financial planning. As a result, the most urgent of tasks (i.e., taking care of the daily needs of the beneficiary) naturally took precedence over less time-pressing issues of the future. Moreover, the issue of annual pre-activation fees possibly depleting the trust account could not be adequately addressed without lowering those fees.

SNTC subsequently raised the matter with the MSF in 2011 and managed to negotiate more funding so that funds could be used to subsidise the fees charged by SNTC. In 2012, the 90–100 per cent subsidies mentioned above kicked in. Due to the high level of subsidies, settlors who were hard-pressed for cash during their lifetimes no longer had to worry that the trust fund could be depleted due to pre-activation fees. As Table 11.4 demonstrates, the trust account would only make a slight loss in the first three years before earning interest from the fourth year onwards:

Table 11.4 *Year-on-Year Projection on Trust Fund*

Refers to what the settlor injects into the trust	What PT charges the settlor* for his/her top-up	What is left in the trust, minus PT's fee on capital	What PT charges the settlor* for interest earned	SNTC's review fee	Total funds left in the trust after fees are subtracted. C/F = Carry Forward	ROI = Return on investment

Pre-Activation Projection on Trust Fund

Year	B/F	Gross Capital Injected	PT Fee on Capital incl GST	Net Capital Invested	Interest Earned	PT Fee on Interest Earned incl GST	Review Fee $250 fully subsidized	Total Fees	Funds Net of Fees C/F	Total Gross Capital Injected to-date	ROI	% OF ROI
1		$5,000.00	$325.00	$4,675.00	$96.28	$5.30		$330.30	$4,766.98	$5,000.00	-$234.02	-4.68
2	$4,766.98	$0.00	$0.00	$4,766.98	$98.15	$5.40	$0.00	$5.40	$4,858.73	$5,000.00	-$141.27	-2.83
3	$4,858.73	$0.00	$0.00	$4,858.73	$100.06	$5.50	$0.00	$5.50	$4,953.29	$5,000.00	-$46.71	-0.93
4	$4,953.29	$0.00	$0.00	$4,953.29	$102.01	$5.61	$0.00	$5.61	$5,049.69	$5,000.00	$49.69	0.99
5	$5,049.69	$0.00	$0.00	$5,049.69	$103.99	$5.72	$0.00	$5.72	$5,147.96	$5,000.00	$147.96	2.96
6	$5,147.96	$0.00	$0.00	$5,147.96	$106.02	$5.83	$0.00	$5.83	$5,248.15	$5,000.00	$248.15	4.96
7	$5,248.15	$0.00	$0.00	$5,248.15	$108.08	$5.94	$0.00	$5.94	$5,350.28	$5,000.00	$350.28	7.01
8	$5,350.28	$0.00	$0.00	$5,350.28	$110.17	$6.06	$0.00	$6.06	$5,454.41	$5,000.00	$454.41	9.09
9	$5,454.41	$0.00	$0.00	$5,454.41	$112.33	$6.18	$0.00	$6.18	$5,560.56	$5,000.00	$560.56	11.21
10	$5,560.56	$0.00	$0.00	$5,560.56	$114.51	$6.30	$0.00	$6.30	$5,668.77	$5,000.00	$668.77	13.38

Since the subsidies were put in place, the take-up rate for SNTC's trust service has steadily increased, with an average of 73 new accounts now being established each year, and more lower- to middle-income families caring for PSNs are now able to benefit from the service.

2 PT's Low Rate of Return

Besides the issue of fees, some potential clients also felt that the interest rate offered by the PT was too low, and hence it was not meaningful to set up a trust whereby the funds would be invested by them.

As the PT is a government body set up by statute (i.e., the Public Trustee Act[3]), it operates in a different manner from private fund managers and takes a conservative approach to making investments. All funds received by the PT for investment (including funds from SNTC's trust accounts) are directed into a Common Fund. The Common Fund is then invested as a whole by the PT, and at the end of the investment period, any interest earned is credited to each account accordingly. The Common Fund is invested in low-risk financial products such as government bonds, and the principal sum of each trust account is guaranteed by the government.

To address the issue of low returns, SNTC makes it a point to explain to potential clients that the objective of its trust service differs from that of private trust services: the primary goal is to safeguard funds for the beneficiary's future use, not to grow the settled sum through investment. Given that the objective is to safeguard the funds settled, the PT provides

---

[3] A copy of the statute can be found here: http://statutes.agc.gov.sg.

an appropriate mechanism because its investments are low risk and the principal sum is government guaranteed. SNTC also highlights to potential clients that the PT's rate of return has historically hovered around 2–3 per cent.[4]

3   Irrevocability of the Trust

The third issue that may have contributed to the low take-up rate relates to the irrevocable nature of an SNTC trust. Irrevocability serves a protective function. Given the vulnerability of the beneficiary, it is important that any monies set aside for him or her will not be withdrawn or taken away by third parties.

However, many potential clients see irrevocability as a disadvantage. They would prefer to retain the flexibility of changing their mind, should (for example) SNTC's terms of service become less attractive than what other service providers offer in future. Some families – especially those who are young – are also uncertain about the future and whether a trust is appropriate for their circumstances.

SNTC addressed this issue by highlighting the protective purpose of irrevocability. Younger families are also advised to attend financial education workshops organised by SNTC from time to time so that they can be apprised of what they can do to better plan for the future. The idea of setting up a trust could always be revisited later, when their financial circumstances become more certain.

4   Lack of Awareness of the Benefits of a Trust

The last factor that may have affected the take-up rate relates to a lack of awareness of how a trust can benefit the PSN in a family. Many families in SNTC's target group are not highly educated; and hence many find the concept of a trust unfamiliar. In most cases, their first encounter with SNTC would also be their first encounter with the concept. Thus, many families take a while to understand the workings of a trust, let alone how it can benefit the PSN.

A perennial challenge for SNTC is thus educating the special needs community as a whole about how a special needs trust works and what its benefits are. This is not an easy task because the concept involves the use of technical terms that are only familiar to lawyers (beneficiary, settlor, trustee, residual beneficiaries, etc.). The challenge is compounded by the

---

[4] The rates are publicly available in the various notifications listed here: http://statutes.agc.gov.sg.

cultural diversity of the Singaporean population, as potential clients may be conversant in only one or two of the many languages and/or dialects spoken in Singapore. Most of SNTC's case managers are bilingual or even multilingual, but even so, they sometimes face the challenge of explaining the trust concept in a language/dialect that does not have the equivalent words to capture the meaning. Outreach events are also conducted only in English and Mandarin (the two main languages spoken in Singapore).

Some of the most common misconceptions of the trust include the following:

(a) The SNTC trust is like other government-provided financial assistance schemes for the special needs community, whereby individuals are given a sum of money by the government (and thus families do not need to use their own money to set up the trust).
(b) The SNTC trust works like a private trust, in that SNTC's main task is to help grow the trust fund.
(c) Once an SNTC trust has been set up, no more work or planning is required on the settlor's part.
(d) SNTC can act as legal guardian or deputy of the LB and make personal welfare decisions on his/her behalf.

B Service Delivery

SNTC's trust service is a 'lifelong' service, in the sense that a client's trust account has to be maintained until the demise of the client or the exhaustion of the funds (whichever occurs earlier). The service comprises six stages – (i) intake assessment; (ii) trust setup; (iii) pre-activation; (iv) activation; (v) post-activation; and (vi) termination. A brief description of each stage is provided below (see Annex A of this chapter for diagrammatic version):

Several challenges were faced by SNTC in terms of service delivery:

Pre-activation: How could case managers effectively influence settlors to take steps to build up the trust fund during their lifetime?

Activation: How could trust administrators ensure that monies due to the trust (e.g., under the settlor's will) would be paid into the trust in a timely manner?

Post-activation: How closely should SNTC follow the settlor's letter of intent with respect to the disbursement of funds? How can the exercise of discretion (when required) be properly guided and documented?

Table 11.5 *Description of SNTC's Trust Service at Different Stages*

S/N	Stage	Description of Service Rendered
1	Intake assessment	• Evaluate the PSN's presenting problems and risk factors • Evaluate the eligibility criteria of the PSN and settlor • Assess whether the case has trust potential – i.e., potential for the trust to be injected with a sizeable amount of funds in future which can meet the PSN's care expenses for at least five years • Explain the trust service to the potential settlor
2	Trust setup	• Assist potential settlor in filling in the trust application form and providing the necessary supporting documents • Process the application to be submitted to the PT • Prepare the necessary legal documents (e.g., Trust Deed) for signature

3	Pre-activation	• Conduct regular reviews with the settlor on
		   - The LB's care plan (i.e. future care arrangements)
		   - How to build up the trust fund
		• Refer the settlor/LB to other social services if necessary

4	Activation	• Work with the appointed caregiver to ensure that the LB's welfare is secure • Monitor the injection of funds, if any (e.g., funds could be due to the trust according to the will of the deceased settlor) • Discuss disbursement plans with the appointed caregiver
5	Post-activation	• Process disbursements and monitor trust balance • Conduct regular reviews with the appointed caregiver • Conduct home visits
6	Termination	• Distribute trust balance to residual beneficiaries

1 Pre-Activation

After a trust has been set up, SNTC reviews the case annually with the settlor. The primary objective of the review is to update the LB's care plan (BCP) and the trust's letter of intent (LOI), so that they reflect the latest information about what the future care needs of the LB are likely to be based on his or her present condition. When the settlor passes on, SNTC will activate the trust and disburse the funds in accordance with the most recent LOI.

However, experience has shown that updating the BCP and LOI is not sufficient to ensure that the trust fulfils its purpose in future. Settlors also need to have a clear plan for building up the trust fund and to act on such a plan. If not, the trust will likely end up as an 'empty trust' – i.e., a trust that has very limited funds and hence is unable to meet the expenses of the LB.

Unfortunately, many settlors cannot afford financial planning services and hence remain ignorant about the various ways in which their trust funds can be built up. To address this issue, SNTC's Community Engagement team has collaborated with various agencies (e.g., Institute of Financial Literacy[5]) and individuals (e.g., lawyers) to organise talks and workshops on financial planning matters such as budgeting, planning for retirement and a special needs child, wills, deputyship, etc. Through these events, settlors learn about ways in which their trust funds can be built up during and after their lifetime.[6] SNTC has also created a Settlor's Guidebook that provides an overview of the three main ways in which the trust fund can be built up (i.e., via a will, insurance nomination or Central Provident Fund nomination[7]). The Guidebook is distributed to potential settlors at the trust setup stage and to settlors during review sessions.

Despite these efforts, two challenges remain. First, SNTC's case managers sometimes face difficult questions from settlors on whether a particular insurance policy can be nominated to the trust. Given the wide variety of insurance products in the market, case managers often lack the knowledge required to answer such questions.

To address this issue, SNTC is planning to seek support for its staff from individuals with financial planning knowledge. This in turn increases internal knowledge on the subject matter and enables SNTC to provide accurate financial information to settlors. Settlors can then

---

[5] See https://finlit.sp.edu.sg/about-us/ for more information.

[6] For instance, settlors can do a will to instruct the executor to liquidate his/her property and inject the sale proceeds into the trust.

[7] The Central Provident Fund (CPF) is a compulsory savings scheme for all Singaporeans to save for their housing, medical and retirement needs. Both Singaporeans and their employers contribute to this account. CPF account holders are able to nominate SNTC to receive the balance in the account on the LB's behalf, upon his/her (i.e., the account holder's) demise. See www.cpf.gov.sg for more information.

make better-informed decisions about their assets. At the same time, SNTC needs to be careful that it does not provide financial advice to its clients, as it is not licensed to do so. The line between providing accurate financial information and giving financial advice must be trod with care.

Second, settlors may face certain obstacles and setbacks unique to their particular case which prevent them from building up the trust fund. For instance, after setting up the trust, some settlors may find that they need to use their assets to provide for other family members and for their own retirement needs. Such expenses are not always foreseeable at the time the trust is set up, as family circumstances may change unexpectedly. Some settlors may also find that they have inadvertently offended their other children, who perceive the establishment of the trust as a sign of the settlor's distrust towards them. In such situations, to prevent further strain on familial relations, settlors may sometimes refuse to top up the trust fund. In these cases, an 'empty trust' may result, and the effectiveness of any intervention by SNTC would be limited.

2   Activation

Once a clear plan to build up the trust fund has been devised and put in place by the settlor, SNTC needs to ensure that the plan (which usually involves actions that are to take place only after the settlor's demise) is fully implemented. This poses a challenge in some cases, especially when the executor of the settlor's will is not forthcoming or cooperative.

The following case studies illustrate the issues that SNTC has faced in ensuring the timely payment of monies due to the trust under the settlor's will, as well as how SNTC dealt with them:

CASE STUDY 1: MS L

Ms L is a 34-year-old woman with Down's syndrome. Her mother, Mdm T, had set up an SNTC trust for her benefit and made a will bequeathing a large part of her estate to SNTC as trustees for Ms L. Mdm T appointed her sister (Ms T) and brother (Mr T) as executor and successor executor respectively.

After Mdm T's demise in February 2012, Ms T relinquished her appointment as Executor and so Mr T took on the role instead. The Grant of Probate was issued in November 2012. However, after sending (via cheque) the first batch of monies due to Ms L's trust account in December 2013, no further action was taken by Mr T to inject the outstanding balance due to the trust. Mr T was also not forthcoming, despite multiple emails from SNTC requesting an account of the outstanding sum.

(*CONT.*)

In October 2015, SNTC's Board passed a resolution to appoint lawyers to take legal action against Mr T. As Mr T failed to prepare his defence on time, a default judgment was prepared, and this was accepted by Mr T. All the monies were finally accounted for by July 2016.

This was the first case (and the only case thus far) in which SNTC has had to resort to legal action to recover the monies due to a trust.

CASE STUDY 2: MR S

Mr S is a 44-year-old man with intellectual disability. His mother, Mrs K, had set up an SNTC trust for his benefit in 2011. In January 2012, Mrs K executed a Settlement Deed that appointed two of her other children (i.e., Mr I and Ms Y) as trustees, and instructed them (among other things) to liquidate her property and inject SGD1 million of the sale proceeds into Mr S's SNTC trust. Mrs K also made a will.

Unfortunately, the contents of both the will and the Settlement Deed were not known to SNTC until two years after Mrs K's demise in August 2012. Mrs K had not provided SNTC with a copy of these documents, and Mr I and Ms Y (who were executors of her will as well) refused to do so. As a result, SNTC did not know for a certainty whether Mrs K had bequeathed anything to Mr S's trust.

Despite its lack of information, SNTC repeatedly asked Mr I and Ms Y to account for the monies due to the trust from Mrs K's estate (if any). Finally, a copy of the Grant of Probate – without a copy of the will attached – and the Settlement Deed was given to SNTC in September 2014; and a few days later, a sum of SGD 1 million was transferred to the trust.

Given Mr S's current expenses, SNTC expects that the sum of SGD 1million will likely be more than enough to meet his needs for the rest of his life. However, even today, SNTC cannot be sure that all the monies due to the trust have been accounted for because a copy of the will was never furnished.

The key lessons learnt from the preceding experiences are as follows:

- **The importance of possessing a copy of the settlor's will.** The two cases mentioned earlier had different outcomes in terms of trust asset realisation because SNTC had a copy of the settlor's latest will in Case 1 but not in Case 2. If SNTC had possessed a copy of the will in Case 2, SNTC would know for certain whether it had been named to receive any monies on behalf of the LB. If SNTC had been so named, it would be sure of its entitlement to the settlor's estate, and thus able to take legal action against the executors if necessary.

- **The importance of collecting key legal documents (will, insurance nomination, etc.) during the pre-activation stage.** These two cases highlight to settlors the importance of keeping SNTC apprised of the latest legal documents pertaining to estate planning. If settlors do not do this, the value that SNTC can provide through its service becomes limited, as SNTC will have no way of ensuring that all monies due to the trust are duly transferred to it. Unfortunately, many settlors do not appreciate the importance of this issue and refuse to share such documents due to confidentiality concerns. Thus, SNTC's case managers intend to use these case studies as real-life examples to persuade settlors who are not inclined to share such information with SNTC.

3   Post-Activation

In the post-activation stage, SNTC's responsibility to disburse the trust funds in the best interests of the LB becomes the central focus. Currently, SNTC has limited case experience in this area due to the relatively low number of cases activated to date. However, the challenges are already apparent.

One of the main challenges in this area relates to the 'best interest' principle. The trust deed that settlors sign with SNTC states the principle in the following clauses (see italics):

> **7 Power of Maintenance & Advancement**
> Upon the occurrence of the Activation Event and during the Trust Period, the Trustee may from time to time having taken into consideration (but not in any way bound by) the Letter of Intent, pay or apply all or any part of the Trust Fund and the income thereof *for the advancement or benefit of the Life Beneficiary.*

> **13 Trustee may have regard to Letter of Intent**
> 13.1 In the administration of the Trust and in the exercise of its powers under the Trust, the Trustee may have regard to the Letter of Intent.
> 13.2 The Trustee is not bound by the Letter of Intent and may, in its absolute discretion, deviate from the financial recommendations and preferences of the Settlor set out in the Letter of Intent if in all the circumstances of the case as are within the actual knowledge of the Trustee *it is in the best interest of the Life Beneficiary to do so.*

In summary, the clauses state that the 'best interest' principle is to govern the use of the trust fund, even if the application of the principle necessitates a deviation from the settlor's letter of intent. Nonetheless, whatever is stated in the letter of intent must be taken into consideration.

While the approach may be easy to state in writing, putting it into practice poses challenges, especially in cases with a multitude of claims but limited funds. For example, the term 'best interests' is very broad, and hence determining whether something is in the best interests of the LB in any particular case will likely involve the consideration of many factors. This in turn gives rise to operational difficulties, whereby case managers and members of the Executive Committee (EXCO) could approach the 'best interest' question differently. Consequently, information that the EXCO considers essential to decision-making may be left out by the case manager and vice versa.

To address this issue, a 'best interest' framework was created in early 2017 to guide SNTC staff and EXCO on the factors that should be considered when deciding whether a disbursement request should be approved or rejected. The framework is based on the following four factors and suggests the sequence in which they should be considered (see Annex B of this chapter for diagrammatic representation):

(a) **Settlor's intentions** – is the expenditure item mentioned in the letter of intent?
(b) **Benefit to LB** – will the LB directly benefit from the expenditure? E.g., –
    (i) Does it concern the LB's basic needs, such as food, accommodation, medical, etc.?
    (ii) If not (a), will it improve the LB's current condition or prognosis? What is the likelihood of improvement?
    (iii) If not (b), will it enhance the LB's quality of life? In what ways will it do so?
(c) **Affordability** – can the LB afford it, given the expenses he will incur for his present and future needs? E.g., –
    (i) Is it a one-off or recurring expense?
    (ii) If this expense is incurred, how much trust funds will be left?
    (iii) Can the balance meet current and future needs? If not, how will future needs be met?
    (iv) Would the expense result in potential savings in future?
(d) **Criticality** – how critical is it for the LB to have this?
    (i) What is likely to happen if the request is not granted?
    (ii) Is it time-sensitive?
    (iii) Are there alternative options that are more cost-effective? If time-sensitive – are these alternatives readily available?

The framework is not exhaustive and acknowledges that there could be exceptional circumstances that need to be considered besides the preceding (or notwithstanding the preceding). Furthermore, the final analysis is an overall assessment of the four factors that inevitably involves some element of subjectivity. Some of the factors in the framework are also difficult to assess (e.g., how does one evaluate affordability in light of future needs that may or may not arise?). Finally, all these elements of subjectivity make it difficult to integrate this part of the work process into an IT system (see the discussions on leveraging on IT the follow). Nonetheless, despite these limitations, the existence of a broad framework is a step forward in improving SNTC's operations, as it ensures that everyone in the organisation has a common understanding of how the 'best interest' principle is to be applied.

Another challenge faced by SNTC in the area of post-activation disbursements relates to the weight that is to be attributed to the settlor's letter of intent as a safeguard against over-claiming and the need to ensure that well-intentioned appointed caregivers (i.e., individuals named by the settlor to care for the LB upon his or her demise) do not find it too burdensome to make claims against the LB's trust fund.

Currently, the letter of intent of each settlor is written based on a template whereby the expenditure item, frequency and estimated cost are written side by side:

General Expenses of the Life Beneficiary

It is my wish that as far as reasonably possible the Trust Fund be used to maintain the Life Beneficiary's accustomed standard of living, and for payment of the Life Beneficiary's expenses. I have set out below some of the general expenses that may be incurred by the Life Beneficiary during the Life Beneficiary's lifetime.

1. Basic Needs

SN	Description	Frequency	Amount
1.1	Pay appointed caregiver or Service Provider for LB's following expenses: 1. Food 2. Transport 3. Allowance not exceeding $100 per month	Monthly	

While the estimated cost is indicated in the letter of intent, this amount is likely to be outdated due to many reasons (inflation, changes in the LB's needs, etc.), especially as time goes by. Hence, SNTC does not process a disbursement request that exceeds the indicated amount as an exceptional request that requires the EXCO's approval. In contrast, disbursement requests that are not mentioned in the letter of intent require the approval of the board (via the EXCO).

However, a question arose as to whether SNTC staff should scrutinise a disbursement request that exceeds the indicated amount more closely, as compared to a disbursement request that falls squarely within the amount indicated by the settlor. On the one hand, increasing the level of scrutiny in such cases could act as a safeguard against extravagant spending on items mentioned in the letter of intent. But on the other hand, the greater level of scrutiny could end up being redundant because, over time, the amount indicated in the letter of intent will become increasingly less relevant as a useful gauge of what is reasonable. Practically speaking, SNTC staff would eventually end up adopting a higher level of scrutiny for almost every request submitted, since almost all of them will exceed the amounts stated in the letter of intent. This would not be ideal, as appointed caregivers should be promptly reimbursed for whatever they spend to care for the LB (as long as it is mentioned in the letter of intent). Furthermore, this modus operandi will not be sustainable when transaction volume grows, since most transactions would then require SNTC's case managers to go through multiple levels of bureaucracy.

This issue described also brings into question whether there is really a need to state the estimated cost of an item in the letter of intent, since settlors will almost certainly be aware that these amounts will become outdated and would consequently not expect SNTC to give them great weight when exercising its discretion as trustee. In light of this, it might be more effective for SNTC to work out the estimated expenditure amounts for a given year with the appointed caregiver instead (this could be done during the annual review sessions conducted with the appointed caregiver). This matter is still being discussed internally as part of the organisation's review of its standard operating procedures. At the same time, SNTC embarked on a study trip to the United Kingdom in November 2017 to learn how other non-profit special needs trust companies deal with the issue.

C   Outreach Efforts

Reaching out to the special needs community was particularly challenging in the initial years of SNTC's operations. Not only was SNTC a new entrant in the disability services landscape; it was also a unique creature because most disability services in Singapore do not look into the future financial security of the PSN.[8] Furthermore, the nature of SNTC's

---

[8] Most disability service providers in Singapore look into the social care, healthcare, rehabilitation, therapy and/or accommodation needs of persons with special needs.

services were such that only some families with special needs loved ones would benefit but not others (e.g., financial assistance is more appropriate for those who do not have assets to set aside for their special needs loved ones in future). In light of these factors, SNTC had to address many misconceptions that members of the special needs community had about its services.

These challenges were compounded by the fact that in the initial years, the MSF funded SNTC based on the number of trust accounts set up in each financial year. Consequently, SNTC's outreach efforts focussed on encouraging families with special needs individuals to set up a trust with SNTC as soon as possible, without a deeper consideration as to whether the settlor had the capability to utilise the trust mechanism to his or her advantage (e.g., via top-ups during his or her lifetime or via wills or insurance nominations thereafter), or whether it would be better for the settlor to set up the trust at a later date. As a result, some settlors subsequently found the trust less useful than it set out to be. SNTC's resources were also channelled to servicing many low-risk cases (i.e., cases where the LB is very young and where the trust is unlikely to be activated anytime soon). This was not ideal.

SNTC raised the matter with the MSF and proposed that the funding model be amended to what is being adopted today (see previous discussions). The MSF agreed with SNTC that the number of care plans drafted was a more accurate indicator of the effectiveness of SNTC's outreach efforts, as all potential clients who have developed a care plan with SNTC's case managers would have heard about SNTC. However, not all who developed a care plan would set up a trust, and they could refuse to do so for reasons beyond SNTC's control.

Once the funding model was amended, SNTC modified its community outreach approach to be more nuanced and targeted. Two main groups of potential clients were identified, with a separate approach adopted for each:

- **Target Group 1: Elderly parents/caregivers (≥ 55 years).** This group is considered 'high risk' because there is less time available for such families to plan ahead for their special needs loved ones. SNTC reaches out to this group by organising talks on specific financial planning matters (estate planning, wills, deputyship, etc.) and by sharing about its services with agencies that regularly come across this group of individuals (healthcare providers, social service agencies, etc.). This group is encouraged to see a case manager and consider setting up an SNTC trust for their special needs loved one.

- **Target Group 2: Young parents/caregivers (< 55 years).** This group is considered 'low risk' because there is a longer runway of time available for such families to plan ahead for their special needs loved ones. SNTC reaches out to this group by organising financial education talks that cover the essentials of planning ahead for their own retirement as well as for their special needs loved ones. SNTC does not encourage this group to set up an SNTC trust at this point in time. However, they are encouraged to meet with a case manager to develop a care plan, as the care plan would provide them with an estimate of how much their special needs loved one would need upon their demise.

The change in outreach strategy has benefited SNTC greatly, as SNTC's limited resources can now be channelled to cases that genuinely and urgently need its services.

D   Client Data Management

To support its outreach efforts and the administration of its trust service, it is necessary for SNTC to maintain up-to-date profiles of its leads, prospective clients and registered clients (i.e., those who have signed up for the trust service). SNTC currently uses a corporate secretarial software – Viewpoint – to maintain the profile of its registered clients while the data of leads and prospective clients are maintained separately outside of this system.

The segregation of client data is necessary as SNTC is entrusted with very sensitive personal information. Hence, access to client data is granted only to authorised staff who absolutely need the information for work, so as to safeguard the clients' confidentiality. Having distinct databases also organises client data better, and enable the different teams in SNTC to reach out to the various groups of clients in a more specific and effective manner.

As SNTC is a nascent trust company, its existing tools are sufficient to maintain its current volume of client data. However, each SNTC trust account is a lifelong commitment for both SNTC and the client, and the number of clients is projected to increase annually. This means that the amount of data handled by SNTC will grow nascent over the years.

SNTC is therefore looking into more sophisticated ways of managing its client database. This will not only enhance the security of the data but also support SNTC in analysing the profiles of its clients and in assessing the effectiveness of its strategies, so as to better plan for its policies and resources in the long term.

E   Leveraging on IT

Viewpoint – the software used to maintain records of SNTC's clients – was given to SNTC in 2011 as part of Viewpoint's corporate social responsibility programme. As SNTC is not a conventional trust company, Viewpoint customised the software to suit SNTC's specific requirements and provided training to its staff to enable them to use the system.

However, SNTC's processes remain largely manual due to the uniqueness of its business model and the complexity of its operations. For instance, SNTC currently uses Microsoft Excel spreadsheets to manually compute the fees levied by the PT for each trust account. This poses operational risks (e.g., input inaccuracy due to human error) and will not be sustainable in the long run, especially with the steady growth of its trust accounts and the future expansion of its programmes.

With a view to automating more of its work processes and enhancing productivity and client satisfaction, SNTC embarked on a small-scale business process re-engineering project to streamline some of its work processes in 2016.

During the course of the project, SNTC explored the possibility of leveraging more on Viewpoint to automate its manual processes. The review led to SNTC rejigging some of its workflows to enable data to be captured only once in the system for multiple uses in the downstream processes. However, a more permanent solution is still lacking, and hence this is still being explored.

In the meantime, SNTC is exploring other functionalities of Viewpoint which could help to support its other work processes until SNTC is able to establish its own system to fully meet its business needs and enhance risk management. While this is a step in the right direction, it is anticipated that IT may still have its limitations when it comes to certain work processes (see the example discussed earlier).

III   Conclusion

SNTC started out and still remains as Singapore's only non-profit trust company. With no predecessor to learn from, the operational struggles faced by the organisation were many, especially during the initial years. In the 10 years since its establishment, SNTC has resolved some of these operational struggles, but several still remain and new ones have arisen.

Fortunately, SNTC has a strong management team as well as board of directors, which has helped it pull through many seasons of change.

Besides actively reviewing its work processes and refining them based on the lessons learnt, SNTC is also looking at meeting a service gap that currently exists in the community today concerning Singaporean elderly. Given its rapidly ageing population and the steady decrease in household sizes, the number of Singaporean elderly with no family support is increasing. Many of these elderly have acquired a modest estate (e.g., usually consisting of one public housing apartment and some savings) during their working lives which can finance their retirement. However, they have no trusted family member or relative to rely on to manage their affairs should they lose mental capacity. As some of SNTC's beneficiaries have caregivers who fall in this group, SNTC is well aware of their situation.

In light of this, SNTC is looking into creating a pre-planning service for this particular group of elderly individuals. The pre-planning service would involve SNTC working with the elderly individual on his/her care plan (i.e., how he/she would like to be cared for upon loss of mental capacity and how he/she would like his/her estate to be managed to finance the care). Once a care plan has been drawn up, SNTC will advise the client to appoint a professional donee or list down his/her preferred professional deputy. Upon the client's loss of mental capacity, SNTC will work with the client's donee or deputy to ensure that the client's care plan is duly carried out. The care plan will instruct (among other things) the donee or deputy to liquidate the client's assets and use the monies to set up an SNTC trust for the benefit of the client. Thereafter, SNTC will act as the client's trustee and administer the funds to meet the client's care needs.

In order for this new service to be operated effectively, certain work processes need to be in place, and SNTC's IT system would need to have the ability to support the work. Hence, SNTC's prior experience will put it in good stead as it develops this new service for the benefit of the elderly in Singapore.

Annex A

Summary Workflow of SNTC's Trust Service

Hotline & email enquiries	Talks & roadshows	Referrals (e.g. from other agencies, MSF)	Walk-ins	Other networks

#1: INITIAL CONTACT
SNTC's Community Engagement Dept identifies PSNs and their caregivers; contacts them & fixes appointments with Case Mgrs

#2: INTAKE ASSESSMENT

Obtain info on potential client's circumstances i.e. establish rapport, inquire about social & financial circumstances, explain SNTC's trust service	Assess trust relevance i.e. evaluate LB's presenting problems & risk factors, eligibility criteria, trust (asset) potential

If trust is relevant

Assess risk activation level
i.e. if a trust is set up, what is the likelihood of it being activated anytime soon?

If high / medium risk — *If low risk*

Assess potential client's interest i.e. is he / she keen & ready to set up a trust now or later?	Recommend trust set-up in future (financial education more appropriate for low-risk cases)

If trust is relevant & potential client is keen

#3: TRUST SET-UP

Prepare for Trust Application Pack (TAP) session i.e. inform potential client of supporting documents required	Complete TAP i.e. ensure application documents are in order	Process TAP	Prepare for signing of Trust Deed

#4: PRE-ACTIVATION TRUST SERVICING: REGULAR REVIEWS

Care Planning i.e. any changes in LB's current & future needs?	Living Arrangement i.e. what is LB's future living arrangement?	Caregiving Arrangement i.e. who will be the Appointed Caregiver or Deputy?	Trust Sufficiency i.e. how to build up the trust fund?

#5: ACTIVATION

Work with Appointed Caregiver on:

Arrangements for LB e.g. interim living arrangements & expenses, transition to a home	Assets injection i.e. ensure Settlor's assets (CPF, insurance, will) are injected into the trust	Verification of Activation Event i.e. what is the process?	Disbursement planning i.e. how should trust $ be disbursed? For what, how much, how often?

#6: POST-ACTIVATION TRUST SERVICING: REGULAR REVIEWS

Processing of claims, disbursement To pay for LB's care needs	Post-Activation Reviews with Appointed Caregiver e.g. any changes to LB's needs?	Periodic home visits i.e. to review LB's well-being

#7: TRUST TERMINATION
Distribution of trust fund balance (if any) to Residual Beneficiaries

Annex B

Best Interests Framework

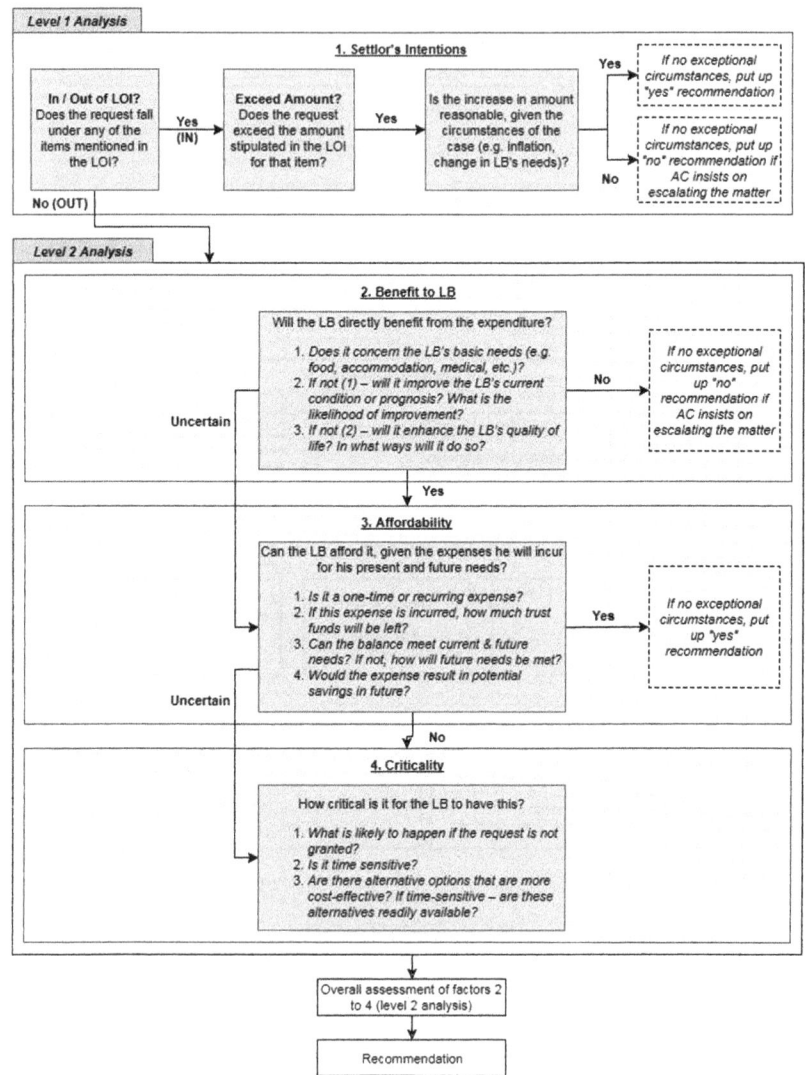

12

A New Perspective on Adult Guardianship and Trusts in Korea

CHEOLUNG JE*

I Introduction

Owing to the prevailing patriarchal family system in Korea, it has long been believed that adults with cognitive impairments, such as adults with dementia or developmental or mental disabilities, ought to be cared for and protected by their families. Under that system, which was legally abolished by the 2005 Civil Code (Act No. 7428), the head of the family, usually coming from the eldest son, was legally obliged to care for family members.[1] The repeal of provisions related to the patriarchal family system reflects the dramatic changes in family structure ushered in by Korea's ongoing process of industrialisation and urbanisation. In contrast to the traditional extended family structure that prevailed in the 1970s,[2] single-person households accounted for 27.8 per cent of all households in 2016, 31.5 per cent of them composed of persons aged 60 and older, with the number of households comprising parents and an adult child and his or her spouse falling to just 3.7 per cent.[3] Such a rapid breakdown in the traditional extended family structure has resulted in social and legal changes in the care system for the elderly and persons with disabilities. On the one hand, the number of nursing homes,

---

* Professor, Hanyang University, Republic of Korea. This research was supported by the Ministry of Education of the Republic of Korea and the National Research Foundation of Korea (NRF-2016S1A3A2924706).

[1] See the 1958 Korean Civil Code, art. 778 (the head of family) and art. 797 (maintenance duty of the head of family), an unofficial English version of which can be found at https:// elaw.klri.re.kr.

[2] In the 1970s, it was common for elder sons to live with and care for their aged parents. Such households, composed of parents and their adult son and his spouse, accounted for 24.6 per cent of all households in that decade, and there were no statistics on single-person households. See the household statistics for 1970 at http://kosis.kr/common/meta_onedepth.jsp?vwcd=MT_ZTITLE&listid=A1.

[3] Ibid.

institutions for persons with disabilities and care hospitals for the elderly has increased substantially over the past few decades to accommodate elderly and disabled persons who used to be cared for in the family home, as shown in Table 12.1.[4]

On the other hand, a new legal framework is needed to ensure that the traditional care function of the extended family is adequately replaced. One area of discussion in this arena is special needs financial planning – trust schemes in particular. However, the main focus of discussion is the reform of Korea's adult guardianship system because the traditional function of the family head seems easily replaceable by that of a non-family member adult guardian. This chapter first deals with the relation between guardianship and trusts as new legal frameworks in Korea and then introduces a new perspective on special needs trusts in the Korean context.

II   Trusts for Persons with Cognitive Impairments: The Current Situation

A   Current Trust Law in Korea

Unlike common law, Korean law treats trusts as contracts. Until passage of the revised Trust Act in 2011, which entered into force in July 2012, trusts could be created only by contracts agreed by trustors (creators) and trustees. Although they can now be created by the declaration of trustors, trusts created by declaration must be written as notarial deeds (article 3 (1), subparagraph 3 of the Trusts Act).[5] Accordingly, it is unsurprising that Korean trust law does not acknowledge any resulting trusts or constructive trusts. Although the Trusts Act was enacted in 1961, it has rarely been applied in Korean legal practice. Trusts for investments by financial institutions, in contrast, are fairly common, and were regulated

---

[4] These statistics are rearranged with reference to National Mental Health Statistics – Pilot Study Part 2, 2016, J. T. Lee, 'Current Situation on Care Hospitals and Tasks for Improvement' (2017) 14 *KIRI Monthly*, available from www.index.go.kr/potal/main/EachDtlPageDetail.do?idx_cd=2773.

[5] Article 3(1) provides that 'a trust may be created in any of the following manners. However, a trust for a specific purpose without any beneficiary (hereinafter referred to as "purpose trust") shall not be created in the manner prescribed in subparagraph 3, expt for public trusts prescribed in the Public Trust Act: 1. A contract between the trustor and the trustee; 2. The will of the trustor; 3. Declaration of the trustor in which the trustor has specified the purpose of the trust, trust property, beneficiary (or a trust administrator under art. 67(1) in case of a public trust prescribed in the Public Trust Act) etc., and designation of himself/herself as the trustee.'

Table 12.1 *Changes in Bed Numbers in Hospitals and Institutions for the Elderly and Disabled*

	2010	2011	2012	2013	2014	2015
Persons with Disabilities Accommodated in Institutions	24,395	25,345	30,640	31,152	31,406	31,222
Persons with Mental Illness in Psychiatric Hospitals and Other Institutions	75,282	78,637	80,569	80,462	81,625	81,105
Elderly in Nursing Homes	107,506	111,417	118,631	121,774	132,387	141,479
Elderly in Care Hospitals		134,930	159,506	189,446	215,841	237,669

by the 1961 Business of Trusts Act before the 2008 Financial Investment Services and Capital Markets Act took effect.

Furthermore, bare trusts or nominal trusts were frequently created during the 1910–1945 colonial period to avoid the disclosure of real property owners to the colonial authorities, and many relevant cases have since been dealt with by the Korean Supreme Court.[6] Nominal trusts for real property were, in principle, made void by the enactment of the 1995 Real Owners of Real Property Registration Act, with trusts for non-commercial purposes subsequently becoming less common. However, the Trusts Act was completely revised in 2011 to facilitate the use of trust schemes for non-commercial purposes. Since then, scholars and practitioners alike have become interested in using trust schemes for the purpose of alternating intestate succession and entitling successive beneficiaries to trust benefits.

There are numerous explanations for the rare use of non-commercial trusts other than nominal trusts in Korea, but what is certain is that foundation and unincorporated associations fulfil some of the needs of such trusts. Both types of association constitute very good schemes for restricting property to special purposes. That being said, however, neither fully meets the needs of non-commercial trusts. First, foundations are subject to the supervision of competent authorities (article 37 of the Korean Civil Code).[7] Given that the control of such authorities can be highly unpredictable,[8] it is nearly impossible to use foundation schemes elastically for private purposes. Second, unincorporated associations pose several difficulties for meeting the needs of non-commercial trusts, even when they are freely established and managed without governmental supervision. Because the management and disposal of property by unincorporated associations is controlled by either those associations' bylaws or the decisions of their general assemblies (article 275 of the Korean

[6] Data on more than 900 Supreme Court cases can be found on the Supreme Court website: http://glaw.scourt.go.kr/wsjo/panre/sjo060.do - 1515652610613.

[7] Article 37 provides that the affairs of non-commercial associations and foundations shall be subject to the inspection and supervision of a competent authority.

[8] The Korean Supreme Court has ruled in many cases that the inspection and supervision of competent authorities are based not on legal provisions but on those authorities' own discretion, e.g., Korean Supreme Court decision 98DU16996 (28 January 2001). The upshot is that inspection and supervision cannot be invalidated without establishing that the competent authority in question has abused its supervision function.

Civil Code),[9] the use of unincorporated associations is necessarily limited to very narrow purposes such as religion and ancestral worship.

It is therefore natural that people with specific concerns about the management of their property would turn their attention to trusts. For example, although state intervention is permissable in exceptional cases,[10] trusts can prevent trust property from being subject to seizure by a trustor's creditors and heirs[11] and make it possible to trace an individual trust property disposed against the trust purpose to some extent.[12] Owing to the elastic nature of trusts, trust schemes have begun to attract the attention of individuals who are considering applying to the family courts for adult guardianship and those who are under adult guardianship.

B   Relation of Guardianship to Trusts

The backdrop to the discussion of trust schemes in relation to adult guardianship is the growing need to protect adults with cognitive impairments, which has become an important social issue in Korea. The number of adults with impaired decision-making abilities exceeded 1 million in 2013, as shown in Table 12.2[13].

---

[9] Article 275(2) of the Korean Civil Code (Act no. 14409) specifies that unincorporated associations are subject to the two following articles, namely arts. 276 (management and disposal of property of unincorporated associations) and 277 (acquisition and loss of rights and duties concerning property of unincorporated associations) of the Korean Civil Code, unless any derogation from those provisions is made by bylaws of, and contracts related to, the establishment of unincorporated associations. Article 276(1) of the Korean Civil Code stipulates that the management and disposal of the properties of incorporated associations are subject to the decision of their general assemblies. With respect to these two provisions, the plenary decision of the Korean Supreme Court, 2004DA60072, 6008, on 19 April 2007, succinctly formulates the ways that properties owned by unincorporated associations should be managed and disposed of.

[10] For instance, the courts can appoint a trust property manager upon the application of interested persons in cases in which beneficiaries cannot supervise trustees owing to minorship or a lack of mental or legal capacity unless the parties to the trust contract agree otherwise (art. 67(3) of the Trusts Act).

[11] Trusts Act (Act no. 12592), art. 22 (Prohibition of Forcible Execution by Trustors Creditors), art. 23 (Prohibition of Succession to Heirs of Trustee) and art. 24 (Prohibition of forcible execution by trustee's creditors) are the relevant provisions.

[12] In the case that trustees dispose of trust properties for a purpose other than that of the trust, registered properties can be traced without any restriction in accordance with art. 4 of the Trusts Act, whereas non-registered trust properties can be traced only if the other party to the transaction at issue knew or recklessly ignored that the properties belonged to the trust in accordance with arts. 75 and 76.

[13] The Korean Ministry of Health and Welfare, *The Number of Persons with Impaired Decision Making Abilities* (2013).

Table 12.2 *Number of Persons with Impaired Decision-Making Abilities, 2013*

Number/ Type	Persons with Dementia	Persons with Brain Injury	Persons with Developmental Disabilities	Persons with Mental Illness
Registered Number	540,755	257,797	190,163	94,638

Table 12.3 *Applications for and Acceptance of Full and Limited Incapacity Declarations from 2001 to 2012*

Year	Applications	Acceptance	Year	Applications	Acceptance
2001	323	176	2007	747	334
2002	421	208	2008	804	391
2003	433	250	2009	944	493
2004	473	274	2010	1,024	515
2005	529	291	2011	1,290	617
2006	663	303	2012	1,342	705

Source: Korean Judicial Statistics (2001–2012)

What is most needed in caring for adults with cognitive impairments is the power and authority to represent them because legal acts are usually indispensable for the management of their property, care and/or medical treatment. Adult guardianship is the traditional legal tool by which legal acts are taken in such management. However, adult guardianship is rarely resorted to under the declaration of legal incapacity regime.[14] As Table 12.3 shows, the number of adult guardianship applications filed during the 2001 to 2012 period was just 4,557.

The scarcity of adult guardianship applications means that family members and others who care for adults with cognitive impairments are in many cases representing them without any formal power or authority, a situation that in turn is accepted by the other parties to the

---

[14] For a brief introduction to the difference between the declaration of legal incapacity regime and the adult guardianship system in Korea, refer to C. U. Je, 'Korean Guardianship', in A. K. Dayton (ed.), *Comparative Perspectives on Adult Guardianship* (Durham: Carolina Academic Press, 2014), p. 191.

Table 12.4 *Number of Applications for Adult Guardian Appointments under New Adult Guardianship System*

Types of Guardianship	2013 (July–)	2014	2015	2016	Total
Full Guardianship	727	1,967	3,013	3,716	9,423
Limited Guardianship	116	245	276	282	919
Specific Guardianship	50	355	181	158	744
Contractual Guardianship	7	8	8	17	40
Total	900	2,575	3,478	4,173	11,126

Source: Unofficial statistics from the Korean Supreme Court Administration (2013–2016)

legal transactions concerned. Such a phenomenon has persisted because it is rare for anyone to object to unauthorised representations unless there are other family members involved who object to the legal transactions. However, unauthorised representations are becoming increasingly difficult to employ in relation to property matters owing to the legalisation of all financial and real property transactions to prevent money laundering. Since the implementation of the new Adult Guardianship Act in 2011,[15] the number of applications for the appointment of adult guardians has rapidly increased, as reported in Table 12.4.

With Korea having achieved aged society status in 2017, increasing numbers of people are expected to resort to adult guardianship in the coming years.[16] The number of adult guardians appointed will also increase. Nearly 93 per cent of adult guardians in Korea are continuous (or full) guardians or limited guardians, who are supposed to serve until the adults under guardianship die unless the guardianship is revoked owing to rehabilitation or the recovery of mental capacity. According to a paper analysing the adult guardianship cases brought before the Seoul Family Court,[17] 87.3 per cent of all adult guardians appointed are family

[15] The official title is 'Amendment of Some Provisions in Korean Civil Code Act' (Act no. 10429). Because Korean guardianship is regulated by the Korean Civil Code, any amendment thereof requires an amendment to the Korean Civil Code. However, the 2011 Adult Guardianship Act is frequently used because it succinctly indicates the purpose and target of the revision.

[16] The number of persons aged 65 and older in August 2017 stood at 7,257,288, accounting for 14.2 per cent of the Korean population. Korea reached aged society status one year earlier than expected. See www.mois.go.kr/frt/sub/a05/ageStat/screen.do.

[17] S. W. Kim, 'The Operation of Guardianship System and the Role of Family Court in Korea' (2017) 722 *Bubjo* 129.

members, 2.7 per cent of whom are co-guardians with professionals. The most commonly appointed family members are adult children, followed by spouses, parents and siblings.

The most frequently cited motives for applying for the appointment of an adult guardian are the management and disposal of the property of a person with cognitive impairments,[18] which reflects the changed legal environment for representation: It has become increasingly difficult for even family members to represent adults with cognitive impairments without evidencing the requisite power and authority. Most applicants therefore seek full guardianship, which confers the necessary power and authority to manage and dispose of the property of the adults under guardianship,[19] to relieve themselves of the burden of proving such power and authority.

The rise in the number of relatives applying for full guardianship has triggered concern amongst family court judges and the competent authorities tasked with protecting vulnerable adults over the potential misuse and abuse of their power and authority. Adults under full guardianship are deprived of their legal capacity, which renders their guardians susceptible to the misuse or abuse of their power and authority. Moreover, family members are immune from indictment on the grounds of misappropriation or embezzlement,[20] meaning there may be insufficient controls in place to supervise relatives appointed as full guardians. The family courts' supervision tends to fall short in deterring guardians from misusing or abusing their power and authority, not only because those courts have insufficient administrative arms, but also because guardians are required to report their activities to the courts only once a year.[21]

---

[18] According to an article analysing adult guardianship applications filed with the Seoul Family Court between July 2013 and September 2016. See S. W. Kim, 'Current Status and Issues of Adult Guardianship' (2016) 30 *Korean Journal of Family Law* 416. According to the article, more than 75 per cent of the applications were motivated by property concerns.

[19] In the case of limited guardianship, a family court judge confers power and authority on guardians, with the individual needs of their wards taken into consideration (art. 959-4 in conjunction of art. 936 of the Korean Civil Code). In court practice, limited guardianship is no different from full guardianship if the extent of the power and authority conferred upon guardians is the same.

[20] There are criminal law provisions concerning relatives' immunity from indictment in property-related crimes. For more details, refer to C. U. Je, 'Korean Guardianship as a Policy for the Protection of Adults with Impaired Decision Making Abilities' (2016) 9 *Journal of International Aging Law & Policy* 104.

[21] According to art. 947 of the Korean Civil Code (Act no. 14409) and art. 38-6 of the Regulation of the Family Law Procedure Act, family court judges can order guardians to report their activities at any time. In practice, however, they generally order guardians to

It is for these reasons that the Seoul Family Court has turned its attention to trusts,[22] recommending that prospective guardians formulate a trust contract with a trust company as soon as they are appointed. The trust company then periodically distributes the proceeds of the trust property to the guardians for expenditure on behalf of the adults under their guardianship. The Seoul Family Court's recommendation applies to cases in which adults with cognitive impairments have a substantial amount of property, and there is reasonable doubt over the prospective guardians' ability to manage that property. The model in question seems to be the Japanese adult guardianship support trust scheme.[23]

C   Adult Guardianship Support Trusts

Korea's adult guardianship support trust scheme can be traced to the trust scheme for the special care of disabled persons, which was introduced in 1998 to safeguard money donated by parents or other relatives for those persons' benefit. To facilitate such donations, gifts of up to 0.5 billion South Korean won (KRW) to a disabled child or relative are exempted from the gift tax.[24] However, the number of trust contracts made for that purpose was only 20 by 2016, with the total value of trust property reaching about KRW9.2 billion (nearly USD8.6 million).[25] There are a variety of reasons for the special care trust scheme's lack of popularity, but two factors have proved decisive. First, the scheme does not guarantee that the trust incomes will be made available to beneficiaries in accordance with the intention of the trust creators, namely to be used for the beneficiaries' daily expenditures, care and treatment, because the trustees, who are commercial in nature, charge additional fees for such dispersal. Second, the tax exemption conditions are so strict that the capital can be neither withdrawn nor spent. The levy of the gift tax is thus effectively deferred until the disabled relative's

---

submit annual reports owing to staffing issues. For instance, Seoul has a population in excess of 10 million, but only three judges in the Seoul Family Court are responsible for all guardianship cases, including minor guardianship cases.

[22] The first contract for an adult guardianship support trust was agreed in January 2017. See http://news.mk.co.kr/newsRead.php?year=2017&no=61058.

[23] For information on the banks providing adult guardianship support trusts in Japan, see www.courts.go.jp/tokyo-f/vcms_lf/290403kinyukikan-ichiran.pdf. In 2015, 9,965 such trusts were concluded: www.courts.go.jp/about/siryo/sintaku/index.html.

[24] Inheritance Tax and Gift Tax Act (Act no. 14388), art. 46, no. 8.

[25] See www.hani.co.kr/arti/economy/finance/747456.html.

death, at which time the trust capital, along with all other properties owned by that relative, becomes subject to succession tax.

Adult guardianship support trusts may also prove unpopular, attracting resistance from appointed guardians because of the additional trust-related costs incurred. In other words, such a trust scheme is unlikely to meet the real needs of persons with cognitive impairments unless adults under guardianship have property sufficient to cover all costs incurred in establishing the trust. It is thus necessary to extend the discussion from special care trusts to special needs trusts.

III   New Approach to Trusts for Persons with Special Needs

A   Theoretical Background to Special Needs Trusts

1   CRPD and Trusts

The UN Convention on the Rights of Persons with Disabilities (CRPD) provides that the legal capacity of persons with decision-making disabilities shall be fully respected rather than restricted or deprived (article 12(2)), and, further, that contracting states shall support those persons' decision-making to ensure they enjoy their legal capacity (article 12(3)). Moreover, the CRPD Committee insists in its General Comment on article 12 that substitute decision-making systems be replaced with supported decision-making systems.[26] Substitute decision-making systems are those in which the legal capacity of disabled persons is restricted or deprived, substitute decision-makers are appointed by persons other than the disabled themselves and/or decisions are made on the basis of the best interests, rather than the will and preferences of the disabled.[27] Instead, the CRPD Committee recommends that persons with decision-making disabilities be encouraged and supported to engage in future planning with respect to such issues as power of attorney and advanced directives.[28]

Both the CRPD provisions and General Comment on article 12 by the CRPD Committee call for fundamental changes to countries' guardianship systems, which have long constituted substitute decision-making systems aimed at protecting those with cognitive impairments. Like their

---

[26] UN Committee on the Rights of Persons with Disabilities, *General Comment No. 1 (2014)*, CRPD/C/GC/1, para. 28.

[27] Ibid., para. 27.

[28] Ibid., para. 17.

counterparts elsewhere in the world, advocates and scholars in Korea stand behind such a change in the guardianship regime, calling for guardianship to be available only as a last resort and to be used and understood not as a property management or personal care scheme, but rather as a form of statutory representation.

In addition, CRPD article 19 also provides that contracting states shall support the independent living of disabled persons in their communities. This provision requires that the traditional policy of institutionalisation to protect persons with cognitive impairments be abandoned, with those persons instead receiving the support necessary to use their property for community living.

The two CRPD provisions together set contracting states the challenge of helping disabled persons to manage their property in such a way that they can engage in independent community living with no restriction or deprivation of their legal capacity and liberty. In responding to that challenge, contracting states have no choice but to replace the adult guardianship system with a supported decision-making scheme whereby guardianship is used as a last resort to support the decision-making of those with impaired decision-making abilities rather than to manage their property and personal care. The power of guardians to possess and manage their wards' property will then be excluded from the proper guardianship role. Contrary to common law guardianship, Korean guardianship is not based on the idea of parens patriae, and hence the family courts will increasingly be confronted with resistance to family court judges exercising any discretion to confer guardians with the power to possess and manage the property of adults under guardianship.

That being said, however, family court judges may order provisional guardians to take possession of those adults' property for management purposes as a preliminary measure until the appointment of guardians, according to article 62(1)[29] of the Family Litigation Procedure Act and article 32(1)[30] of the Family Litigation Regulation. After the appointment

---

[29] It provides that 'In the case where a family litigation case, an adjudication for non-litigation case, or a conciliation is pending, the family court, conciliation committee, or a judge in charge of conciliation may, either ex officio or upon request of a party, issue an order to prevent the other party or other interested persons from altering the current status or disposing of the goods, and take proper measurements, such as a measure for preserving the property related to the case, a measure for custody and fostering of the related persons etc., if the order is specially required for the settlement of the case.'

[30] It provides that 'when family court judges appoint provisional guardians in the proceedings related to full guardianship, limited guardianship, specific guardianship or

of guardians, family court judges may order guardians to take the appropriate measures required, if any, to discharge their duty (article 947, Korean Civil Code[31]). However, the direct possession and management of the property of adults under guardianship may not be required as a legal power in discharging that duty unless permitted for a very limited period of time. This means that a family court order to confer upon guardians the power to possess/manage the property of adults under guardianship would infringe the latter's basic rights protected by article 10 of the Korean Constitution, namely the guarantee of a private life and right to self-determination, unless specific reasonable grounds were provided to back up such an order. Because guardianship by means of a family court order is effectively an intervention into the private life of adults under guardianship and a restriction of their right to self-determination, such an order should be made solely on the basis of the principles of necessity and proportionality.[32] Accordingly, the management of property by way of possession should be considered only in the exceptional case that persons under guardianship require protection as a matter of urgent necessity.

In this regard, trusts appear to be a promising candidate for making advance arrangements for disabled persons to manage their property even in the case of future incapacity. Indeed, trusts have traditionally been considered an alternative to guardianship in terms of guardians and trustees enjoying similar degrees of power and authority and being obligated to fulfil a similar fiduciary duty.[33] However, the relation between guardianship and trusts will change if supported decision-making systems become widespread: trusts will be created to address the issue of how the property management role previously played by

contractual guardianships a preliminary measure according to art. 62 of the Family Litigation Procedure Act, legal provisions which would apply if requested guardians or supervisory guardians in the pending cases were appointed shall be applied to those preliminary guardians with necessary modifications.'

[31] It provides that 'in administering the property and personal matters of an adult und full guardianship, the full guardian shall administer such affairs in a manner conforming to the welfare of the adult under full guardianship with diverse circumstances considered. In such cases, the full guardian shall respect the will of the adult under guardianship unless it conflicts with the welfare of that adult.'

[32] Such an interpretation can be found in C. U. Je, 'Adult Guardianship and Lasting Power of Attorney'(2017) 722 *Bubjo* 96.

[33] For a brief introduction, see J. H. Pietsch, 'Alternatives to Guardianship and Supported Decision Making', in A. K. Dayton (ed.), *Comparative Perspectives on Adult Guardianship* (Durham: Carolina Academic Press, 2014), p. 290.

guardians can be filled. In other words, there is no more appropriate candidate for that role in Korea than the trust. Under Korean law, trusts can be created by contract, meaning that those who want to prepare for future incapacity resulting from dementia, mental illness or another disability can create a trust contract to the effect that their property will be managed in accordance with their will and preferences, thereby reducing both the need to resort to adult guardianship and state intervention into the private sphere. In that sense, trusts can be a future planning tool for supported decision-making in Korean law, recommended by the UN CRPD committee.[34] In an aged society in which increasing numbers of people require decision-making support owing to dementia, mental disabilities and old age, and in a human rights-respecting society wherein self-determination and supported decision-making are valued, trust schemes are the most appropriate candidate to replace guardianship as a substitute decision-making system, at least in the property management arena.

2   Drawbacks of Adult Guardianship Support Trusts

Trusts can be used not only as a future planning tool for the management of trust creators' property, but also as a property management scheme for persons with decision-making disabilities who have missed the opportunity to prepare for their incapacity. Adult guardianship can be implemented to make a trust contract for those who require property management support. In principle, such guardianship will last only until a proper trust contract is concluded and the trustee begins to serve. In this regard, it is not necessary to create adult guardianship support trusts for the purpose of preventing guardians from misusing their power and authority. First, the power and authority of full guardians and trustees overlap with respect to property management and thereby incur double costs. Second, even when guardians' power and authority may be restricted to making daily expenditures on behalf of the adults under guardianship once trustees begin to serve, all changes to the former's power and authority, as well as their revocation or replacement, are subject to court orders, which imposes both social and personal costs. Finally, personal will and preferences may be insufficiently reflected in

---

[34] Para. 17 of the General Comment on art. 12 CRPD by UN CRPD Commission says that the opportunity to make a future plan in advance where will and preference mentioned in the documents will be followed at the time when they cannot communicate their wish and preference to other shall be given to even persons with disabilities. Trusts can be such a future plan in Korean law.

the adult guardianship process because Korean family court judges, who are generally rotated to courts with different functions every two to three years, do not have sufficient expertise on persons with decision-making disabilities.

B A Pilot Project for Developmental Disability Trusts in Korea

Since July 2015, the Korea Autism Society began to provide trust services for both parents of children with developmental disabilities and adults with developmental disabilities as a pilot project, which was financially assisted by ASAN Foundation for three years. The purpose of this pilot project is for Korea Autism Society to petition government and Parliament to enact special needs trust law. With the end of ASAN Foundation assistance for the pilot project approaching, Korean Autism Society began to lobby for the enactment of the introduction of special needs trusts system.[35]

1   A New Trust Purpose

As noted, trusts are traditionally used for investment purposes in Korea. The only difference between adult guardianship support trusts and traditional investment trusts is that the benefit of the former accrues to the adults under guardianship, who are the trust beneficiaries. However, trusts could be created to manage the trust creators' property in the same way that they or the protected persons did themselves even before the cognitive impairments resulting in property management difficulties took place. The purpose of such trusts would thus be property management in accordance with the will and preferences of persons with decision-making disabilities. These developmental disability trusts could be managed by non-profit organisations rather than trust companies, which are subject to the 2008 Financial Investment Services and Capital Markets Act. Suppose that a person with dementia received income from a salary, pension or interest on a savings account prior to suffering dementia – which he or she spent on daily expenditures, care and medical treatment – and that his or her money and property are now in an investment trust. The requirement to adhere property management to that person's will and preferences would ensure that all expenditures on his or her behalf proceeded in the same way as before the dementia

---

[35] For more about the pilot project, refer to the website, www.autismkorea.kr.

occurred. A trust created for that purpose would deliver the dementia sufferer's property and income to trustees, who would cover his or her expenditures. The adult guardianship system could be opened up to allow a trust contract even if the person in question lacked the capacity to agree to such a contract.

In cases where a person is diagnosed with cognitive impairments that may develop into dementia, he or she could formulate a trust contract as a means of future planning for property management. The primary purpose of such a contract would be to ensure that that person can live independently in the community and have the necessary means to cover daily expenditures, care and treatment. That purpose can be directly converted into the purpose of the trust. Investments made to increase the value of property can hardly be said to accord with the will and preferences of persons with impaired decision-making abilities. Such investments are an indirect way of meeting future needs and are thus accompanied by a variety of risks. A person with cognitive impairment could easily be unduly influenced in investment-related decision-making.

In summary, persons with decision-making disabilities require trusts for the purpose of ensuring their ability to live independently in the community with sufficient means to cover their daily expenditures, care and treatment. Such trusts should be provided for in Korea. Investment trusts could still be created to secure managing trustees in the case that the use of such trusts accords with the will and preferences of persons with decision-making disabilities.

2   Non-Profit Trusts as a Reasonable Accommodation for the Property Management Required by Persons with Decision-Making Disabilities

The will and preferences of persons with decision-making disabilities may change over time for a variety of reasons, such as life cycle shifts or special needs arising from disease, accidents or unexpected changes in circumstances. Those new needs should be reflected in the trust purpose. Moreover, assistants, protectors or carers may well be necessary for beneficiaries to live independently with the benefit of the trust property and play a key role for persons with decision-making disabilities, and accommodation should thus also be made for them in the trust. Their role can in a sense be compared to that of traditional adult guardians. Just as adult guardians are subject to supervision by the family courts, assistants, protectors and carers need administrative and personal mentors and supervisors to carry out their duties and responsibilities, a role that can be performed by trustees. If the trusts are operated by non-profit organisations, they can be considered to be making reasonable accommodation for the property management required by persons with decision-making disabilities.

The Autism Society of Korea has offered trusts to persons with developmental disabilities since July 2015.[36] The main contract governing this trust scheme contains the following elements.[37] First, an individual assessment process covering the present and future needs of the individual beneficiary must take place. That process is similar to the individual assistance plan process in the public benefit delivery system.[38] Second, all property transferred to the trustee is, in principle, expected to be spent in a way that allows the person with developmental disabilities to live independently in the community. Exhausting the trust property is considered beneficial to both society and the beneficiaries because doing so allows the latter to participate in economic activities as effective consumers. Otherwise, property owned by persons with developmental disabilities might either remain uncirculated in the market or be exploited or extravagantly spent by third parties. Third, individual supporters should be assigned to beneficiaries to aid the latter's decision-making in relation to money transmitted by trustees. In cases where the beneficiaries lack the capacity to make any decisions concerning legal transactions, the trustees then transmit money to the individual supporters, who can be family members, friends, guardianship associations or staff members of the trustee organisations. The difference between guardians and supporters is that the former are appointed, revoked and replaced by family court orders, whereas the latter are appointed, revoked

---

[36] For information on the introduction of developmental disability trusts, see www.autismkorea.kr/2014.

[37] This 'pilot project for developmental disability trust' model is based on research by C. U. Je, 'Feasibility of the Special Needs Trust Schemes for the Protection of Persons with Severe Developmental Disability' (2014) 66 *Comparative Private Law* 1139; C. U. Je, 'The Needs for the Trusts for Persons with Developmental Disabilities and Its Applications in the Praxis' (2015) 32(4) *Hanyang University Law Review* 425.

[38] Article 15(1) of the Social Benefit Application, its Provision and Discovery of the Entitled Recipients Act (Act no. 13994) provides that an individual assistance plan for a beneficiary of public benefits shall be made with respect to (1) types, methods, quantity and duration of any public benefit; (2) providers of public benefit; (3) Mutual relationship between multiple providers of public benefits, if applicable; (4) connection and its method between providers of public benefits and non-governmental organisations providing welfare services to the beneficiary, if any decision to provide any public benefit to the beneficiary is made in accordance with art. 9(1) of this Act.

and replaced in accordance with the procedures set out in the trust contract.

The role of the trustee (the Autism Society of Korea) is to make sure that the present and future needs of persons with developmental disabilities (the beneficiaries) are correctly assessed, that the financial resources needed to meet those needs are properly transferred and that the beneficiaries' individual supporters are properly advised and supervised. All functions of the trustee are to be performed in accordance with individual trust contracts. In this regard, developmental disability trusts differ from traditional investment trusts and commercial trusts, and even from the aforementioned special care trusts for disabled persons offered by banks. Their delivery system is illustrated in Figure 12.1.

In the past two years, the Autism Society of Korea has attracted significant attention from disabled persons and their family members. It has assessed nearly 50 cases and concluded 36 trust contracts, as shown in Table 12.5. In all cases, the trust creators are either persons with developmental disabilities or their parents. When the former lack the capacity to understand the trust contract or do not have living parents, the Autism Society supports applications for the appointment of dedicated guardians to support them. It then allows the applicant to submit

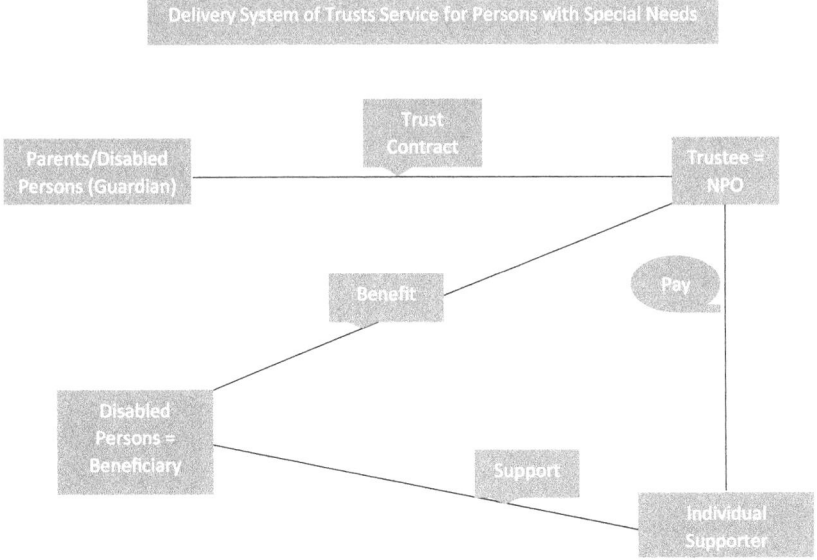

Figure 12.1   Delivery System for Developmental Disability Trusts

Table12.5 *Current Situation of Trust Contract Performance by the Korean Autism Association*

Creator Type	Assessments	Contract Process	Contracts Concluded	End
Parents	26	1	23	2
Persons with Developmental Disabilities Living in the Community	12	2	9	1
Persons with Developmental Disabilities Living in Institutions	7	1	4	2
Total	45	4	36	5

the trust contract document, which will subsequently be concluded by the guardian, to the family courts for a relevant order.[39]

The property transferred by developmental disability trusts has, in most cases, taken the form of cash, although real property has been transferred in several cases.

IV   Conclusion: Future of Special Needs Trusts in Korea

Under the Autism Society of Korea's pilot trust scheme, any type of property – be it money, movables or real property – can be transferred to the trustee – i.e., the Autism Society – for the benefit of persons with developmental disabilities. The only criterion is that the property so transferred be suitable to meet the beneficiary's present and future needs. Transferred money is managed by a bank in an ordinary deposit account.

The experience of this pilot scheme, which has now been in operation for more than two years, reveals several major issues. First, one of the best ways to manage transferred money is to collectively manage and invest it, with the individual beneficiaries entitled to a share of that collectively managed and invested money. Such management can have a real effect on the economy. However, the Autism Society has difficulty

---

[39] However, many Korean family court judges have proved reluctant to allow guardianship in the case of developmental disability trust creation. That reluctance may stem from their limited knowledge of such trusts or doubts over the Korean Autism Society's ability to act as trustee.

exploiting that method because article 37(2)–(3) of the Korean Trusts Act specifies that trustees must manage trust property separately from other property, and article 41 that they must not invest transferred money in any assets other than ordinary savings accounts and government bonds.

Another issue is how to subsidise the special needs trust management fees for low-income beneficiaries. The most suitable way would be to subsidise the trustee rather than levy fees on the beneficiary. However, doing so would require new legislation, and the Autism Society is actively petitioning members of the National Assembly to enact a relevant law.

Finally, there is a need to exclude property transferred to special needs trusts from the property on which the national benefits guaranteeing a minimum living standard are calculated.[40] That standard currently falls short in meeting the needs of people with cognitive impairments. The inclusion of property transferred to special needs trusts in the national benefit calculation may be inhibiting parents and relatives from creating trusts contracts on behalf of their disabled children and relatives out of fear that those children/relatives will lose their benefit eligibility. Although this is a matter of ethics, practical policies cannot take into consideration individual behavior and selfish motives. It is thus recommended that property transferred to special needs trusts be granted special status. In this regard, Korea could learn from the US and Canadian examples.

---

[40] National Assistance Act (Act no. 14880), art. 6-3, which guarantees a national minimum living standard for Koreans, provides for the calculation of a minimum income, based on which persons' eligibility for national assistance benefit is determined. According to that provision, all trust property belongs to the category of financial assets, and is thus regarded as income.

13

Reforming Enduring Powers and Launching a Special Needs Trust in Hong Kong

LUSINA HO[*] AND REBECCA LEE[#]

I Introduction

The Hong Kong population is rapidly ageing as a result of increased longevity, and faces a pressing need to enhance the financial planning instruments available to individuals with cognitive impairment. Whether their impairment is inborn or the result of illness or accident, such individuals are dependent on others to manage the financial assets available for their benefit. Unfortunately, the growing prevalence of nuclear and single-parent families has made it increasingly difficult to rely solely on the families of the individuals concerned to support, let alone maintain, them. For individuals born with a cognitive impairment such as Down's syndrome, improved life expectancy means that they will likely survive their parents for a longer period than in the past, and thus face a considerable risk of disruption to the care they previously enjoyed.

Accordingly, there is increasing demand amongst such parents for reliable financial arrangements for their children once they no longer have capacity to do so. One such planning mechanism is the enduring power of attorney (EPA) – a simple, cost-effective agency arrangement that 'endures' even after the principal has lost mental capacity – where appointed donees are granted the power to manage the financial affairs of the donor when the latter no longer has the necessary mental capacity to do so. Parents may also set up a private family trust and engage the service of a family or professional trustee to manage the assets. However, these existing legal tools in Hong Kong are inadequate. The EPA

[*] Professor, Faculty of Law, The University of Hong Kong.
[#] Associate Professor, Faculty of Law, The University of Hong Kong. This research is supported by the RGC General Research Fund 2016–2017 (project number: 17612916). We are grateful to Oscar Chan, Jason Fee and Alex Yeung for research assistance.

legislation was enacted in 1997 and has not been substantially reviewed until recently. Besides, only families with substantial wealth can afford the fees charged by professional trustees of private trusts. In response to these challenges, the Hong Kong government recently proposed new enduring power legislation designed to reinvigorate the antiquated law on enduring powers and enhance public awareness of this important financial planning tool. Furthermore, it also recently decided to establish a special needs trust (SNT), an affordable trust designed specifically for persons with special needs by pooling together funds contributed by individual participating settlors for management and investment to allow the sharing of operational fees, thereby reducing the fees paid by individual participants. The SNT is a relatively recent legal device in other jurisdictions, and the current model proposed for Hong Kong in which the government lead and manage the SNT would also be amongst the first of its kind in the world. This chapter will review these two long-anticipated efforts of the Hong Kong government.

II Reforming Enduring Powers of Attorney for Individuals with Cognitive Impairment in Hong Kong

A Enduring Power of Attorney

Hong Kong introduced EPAs in 1997 by enacting the Enduring Power of Attorney Ordinance (EPAO), which replicated the subsequently repealed UK Enduring Power of Attorney Act 1985. Whilst the UK legislation was overhauled by the Mental Capacity Act 2005, there have only been minor amendments to the EPAO in 2011. Although an EPA constitutes an affordable and effective means of financial management, there are a number of obvious drawbacks to its use.

Firstly, even when an individual with cognitive impairment has the requisite mental capacity to do so, stringent formalities involved in executing an EPA limits its practical application. Further, the risk of abuse inherent in the individual subsequently becoming incapacitated and thus being unable to monitor the donee is pertinent. Additional safeguards are required to protect incapacitated donors.

Secondly, onerous formality requirements in demanding both a medical doctor to certify the mental capacity of the donor and a solicitor to be present on the same occasion to witness the execution of an EPA was a major hindrance to EPA's wider use, and was relaxed in 2012 to allow the solicitor to confirm the apparent mental capacity of the donor within

28 days of the power's execution in the doctor's presence.[1] By way of comparison, Singapore's Mental Capacity Act provides for simple lasting power of attorney certification by a qualified psychiatrist, qualified medical practitioner or solicitor.[2]

Finally, in terms of the scope of authority of an EPA, the absence of 'general power' and 'personal care' enduring powers is a major deficiency. As noted, the EPAO was drafted along the lines of the UK's now repealed Enduring Powers of Attorney Act 1985. Unfortunately, it incorporated a restriction on the delegation of a general power under an EPA 'in apparent ignorance of the fact that no such restriction had been adopted (or, indeed, recommended) in England and Wales'.[3] As the granting of a general power would render an EPA invalid, the donor needs to choose from a list of default powers in the prescribed standard form. The lack of provision for personal care EPAs also poses a problem for an attorney in circumstances in which he or she is unable to make decisions concerning the donor's property and affairs without also becoming involved in personal care matters.[4]

The limitations of the EPA regime in Hong Kong are reflected in the appallingly low number of registered attorneys. In the 10 years following the EPAO's enactment, only 21 EPAs were registered.[5] After the relaxation of the dual-witness requirement, the number of registered EPAs climbed to 383 between 2013 and 2016,[6] but that remains a far cry from the more than 20,000 registration applications seen in Singapore from 2010 to 2016.[7]

B   Proposed Continuing Power of Attorney Regime

In order to reform the currently deficient EPA regime, the Law Reform Commission published a report in 2011, recommending the extension of

---

[1] EPAO, s. 5(2)(a)(ii).
[2] Mental Capacity Regulations 2010 (Singapore), Reg. 7(1).
[3] Law Reform Commission of Hong Kong, *Report on Enduring Powers of Attorney: Personal Care* (2011), para. 4.4.
[4] Law Reform Commission of Hong Kong, *Consultation Paper on Enduring Powers of Attorney: Personal Care* (2009), para. 1.4.
[5] Law Reform Commission of Hong Kong, *Report on Enduring Powers of Attorney* (2008), para. 3.2.
[6] P. Wong, 'The Law of Enduring Powers – A New Vista', 18 February 2017, available from www.adultguardianship.org.hk/conf2017/4. Mr Peter WONG.pdf.
[7] K. Cheng, 'More S'poreans Sign Up for Lasting Power of Attorney', *Today Online*, 28 January 2016, available from www.todayonline.com.

the scope of an EPA to cover not only decisions on a donor's property and financial affairs, but also decisions on a his or her personal care. Subsequently, the Department of Justice (DoJ) convened an inter-departmental working group to study the 2011 Report and, in December 2017, proposed the creation of a new Continuing Power of Attorney (CPA) regime. A consultation paper was published by the DoJ on a new CPA bill, detailing its own findings and recommendations along with details of the bill. The proposed CPA regime will be implemented by enacting a new Continuing Power of Attorney Ordinance (CPAO) to avoid confusion with the EPAO, and EPAs executed prior to commencement of the CPAO will continue to be governed by the EPAO, which will operate in parallel.[8] The CPA regime will bring about a number of changes as detailed in the following paragraphs.

Most significantly, a CPA will afford the attorney the power to make personal care decisions beyond merely financial decisions already permitted for EPAs[9] and the corollary power to access the donor's electronic healthcare records to inform such decisions. The scope of healthcare decision-making encompasses, inter alia, the donor's accommodation, education, work and holidays.[10] However, much like Singapore, the attorney will not have the authority to authorise removal of the donor's organs for transplant or his or her sterilisation or admission to a mental hospital; decide on life-sustaining treatment or an advance directive; or subject the donor to medical research, electroconvulsive therapy or reproductive technology procedures.[11] In conferring the new powers, the CPAO will remove the restriction under section 8(1)(b) of the EPAO on conferring a general power, and the donor will no longer be bound by the prescribed form relating to the attorney's specific power to act in relation to all of the donor's property and financial matters.[12] Accordingly, under the new regime, the donor may authorise the attorney to act in relation to all of the donor's property and affairs, which may be given subject to conditions and restrictions. It is noteworthy that whilst both

---

[8] Department of Justice, *Consultation Paper on the Continuing Power of Attorney Bill* (December 2017), para. 3.

[9] Continuing Power of Attorney Bill (Consultation Draft December 2017), cl. 3(1).

[10] Department of Justice, *Consultation Paper on the Continuing Power of Attorney Bill*, ibid., Annex A: Summary of the Recommendations of the Law Reform Commission (LRC) ('Summary of Recommendations'), Recommendation 4.

[11] Law Reform Commission of Hong Kong, *Enduring Powers of Attorney: Personal Care*, n 3, paras. 3.9, 3.28.

[12] Ibid., para. 4.16.

natural persons who are not bankrupt and trust corporations can serve as attorneys vis-à-vis financial matters, only natural persons can handle personal care matters.[13] The prescribed form for the CPA will be revised to reflect changes in the aforementioned scope of authority extended to attorneys. Further details of the prescribed form will be set out at a later stage in subsidiary legislation.

The creation of CPAs replicates the requirements of EPAs for dual, but not necessarily simultaneous, witnesses (as previously discussed).[14] Similar to the EPA system, CPAs must be registered with the Registrar of the High Court, and registration does not immediately mean the court will accept its validity.[15] The Registrar can cancel a CPA registration upon revocation of the same by the Guardianship Board or courts or the removal of the attorney by the Guardianship Board or courts without replacement.[16] The number of nominees to be notified before an application for the registration of a CPA has also been increased from two to five, but just like under the EPA regime, failure to notify does not invalidate a CPA, although the Guardianship Board or courts may take such failure into account in drawing adverse inferences in legal proceedings relating to the continuing power.[17]

The new CPA regime attempts to promote respect for the wishes of the donor. In addition to existing fiduciary duties owed by attorneys under the EPA regime, which is transferred to the new CPA regime, the proposed CPAO contains further provisions referring to the will and preferences of the donor. Accordingly, in addition to the usual duties to avoid conflicts of interest, to act honestly and with due diligence, and to keep accounts and segregate assets,[18] attorneys must now take into account the ascertainable wishes and feelings of the donor and consult his or her caregiver or any other person named by the donor if practicable and appropriate.[19] However, an attorney may be relieved of liability if his or her acts are deemed to be honest and reasonable.[20]

Another striking feature of the proposed CPAO is its empowerment of the Guardianship Board. Under section 11 of the EPAO, supervisory

---

[13] Continuing Power of Attorney Bill (Consultation Draft December 2017), cl. 8.
[14] Ibid., cl. 28–31. See also Summary of Recommendations, n 10, Recommendation 7.
[15] Ibid., cl. 38.
[16] Ibid., cl. 42.
[17] Ibid., cl. 41(2).
[18] Ibid., cl. 18.
[19] Ibid., cl. 19.
[20] Ibid., cl. 77.

powers are exercised by the courts alone, and it is only upon the application of an interested party that the courts may order a production of accounts, removal of attorneys or revocation of an EPA. To simplify this process and to reduce costs, the Guardianship Board will now be empowered to perform the following functions: upon the application of an interested party, or on its own initiative, the Guardianship Board may make one or more decisions specified in Division 5 of the proposed CPAO – including declaring the validity of a CPA; rejecting or affirming a donor's revocation of a CPA; revoking, varying or suspending a CPA; or ordering an account.[21] The difference with the EPA regime is that the Guardianship Board will serve as the first point of contact for all interested parties, as the courts will no longer accept applications for proceedings directly from those parties. Instead, they will handle applications referred to them by the Guardianship Board[22] and appeals against decisions of the Guardianship Board,[23] and when addressing such applications and appeals, the courts will also be able to make one or more of the decisions specified in Division 5.[24] It is in this capacity that the courts will continue to play an active supervisory role under the new CPA regime.

The proposed CPAO will effect positive changes to the EPA regime: It will expand the scope of authority to personal care and place greater emphasis on the wishes of the donor while streamlining the process by designating the Guardianship Board rather than the courts as the first point of contact. However, the CPA bill leaves open a number of unexplored possibilities, such as 'supported decision-making',[25] greater guidance and support for attorneys and additional safeguards to protect donors. Even if EPAs in Hong Kong are reformed in line with the best international practice, they remain vulnerable to the difficulty of identifying individuals who are willing and able to take up such an onerous role gratuitously throughout the lifetime of an individual with cognitive impairment. Furthermore, most individuals with cognitive impairment lack sufficient mental capacity to satisfy the requirement to plan for the day they lack such capacity. Moreover, the issue of capacity can become

---

[21] Ibid., cl. 68–73.

[22] Ibid., cl. 62(2).

[23] Ibid., cl. 74–76. See also, Summary of Recommendations, n 10, Recommendation 11(3).

[24] Ibid., cl. 66. See also, Summary of Recommendations, n 10, Recommendation 11(1).

[25] State parties have an obligation to review their guardianship and trusteeship laws to replace substitute decision-making with supported decision-making regimes: see UN Committee on the Rights of Persons with Disabilities, *General Comment No. 1 (2014)*, CRPD/C/GC/1, para. 26.

highly complex, particularly when an individual's ability to make reasoned decisions fluctuates with the severity of his or her illness. In this case, an SNT provides the most viable alternative.

III   Launching a Special Needs Trust in Hong Kong

A   Advocacy for Change

The SNT is a variation of a private trust, which is a flexible and reliable legal tool for financial management, as it does not end with the death or termination of the settlor or trustee. Although the cost of a private trust is prohibitive for families of modest means, the Hong Kong government's SNT will achieve cost savings by pooling the funds contributed by numerous settlors for management and investment, thereby reducing the fees levied.

As of yet, there is still no comprehensive policy or legislative frame-work for the development of advocacy schemes for vulnerable adults. There have, however, been a number of disabled persons organisations (DPOs)[26] that have engaged in advocacy and lobbied the government for legislative reforms aimed at securing the rights and protecting the inter-ests of vulnerable sections of the community due to repeated concerns expressed over the lack of a good special needs financial planning instrument in Hong Kong. The Concern Group of Guardianship System and Financial Affairs ('Concern Group') is an example of such ad hoc organisations:[27] a non-governmental local advocacy group established in late 2013 that focusses on improving the guardianship and related systems for individuals with cognitive impairment. The Concern Group is more than just a mutual support group; it is also an expressive, task-oriented group that mobilises its members – most of whom are the

---

[26] Disabled persons organisations are defined in the CRPD (Committee on the Rights of Persons with Disabilities, *Report of the Committee on the Rights of Persons with Disabil-ities on Its Eleventh Session (31 March–11 April 2014)* (2014), CRPD/C/11/2, Annex II 'Guidelines on the Participation of Disabled Persons Organizations (DPOs) and Civil Society Organizations in the work of the Committee on the rights of Persons with Disabilities') as organisations comprising a majority of persons with disabilities, with such persons accounting for at least half their membership, and governed, led and directed by persons with disabilities.

[27] The Concern Group was established by a group of parents and caregivers of persons with cognitive impairment. Its mission is to strive for a better adult guardianship system by examining the current system's weaknesses and exploring improved policies and insti-tutions. It is hoped that its efforts will enhance the personal care and financial manage-ment arrangements available for individuals with cognitive impairment in Hong Kong.

parents of children with cognitive impairment and/or representatives of other DPOs – to press for specific reform initiatives. The 2016 Policy Address of the Hong Kong government responded to the request of the Concern Group and other DPOs by setting up a taskforce to explore the feasibility of setting up an SNT in Hong Kong to provide affordable financial services to individuals with special needs.[28]

But despite the sporadic advocacy efforts of DPOs, there has hitherto been little systematic research conducted on the views and experiences of the parents of individuals with special needs concerning the existing financial planning mechanisms available in Hong Kong, a situation that renders advocacy even more challenging. Thus, to provide a foundation for the establishment of an SNT in Hong Kong, a questionnaire survey of parental opinions on the usefulness of existing mechanisms and possibility of introducing an SNT in Hong Kong was carried out in 2016 by the authors in conjunction with the Concern Group ('2016 Questionnaire'). The target respondents were parents and caregivers of individuals with intellectual disability.[29]

The findings of the 2016 Questionnaire revealed strong demand for the establishment of an SNT in Hong Kong, and an overwhelming majority of the parents surveyed named the Hong Kong government as their top choice for trustee.[30] Following the enthusiastic response to the questionnaire, the Chief Executive of the Hong Kong SAR proposed in her Policy Address in October 2017 that the government take the helm in the SNT's establishment,[31] which was followed by the 2018 Budget, where HKD50 million was allocated by the Hong Kong government to

---

[28] The Chief Executive's 2016 Policy Address, para. 158, available from www.policyaddress.gov.hk/2016.

[29] According to Hong Kong government statistics, there are between 71,000 and 101,000 persons with intellectual disability in Hong Kong: Census and Statistics Department, *Social Data Collected via the General Household Survey: Special Topics Report No. 62 – Persons with Disabilities and Chronic Diseases* (Hong Kong: Census and Statistics Department, 2014); Census and Statistics Department, 'Persons with Disabilities and Chronic Diseases in Hong Kong' (January 2015) *Hong Kong Monthly Digest of Statistics*, para. 3.1. This number represents 1.0–1.4 per cent of the Hong Kong population.

[30] For details, see R. Lee, L. Ho and the Concern Group, 'Ascertaining the need for Special Needs Trusts in Hong Kong: Report on Key Findings and Observations (Faculty of Law, The University of Hong Kong, January 2017); and L. Ho and R. Lee, 'Introducing the Special Needs Trust to Hong Kong' (2017) 23 *Trusts & Trustees* 1111.

[31] The Chief Executive's 2017 Policy Address, para. 190, available from http://policyaddress .gov.hk/2017.

establish a dedicated SNT office.[32] The SNT office opened in December 2018 and accepted the establishment of SNT accounts from March 2019.[33] It is the government's mission to provide a reliable, affordable and sustainable SNT service to persons whose special needs (such as intellectual disability, autism or mental illness) render them unable to manage their own property affairs.

B   Advantages of an SNT

Given the lack of satisfactory, affordable financial planning services for individuals with special needs, SNTs offer an attractive alternative with numerous advantages. Firstly, an SNT overcomes the practical impossibility of finding a suitable, reliable trustee whose service will continue throughout, if not beyond, the life of the dependent with special needs. Secondly, the financial assets devoted to the dependent are managed by a professional trustee, which both reduces the risk of financial abuses by caregivers and relieves them of the burden of managing the finances of the individuals concerned, thus allowing them to focus on looking after their personal welfare. Thirdly, an SNT allows dependents with special needs to participate in the decision-making process concerning their caregiver if such participation is set out in the letter of intent (explained in Section IV.B). Fourthly, the trust administration fee is reduced to a minimum level because the trustee, being either a government unit or a non-governmental organisation (NGO), is non-profit-making and charges fees only to cover necessary expenses. Insofar as the funds are placed with a professional investment manager, fund management fees are inevitable, but they are kept to a low level by the simple, standardised nature of the trust plan. This means that in practice, the dependent beneficiaries enjoy trust services that are normally only available to high-net-worth individuals. Finally, from the government's perspective, the continuation of secure, stable private funding for dependents with special needs alleviates the burden of social welfare provision.

---

[32] Speech by the Financial Secretary, the Hon Paul MP Chan moving the Second Reading of the Appropriation Bill 2018 (28 February 2018), *The 2018–19 Budget*, para. 176, available from www.budget.gov.hk/2018/eng/pdf/e_budget_speech_2018-19.pdf.

[33] Information about the SNT service is available at the website of the Social Welfare Department of the Hong Kong government: www.swd.gov.hk.

IV   Operational Framework of the SNT Model for Hong Kong

A   Parties

The key parties essential to the Hong Kong SNT are the trustee, the settlor, the caregiver, the beneficiary and a representative of the trustee who interfaces with the caregiver and beneficiary. The roles and functions of these five parties are discussed in turn in the following paragraphs.

Unlike in Singapore, where the trustee is a separately incorporated trust company (the Special Needs Trust Company, SNTC), in Hong Kong the trustee is the Director of Social Welfare Incorporated (DSWI), constituted as a corporate sole under the Director of Social Welfare Incorporation Ordinance (DSWIO).[34] Under section 4 of the DSWIO, the DSWI is capable of serving 'as trustee of any trust created for the benefit of persons in the care of the Social Welfare Department or of any trust created in connection with the work of the said Department'.

In theory, it is possible for an NGO to retain custody of the trust asset and make investment decisions. However, in practice, it is crucial that the two roles (custody and investment) are taken up by the government or a statutory body supported by it; this is because of potential settlors' lack of confidence in non-governmental trustees and the practical impossibility of collecting sufficient funds upfront to meet the necessary threshold for achieving economies of scale in investing the trust assets. The 2016 Questionnaire findings confirm that the government's assumption of trusteeship (alongside parental representation in the governing board of the SNT) will boost the likelihood of parental/caregiver participation in the SNT. The parent respondents demonstrated strong support for the establishment of a government-managed SNT, with nearly half (44 per cent) indicating that they would be 'likely' or 'very likely' to participate in such a trust. That finding is not difficult to understand. Firstly, parents/ caregivers are understandably reluctant to transfer their wealth to an NGO that is only monitored, rather than run, by the government, particularly if the NGO is new and thus has a short track record. Secondly, a new NGO would unlikely reach a scale sufficient to afford in-house professional investment and would inevitably need to engage the services of professional trustees or financial institutions, thereby raising the management cost of the SNT to a level unattractive to potential users. It is encouraging to see that the Singaporean approach

---

[34] Cap. 1096 of the Laws of Hong Kong.

of placing assets with the government for custody and investment has been adopted by the Hong Kong government. It is likely that a low-risk investment strategy that requires little maintenance will also be stipulated in the terms of the trust, as the purpose of the SNT is to ring-fence funds from potential abuse, not to realise investment profits. A government-led SNT can also ensure both prudent management of the trust fund and fund disbursement will be in accordance with the settlor's wishes. The DSWI will be guided by the relevant provisions of the SNT and other legislation. Section 5 of the DSWIO expressly provides that the DSWI's power to invest funds is to be exercised in accordance with the Trustee Ordinance and the trust terms.

Further, naming the DSWI the trustee is a sustainable arrangement. As a corporate sole, the director has a perpetual and permanent legal status, allowing it to provide financial services even after a settlor's death. Caregivers can then receive funds periodically to establish a sustainable support system for the individuals with special needs concerned.

The Hong Kong SNT accepts any parent, sibling or relative of an eligible individual to be the settlor. To avoid the possibility of conflicting care plans, only one of these eligible settlors can establish the SNT account, leaving it to the family members to decide whom to take up this role based on their age, health and financial resources. This means that divorced parents will need to decide on uniform caregiving arrangements for the individual concerned through negotiation and communication, and it is not possible for them to establish separate SNT accounts for the beneficiary. Relevantly, after the account is activated, any person may make a cash gift to the SNT account, subject to the agreement that the gift will be deployed in accordance with the care plan already laid down by the settlor. To keep administrative costs to an acceptable level, the minimum amount of each gift should not be less than six months of the latest median monthly employment earnings of employed persons in Hong Kong. In the third quarter of 2018, the figure is HKD17,000.[35] This flexibility crucially expands the network and duration of financial support available to the beneficiary.

At the same time as when the settlors establish the SNT accounts, they should also appoint a list of caregivers with an indication of priority. The caregiver is the person designated by the settlor to take care of the beneficiary after the settlor's death in accordance with the wishes of the

---

[35] Census and Statistics Department, Hong Kong Government, available from www.censtatd.gov.hk.

settlor. The government is also seeking to mobilise non-profit organisations to provide the service of institutional caregivers on a self-funded basis.

The beneficiaries must be Hong Kong residents who are ordinarily resident in Hong Kong. Whilst the term 'children with special needs' was used in the 2017 Policy Address to refer to potential beneficiaries, the service is now available to a broader spectrum of individuals with special needs such as intellectual disability, autism and mental illness, as long as their special needs render them unable to manage their property and financial affairs.[36] These will include individuals who meet the eligibility requirements for obtaining rehabilitation services provided by the Social Welfare Department or the eligibility requirements for enrolment in special schools registered with the Education Department. Individuals suffering illness will need to be medically certified to be unable to manage their own financial affairs.

Singapore provides a successful example in having a case manager assigned to each SNT account. The SNTC comprises a board of trustees – who are volunteers drawn from the legal, medical and financial professions, but the day-to-day interface with beneficiaries is monitored by case managers who conduct periodic home visits to check on the beneficiaries' well-being after their settlors have passed away. To date, the SNTC has served more than 400 clients with a wide spectrum of special needs, including persons with autism, Down's syndrome, intellectual disability, dementia and mental illness. Although the Hong Kong government does not label its client-management staff at the SNT office as case managers, it does undertake to provide a similar service. For example, when the settlors are still living, SNT office staff will review the care plan with the settlors at least once a year. This may not be at a face-to-face meeting, but if there is a change of circumstance that requires more extensive adjustment to the care plan, face-to-face consultation will be available. After the settlors pass, there will be a monthly visit to the beneficiary in the first three months of the activation of the trust account; thereafter, the frequency of the meetings will be adjusted according to the beneficiary's needs, and in any event, there will be a meeting at least once every year.

---

[36] Indeed, it is useful to note that it would not be desirable for persons without such impaired ability to be engaged as an SNT beneficiary because the SNT's operation necessarily entails encumbrances on the beneficiary's use of assets.

B   Operational Mechanisms of the SNT Accounts

The operational mechanisms of an SNT account under the Hong Kong SNT can be divided into four stages: establishment, activation, operation and termination.

1   Stage One: Establishment

To establish an SNT account, the settlor executes a Deed of Trust in the presence of a solicitor, wherein he or she defines who the beneficiary is. This is accompanied by the Letter of Intent, which sets out his or her wishes as to how the trust assets are to be used; and the Care Plan provided by the settlor, which instructs the subsequent caregiver on how the trust funds are to be used in caring for the beneficiary with details of the care that the settlor wishes the beneficiary to receive, along with a rough estimate of the expenditure required to sustain the level of care specified.

Separately, the settlor needs to execute a will in the presence of a solicitor, providing that a portion of his or her assets is to be transferred to the SNT upon his or her death. Use of a will grants the settlor flexibility in managing his or her assets during his or her lifetime, as those assets pass to the trust only after he or she has passed away. It also allows for more investment possibilities, which may generate more assets for the use of the settlor and beneficiary. Although the Hong Kong government will not provide will-drafting services, it will offer settlors a standard clause to insert into their wills to enable the transfer of assets into the SNT account when they die.

Apart from executing the above-mentioned documents, the settlors must also make an initial contribution into the SNT account at the time of establishment. The Hong Kong SNT also only accepts fund contributions, as opposed to other assets such as shares or real property, in order to reduce administrative costs. The minimum amount of initial contribution comprises two parts. First, it includes one year of the beneficiary's expenses as set out in the care plan, which must not be lower than one year of expenses calculated based on the latest median monthly employment earnings of employed persons, which is currently at HKD17,000 per month.[37] Second, it includes one year of trust management fee, which

---

[37] The same amount is used to define the maximum monthly amount that can be disposed by an adult guardian under Section 44B(8) of the Mental Health Ordinance of Hong Kong.

is currently set at a flat fee of HKD21,000 per year. In other words, if a settlor establishes an SNT account in February 2019, the minimum amount of initial contribution will be HKD17,000 × 12 (HKD204,000) plus HKD21,000, which comes up to HKD225,000. The purpose of the initial contribution is to allow the trust to be activated immediately upon the settlor's passing, without having to wait for the completion of probate.

Subsequent to the establishment of an SNT account and creation of a will, it may take 20 years or more before the SNT account is fully activated for pooled investments upon the settlor's death. During the intervening period, DSWI representatives will contact settlors annually to confirm whether the original care plan remains appropriate or whether adjustments are required to meet the beneficiaries' needs in a timely fashion. The initial contributions will not be invested beyond being placed in a savings bank account, as the funds may need to be put into immediate use at any time. Once established, the SNT account cannot be revoked unless the beneficiary passes on before the settlor or the settlor no longer resides in Hong Kong ordinarily, in which case the trust will be terminated and the fund returned to the settlor.

2   Stage Two: Activation

Activation of the SNT account takes place after the settlor's death when the SNT trustee receives notice of the settlor's passing. At its initial launch, the Hong Kong SNT does not provide for activation in circumstances such as the settlor's onset of incapacity or deterioration of health; it is likely that the current restriction will be reviewed at the next occasion. Upon activation, the trustee will start to make monthly distributions to the caregiver out of the initial contribution. The second, substantial contribution is made when the executor transfers funds to the SNT account pursuant to the settlor's will.

3   Stage Three: Operation

Different parties perform different tasks during the operation of the SNT account. The DSWI, as trustee of the SNT, has three duties: first, to invest the funds; second, to distribute the funds to the caregivers in accordance with the letters of intent and care plans; and, third, to visit the beneficiaries periodically to provide support and review the care plans.

With respect to investment of funds, it is not the SNT's objective to generate significant returns on the assets entrusted to it, but rather to make prudent investments with the hope of counteracting inflation. Investment of the SNT funds will be overseen by an investment consultation committee formed by the SNT office and comprising professionals from the finance and investment industries, as well as representatives of parents of dependents with special needs. The consultation committee will be tasked with ensuring that the investment portfolio selected by the trustee corresponds with the risk profile and investment objectives of SNT users.

However, to keep operational costs low, unlike users of the Mandatory Provident Fund, which is a compulsory pension and savings scheme in Hong Kong, SNT users will not be able to choose from multiple providers or multiple investment portfolios, as the SNT's primary objective is to offer a cost-efficient financial solution to families with dependents with special needs. Any profits that the SNT makes from its investments will be channelled back to the beneficiaries as part of the assets in their SNT accounts.

With respect to distribution duties, the trustee will make periodic disbursements to caregivers in accordance with the letters of intent and care plans provided by the settlors. Caregivers will not receive the entirety of settlors' assets at once to reduce the risk of asset misuse. The trustee also has the power to remove the caregiver in a range of circumstances such as his or her death, bankruptcy, imprisonment, refusal to discharge duties or resignation, emigration or habitual unavailability for contact, change of circumstances and capabilities that renders him/her unsuitable to be a caregiver, abuse of the beneficiary, appropriation of the beneficiary's assets, or negligence. The caregiver may also be removed by an order of the court or when the trustee is of the view that his/her removal is in the best interest of the beneficiary. The next nominated caregiver will then be appointed in place, and in the absence of such a person, the trustee will appoint a suitable person bearing in mind the best interests of the beneficiary.

With respect to support for the beneficiary, staff from the SNT office will meet with beneficiaries at least once every year to review if they receive the level of care stipulated in the care plan. If a case manager identifies any deficiency in a beneficiary's treatment, he or she is duty bound to refer the matter to a social worker for further action.

When caregivers receive the aforementioned periodic disbursements, they must use them to care for the beneficiaries in the manner prescribed by the care plan. Settlors are advised to designate a number of alternate caregivers in sequence, lest any one of them be found unfit or unable to perform his or her duties. The government is facilitating the provision of institutional caregiver service by non-governmental welfare organisations.

Finally, a service consultation committee comprising parent and set-tlor representatives will also be formed to continue to advise the SNT trustee on the operation and improvement of the trust service. The government has also undertaken to review the SNT service within two years from its establishment.

4   Stage Four: Termination

An SNT account will be terminated, among other things, upon the exhaustion of funds in the account, the death of the beneficiary or when the beneficiary no longer resides in Hong Kong ordinarily. A beneficiary who has exhausted the trust fund will continue to be cared for by the 'safety net' provided by the Social Welfare Department, possibly through the receipt of Comprehensive Social Security Assistance or Disability Allowance. Any residuary fund in the account upon the passing of the beneficiary will be distributed according to his will, or, in the absence of a will, according to the statutory regime for intestate sucession.

5   Cost

Responses to the 2016 Questionnaire indicated that more than half of the parents surveyed would not use SNT services if the annual fees charged were more than 1 per cent of the trust assets in the SNT account. In response, the government is seeking to keep the annual fee to a flat rate of HKD21,000 based on partial recovery of staff cost in the administration and management of SNT accounts.[38] The fee level will be adjusted in accordance with staff salary increment. Relevantly, staff cost devoted to social services pertaining to the trust, such as the periodic visit of beneficiaries, as well as overheads and other costs will be absorbed by the government. No additional set-up or investment fees will be charged.

Charged at a flat rate, the fee will be at about 1 per cent if there is HKD2.1 million in the trust account. As with all flat fees, users with a higher amount of trust funds in effect pay a lower rate. Nonetheless, as the SNT is a government-operated scheme that provides the same pack-age of service to every user and charges a fee based on the average cost of service for each account, this is an understandable measure especially at the initial launch of the service. In the future, when statistics about the

---

[38] According to the government's information forums held in early 2019, the fee is calcu-lated on the basis of the cost of staff at the SNT office, on the assumption that there are 300 cases.

number and profile of users are available, there may be room to consider the viability of alternative mechanisms.

6   Continued Eligibility for Public Assistance

The government has also made it clear that assets held in the SNT account are to be treated as a resource available to the beneficiaries for the purpose of means-tested public assistance programmes in Hong Kong. However, non-means-tested social benefits such as disability allowances will not be affected. While settlors may wish to have the best of both worlds, it is not easy for a government department who manages both the SNT and the means-tested public assistance programmes to take into account the assets in one but treat them as unavailable in the other.

V   Conclusion

Individuals with cognitive impairment are often unable to manage their own financial affairs. The proposed reform of the EPA regime and establishment of a Hong Kong SNT will go a long way towards enhancing financial planning mechanisms available to parents of children with cognitive impairment. The proposed SNT was brought about by the joint efforts of civil society, academic research and the Hong Kong government. The speed at which it proceeded from conception to launch of service is phenomenal. It will be an affordable trust that provides peace of mind to many parents who would otherwise not be able to enjoy professional trust service. Most importantly, Hong Kong distinguishes itself from all other SNT regimes in the world, in that the social welfare unit of the government took up responsibility in managing the trust. It will be amongst the first of its kind in the world, and provides an example of a government-run SNT system that is both feasible and affordable.

INDEX

ABLE Account, 25, 263–264, 292
Abuse
  Elder, 231–232
  Financial, 134, 195, 198, 212,
    229–231
  of Power, 67
  of Rights, 203
  Safeguards against, 147, 191
Adult Guardianship
  Adult Guardian. *See* Guardian
  Adult Guardianship Support Trust
    (Korea), 337, 341–342
  Assessment, 38, 42
  Australia, 3, 7–8, 15, 24, 194
  Canada, 30, 51
  England & Wales, 117
  Guardianship Order, 38, 41
  Japan, 61–62, 65–66, 71, 73–74
  Korea, 330, 333–335
  Personal Matters, 40
  Property Management, 339
  Property Matters, 40
  Taiwan, 87–89, 91–93, 110
  Tribunal (Australia), 11, 181, 187
  Voluntary Guardianship (Taiwan),
    111
Advisorship, 62–63, 77
Affordable, 195, 309

Best Interests, 8, 32, 34–36, 106, 143,
  146, 191, 216, 221, 319, 328, 338

Conflict
  of Interest, 37, 54, 70, 93, 107, 182
  Transaction, 185, 188, 191, 198, 200,
    203
    Fiduciary Principles, 199

Continuing Power of Attorney. *See* also
  Enduring Power of Attorney
  Hong Kong, 351
  Japan, 62, 64, 78
Court of Protection (England & Wales),
  120, 123–124, 129, 139, 143–144
  Visitor, 128
Curatorship, 61, 77
  Curator, 118

Decision-Making, 11–12, 32, 40, 146
  Authority, 52
  Capacity, 12, 32, 35, 121, 138, 150,
    161, 181–182, 185, 197, 200
  Co-, 32–33, 38
  Disabilities, 338, 342–343
  Impaired, 333, 339
  Proxy, 7, 11–12
  Substituted, 8, 11–12, 21, 23–24,
    32–33, 36, 52, 71, 152, 155, 161,
    181, 188, 191, 203, 338
  Supported, 3, 10–12, 22, 24, 32–33,
    36, 52, 71, 122, 150, 161, 190,
    199, 338–340
Dementia, 5, 10, 61, 65, 87, 159, 180,
  201, 212, 329, 334, 342
Deputy
  Appointment, 129
  Duties, 143
  Supervision, 127–128
  Supervision Fee, 144
  Types of, 127
Deputyship (England & Wales), 143
  Advantages, 143
  Deputy. *See* Deputy
Developmental Disability Trust
  (Korea), 342

Disability, 12, 16, 20, 45, 49, 255, 269,
      280, 284
   Cognitive Impairment, 6, 10, 13, 16,
      30–31, 43, 50, 54, 62, 329, 333,
      339, 343, 348
   Developmental, 266, 329, 334,
      342
   Intellectual, 5–7, 10, 13, 23, 31, 33,
      212
   Mental, 31, 49, 63, 134, 152, 216
   Mental Capacity. *See also* Mental
      Capacity
   Mental Illness, 5, 10, 266, 331,
      334

Elderly, 87, 91, 96, 103, 212
Enduring Power of Attorney, 138
   Applications to Court, 170
   Australia, 3–4, 7, 179, 190
   Complaint Mechanisms, 173
   Donor, 152
   Eligibility, 169
   England & Wales, 132, 134
   Formalities, 349
   Hong Kong, 348
   Ireland, 149
   Limited Authority to Make Gifts, 136
   Nature and Effect, 137
   Objections to Registration, 135
   Principal, 185
   Registration, 135, 138, 156, 171, 174,
      190, 194
   Reporting Obligations, 172
   Representative, 184–185, 191
   Revocability, 136
   Role of Court, 136, 158
   Safeguard, 191
Estate Planning, 30, 49

Family Structure, 215
Financial
   Affairs, 120–121, 123, 129, 145,
      212
   Assistance, 31
   Decision-Making, 280
   Exploitation, 219, 303
   Management, 280
   Matters, 305
   Planning, 244

Gift, 17, 126
Government Assistance
   Entitlement, 43, 47
Guardian, 32, 35, 38, 54, 77, 87, 93,
      339–340
   Appointment, 339
   Co-, 336
   Continuous, 335
   Enduring, 182
   Fiduciary Duty, 340
   Limited, 335
   Property, 54
   Provisional, 339
   Third-party, 67

Henson Trust, 25, 43, 49–50, 53, 57
   Trustee, 54
Hong Kong Special Needs Trust
   Activation, 361
   Distribution, 362
   Establishment, 360
   Fees, 363
   Government Trusteeship, 357
   Investment, 362
   Operation, 361
   Public Assistance, 364
   Termination, 363

Insurance, 31, 45, 129, 231
Investment, 31, 45, 310, 312

Lasting Power of Attorney. *See also*
      Enduring Power of Attorney
   Court of Protection, 140
   Donor, 140
   England & Wales, 125, 132, 139,
      144–145
   Form, 139
   Limited Authority to Make Gifts, 140
   Objections to Registration, 140
   Registration, 140, 217
   Singapore, 216, 229
Legal Capacity, 90, 152, 165
   Limited, 90

Means-Testing, 4, 17–18, 44, 50
Medicaid, 244, 264, 269–273
   Means-Tested, 269
   Payback Trust, 274, 280

Medicare, 272
Mental Capacity
  Assessment, 77, 122
  Legal Capacity, 164
  Test, 159
Mental Incapacity
  Definition, 154
Midwest Special Needs Trust
  Account, 250
  Administration, 250
  Background, 241
  Beneficiary, 249
  Co-Trustee, 247
  Creation, 240, 255
  Distribution, 249
  Eligibility, 246
  Fees, 250
  First-Party Trusts, 245, 252, 264
  Investment, 254
  Operation, 257
  Settlor, 247
  Tax, 252
  Termination, 259
  Third-Party Trusts, 252
  Trustee, 247

National Disability Insurance Scheme
    (Australia), 5, 13–14, 16, 21

Power of Attorney
  Automatic Revocation, 133–134
  Canada, 52
  Continuing. See Continuing Power
    of Attorney
  Decision-Making, 155
  Deputy, 217
  Donee, 216
  Donor, 132–133
  Durable. See Durable Power of
    Attorney
  Fiduciary Duties, 185, 352
  Formalities, 153, 166, 217
  General, 179
  General Authority, 154
  Lasting. See Lasting Power of Attorney
  Principal, 182
  Register, 123
  Scope of Authority, 217
  Supportive Attorney, 188

Property Management, 106, 280, 340, 343
Public Benefit, 280, 285
Public Guardian
  Australia, 9, 12
  England & Wales, 123–124, 127–129,
    140, 143–144
  Singapore, 217
Public Guardian and Trustee (Canada),
    31, 35, 49, 54
Public Support System, 73
Public Trustee
  Australia, 9, 12, 17
  Singapore, 310, 312

Quality of Life, 43, 53, 63

Registered Disability Savings
    Programme
  Property Guardianship Order, 53
Registered Disability Savings
    Programme (Canada), 15,
    25–26, 49, 53
Representative Payee, 6–7
Resource, 245, 270, 273
Retirement, Survivors and Disability
    Insurance, 269, 271
  Not Means-Tested, 271

Safeguard, 12, 22, 24, 37, 41, 70, 103,
    134, 147, 153, 191
Saskatchewan Assured Income for
    Disability, 34, 45–46
Scope
  of Authority, 52, 126
  of Duty, 106
  of Power, 93, 168
Self-Determination, 32, 63, 69, 71, 78,
    161, 340
Singapore Special Needs Trust
  Account, 308
  Activation, 317
  Beneficiary, 305, 312
  Care Plan, 308, 315
  Case Manager, 314, 316
  Fees, 220, 309–310
  Investment, 312
  Irrevocability, 313
  Letter of Intent, 315, 319
  Low-Income, 309

Singapore Special Needs Trust (cont.)
    Outreach, 322
    Post-Activation, 319
    Pre-Activation, 310
    Public Trustee, 221, 224, 303
    Settlor, 317
    Special Needs Trust Company, 305,
        308, 312, 314
Social Assistance, 17, 43, 53
    Eligibility, 50
Social Security Disability Insurance
    (US), 244
Social Welfare, 106, 214–215
Special Disability Trust (Australia),
    18–19, 21
Special Needs Savings Scheme
    (Singapore), 26, 223
Special Needs Trust, 17, 244, 342
    Account, 221, 250, 305, 312
    Beneficiary, 221, 244
    Care Plan, 221
    Caregiver, 221
    Fee, 220–221
    Hong Kong, 354, See also Hong
        Kong Special Needs Trust
    Investment, 221
    Korea, 342, 346–347
    Letter of Intent, 221
    Missouri, 240, See also Midwest
        Special Needs Trust
    Settlor, 221, 244
    Singapore, 220, See also Singapore
        Special Needs Trust
    Singapore Special Needs Trust
        Company, 25
    Trust Asset, 221
    Trustee, 244
    Wisconsin. See also Wispact Trust
Supplemental Needs Trust, 268, 273,
    279–280
    Self-Funded Trusts, 274, 280
    Third-Party Trusts, 273, 280
Supplemental Security Income, 244,
    269–271, 273
    Eligibility, 270

Tax, 19, 26, 31, 49, 252, 269
    Exemption (Korea), 337
    Gift (Korea), 337

Income (USA), 271
Succession (Korea), 338
Trust, 5, 18, 20, 75, 90, 92–93, 103, 333,
    340
    Beneficiary, 18, 20, 43, 45, 49, 90,
        104, 273, 337
    Care and Maintenance, 104
    Discretionary, 18, 45, 273, 280
    Mandatory, 102
    Property, 90–92, 106, 337
    Self-Benefit, 91, 108
    Settlor, 90, 92, 104
    Taiwan, 90
    Termination, 109
    Trust Agreement or Contract,
        45, 91
    Trust Supervisor, 92, 107
    Trustee, 17, 20, 44–45, 50, 55, 90,
        104–106, 273, 337
    Voluntary, 111

UN Convention on the Rights of
    Persons with Disabilities, 3, 8,
    10–12, 16, 22–24, 33, 37, 61, 68,
    71, 77, 87, 147, 149, 161, 180,
    188, 190, 338–339
Unauthorised Representation, 335

Will, 5, 9, 45, 49, 90
Wispact Trust, 271, 276
    Account, 271, 275
    Advisor, 275, 278
    Beneficiary, 271, 284
    Beneficiary Specialist, 285
    Contribution Agreement, 277, 285
    Distribution, 276, 278, 286, 290
    Eligibility, 282
    Fee, 278, 294
    Investment, 278
    Manager, 276
    Master Trust, 276–277
    Protector, 276
    Retained Fund, 282, 296
    Self-Funded, 283
    Self-Funded Trusts, 284
    Third-Party Trusts, 284
    Trustee, 276

Yokohama Declaration, 61, 72–73, 82